NTAL RETARDATION

A life cycle approach

MENTAL RETARDATION
A *life cycle approach*

PHILIP C. CHINN, Ed.D.

Special Assistant to the Executive Director on Minority Concerns
and Development, Council for Exceptional Children,
Reston, Virginia

CLIFFORD J. DREW, Ph.D.

Professor, Department of Special Education,
Professor, Department of Educational Psychology,
Associate Dean, Graduate School of Education,
University of Utah,
Salt Lake City, Utah

DON R. LOGAN, Ed.D.

Professor and Chairperson, Department of Special Education,
University of Utah,
Salt Lake City, Utah

SECOND EDITION

with 48 *illustrations*

The C. V. Mosby Company

ST. LOUIS • TORONTO • LONDON   1979

Illustration in lower right-hand corner of cover is
Mr. Bernard Casper, Murray Ridge Production Center, Inc., Elyria, Ohio.

SECOND EDITION

Printed in the United States of America

The C. V. Mosby Company
11830 Westline Industrial Drive, St. Louis, Missouri 63141

Library of Congress Cataloging in Publication Data

Chinn, Philip C   1937-
    Mental retardation.

    Bibliography: p.
    Includes index.
    1. Mentally handicapped. I. Drew, Clifford J.,
1943-   joint author. II. Logan, Don R., 1931-
joint author. III. Title.
HV3004.C47 1979   362.3   78-31835
ISBN 0-8016-0968-2

GW/VH/VH 9 8 7 6 5 4 3 2 1   02/C/256

Preface

The preface to the first edition of this volume made note of a public awakening relative to the problems of the handicapped. Reference was made to increased public and private funding, accumulating research, and a continually growing commitment to meeting the needs of retarded individuals. As this second edition is being published, these same influences are operating, although the current scene might not be easily recognized by the readers of the first edition. The vigor and energy found in all areas pertaining to the handicapped, particularly the retarded, can only be characterized as intense—so intense, in fact, that we often find ourselves painfully impatient with those in our personal and professional environments who are not involved. The level of activity found today would surely surpass the fondest dreams and wildest imaginations of those historical educators and scientists who provided the initial foundations on which we build.

This second edition reflects the issues, influences, and perspectives that have surfaced during the 4 years since the first edition was published. In some cases these represent scientific advances, in others, controversial sociocultural issues. The field of mental retardation is complex, fluid, and multidimensional. For the reader who is taking a first step it is important to be forewarned that there are few, if any, simple answers. The reader should also know, however, that there may not be another field that holds such intrigue and so many implications for the human condition in general. Mental retardation is an area that can hardly be restricted by the term "topic." It is like an addictive narcotic to those who dare to take the first step.

The intended audience for this edition remains much the same as that of the first edition. Several groups are targeted, including the incipient professional who anticipates central involvement with the retarded as well as those who attend to the retarded as a concern peripheral to another focus. Additionally, it is anticipated that much of the information and discussion

v

will be of interest to parents, families, and friends of retarded individuals who find themselves faced with the dilemmas that so frequently accompany such circumstances.

In order to serve these varied audiences we have addressed a variety of topics. This edition continues to adhere to the fundamental concepts that guided the preparation of the first. We have attempted to be most serious about the life cycle, thus the reader will find the major portion of the text framed in a developmental manner—from conception through the aging process. Furthermore, we have sought to emphasize a multidisciplinary conceptualization as the fundamental backdrop of our presentation. A multidisciplinary concept has always been important in mental retardation. The reader will find, however, that the need for this approach is vastly more important today than ever before, and it will continue to emerge as the only sensible manner in which to view the field of mental retardation.

This second edition represents a major expansion from the material presented in 1975. The reader will find several new chapters as well as substantial expansion and revision of others. A conscientious effort has been made to give greater attention to the latter phases of the life cycle. Additionally, new material has been prepared examining legal, social, and ethical issues—matters that have accelerated both in visibility and importance at a dramatic rate.

We are indebted to the many students and colleagues who provided invaluable feedback that suggested the revisions and additions. So, to the beginning reader, we invite you to become involved with us, to share the intrigue, excitement, and challenges of the field of mental retardation. To our colleagues who are already involved, we hope that you will find this volume a contribution that facilitates your teaching, research, and exploration of the many issues that continue to emerge and require attention.

P. C. C.
C. J. D.
D. R. L.

Contents

PART ONE

Introduction

CHAPTER 1

Concepts, definitions, and classifications

(Photograph by Peter Poulides.)

INTRODUCTION

"What is mental retardation?" This is a question that would seem rather simple to answer, yet it is a question that has plagued educators and psychologists for many years. As in many areas of behavioral science, this question is deceiving in its simplicity, but an answer that is in any way complete is exceedingly difficult to articulate. In reviewing the literature relating to mental retardation, one finds that the response to the question has received a great deal of attention, particularly during the past 25 years. This chapter examines mental retardation from the standpoint of a concept, definitions, and classification systems that have been used both historically and on a current basis. Review of this material and that found in the following chapters will provide the reader with an overview of mental retardation. It will become evident that the problem is multifaceted. Mental retardation is an educational problem, a social problem, a medical problem, a legal problem, and always a family problem. What we have attempted, in this volume, is to place mental retardation in its broadest perspective, squarely in the center of human existence because, above all, mental retardation is a human problem. It cannot be viewed from a narrow focus if one wishes to obtain an accurate and comprehensive perspective.

MENTAL RETARDATION AS A CONCEPT

An examination of the mental retardation literature suggests strongly that the conceptual issues are complex and a considerable lack of clarity still exists. Frequently professionals seem to respond to our initial question of defining mental retardation by discussing what it is not and by describing causes. Refinement of the concept of mental retardation remains elusive.

The history of mental retardation predates many of the other areas that are considered handicapping conditions. Hippocrates and Confucius provided descriptions of mental retardation that date several hundred years BC. Even if these early accounts are disregarded, the area of mental retardation has a far-reaching past. Doll (1966) noted that "this is no flash-in-the-pan subject. Our field has an honorable history of 150 years." With such a lengthy record of attention it is of some interest why confusion and vagueness remain concerning classification and definition.

A variety of factors contribute to this lack of precision in definition. It is commonly accepted that mental retardation is related to a reduced level of intelligence. The concept of intelligence, perhaps more than any other factor, has played a central role in the definition of mental retardation. As Robinson and Robinson (1976) note, all of the controversy concerning the nature of intelligence has a direct impact on the field of mental retardation. As a consequence, part of the difficulty in defining mental retardation relates to the notion of permanence of intelligence.

Mental retardation has always been an area in which many disciplines have operated. This has contributed significantly to the problems of definitional and conceptual clarity. Iscoe (1962) highlighted this issue by noting that "even more than with normal children, no one discipline can claim the exceptional child as its unique area of study and concern." There has never been a legitimate "science" of mental retardation in and of itself. The problem of mental retardation has been addressed by psychiatrists, sociologists, psychologists, educators, anthropologists, and many others, each with a separate perspective and language. Consequently, the many different definitions and classification systems often tend to focus on the constructs of the particular profession rather than on the retarded individual; thus the sociologists set out to study retardation as a social problem, the psychologists as a psychological problem, and the physicians as a medical problem. There are even wide variations evident within professional areas, such as between clinical and experimental psychology. We do not intend to negate the value of a multidisciplinary attack on any problem. What is intended is to highlight the fact that the central conceptual focus, the retarded individual, is in danger of being ignored. The present text intends to present the areas of mental retardation from a multidisciplinary perspective but to maintain focus on the concept of the retarded individual.

Nearly 20 years ago Heber (1962) noted that "historically, mental retardation has been a social, administrative and legal concept, rather than a scientific one." The absence of a functional conceptualization has seriously detracted from preparation of professionals who work with the retarded. While a high degree of sophistication has developed in certain technical aspects of programming for children (for example, reinforcement procedures), the absence of effective conceptualization of mental retardation has frequently resulted in a discrepancy between professional skill and job or task requirements. Recent efforts consequently have been exerted toward formulating conceptual frameworks that will facilitate more effective professional preparation.

Cantor (1960) identified two major criteria for assessing abstract concepts: (1) the *clarity* of a definition and (2) its *usefulness*. These two criteria obviously relate to different facets of a definition. The first involves how well the definition communicates—do you know what I mean by my definition? The usefulness criterion involves the degree to which a concept facilitates making predictions and decisions. Using these criteria, it becomes evident that the conceptual framework is intertwined in an essential relationship with both definition and classification. Research in mental retardation clearly indicates that it is not a simple phenomenon. The problem is a fluid one both between and within disciplinary areas. The conceptual framework for mental retardation, if it is to be functional, will necessarily be complex.

DEFINITION OF MENTAL RETARDATION

The definition of mental retardation presented by the American Association on Mental Deficiency (AAMD) involves two dimensions—adaptive behavior and measured intelligence. The AAMD definition states that, "Mental retardation refers to significantly subaverage general intellectual functioning existing concurrently with deficits in adaptive behavior, and manifested during the developmental period" (Grossman, 1977, p. 11).

In publishing the above definition, the AAMD took steps to comply with Cantor's (1960) criterion of clarity for concepts. Each of the important terms in the statement was specifically defined in the published manual. For convenience, the complete articulation of these term definitions has been excerpted from the manual and is presented in the Appendix to this chapter. In reviewing this material the reader may identify areas where clarity in a strict sense is lacking. Our use of the word clarity in this context is not in a literal sense, but relative to previous definitional efforts.

Some professionals have viewed the inclusion of adaptive behavior in the AAMD definition as placing clarity in jeopardy (Clausen, 1972; Penrose, 1972). Despite the longevity of the idea in relation to mental retardation, measurement of adaptive behavior has not achieved the sophisticated precision that would be desirable. Clausen (1972) contended that adaptive behavior is representative of an ". . . ill-defined elusive concept, the inclusion of which results in added confusion, rather than increased clarity. . . ." The interested reader is directed to Symposium No. Seven in the annotated references of this chapter for a more detailed discussion of the issues involved in this topic (p. 39).

The inclusion of adaptive behavior represented a rather dramatic broadening of formally stated criteria for viewing mental retardation. This particular criterion does, however, raise certain issues that should be kept in mind for a variety of dimensions that may be relevant as attributes of mental retardation. A retarded person may be viewed as essentially one requiring some sort of action on the part of the community, either for the protection of the individual or others in the community. Two factors usually enter into this perception: (1) the retarded individual's deficits or level of functioning and (2) the threshold of community tolerance. When such action is taken depends on the degree to which the individual deviates from community norms—from those zones of behavior or performance that are deemed acceptable by society.

Mentally retarded people usually come to the attention of someone in the community of persons surrounding them because their behavior deviates sufficiently from the norm to be noticeable. This is true regardless of the degree of retardation. Identification of the more severely handicapped individual may occur at birth or during the first few days of life. This usually happens because some anomaly, either physical or behavioral, is sufficiently obvious that it is observable. For the retarded who are less deviant, identification may not occur until much later, as they begin to develop language or enter school. Initial suspicions of deviancy may then be further investigated through formal diagnostic evaluation and clinical observation by professional personnel. More details about diagnosis and evaluation are provided later in the text.

PREVALENCE OF MENTAL RETARDATION

How frequently do individuals evidence sufficient deviancy to be considered mentally retarded? A precise answer to this question is difficult to obtain for a variety of reasons. Accurate accounting is neither easy nor economically feasible. The difficulty of obtaining a consistent definition in order to determine actual frequency makes the task even more formidable. Estimates of the prevalence of mental retardation generally range from about 1 to 3 percent of the general population, with the 3 percent figure being most consistently cited. Translating this projection into numbers is difficult, although Scheerenberger estimated that in the United States in 1964 there were 5.4 million individuals who were mentally retarded. He further projected that by 1970 there would be 6.5 million retarded people residing in the United States. Figures such as these defy confirmation because of the astronomical cost of a complete census on such a population.

By far the largest proportion of these individuals fall into the mildly retarded range. The AAMD estimated that 2.5 percent of the total population were mildly retarded (Grossman, 1973). The moderate level of mental retardation, on the other hand, is generally thought to involve about 0.3 percent of the total population, and the severe and profound levels combined involve approximately 0.1 percent. The reader will note that these figures do not total exactly 3 percent, although they are quite close. This emphasizes the difficulty encountered in operating with estimates and definitions from a variety of sources and viewpoints. In no way should prevalence estimates be viewed as solid established facts—they are *estimates*. With respect to the population of mentally retarded per se, these figures suggest that somewhat over 86 percent of the group functions at the mild level of retardation, about 10 percent at the moderate level, and between 3 and 4 percent at the severe and profound levels.

Considerable variation is found in the incidence of mental retardation as one views different chronological age levels. Research has consistently indicated the highest incidence of retardation occurs during the years of formal schooling, with rather dramatically reduced numbers being identified both at the preschool and postschool levels. This distribution relates both to level of retardation and to tasks that are presented to the individual at different ages. Prior to entering the formal school environment very little is required that cannot adequately be performed except by the more severely handicapped child. Thus those individuals identified as retarded prior to about age 6 are primarily the moderately, severely, and profoundly retarded. As noted earlier, these lower levels of retardation constitute a small percentage of all retarded persons, particularly in relation to the percentage falling into the mild range of intellectual functioning.

The highest incidence of identified mental retardation occurs during the school years, approximately ages 5 to 18. This is an understandable phenomenon in light of the environmental tasks presented. As children enter school, they encounter a rather concentrated emphasis on abstraction and the acquisition of academic skills. This places retarded children in a very visible position since abstract skills are their area of greatest difficulty. The majority of retarded individuals identified at this stage are in the mild range of intellectual deficit.

Subsequent to the years of formal schooling the incidence of identified mental retardation decreases dramatically. Several factors contribute to this trend, which has often been noted as the phenomenon of the "disappearing

Table 1. Retardation incidence per 1,000 school-age children by educational classification and SES level of community*

Degree of impairment	SES level		
	High	Middle	Low
Totally dependent (IQ below 20)	1	1	1
Trainable (IQ 20 to 50)	4	4	4
Educable (IQ 50 to 75 or 80)	10	25	50
Slow learner (IQ 75 or 80 to 90)	50	170	300

*IQ ranges are given for the convenience of the reader. They represent approximate ranges that vary to some degree depending on the source of data.

retardate." From what was noted, one of these factors is obviously related to the fact that a majority of mentally retarded persons have been identified by the time the formal school years end. Another factor is operative, however, which deserves considerable attention with respect to curriculum planning. On termination of the tasks of formal education—emphasizing abstract concepts—the retarded are placed back into an environment where the requirements are less focused on their area of difficulty. Thus they seem more able to adapt in the postschool environment than in that presented by formal education. Some professionals have suggested that this may indicate the school curriculum is out of phase with later life and thus may not represent effective education (Spicker and Bartel, 1968; Drew, 1972). This is explored more fully in later chapters relating to education of the retarded.

The incidence of mental retardation also varies as one views socioeconomic status (SES). Table 1 summarizes the approximate incidence rate of retardation per 1,000 school-age children by educational classification and SES level of the community. As indicated in Table 1, there is no evident difference in incidence as a function of SES level in the dependent and trainable levels of impairment. The educable and slow-learner levels, however, indicate an increasing incidence as SES level decreases. These figures suggest that in the lower levels of retardation, where greater central nervous system damage pervades, SES levels are somewhat equally vulnerable. The milder impairments, however, seem more sensitive to environmental influences with respect to incidence. In light of the fact that the majority of retarded individuals fall into these upper levels, the social dimensions of mental retardation become highlighted. This also is discussed at greater length in later chapters.

HISTORY AND BACKGROUND OF DEFINITION
AND CLASSIFICATION
Definition

Both definitions and classification systems concerned with the retarded have experienced considerable change through the years. Definitions of mental retardation have been problematical from at least two general standpoints. First, a historical examination of definitions indicates that there has often been a focus on the adult to the relative exclusion of other age groups. The second area of difficulty relates to which factors should be included in a definition of mental retardation. This latter problem has provided a very visible arena of professional disagreement.

For what ages. Earlier definitions of mental retardation varied to some degree with respect to age focus. Tredgold (1937) and Benda (1954), for example, offered the following definitions that describe adult behavior.

> . . . a state of incomplete mental development of such a kind and degree that the individual is incapable of adapting himself to the normal environment of his fellows in such a way as to maintain existence independently of supervision, control or external support (Tredgold, 1937).
> A mentally defective person is a person who is incapable of managing himself and his affairs, or being taught to do so, and who requires supervision, control, and care for his own welfare and the welfare of the community (Benda, 1954).

Such a focus did not provide adequate latitude for the full range of attentions that were surfacing in mental retardation. The emphasis on adult behavior was particularly troublesome for professionals who were primarily inclined to work with children. Doll's (1941) definition was in obvious contrast in that it highlighted the appearance of the handicap as a developmental phenomenon. Although other controversies revolved around Doll's definition, it was an important forerunner for what was to follow with respect to the chronological age dimension. As noted, Doll addressed the issue of mental retardation in childhood. However, he also provided broad latitude by including the adult as well as the younger retarded. Doll's (1941) approach was specific in stating that retardation represented mental subnormality, ". . . which has been developmentally arrested . . ." that ". . . obtains at maturity." This full range of chronological ages is essential if the necessary breadth of the retardation problem is to be addressed.

In 1957 a project was begun under commission from the AAMD. The purpose of this activity (a part of a larger Project on Technical Planning in Mental Retardation) was to develop a manual on definition and classification terminology concerned with retardation. The resulting product that was adopted as a formal statement of definition by the AAMD (Heber, 1961; Grossman, 1973, 1977) was presented earlier (p. 6). This definition represented several significant changes in the area of definition and classification of mental retardation.

The AAMD definition addresses the problem of latitude in chronological age very specifically. It approaches mental retardation from a developmental framework but also attends to the adult retarded within the concept of adaptive behavior. Although similar to Doll's (1941) definition, from the standpoint of ranging from infancy to adult, the terminology is substantially different in order to avoid other definitional problems, such as incurability.

What to include. As noted earlier, a second general problem area has been the inclusion or exclusion of particular factors with respect to definition.

SOCIAL ADAPTATION. The majority of efforts at defining mental retardation through the years have, in one fashion or another, involved concepts of social adaptation or adjustment. These have reflected considerable professional consensus that important factors beyond measured intelligence are involved in mental retardation. It is of some interest that, despite this apparent conceptual consensus, a thrust toward formal functional measurement of social adaptation has only been evident in recent years. Although sporadic attempts were made to assess other behavioral dimensions, measured intelligence has primarily served as the criterion of mental retardation. This should not be taken to mean that recent influences (such as the 1961, 1973, and 1977 AAMD definitions) have generated immediate large-scale changes in the field, encompassing adaptive behavior as a measured criterion for diagnosis. Many services are still operationally functioning with the single criterion of intelligence. However, movement has been accomplished toward functionalizing the adaptive behavior criterion as a diagnostic factor.

CONSTITUTIONAL ORIGIN. Considerable controversy has been generated by two factors that have appeared from time to time during the historical evolvement of mental retardation definitions. These factors are best exemplified by Doll's (1941) definition, which specifically stated that mental subnormality ". . . is of constitutional origin" and "is essentially incurable." These two criteria generated considerable debate and became problematical on various fronts. Although not clearly defined, Doll's discussion of constitutional origin centers around the idea of biological pathology as the cause of the mental deficiency. He specifies that this may involve inherited biological problems or developmental alterations that biologically generate mental retardation.

The constitutional origin criterion posed particular difficulties with respect to that segment of the retarded population that does not present identifiable etiology. Primarily with the group that is termed "cultural-familial," adherence to a constitutional origin criterion required one of two decisions: either this group, for which constitutional origin could not be identified, should not be considered retarded, or one must operate on the basis of an assumed but unidentifiable constitutional origin. Both of these alternatives present problems. The former tends to ignore the greatest proportion of the population that functions at a retarded level. If taken literally, this approach could deter delivery of much needed services to these persons. The latter alternative sets a basic premise of the definition on extremely weak vulnerable grounds. Recent thinking has virtually achieved consensus that the constitutional origin criterion is too restrictive and cannot serve in a functional conceptualization of mental retardation.

INCURABILITY. The criterion of incurability has now met a similar fate to that of constitutional origin. However, the concept of incurability enjoyed considerable endorsement in past years, with resultant problems. One of the difficulties to which incurability contributed substantially was a pessimistic attitude toward expenditure of effort and resources for work with the retarded. Although a more realistic attitude is becoming increasingly prevalent, many would still relegate the allocation of resources for the mentally retarded to the lowest priority level.

Another difficulty presented by the concept of incurability involved situations in which an individual was diagnosed as mentally retarded at point A but later, at point B, evaluation did not reveal retardation. Such a situation may exist because of a number of specific factors but generally involves two broad possibilities. Obviously an error could have been committed such that either of the measurements indicated a false diagnosis. The second general possibility would be that indeed the individual was mentally retarded at point A but because of factors intervening between the measurements (such as specific instruction, maturational change) retardation no longer exists at point B.

In any case, individuals did seem to surface as mentally retarded at one point but not at another. If the second general possibility were true, strict adherence to the concept of incurability was not possible. By definition such a situation could not occur. Consequently a complementary concept of pseudo-retardation (sometimes termed pseudo-feeblemindedness in early literature) evolved. The term pseudo-retardation is an example of the need to explain or strengthen weak concepts by the development of compensatory concepts. Often, as with the case of pseudo-retardation, these compensatory concepts were equally weak or lacking in sound logic. Benton (1956) discusses the concept of pseudo-feeblemindedness from two frameworks, errors in diagnosis and the difference between an existing condition and some "true" mental retardation. He states emphatically that the situation of diagnostic error ought not ". . . be given the status of a clinical entity . . ." which is the case if pseudo-feeblemindedness is used in this way. Benton states that pseudo-feeblemindedness is not a relevant concept for use in cases of error in diagnosis, which essentially denies the first general explanation made necessary by incurability. An error in measurement is just that—an error in measurement. It is much sounder logic to recognize it as such rather than to search for a clinical entity as an excuse.

Benton describes pseudo-feeblemindedness from a second framework as ". . . a condition of behavioral retardation or deficiency which is ascribable to factors other than those customarily held to be the essential antecedent conditions of 'true' mental defect." This framework combines, somewhat, both the concepts of constitutional origin and incurability. The idea that there exists "true" mental retardation (and thus "false" or pseudo-retardation) was cumbersome, to say the least. First, it implied that there were agreed on causes that were identifiable. Such an implication relates to the criterion of constitutional origin, which has previously been discussed with respect to its weaknesses. Second, the situation of retardation at point A but not at a later point B defies the incurability concept in that the individual must not really have been retarded at the first measurement or retardation would have also been present at the second.

This complex set of interrelated concepts was further complicated by a controversy that was ongoing in the field of measured intelligence. The question was historical and involved whether intelligence tests assess functioning or potential capacity. More recent trends in professional consensus seem to be favoring functioning, although the issue is not completely dead. Interpretation of intelligence scores as measures of functioning dramatically clarifies the issues involved with incurability, pseudo-retardation, and, more generally, the definition of mental retardation.

From the standpoint of intelligence as behavioral functioning it is quite reasonable to expect situations in which an individual functions as mentally retarded at one time and not at another. Intervening experiences may have altered the level of functioning on the second measure to such a degree that the person does not exhibit a behavioral deficit. Such a viewpoint denies the incurability criterion and certainly makes the concept of pseudo-retardation unnecessary and nonfunctional.

It was noted earlier that the AAMD definition (Grossman, 1973, 1977) represents several substantial departures from the general trend of definitional efforts. One of these important changes was the formalization of a position concerning the framework from which intelligence measures are viewed. The AAMD definition specifically rejects the principle of potential intelligence and views mental status as representative of behavioral functioning level at the time of assessment. These conceptual changes in definitional position should not be interpreted as suggesting that professionals now view all mental retardation as "curable." Such a position would be totally unrealistic. It is the case, however, that the restriction of incurability has been largely discarded from definitions because it is a nonfunctional framework from which to view the broad problem of mental retardation. Two major advances have been evident in this evolution of definition and philosophy. Mental retardation is on much firmer conceptual ground than it was previously. In addition, the changes represented by the AAMD definition legitimatize the conceptual framework by bringing it closer in harmony with the realities presented by mental retardation as viewed in the community.

COMMENTS. Despite the advances just discussed, definitions for mental retardation still face some philosophical problems that will strongly affect decisions regarding services. Perhaps the most serious problem is simple and obvious. It does not seem efficacious to spend time and effort defining mental retardation without asking, "What is the purpose or objective of this definition?" The purpose or objective of definition, of course, was not completely ignored. Obviously each of the early workers who presented definitions was progressing in a given interest area, probably with objectives clearly in mind. These purposes were, however, most probably in line with the particular segment of effort involved and thus not attentive to the broader problems of mental retardation. It is our contention that the confusion evident in the historical evolvement of an encompassing definition of mental retardation is characteristic of an effort proceeding without overall purpose or direction. The absence of overall purpose is perhaps most obvious in the area of educational programming. If Cantor's (1960) second criteria for a concept were attended to, then a definition should be useful. Yet we find the definition of mental retardation being of questionable utility for educational programming, a facet of services that touches a very large proportion of the retarded population. This issue surfaces again as we consider classification schemes. It is discussed more fully in Chapters 8 and 9.

Classification

The historical development of classification schemes for mental retardation has evidenced confusion in concept and direction nearly parallel to that apparent in definition efforts. Perhaps the most serious difficulty with classification schemes relates to the choice of parameters for classification. This problem has been particularly troublesome in the mental retardation field, again partially because of the wide variety of disciplines interested in the phenomenon. Other difficulties related to the range of disciplines involved have been generated by the purpose or objective underlying the classification process. A given difference in purpose held, for example, by school administrators and physicians does not necessarily mean that the classification schemes are mutually exclusive or in conflict. It has been the case, however, that compatibility or joint focus has seldom been evident between professions.

Parameters for classification. A survey of the literature reveals that a rather wide variety of parameters have served for different classification schemes, both historically and in current approaches. Although used with varying frequency, six general parameters for classification seem evident: (1) symptom severity, (2) symptom etiology, (3) syndrome description, (4) adaptive behavior, (5) educability expectations, and (6) behavioral manifestations.

SYMPTOM SEVERITY. The most common criterion used in relation to the symptom severity parameter has been measured intelligence. Classification on this basis, of course, necessitates grouping by IQ scores in some fashion and identifying these groups with a designative term or label. For example, several early classifications used such terms as borderline retardate, moron, imbecile, and idiot. Terman (1916) used these labels with IQ unit groups of 70 to 79 for borderline, 50 to 69 for moron, 25 to 49 for imbecile, and 25 or below for idiot. Wechsler (1958) used the same terminology but with slightly different IQ units of 30 to 49 for imbecile and 29 or below for idiot. Use of the terms moron, imbecile, and idiot has for the most part been discontinued in the

United States because of negative connotations. However, they are still found in some literature from other countries. Grouping by measured IQ remains in heavy use, as exemplified by the AAMD classification. Using the terminology of mild, moderate, severe, and profound retardation, the AAMD IQ units are based on standard deviation of the test used. For example, on the revised Stanford-Binet these ranges are 52 to 67, 36 to 51, 20 to 35, and below 20 for the respective categories noted before. The AAMD classification is discussed more fully later in this chapter. Table 2 summarizes selected symptom severity classification.

One of the difficulties with symptom severity classification involves identifying a given individual as, for example, moderately retarded on the basis of an IQ score of 50. The measurement error involved in intelligence tests is generally considered to be 5 IQ points in either direction of the actual score obtained. Thus it is possible that the person's score might fall anywhere from 45 to 55 on the basis of error alone. In this particular example such error in measurement makes a difference with respect to which classification is used (since a score of 55 would fall well into the mildly retarded category). Such an example serves to emphasize the fact that a score should not be treated as a precise statement and also that a label or category is far from ironclad. As the reader progresses into the field of mental retardation, it will become increasingly apparent why the entire process of classification labeling is under close scrutiny.

SYMPTOM ETIOLOGY. The second general parameter for classification is the etiology of symptoms. Etiology has primarily involved the biomedical aspects of mental retardation. As such, this parameter is most often viewed in a medical context and has on occasion been termed medical classification. The AAMD Manual on Terminology and Classification included an etiological classification* with the following ten categories:

1. Following infection and intoxication (e.g., congenital rubella, syphilis)
2. Following trauma or physical agent (e.g., mechanical injury at birth)
3. With disorders of metabolism or nutrition (e.g., phenylketonuria or PKU, galactosemia)
4. Associated with gross brain disease, postnatal (e.g., neurofibromatosis, intracranial neoplasm)

*From Grossman, H. J. (Ed.). *Manual on terminology and classification in mental retardation.* Washington, D.C.: American Association on Mental Deficiency, 1977.

Table 2. Selected symptoms severity classifications

Measured intelligence*

Source	90–80	79–70	69–50	49–30	29–10
Terman (1916)		Borderline—IQ 70 to 79	Moron—IQ 50 to 69	Imbecile—IQ 25 to 49	Idiot—IQ 24 or below
Weschler (1958)		Borderline—IQ 70 to 79	Moron—IQ 50 to 69	Imbecile—IQ 30 to 49	Idiot—IQ 29 or below
American Association on Mental Deficiency (1961)	Borderline intelligence—−1 S.D., IQ 68 to 83	Mildly mentally retarded—−2 S.D., IQ 52 to 67	Moderately mentally retarded—−3 S.D., IQ 36 to 51	Severely mentally retarded—−4 S.D., IQ 20 to 35	Profoundly mentally retarded—−5 S.D., IQ 19 or below
American Association on Mental Deficiency (1973, 1977)		Mildly mentally retarded—2 S.D., IQ 52 to 67	Moderately mentally retarded—3 S.D., IQ 36 to 51	Severely mentally retarded—4 S.D., IQ 20 to 35	Profoundly mentally retarded—5 S.D., IQ 19 or below
American Psychiatric Association	Mildly or slightly mentally deficient—IQ 70 to 85	Moderately mentally deficient—IQ 50 to 69	Severely mentally deficient—IQ below 49		

*IQ ranges from Stanford-Binet standard deviations.

5. Associated with diseases and conditions resulting from unknown pre-natal influence (e.g., hydrocephalus, microcephaly)
6. Associated with chromosomal abnormality (e.g., Down's syndrome)
7. Associated with gestational disorders (e.g., prematurity)
8. Following psychiatric disorder (e.g., autism)
9. Associated with environmental influences (e.g., cultural-familial retardation)
10. Associated with other conditions

Approximately 75 to 85 percent of the total population of retarded persons fall into categories 9 and 10, with the remaining 15 to 25 percent distributed between categories 1 to 8. Categories 9 and 10, on closer scrutiny, are somewhat of a miscellaneous category that essentially specifies the absence of verifiable structural characteristics. From this it is evident that the other categories often involve retardation associated with observable or at least verifiable existing characteristics. As noted, these eight etiological classifications account for a relatively small portion of all mental retardation.

SYNDROME DESCRIPTION. The third approach to classification involves the description of syndromes by symptom grouping. As with etiology, the syndrome description approach has been used with greater frequency by medical workers than by others. Syndromes are usually identified by observation of a pattern of physical and behavioral characteristics, although physical descriptions have predominated. Of course, in any given case a syndrome may involve such characteristics in varying degrees and patterns.

The syndromes (such as Down's syndrome or mongolism, microcephaly, hydrocephaly) seem to portray the epitomized connotation of mental retardation often held by people not working in the field. It is not uncommon for the visual image of a mongoloid person to be thought of when mental retardation is mentioned in a lay context. This may be because the defining characteristics for syndromes are often very visible or because the syndrome approach to classification has enjoyed a rather long history, which may also be influential. Syndrome names usually include either the name of the pioneering worker in the study of that syndrome or, in many cases, the technical clinical terminology involved in diagnosis (as in neurofibromatosis). For a more detailed treatment or reference to a particular syndrome, we recommend either Carter's (1975, 1978) volumes on medical aspects of mental retardation or the syndrome atlas by Gellis and Feingold (1968).

ADAPTIVE BEHAVIOR. Adaptive behavior or related concepts have been involved in definition and classification for a major portion of the history of effort in mental retardation. Only in about the past two decades, however, have conceptualization and measurement progressed to a point that adaptive behavior is viewed as a functional parameter of classification. Primary impetus for this movement came from the work of Sloan and Birch (1955), which was adapted for the AAMD Manual on Terminology and Classification in 1961 (Heber, 1961) and further developed by later revisions of this manual (Grossman, 1973, 1977). One of the important factors in adaptive behavior as a classification parameter is that it attends rather specifically to human development. Reference to the Appendix of this chapter provides the generic framework for adaptive behavior as articulated by the AAMD Manual (Grossman, 1977). Table 3 summarizes the illustrations of adaptive behavior levels by ages presented in this manual.

Table 3. Example adaptive behavior levels by age*

Age and level indicated	Illustrations of highest level of adaptive behavior
Age 3 years and above: *profound* (NOTE: All behaviors at greater degree of impairment would also indicate *profound* deficit in adaptive behavior for persons 3 years of age or above.)	*Independent functioning:* Drinks from a cup with help; "cooperates" by opening mouth for feeding *Physical:* Sits unsupported or pulls self upright momentarily; reaches for objects; has good thumb-finger grasp; manipulates objects (plays with shoes or feet) *Communication:* Imitates sounds, laughs or smiles back (says "Da-da," "buh-buh" responsively); no effective speech; may communicate in sounds, gestures, or signs *Social:* Indicates knowing familiar persons and interacts nonverbally with them
Age 3 years: *severe* Age 6 years and above: *profound*	*Independent functioning:* Attempts finger feeding; "cooperates" with dressing, bathing, and toilet training; may remove clothing (socks) but not as an act of undressing as for bath or bed. *Physical:* Stands alone or may walk unsteadily or with help; coordinates eye-hand movements *Communication:* One or two words (Mama, ball), but predominantly vocalization *Social:* May respond to others in predictable fashion; communicates needs by gestures and noises or pointing; plays "patty-cake"; plays imitatively with little interaction; occupies self alone with "toys" for a few minutes

*Adapted from Grossman, H. J. (Ed.) *Manual on terminology and classification in mental retardation.* Washington, D.C.: American Association on Mental Deficiency, 1977.

Continued.

Table 3. Example adaptive behavior levels by age—cont'd

Age and level indicated	Illustrations of highest level of adaptive behavior
Age 3 years: *moderate* Age 6 years: *severe* Age 9 years and above: *profound*	*Independent functioning:* Tries to feed self with a spoon with considerable spilling; removes socks, pants; "cooperates" in bathing; may indicate wet pants; "cooperates" at toilet *Physical:* Walks alone steadily; can pass ball or objects to others; may run and climb steps with help *Communication:* May use four to six words; may communicate many needs with gestures (pointing) *Social:* Plays with others for short periods, often as parallel play or under direction; recognizes others and may show preference for some persons over others
3 years: *mild* 6 years: *moderate* 9 years: *severe* 12 years and above: *profound*	*Independent functioning:* Feeds self with spoon (cereals, soft foods) with considerable spilling or messiness; drinks unassisted; can pull off clothing and put on some (socks, underclothes, boxer pants, dress); tries to help with bath or hand washing but still needs considerable help; indicates toilet accident and may indicate toilet need *Physical:* May climb up and down stairs but not alternating feet; may run and jump; may balance briefly on one foot; can pass a ball to others; transfers objects; may do simple form-board puzzles without aid *Communication:* May speak in two or three word sentences (Daddy go work); names simple common objects (boy, car, ice cream, hat); understands simple directions (put the shoe on your foot, sit here, get your coat); knows people by name; if nonverbal, may use many gestures to convey needs or other information *Social:* May interact with others in simple play activities, usually with only one or two others unless guided into group activity; has preference for some persons over others
6 years: *mild* 9 years: *moderate* 12 years and above: *severe* 15 years and above: *profound*	*Independent functioning:* Feeds self with spoon or fork, may spill some; puts on clothing but needs help with small buttons and jacket zippers; tries to bathe self but needs help; can wash and dry hands but not very efficiently; partially toilet trained but may have accidents *Physical:* May hop or skip; may climb steps with alternating feet; rides tricycle (or bicycle over 8 years); may climb trees or jungle gym; plays dance games; may throw ball and hit target *Communication:* May have speaking vocabulary of over 300 words and use grammatically correct sentences. If nonverbal, may use many gestures to communicate needs. Understands simple verbal communications including directions and questions ("Put it on the shelf." "Where do you

Table 3. Example adaptive behavior levels by age—cont'd

Age and level indicated	Illustrations of highest level of adaptive behavior
15 years and above: *profound*—cont'd	live?''); (Speech may be indistinct sometimes.) May recognize advertising words and signs (ice cream, stop, exit, men, ladies); relates experiences in simple language *Social:* Participates in group activities and simple group games; interacts with others in simple play (''store,'' ''house,'') and expressive activities (art and dance)
9 years: *mild* 12 years: *moderate* 15 years and older: *severe*	*Independent functioning:* Feeds self adequately with spoon and fork; can butter bread; needs help with cutting meat; can put on clothes and can button and zipper clothes; may tie shoes; bathes self with supervision; is toilet trained; washes face and hands without help *Physical:* Can run, skip, hop, dance; uses skates, sled, and jump rope; can go up and down stairs alternating feet; can throw ball to hit target *Communication:* May communicate in complex sentences; speech is generally clear and distinct; understands complex verbal communication, including words such as ''because'' and ''but.'' Recognizes signs, and words, but does not read prose material with comprehension. *Social:* May participate in group activities spontaneously; may engage in simple competitive exercise games (dodge ball, tag, races). May have friendship choices that are maintained over weeks or months *Economic activity:* May be sent on simple errands and make simple purchases with notes; realizes money has value but does not know how to use it (except for coin machines) *Occupation:* May prepare simple foods (sandwiches); can help with simple household tasks (bedmaking, sweeping, vacuuming); can set and clear table *Self direction:* May ask if there is ''work'' for him to do; may pay attention to task for 10 minutes or more; makes efforts to be dependable and carry out responsibility
12 years: *mild* 15 years and over: *moderate*	*Independent functioning:* Feeds, bathes, dresses self, may select daily clothing; may prepare easy foods (sandwiches) for self or others; combs and brushes hair; may shampoo and curl hair; may wash, iron, and store own clothes *Physical:* Good body control; good gross and fine motor coordination *Communication:* May carry on simple conversation; uses complex sentences. Recognizes words, may read sentences, ads, signs, and simple prose material with some comprehension

Continued.

Table 3. Example adaptive behavior levels by age—cont'd

Age and level indicated	Illustrations of highest level of adaptive behavior
15 years and over: *moderate*—cont'd	*Social:* May interact cooperatively and competitively with others *Economic activity:* May be sent on shopping errands for several items without notes; makes minor purchases; adds coins to dollar with fair accuracy *Occupation:* May do simple routine household chores (dusting, garbage removal, dishwashing; preparing simple foods that require mixing) *Self direction:* May initiate most of own activities; attends to task 15 to 20 minutes (or more); may be conscientious in assuming much responsibility
15 years and adult: *mild* (NOTE: Individuals who routinely perform at higher levels of competence in adaptive behavior than illustrated in this pattern should NOT be considered as deficient in adaptive behavior. Since by definition an individual is not retarded unless he shows significant deficit in *both* measured intelligence and in adaptive behavior, those individuals who function at higher levels than illustrated here cannot be considered to be retarded.)	*Independent functioning:* Exercises care for personal grooming, feeding, bathing, toilet; may need health or personal care reminders; may need help in selection and purchase of clothing *Physical:* Goes about home town (local neighborhood in city, campus at institution) with ease, but cannot go to other towns alone without aid; can use bicycle, skis, ice skates, trampoline, or other equipment requiring good coordination *Communication:* Communicates complex verbal concepts and understands them; carries on everyday conversation, but cannot discuss abstract or philosophical concepts; uses telephone and communicates in writing for simple letter writing or orders but does not write about abstractions or important current events. *Social:* Interacts cooperatively or competitively with others and initiates some group activities, primarily for social or recreational purposes; may belong to a local recreation group or church group, but not to civic organizations or groups of skilled persons (photography club, great books club, or kennel club); enjoys recreation (bowling, dancing, TV, checkers, but either does not enjoy or is not competent at such activities as tennis, sailing, bridge, piano playing, or other hobbies requiring rapid, involved or complex planning and implementation) *Economic activity:* Can be sent or can go to several shops to make purchases of several items without a note to shopkeepers; can make change correctly, but does not use banking facilities; may earn living but has difficulty handling money without guidance *Occupation:* Can cook simple foods, prepare simple meals; and perform everyday household tasks (cleaning, dusting, dishes, laundry); as adult can engage in semi-skilled or simple skilled job *Self direction:* Initiates most of own activity; will pay attention to task for at least 15 to 20 minutes; conscientious about work and assumes much responsibility but needs guidance for tasks with responsibility for major tasks health care, care of others, complicated occupational activity)

EDUCABILITY EXPECTATIONS. Educability expectation is viewed as a parameter of classification by Scheerenberger (1964). This approach to classification is also known as educational classification. Preference for including the term expectation is based on the essential characteristic of this approach, which is a statement or prediction of expected achievement. Generally there are three categories, educable, trainable, and custodial; some professionals have included a fourth classification of dull-normal, which ranges just above the educable in terms of measured IQ (approximately 75 or 80 to 90). Measured IQ ranges associated with the other categories include 50 to 75 or 80 for the educable, 20 to 49 for the trainable, and below 20 for the custodial. Table 4 summarizes classifications by educational expectations.

Table 4. Classification by educational expectation

Terminology	Approximate IQ range*	Educational expectation
Dull-normal	IQ 75 or 80 to 90	Capable of competing in school in most areas except in the strictly academic areas where performance is below average
		Social adjustment that is not noticeably different from the larger population, although in the lower segment of adequate adjustment
		Occupational performance satisfactory in nontechnical areas, with total self-support highly probable
Educable	IQ 50 to 75 or 80	Second- to fifth-grade achievement in school academic areas
		Social adjustment that will permit some degree of independence in the community
		Occupational sufficiency that will permit partial or total self-support
Trainable	IQ 20 to 49	Learning primarily in the areas of self-help skills, very limited achievement in areas considered academic
		Social adjustment usually limited to home and closely surrounding area
		Occupational performance primarily in sheltered workshop or an institutional setting
Custodial	IQ below 20	Usually unable to achieve even sufficient skills to care for basic needs
		Will usually require nearly total care and supervision for duration of lifetime

*IQ ranges represent approximate ranges, which vary to some degree, depending on the source of data.

Although weaknesses would be involved in any classification scheme, the educability expectation approach is particularly vulnerable from a variety of standpoints. To permit adequate treatment of such weaknesses, they will be scrutinized and specifically addressed in a section devoted to that topic later in this chapter.

BEHAVIORAL MANIFESTATION. The sixth classification mentioned focused on behavioral manifestations. This approach has enjoyed considerable popularity in certain areas of the psychology of learning as well as in some educational applications. Only recently, however, has it been suggested as a relevant approach to classification for mental retardation. Based on behavioral observation of task performance, this approach differs conceptually from the previously discussed classification schemes. Essentially this framework is not concerned with grouping but is based on what skills a given individual has or does not have (more precisely, to what degree the task can be performed. The focus, then, is the individual skill level rather than the individual in terms of a category. This difference in approach removes the normative reference or interindividual comparison basis (child's performance compared with others) and places assessment more in the context of an intraindividual (the child's performance compared with no others but self) or criterion-referenced framework. As stated by its proponents, the behavioral approach promises considerable relevance for educational programming, an area where other approaches have been particularly weak. It does not necessarily serve all purposes well, however. There are legitimate reasons for grouping, such as administrative needs or determination and allocation of funds for programs.

Current definitions and classifications in other countries

Definitions and classifications in current usage have been discussed to some degree in earlier sections of this chapter. These treatments have, however, remained nearly exclusively within the geographical boundaries of the United States. It is useful for the student of mental retardation to be aware of other approaches to this phenomenon and to have an idea of how they compare. The purpose of this section is to provide a brief overview of approaches used in other countries and a comparative picture of how they relate to approaches being used in the United States. At the outset the reader should be aware that in many cases limited information is available from other nations.

Soviet Union. Descriptions of scientific philosophies and methods used in one country by scientists of another country are often subject to misinterpretation. Whether because of inadequate information, bias, or some other factor, such inaccuracies do occur and often serve to deter communication as well as to promote discord. It is our opinion that this type of difficulty *may* have been operative as others have interpreted the approach to mental retardation taken by the Soviet Union.

Most generic descriptions of the approach to mental retardation in the U.S.S.R. have suggested that the only mental subnormality acknowledged is that accompanied by central nervous system damage. Indicative of this interpretation is Scheerenberger's (1964) discussion, which states that in the Soviet Union ". . . mental retardation is dependent upon the occurrence, or suspected occurrence, of brain injury." Although providing more latitude than many interpretations, Scheerenberger's treatment is somewhat out of harmony with the impression conveyed by the Russian scientist Luria (1963) as he describes research in the U.S.S.R. Interpretations by scientists in the United States and elsewhere seem to be subject to an error of incompleteness rather than direct bias, if we are reading Luria accurately.

Luria's description of the Soviet Union's approach does very strongly emphasize the concept of nervous system impairment. In this respect the interpretations noted before are harmonious. The difference seems to emerge in terms of the way in which the emphasis is stated. As described by Luria (1963), the Soviet viewpoint is that failure to attempt identification of nervous system impairment, either central or peripheral, precludes ". . . genuinely scientific analysis of the symptoms." One could certainly take issue with the potential profit of such a philosophical base, but the scientist is more responsible for the soundness of method than for the philosophical framework. The emphasis that is conveyed by Luria, however, is somewhat different from that generally given in the interpretations of others.

The Soviet approach also emphasizes mental retardation as a developmental phenomenon. Luria indicates three ways in which retardation can occur. The first involves ". . . a definite link indispensable to the normal development of mental activity becomes deranged owing to an early (more often intrauterine) disease and sometimes to an inborn defect." Luria emphasizes that U.S.S.R. scientists do not believe all retardation to be inborn or hereditary. The second manner in which retardation can occur, according to Luria, involves the defective link ". . . hindering the further mental development of the child, is formed by a certain defect in a particular mental func-tion . . ." such as visual or auditory signal analysis. "Finally, in still other cases a retardation of the development of cognitive processes and of the higher psychological systems may be caused by defects in the intercourse of the child with adults, as well as by defects in training." This latter statement is one that is particularly uncommon to interpretations of the Soviet approach to mental retardation. Although maintaining the stand of inferred nervous system impairment, Luria is essentially saying that retardation may occur by influences of deprivation either in training or early childhood inter-action with adults. The case being suggested is that actual changes in the nervous system may occur because of these influences in the environment. Such speculation is not without support even by research efforts in the United States, where autopsy of animals subjected to extreme environmental influences has revealed a variety of changes in nervous system material (John, 1967).

Argentina. Central nervous system impairment generated by biological etiology has been the concept of mental retardation generally used in Argen-tina. Environmental influences are usually not thought to be involved in causation of retardation. The primary classification scheme in use is the symptom severity model with measured intelligence as the criterion. The term mentally weak has been commonly used to make generic reference to mental retardation. This term is also used in combination with the category labeled teachables, which is characterized by an IQ range of 50 to 70; mea-sured IQs ranging from 25 to 50 are associated with the category termed imbeciles or trainables; and IQs of 0 to 25 fall into the lowest category, which is designated as idiot or custodial.

Australia. Symptom severity also has been the general approach to classi-fication of mental retardation in Australia. Primarily utilizing the AAMD classification scheme, both measured intelligence and social adaptability serve as criteria. In line with the AAMD approach, Australians carefully con-sider developmental history in diagnosis. Categories in terms of IQ ranges are usually from 55 to 79 for mildly handicapped or slow learners; approxi-mately 30 to 50 for moderately handicapped, intellectually limited, or train-able, and below 30 for severely retarded.

Great Britain. From a legal framework there have been two categories of mental retardation in Great Britain, "mental subnormality" and "severe subnormality" (Tizard, 1965). This terminology is a result of the Mental

Health Act of 1959 and is legislatively defined in social and developmental terms. Subnormality is defined as "a state of arrested or incomplete development of mind (not amounting to severe subnormality) which includes subnormality of intelligence and is of a nature or degree which requires or is susceptible to medical treatment or other special care or training . . ." (Stevens and Heber, 1968). Severe subnormality is defined as "a state of arrested or incomplete development of mind which includes subnormality of intelligence and is of such a nature or degree that the patient is incapable of living an independent life or of guarding himself against serious exploitation, or will be incapable when of age to do so" (Stevens and Heber, 1968). The former term—mental subnormality—is also used generically, irrespective of the severity. The upper limit is not specifically delineated but usage seems to focus on an upper measured IQ limit of 70 (Tizard, 1965; Stevens and Heber, 1968).

British scientists working in mental retardation occasionally still use terminology that predates the 1959 Mental Health Act. Terms such as mentally defective and mentally deficient as well as feebleminded, imbecile, and idiot are found in the British literature and are defined for research and clinical purposes aside from those involved in legislative definitions. The latter three terms are essentially based on a symptom severity framework with general IQ ranges of 50 to 70 for the feebleminded, 20 to 50 for imbecile, and below 20 for the idiot classification.

France. France essentially defines mental retardation with the intelligence test. This is not surprising since it was Binet's task to identify children with learning problems when he developed his intelligence assessment instrument. Lafon and Chabanier (1966) suggest considerable diversity of approach within the French professional community working in the area of mental retardation. From a research framework they suggest two primary philosophical camps, the "psychological" (phychometrics, social psychology, and sociology as techniques) and the "organic" (focusing on a search for organic etiology).

Lafon and Chabanier suggest a classification scheme that seems to represent a synthesis of several frameworks, including clinical, educational, and measurement concerns. Their proposed classification reads as follows:

1. A threshold or marginal category, important but particularly difficult to define, including children who are not defective but are unable to attain the average level of their classmates. These are children with a limited intel-

ligence representing, so to speak, the lowest level of normal intelligence. They are characterized by a certain slowness in performing their school work and they have serious difficulties in conceptualization. As a rule they are at the bottom of their class. Their IQ lies between 80 and 100. They are only unadapted within the academic framework, which distorts the current educational structure.

2. Persons with a mild mental deficiency (IQ 65 or above), capable of an independent life and adjustment to a working community.

3. Persons in whom a mild mental deficiency is complicated by associated disorders. These children are not, strictly speaking, intellectually inferior to those of group 2, but the "extra burden" they carry makes their social adjustment more difficult.

4. Moderate mental deficiency (minimum IQ 50). Comparative independence and adaptation to simple work is possible after rehabilitation, but these cases usually require special care throughout their lifetime.

5. Severe mental deficiency (IQ 30 to 50). This "semieducable" group is capable of some social adjustment in a sheltered environment.

6. Profound mental deficiency, "profoundly retarded" group (IQ less than 30). These cases are educable only very slightly or not at all, and their adaptation to group life is doubtful and risky (p. 255).

Comments. As discussed earlier, several classification frameworks are used in the United States. The AAMD manual of terminology includes three parameters in an attempt to meet the diverse needs of professionals working in the field of mental retardation. The etiological classification scheme has been used by medical workers and others primarily involved in diagnosis and treatment of clinical forms of retardation. The adaptive behavior and measured intelligence parameters are ostensibly used in combination for a variety of service purposes. Measured intelligence in the AAMD scheme is essentially a symptom severity approach similar to the educational classification of educable, trainable, and custodial mental retardation. Although the educational scheme involves statements of expected achievement, the primary classificatory technique is measured intelligence.

The variety in international approaches to mental retardation is highly apparent from even the cursory overview given here. Certain countries are well settled into a particular philosophical framework and are pushing ahead in efforts aimed at progress from that framework. Others evidence much more variety, occasionally confusion, with respect to both definition and classification. Certain factors seem to thread through the schemes of several countries, although seldom through all. A developmental emphasis is present in the definition and classification systems of several countries, even those with highly divergent philosophical positions (for example, the U.S.S.R., Great Britain, the United States). Similarly the social adaptation factor is present as at least a partial international concern (for example, in the United States, Great Britain, France). Perhaps the most common factor cutting across international borders is that of symptom severity in terms of measured intelligence.

PURPOSES AND USES OF DEFINITIONS
AND CLASSIFICATIONS

Statements of definition and classification are generated for a wide variety of reasons. At times these schemes provide a conceptual picture of that which is being defined or classified. In serving the conceptual function such postulates often contribute to communication in a professional short-hand fashion. Beyond these roles, however, remains what may be the most vital function of definition and classification schemes—the translation of statements into action or operational terms.

The adequacy with which a classification scheme translates into practice is perhaps the acid test of the scheme itself. There are a number of factors that influence the ease with which this translation can occur. Two factors seem to be particularly evident from our previous discussion of definitions and classification. The first concerns the degree to which the scheme is in harmony with reality; the second relates to how well the purposes or objectives of the group using a definition or classification are served.

If a classification or definition scheme does not relate to the reality of actual circumstances, it is of questionable value and will probably fall into disuse. Perhaps the best example of such a situation in mental retardation involves the concepts of constitutional origin and essential incurability. Constitutional origin was out of phase with reality because it could not be verified in many individuals who are functioning as retarded. This situation required that constitutional origin either be assumed or, if strict adherence to the definition were maintained, services could not legitimately be rendered. The idea of incurability was similarly out of harmony with reality, as exemplified by the necessity of a compensatory concept of pseudo-feeble-mindedness.

Attention is also addressed to the second influence of how well the purposes or objectives of the group using a scheme are served. Purposes and objectives concerned with mental retardation have been nearly as numerous and diverse as the disciplines involved. Heber (1962) noted that mental retardation has historically been treated as ". . . a social, administrative, and legal concept, rather than a scientific one." A synthesis of the literature reveals little reason for disagreement with this statement and furthermore highlights the absence of discussions of mental retardation with clearly stated educational purposes in focus.

Most current as well as historical attempts at defining and classifying the mentally retarded have approached this process from a "grouping" standpoint. Grouping, or placing together those alike on some dimension, serves certain types of purposes very well; yet other objectives are only met minimally or not at all by such an approach. For example, a grouping framework serves administrative convenience quite efficiently. Students may be counted easily, funds distributed by type of child, and justifications of service rendered to legislatures. Similarly, for legal purposes a grouping process also serves well. If a given individual is placed in a particular category, decisions can be made concerning legal responsibility for action, or guardianship can be determined with relative ease. It is important for the reader to be cognizant that this discussion is couched in the perspective of the person or agency whose purpose is involved. In both of the above examples a certain degree of impersonality is involved in the decision-making. Administrative personnel, legislators, and legal agencies are often working with numbers and names rather than individuals, even though the numbers and names represent individuals. We are not addressing the question of how well the individual is served by such decisions. From the individual's standpoint "service" or "justice" may be marginal or absent.

We do not intend to detract from or negate the extreme value that has been accrued and the progress that has been made in the field of mental retardation because of classification by grouping. In fact, impetus provided by legislation and administration of funds at local, state, and federal levels has permitted dramatic service improvements over the past few years. The issue is that the adoption of classification frameworks that may be utilized effectively in one disciplinary segment may not serve well for another segment whose purposes are different.

For the most part, educational classifications of retardation have employed the grouping approach that has been utilized effectively in other contexts. Unfortunately, for the purposes of instruction, particularly with problem learners, such an approach may not be efficient. Evidence has accumulated that rather consistently indicates this, and educators of the retarded are recognizing the ineffectiveness of classification from a conceptual standpoint.

The previous discussion of educational classification indicated two approaches involved in categorization. The first, termed educability expectation, was exemplified by Kirk's (1962) statements of expectation for the educable and trainable retarded. The reader should be reminded, however, that symptom severity with respect to IQ was also used with ranges of approximately 75 or 80 to 90 for the dull-normal, 50 to 75 or 80 for the educable, 20 to 49 for the trainable, and below 20 for the custodial. The IQ range approach essentially serves a grouping function, while the statements of expectation would seem to provide guidelines for prognosis. As noted earlier, a variety of administrative purposes are served by grouping, such as convenient allocation of fiscal resources. Problems arise, however, when educational programs adopt these purposes rather than specifying purposes, objectives, and resulting classificatory schemes more in harmony with the instructional process itself. This issue has been raised in the literature, and concern has been expressed when review seems to indicate that the curriculum for the retarded reflects convenience in administrative arrangement as much as, if not more than, consideration of the type of student being taught (Spicker and Bartel, 1968; Drew, 1971).

In reviewing a number of sources discussing mental retardation, an interesting phenomenon begins to emerge. Since the topics of classification and definition are related to diagnosis and evaluation, one rather serious deficit seems evident with respect to both assessment and conceptualization. The conceptual weakness revolves around the relationship among evaluative assessment, classification, and, ultimately, programming. We have evaluated; this is the classification; now what? Benton's (1962) discussion of this topic suggests letting nature take its course, that we can ". . . predict a typical course and outcome with a fair degree of confidence." This reflects quite closely the educability expectation approach taken by Kirk (1962). The diagnostic purposes seem to be adequately served if the only inclination is a passive response—passive in the respect that no active educational or instructional intervention is implied. Recent trends in instructional philosophy and technique would not support a passive predictive approach but instead would dictate active intervention with specific behavioral objectives.

SOME SUGGESTIONS FOR IMPROVEMENT

Since we are not absolutely satisfied with the instructional usefulness of existing definitional and classification schemes in mental retardation, the next appropriate step is to suggest improvement. This section will focus on that effort.

Although definitions per se are not always precise, definitions of mental retardation have had compounded difficulties by the fact that measurement is specified (Heber, 1961; Grossman, 1973, 1977). Thus, one facet of the AAMD definition that has been viewed justifiably as an important strength has also been instrumental in promoting some difficulties. Because of the absence of stated purpose for educational programming, there is an apparent lack of purpose underlying a combination of definition-classification *and* assessment techniques. The grouping approach promoted both in the definition and classification schemes and the measurement technique involving evaluation that has long been known as normative referenced assessment. Normative referenced evaluation has not historically been of much value for educational programming. Thus, more conceptually sound and pragmatically oriented evaluation approaches have been developed in areas other than mental retardation. Regardless of origin, these concepts need to be explored in terms of the instruction for retarded persons if such educational programming efforts are to become more effective.

Normative-referenced evaluation involves the type of psychological testing with which most people are well acquainted. Probably the best-known assessment of this nature is the intelligence test. Essentially, normative-referenced evaluation provides a measure of an individual's functioning in comparison to some standard or group norm. From this framework a score provides an indication of whether the child stands above or below another student or some hypothetical average student. This type of evaluation is of value for purposes of grouping and beyond that has relevance for certain educational decisions (Drew, Freston, and Logan, 1972). As suggested by earlier discussions, however, the purposes served by such an evaluation approach have several limitations in the total arena of instructional programming. It therefore cannot be expected to provide all the information necessary for the actual teaching process. Such a global acceptance of the normative measure in the past has led to a diminished educational effectiveness with the mentally retarded and a great deal of frustration focused on psychometric information in general.

A counterpart evaluation concept has come into recent focus to meet a variety of needs not being attended to by normative-referenced assessment. Criterion-referenced evaluation does not place the individual's performance in a relative or comparative context with either other students or a normative standard. Often focusing on more specific skills, criterion-referenced assessment is viewed more as an absolute level of performance. It focuses on the actual level of mastery that an individual exhibits or, from a different perspective, the level at which the student becomes unable to perform a given task. This type of information is more useful to the teacher in that it indicates where to begin instruction. Criterion-referenced evaluation has enjoyed considerable popularity in recent years. Despite the obvious utility for certain aspects of instruction, criterion-referenced evaluation in isolation does not provide all of the information needed for a well-reasoned total educational effort. Concerted energy has most recently been focused on the development of more effective total evaluation models (Hammill, 1971; Bloom, Hasting, and Madaus, 1971; Drew, Freston, and Logan, 1972). These efforts are discussed in detail in Chapter 4.

APPENDIX

This definition information is excerpted from *A Manual on Terminology and Classification in Mental Retardation* published by the AAMD.

DEFINITION

The definition of mental retardation in this manual is slightly changed to reflect the deletion of the borderline category. The definition used for the current manual is:

> Mental retardation refers to significantly subaverage general intellectual functioning existing concurrently with deficits in adaptive behavior, and manifested during the developmental period.

General intellectual functioning is defined as the results obtained by assessment with one or more of the individually administered general intelligence tests developed for that purpose.

Significantly subaverage is defined as IQ more than two standard deviations below the mean for the test.

Adaptive behavior is defined as the effectiveness or degree with which an individual meets the standards of personal independence and social responsibility expected for age and cultural group.

Developmental period is defined as the period of time between birth and the eighteenth birthday.

COMMENTARY

Mental retardation as defined denotes a level of behavioral performance without reference to etiology. Thus, it does not distinguish between retardation associated with psychosocial or polygenic influences and retardation associated with biological deficits. Mental retardation is descriptive of current behavior and does not necessarily imply prognosis. Prognosis is related to such factors as associated conditions, motivation, treatment, or training opportunities more than to mental retardation itself.

The two-dimensional nature of this definition, originally formulated in earlier published versions of AAMD manuals, represents a fundamental conceptualization of the mental retardation symptom complex and is a crucial aspect of the classification scheme. Knowledge of the relationship between intelligence and adaptive behavior is still incomplete. It has not been determined with a high degree of precision what level of intelligence individuals need to cope adequately with the environmental demands of their subcultures or of the larger society. Intellectual functioning is assessed with one or more of the individually administered general intelligence tests. Such assessments measure current intellectual functioning only. Intellectual status may change, as may adaptive behavior. Adaptive behavior is a product of the interactions of an individual's abilities and skills with the expectations of society and of the opportunities to learn. Thus, individuals of the same level of measured intelligence may differ meaningfully in their social adaptation. For a person to be diagnosed as being mentally retarded, impairments in intellectual functioning must coexist with deficits in adaptive behavior.

Significantly subaverage general intelligence refers to performance which is more than two standard deviations below the mean (usually 100) of a standardized general intelligence test and is represented by an IQ of 67 or below on the Stanford-Binet and an IQ of 69 or below on Wechsler's scales. For several reasons, these upper IQ limits are proposed only as guidelines rather than as rigid limits. The assessment of intelligence is subject to some variation because of such factors as test construction, circumstances of administration, and measurement errors. Despite these limitations, intelligence test scores represent more reliable and valid measures of ability and performance than do either adaptive behavior measures or clinical judgment.

The arbitrary IQ ceiling values are predicated on data supporting a positive correlation between intelligence and adaptive behavior. This correlation declines in significance at the upper levels of mild retardation, and some individuals with an IQ below the ceilings may not demonstrate impaired adaptive behavior. Conversely, other individuals with scores slightly above these ceilings may be diagnosed as mildly retarded during a period when they manifest serious impairments of adaptive behavior. In such cases, the burden is on the examiner to avoid misdiagnosis with its potential stigmatizing effects, and to rule out such factors as emotional disorders, social conditions, sensory impairment, or other variables that might account more readily for observed deficits in adaptive behaviors.

In combination, and in the hands of qualified professionals, use of measures of intelligence and of adaptive behavior and of clinical judgment may minimize errors in the diagnosis of mental retardation.

Since these expectations of adaptive behavior vary for different age groups, *deficits in adaptive behavior* will vary at different ages. These may be reflected in the following areas:

During *infancy and early childhood* in:

1. *Sensory-motor skills development*
2. *Communication skills* (including speech and language)
3. *Self-help skills*
4. *Socialization* (development of ability to interact with others)

During *childhood and early adolescence* in:

5. *Application of basic academic skills in daily life activities*
6. *Application of appropriate reasoning and judgment in mastery of the environment*
7. *Social skills* (participation in group activities and interpersonal relationships)

and

During *late adolescence and adult life* in:

8. *Vocational and social responsibilities and performances*

During infancy and early childhood, sensory-motor, communication, self-help, and socialization skills ordinarily develop in a sequential pattern reflective of the maturation process. Delays in the acquisition of these skills repre-

INTELLECTUAL FUNCTIONING

	Retarded	Not retarded
Retarded	Mentally retarded	Not mentally retarded
Not retarded	Not mentally retarded	Not mentally retarded

ADAPTIVE BEHAVIOR

Fig. 1-1.

sent potential deficiencies in adaptive behavior and become the criteria for mental retardation.

The skills required for adaptation during childhood and early adolescence involve complex learning processes. This involves the process by which knowledge is acquired and retained as a function of the experiences of the individual. Difficulties in learning are usually manifested in the academic situation but in evaluation of adaptive behavior, attention should focus not only on the basic academic skills and their use, but also on skills essential to cope with the environment, including concepts of time and money, self-directed behaviors, social responsiveness, and interactive skills.

In the adult years, vocational performance and social responsibilities assume prime importance as qualifying conditions of mental retardation. These are assessed in terms of the degree to which the individual is able to maintain himself independently in the community and in gainful employment as well as by his ability to meet and conform to standards set by the community.

It is these deficiencies in adaptive behavior which usually determine the need of the individual for programs or services or legal action as a mentally retarded person.

In *infancy and early childhood,* deficits in sensory-motor development, in acquisition of self-help and communication skills, and development of socialization skills point to the needs for medical services, for early childhood education, or for family guidance.

During *childhood and early adolescence,* deficits in learning and coping skills indicate needs for specialized educational, prevocational, and recreational programs.

In the *late adolescent and adult years*, deficits determine the needs for vocational training, placement, and a variety of supportive services.

The relationship between intellectual functioning, adaptive behavior, and mental retardation is illustrated in Fig. 1-1.

Within the framework of the definition of mental retardation, an individual may meet the criteria of mental retardation at one time in life and not at some other time. A person may change status as a result of changes or alterations in intellectual functioning, changes in adaptive behaviors, changes in the expectations of the society, or for other known and unknown reasons. Decisions about whether an individual is classified as mentally retarded at any given time are always made in relation to behavioral standards and norms and in comparison to the individual's own chronological age group (Grossman, 1977, pp. 11-15).

STUDY QUESTIONS

1. In what ways did the "constitutional origin" and "incurability" factors found in early definitions of mental retardation cause problems? How have they been dealt with in more current definitions?
2. In what ways are definitions and classifications similar between the United States and other countries? How are they different? How would these similarities and differences influence statistical comparisons of incidence of mental retardation between countries?
3. How does the incidence of mental retardation vary in terms of socioeconomic status? As one views various degrees of mental retardation severity, what might be suggested regarding various influences or causation?

REFERENCES

Benda, C. E. Psychopathology of childhood. In Mussen (Ed.), *Manual of child psychology*. (2nd ed.) New York: John Wiley & Sons, Inc., 1954, Pp. 1115-1116.

Benton, A. L. The concept of pseudofeeblemindedness. *Archives of Neurology and Psychiatry*, 1956, **75**, 379-388.

Bloom, B. A., Hastings, J. T., and Madaus, G. F. *Handbook on formative and summative evaluation of student learning.* New York: McGraw-Hill Book Co., 1971.

Cantor, G. N. A critique of Garfield and Wittson's reaction to the revised manual on terminology and classification. *American Journal on Mental Deficiency*, 1960, **64**, 954-956.

Carter, C. H. *Handbook of mental retardation syndromes.* (3rd ed.) Springfield, Ill.: Charles C Thomas, Publisher, 1975.

Carter, C. H. *Medical aspects of mental retardation.* Springfield, Ill.: Charles C Thomas, Publisher, 1978.

Clausen, J. Quo vadis, AAMD? *The Journal of Special Education*, 1972, **6**, 51-60.

Doll, E. A. The essentials of an inclusive concept of mental deficiency. *American Journal of Mental Deficiency*, 1941, **46**, 214-219.

Doll, E. A. Innovations in the field of mental retardation. *Proceedings of the Second Colloquium on Exceptional Children and Youth*, Austin: The University of Texas Press, 1966, Pp. 12-35.

Drew, C. J. Research on social adjustment and the mentally retarded: functioning and training. *Mental Retardation*, 1971, **9**, 26-29.

Drew, C. J., Freston, C. W., and Logan, D. R. Criteria and reference in evaluation. *Focus on Exceptional Children*, 1972, **4**, 1-10.

Gellis, S. S., and Feingold, M. *Atlas of mental retardation syndromes.* Washington, D.C.: U.S. Government Printing Office, 1968.

Grossman, H. J. (Ed.) *Manual on terminology and classification in mental retardation.* Washington, D.C.: American Association on Mental Deficiency, 1973.

Grossman, H. J. (Ed.) *Manual on terminology and classification in mental retardation.* Washington, D.C.: American Association on Mental Deficiency, 1977.

Hammill, D. D. Evaluating children for instructional purposes. *Academic Therapy*, 1971, **6**, 341-353.

Heber, R. A manual on terminology and classification in mental retardation. (2nd ed.) *American Journal of Mental Deficiency, Monograph Supplement*, 1961.

Heber, R. Mental retardation: concept and classification. In E. P. Trapp and P. Himelstein (Eds.), *Readings on the exceptional child: research and theory.* New York: Appleton-Century-Crofts, 1962, Pp. 69-81.

Iscoe, I. The functional classification of exceptional children. In E. P. Trapp and P. Himelstein (Eds.), *Readings on the exceptional child: research and theory.* New York: Appleton-Century-Crofts, 1962, Pp. 6-13.

John, E. R. *Mechanisms of memory.* New York: Academic Press, Inc., 1967.

Kirk, S. *Educating exceptional children.* Boston: Houghton-Mifflin Co., 1962.

Lafon, R., and Chabanier, J. Research on mental deficiency during the last decade in France. In N. R. Ellis (Ed.), *International review of research in mental retardation.* New York: Academic Press, Inc., 1966, Pp. 253-277.

Luria, A. R. Psychological studies of mental deficiency in the Soviet Union. In N. R. Ellis (Ed.), *Handbook of mental deficiency: psychological theory and research.* New York: McGraw-Hill Book Co., 1963, Pp. 353-387.

Penrose, L. S. Mental deficiency. *The Journal of Special Education*, 1972, **6**, 65-66.

Robinson, N. M., and Robinson, H. B. *The mentally retarded child: a psychological approach* (2nd Ed.), New York: McGraw-Hill Book Co., 1976.

Scheerenberger, R. C. Mental retardation: definition, classification, and prevalence. *Mental Retardation Abstracts*, 1964, **1**, 432-441.

Sloan, W., and Birch, J. A rationale for degrees of retardation. *American Journal of Mental Deficiency*, 1955, **60**, 258-264.

Spicker, H. H., and Bartel, N. R. The mentally retarded. In G. O. Johnson and H. D. Blank (Eds.), *Exceptional children research review*, Washington, D.C.: Council for Exceptional Children, 1968, Pp. 38-109.

Stevens, H. A., and Heber, R. An international review of developments in mental retardation. *Mental Retardation*, 1968, **6**, 4-23.

Terman, L. *The measurement of intelligence.* Boston: Houghton-Mifflin Co., 1916.

Tizard, J. Introduction. In A. M. Clarke and A. D. B. Clarke (Eds.), *Mental deficiency: the changing outlook.* (revised ed.) New York: The Free Press, 1965, Pp. 3-22.

Tredgold, A. F. *A textbook of mental deficiency.* (6th ed.) Baltimore: Wood, 1937.

Wechsler, D. *The measurement and appraisal of adult intelligence.* (4th ed.) Baltimore: The Williams & Wilkins Co., 1958.

ANNOTATED BIBLIOGRAPHY

The following are resources for the reader who desires to explore topics in greater depth than is possible in an introductory treatment.

Carter, C. H. *Medical aspects of mental retardation.* Springfield, Ill.: Charles C Thomas, Publisher, 1978.

This volume is an extremely comprehensive catalogue of medical factors involved in mental retardation. It presents detailed descriptions of medical dimensions of the clinical syndromes of retardation.

Gelof, M. Comparison of systems of classification relating degree of retardation to measured intelligence. *American Journal of Mental Deficiency*, 1963, **68**, 297-317.

The author provides a detailed discussion of classification systems developed by a variety of organizations and professionals. The approach focuses on a comparison of different systems (including some aspects of definition) with respect to terminology, criteria, and philosophical position. Extremely comprehensive presentation; includes a detailed table comparing visually the various systems of classification.

Stevens, H. A., and Heber, R. An international review of developments in mental retardation. *Mental Retardation,* 1968, **6,** 4-23.

The authors have provided a valuable service by describing various dimensions of the mental retardation problem in a number of countries throughout the world. Topics of discussion include (1) concept and prevalence, (2) residential and hospital facilities, (3) educational services, (4) rehabilitation and employ-

ment services, (5) medical diagnosis and treatment, (6) prevention, (7) research, (8) personnel, (9) parent and other nongovernmental organizations, and (10) unique problems. Represents a valuable collection of information for the student interested in an international overview.

Symposium No. Seven. *The Journal of Special Education,* 1972, **6,** 51-106.

This symposium includes articles by eight authors. Clausen's article *"Quo Vadis, AAMD?"* serves as the initial stimulus position. Discussion focuses on the inclusion of adaptive behavior in the AAMD definition. For the student interested in this area, this is certainly a worthwhile exploration of issues.

CHAPTER 2

A multidisciplinary viewpoint

(From Marsh, G. E., Gearheart, C. K., and Gearheart, B. R. *The learning disabled adolescent: program alternatives in the secondary school.* St. Louis: The C. V. Mosby Co., 1978.)

INTRODUCTION

It can be argued that reality is a collection of individual perceptions that are collectively experienced. Certainly, cultural factors are very influential in shaping people's perceptions of their environment and their subsequent behavioral reactions. Such cultural differences are readily observed between cultures, and even within a culture there are subgroups that are manifestly different from each other and the larger dominant group. These differences are demonstrated in speech patterns, language differences, clothing styles, values, and so on. That such cultural differences—particularly in values, attitudes, and philosophy—influence the way a culture views the mentally retarded is also readily apparent, although not as easily observable.

In much the same way there are distinguishable differences between professional groups within a society. It is apparent to even the lay person that professional jargon is not the same across groups. There is a need for different terms to more succinctly describe a syndrome, a reaction, a type of legal action, and so on. At the same time, although it is not as obvious, different professional groups involved with the mentally retarded approach their tasks from different psychological, philosophical, and physiological frameworks. This difference in orientation results from the psychological factors that led persons into their particular disciplines and the training philosophy inherent in each discipline. It is a given that each discipline initially sees a mentally retarded individual from its own perspective, and legitimately so. This should not preclude the various professions that are concerned with the mentally retarded from being both aware of and appreciative of the contributions of their colleagues in related areas.

Comprehensive delivery of services for the retarded (or any person with special needs) is far beyond the scope of any single discipline. No individual profession includes the breadth and depth of expertise and resources ultimately necessary during the lifetime of a retarded citizen. There is therefore a genuine need for collaborative efforts among disciplines in order to accomplish all that must be done.

Chapter 1 discussed various approaches to classification and definition of mental retardation. It is now evident that the concept of mental retardation is one that changes, sometimes quite dramatically, depending on who is defining it and under what conditions it is being considered. Conceptual differences have traditionally existed among the various professions or disciplines that serve the retarded. Likewise, concepts have taken on different characteristics as a function of history. The purpose of this chapter is to discuss some of the issues, problems, and potential solutions involved in multidisciplinary efforts.

A BRIEF HISTORICAL PERSPECTIVE

Mental retardation has existed in one form or another in all societies throughout time. This in no way means that the same classifications for retarded persons have remained unchanged. The mentally retarded have been described in different terms, involving many diverse conceptualizations and varying characteristics, depending on societal and situational influences that were operating. In fact, as one looks back over the history of mental retardation, the picture is reminiscent of the chameleon, appearance changing depending on the environment. The concept of mental retardation has been elusive for a variety of reasons, not the least of which has been the temporal factors associated with economic, social, and political climates of the various cultures existing throughout history.

Although the earliest written reference to mental retardation is dated 1552 BC (the therapeutic papyrus of Thebes), anthropological studies have generated evidence of mental retardation substantially predating this time. Severe head injuries were quite common during prehistoric existence and most certainly resulted in frequent mental aberrations. Additionally, human skulls that date to the Stone Age have been discovered that indicate that crude surgical operations had been performed. Such surgical procedures were apparently intended to "cure" what was perceived as abnormal behavior. The methods used were based on the assumption that abnormal behavior was caused by evil spirits and that opening a hole in the skull permitted imprisoned demons to escape. Certainly not all such operations were performed on mentally retarded persons. Whatever the reason, however, the treatment surely produced retarded-like behavior as a result of the crude procedures, which inevitably caused brain damage.

Through the ages, human understanding and treatment of mental retardation has been influenced considerably by the socioeconomic conditions of the times. Mental and physical defects were naturally viewed by primitive nomadic tribes with fear and disgrace, in large part because of the stigma attached to such conditions by religious beliefs as well as superstitions and myths. Other influences on the way the handicapped were viewed resulted from the economic drain on the tribe by these individuals. Nomadic tribes in particular could ill afford to be burdened by nonproductive members who consumed their limited food and water supplies but did not tangibly contribute to the group's common welfare. Even as tribal civilization progressed and a less nomadic existence prevailed, the retarded were frequently viewed somewhat harshly. Farming and maintaining herds had become a way of life, but the threat of famine remained constantly on the horizon. The economic picture for the handicapped was therefore somewhat similar to what it had been during more nomadic times. Neither the religious nor the economic perspective was conducive to the care and maintenance of the retarded—nonproductive citizens were expendable.

Political authority also has represented a potent power base throughout history in terms of determining the lot of the mentally retarded. At times such authority provided very harsh circumstances for handicapped individuals, whereas at other times a much more humane approach prevailed. During the latter part of the sixth century Pope Gregory issued a decree that instructed the faithful to assist those who were handicapped by virtue of being crippled. This period saw various types and degrees of care provided for the handicapped, including the retarded, who were broadly referred to at that time as idiots. In a similar vein, the English under the rule of King Henry II during the twelfth century enacted legislation known as *de praerogative regis.* This statute made individuals who were "natural fools" wards of the King and for the first time distinguished between those whom we would now view as mentally retarded and mentally ill. These are merely isolated examples of efforts on behalf of the retarded. History is replete with other situations that were in diametric opposition and that generated extremely discriminatory and repressive practices. The retarded, as well as those with other handicapping conditions, have long been at the mercy of the more able majority.

Although we have been speaking in historic terms, issues concerning the lives of the mentally retarded remain as one of our most pressing problems today. Many times we look at the postures of early society as being extremely primitive and uninformed. However, a serious examination of current thinking and practices results in a much more balanced perspective. The fight of numerous advocacy groups in the courts and other arenas is public testimony to the fact that many issues remain to be settled. It is quite likely that future professionals will view our present-day efforts and postures as being nearly as primitive as we now consider those of the past.

A historical discussion of mental retardation, regardless of how brief it might be, cannot ignore the specter of the sterilization question, which has come to the fore periodically. The sterilization issue has always been deeply embroiled in numerous other questions such as nature versus nurture, political and economic issues, and moral and social undesirability. However, publicity was so extensive and emotionally charged that the issue of sterilization became a prominent dispute in and of itself.

Very influential in generating the sterilization controversy were some early geneological studies. One such study reported by Goddard (1913) received particularly widespread attention. Goddard traced the descendants of a revolutionary war soldier who he called Martin Kallikak. At one point in time Kallikak had an encounter with a barmaid and fathered an illegitimate child. The descendants of this union were reported to be primarily thieves, prostitutes, and other social-moral undesirables. Kallikak later married a girl of normal intelligence and distinctly higher social status. Descendants of this union were purportedly normal and, in some cases, superior. The resulting conclusion was that, because of genetics, one group was doomed to a life of degeneracy whereas the other was almost certainly destined to be successful. As a result of such reports, a sterilization movement was begun in the early part of this century. A number of intelligent people sincerely believed that enough was known ". . . about human genetics to permit a rational program of eugenics that would lead to an improvement of the human race" (Cranefield, 1966). Because of the fear of mental retardation, support for such controlling methods as sterilization and incarceration became relatively widespread. The result was an almost immediate and virtual destruction of special schools in some states. The purpose of the schools now became custodial care to prevent reproduction. This represented a considerable philosophical shift, since there had previously been at least guarded optimism that institutions would be able to provide education and training for their retarded inmates.

With the shift in purpose, the institutionalized retarded were viewed as permanent residents. They were in no way trained for an eventual return to society. Such actions represented simplistic solutions in terms of preventing "problem" members of society from having children (who might in turn also become problem citizens). This approach also provided a means of denying responsibility for undesirable social conditions for at least some proponents of institutionalization and sterilization.

Although sterilization remains an issue (many states still have legal provision for sterilization), there has been a fortunate reevaluation of the situation. This has been the result of considerable expansion of knowledge concerning heredity as well as advances in the training of the mentally retarded. With increased sophistication in research methodology, serious questions began to be asked about previous studies, such as Goddard's. For example, professionals are much less inclined to discount the effect of environmental influences on human development than was once the case. It is quite probable that the descendants of Kallikak and the barmaid were victims of unfortunate environmental influences as well as heredity. On the other hand, the descendants of the second union were certainly blessed with more favorable educational, social, and family influences. A rational perspective requires careful consideration of both dimensions in order to avoid decisions and practices based on inadequate evidence.

RETARDATION AND THE DISCIPLINES

Reference has been made, both in the present and preceding chapters, to the variety of disciplines concerned with mental retardation. With the very brief discussion of historical factors behind us, this chapter now turns to the various dimensions of interdisciplinary collaboration on the complex problem of mental retardation.

Disciplinary perspectives and factionalism

In a very real sense, the mentally retarded are no different from the rest of the population. A total life concept of necessary services for those of normal intelligence involves medicine, education, psychology, sociology, anthropology, social work, and religion, to name only a few. Likewise the mentally retarded may require attention from all of these diverse factions but to an even greater degree. Here is where the previous notation concerning "no different" becomes an obvious overstatement. During the lifetime of retarded citizens, it is highly probable that they will interact with a broader range of disciplines than their more able counterparts. This even more dramatically highlights a need to consider the multiple of professions dealing with the retarded.

Education—special education in particular—has probably been more centrally concerned with the problem of mental retardation than has any other discipline or profession. Others, such as sociology, medicine, and psychology, have been more tangentially involved, since retardation only represents a small proportion of their broader mission. Despite the focus of effort, special education for the most part has operated from a rather limited perspective—that of instruction. To the degree that special educators' perspective has been limited, so has their effectiveness in terms of meeting the needs of the mentally retarded. Experience over the years has clearly indicated that academic needs are less effectively met when one does not remain cognizant of physiological, social, and emotional influences on the child. These broad terms include a myriad of specific factors, such as medication, family influences, socioeconomic status, cultural background, and peer relations. It is rather difficult to teach children effectively if family strife has kept them awake most of the night and is generating severe emotional turmoil. Thus even the discipline that has the mentally retarded as its central mission is less effective in the absence of interaction with other professions.

The discipline of psychiatry has a very lengthy history in mental retardation. Potter (1971) noted that, when the American Association on Mental Deficiency was organized in 1876, it began with eight charter members, all of whom were psychiatrists. Although a psychiatry leadership was strongly evident in past years, this has changed rather dramatically for a number of reasons. Menolascino (1970) reported that only slightly over 6 percent of the AAMD membership was represented by psychiatrists in 1968.

Psychiatrists, when they have dealt with the mentally retarded, have primarily focused on the more severely handicapped. This has resulted in a rather inaccurate perspective with regard to the broad spectrum of mental retardation. In addition, past approaches have tended to operate from a "curative," traditional medical model. In view of such a posture, plus the selected population receiving most of the psychiatric attention, it is little wonder that the profession in general has become somewhat discouraged and uninterested in mental retardation. However, leaders and forward thinkers in psychiatry have recently advocated a rather dramatic shift in viewpoint from the microscopic approaches of the past. Menolascino (1970) has suggested that the psychiatrist should begin to function more as a generalist than in the past. This would involve an approach that is much more integrated with the many facets of the retardation problem, including a community mental health viewpoint, which involves the more mildly retarded individuals. Potter (1971) similarly sees the role of the psychiatrist shifting. He notes that the modern psychiatrist, at least in America, is more of a behavioral scientist than a medical scientist. With such forces at work within the discipline there is considerable hope that disciplinary territories will become less distinct, certainly a potentially positive shift for more adequate delivery of services to the retarded.

The medical profession has long been involved in mental retardation in a number of ways other than psychiatry. First of all, the physician is very frequently the first professional who is active in identification, diagnosis, and parent counseling. When the retardation is evident at birth (for example, the more severely handicapped either by birth trauma or congenital condition), the physician is usually the first professional to come in contact with the child. When retardation is not evident at birth but development is slower than usual, the physician is also frequently the first professional consulted. This does not necessarily occur because the physician is the best equipped for diagnosis. Instead it tends to occur because most parents do have a family physician or pediatrician with whom they consistently work. At this point, if something appears to be "not quite right," the parents will most likely turn to the professional they are accustomed to consulting.

In most cases the physician views retardation from the standpoint of a medical, that is, basically a physiological, problem. Although progressive changes are evident in the medical field, physicians are still often ill-prepared to conceptualize the ramifications of mental retardation beyond the medical perspective, which includes other disciplines. This substantially limits the effectiveness with which they can approach the total retardation problem. It certainly deters them from providing maximally effective parent counseling, which, as noted previously, has often been one of their tasks. Recent changes in medical training promise considerable improvement relative to the physician's global impact in the mental retardation field. As with other disciplines, the nature of these changes appears to represent a broadened perspective that crosses into other areas previously not addressed.

One other important subarea of the medical field certainly warrants mention—that of medical research. Advances in medical research have had a dramatic impact on certain types of mental retardation. Because of intense efforts in investigating some of the clinical syndromes, such as PKU and hypoparathyroidism, it has become possible and even common practice to implement procedures that will prevent mental retardation. To reach this point, however, collaboration across disciplinary lines was required. Once the causal factor was identified through medical research, it became necessary to turn to those skilled in chemistry and nutrition in order to implement actual preventative measures. Thus even in what appears to be a very limited area, that of preventing a few selected types of mental retardation, the importance of interdisciplinary effort is evident.

Anthropology is a discipline that has focused very little attention on mental retardation and yet might offer some extremely important insights into the broader perspective of the problem. Edgerton (1968) describes the anthropological study of mental retardation as essentially nonexistent and makes a plea for drastically expanded efforts in this regard. An earlier work by Edgerton (1967) represents the most visible contribution by a worker in this profession and has resulted in significant information concerning the retarded person's adaptation to his environment. Although the data provided by Edgerton's 1967 study was important in and of itself, his work makes contributions that appear to have far-reaching implications in other ways.

From the standpoint of research methodology, anthropology offers some intriguing possibilities. The anthropological approach to research is basically one of observing and recording information about an organism in its natural environment. This is a substantially different approach from that usually utilized in the study of mental retardation. More often than not, mental retardation researchers have adopted an experimental psychology research method, whereby the organism is studied in terms of performance or reaction to some artificially imposed treatment or situation. Consequently we know very little about the performance or adaptation of the retarded in their natural habitat. The anthropological method of investigation may provide very useful information that will complement the knowledge base that presently exists. In fact, it has been suggested that educational planning might profit substantially from knowledge about how the retarded individual operates in a natural setting (Drew, 1971). At any rate, anthropology represents a discipline that to date has not been heavily involved in mental retardation but one that may contribute very meaningfully in an interdisciplinary effort.

Sociology is an area that has been involved in mental retardation, at least tangentially for a number of years (Farber, 1968; Mercer, 1973). The work of Mercer and Lewis (1977) in developing a pluralistic model for assessment is but one example, albeit an excellent one, of a multidisciplinary approach to diagnosis. Their system of multicultural pluralistic assessment (SOMPA) is derived from an interdisciplinary conceptualization of the problem with a definite sociological base. However, the potential contribution of sociology toward our understanding of the retarded in a larger societal framework has been largely untapped. For example, Wolfsenberger's (1972) work relating to normalization is an area that would appear to be particularly fruitful from a sociological perspective.

Many other disciplines and subareas within disciplines have interacted with problems associated with mental retardation in one fashion or another. A full discussion of each and a detailed examination of the respective frameworks is far beyond the scope of this text; entire textbooks have been written that attend to only a single area as it relates to mental retardation (for example, social work, Schreiber, 1970; psychiatry, Menolascino, 1970, 1971). The preceding discussion of selected areas is intended to exemplify disciplinary perspectives as well as to stress the absence of essential interaction between disciplines. Other areas could easily have been selected for inclusion because of their attention (or lack of it) to mental retardation. Certainly psychology has contributed from many standpoints. Knowledge about mental retardation never would have progressed as far as it has without the data and knowledge generated from experimental psychology. Likewise, the testing and evaluation provided by psychometricians and school psychologists have long been a part of the overall picture in programming for the mentally retarded. This discipline, as others, has frequently operated independently, within the confines of its own terminology and perspective. The consequent reduction in effective contribution to education has been previously documented (Drew, Freston, and Logan, 1972) and perhaps exemplifies as dramatically as possible the importance of interdisciplinary collaborations. The law has periodically been an important force in the area of mental retardation. Unfortunately, the legal profession has often found it necessary to operate in an adversary role, opposed to other disciplines. Such a situation is exemplified by the case of *Covarrubias v. San Diego United School District*, in which special class placements were challenged by an injunction negating further placements until changes were made in procedures. Only recently have collaborative alliances been formed between the legal and other professions (Turnbull and Turnbull, 1975).

The foregoing discussion has outlined various disciplinary perspectives. As one reviews such perspectives it becomes evident that efforts within a profession, in isolation of meaningful interdisciplinary collaboration, often result in less effective delivery of service to the retarded. This discussion should not be taken to mean that a totally pessimistic outlook prevails. Although change has been slow, there are indications that considerable progress is being made toward bridging gaps between disciplinary perspectives as well as diminishing disciplinary friction. The latter will be examined shortly.

At least two influences have prompted such progress. First of all, experience has shown that the person being served—the mentally retarded person—is the one who is the ultimate victim of inadequate cooperation. Thus it has become clear to many that the actual reason for existence of certain professional efforts (the retarded individual) has been the one that suffers. This has provided considerable impetus to rectify the situation. The second influence that has promoted change involves the realization that something can actually be done to promote interdisciplinary collaboration and that it may not be so terribly difficult to accomplish. Differences in perspective as well as disciplinary friction are at least partially generated by knowledge that is limited to professional boundaries. In most situations where progress has been evident the individuals have accumulated at least some knowledge about the perspective of the cooperating discipline. This has not meant that a professional in one discipline has had to acquire advanced expertise in the other area, but it has involved the acquisition of at least enough information that an understanding of the other perspective is possible. Occasionally the broadened knowledge base may also indicate that what appeared to be differences in perspective were actually not as divergent as they were thought to be.

Friction between disciplines is not frequently discussed openly but remains operative at a sub rosa level. It is a fact of life, regardless of how undesirable or irrational it may be. The present examination is sequenced, following the note on improvement in interdisciplinary cooperation, to provide the reader with the recognition that progress is being made, a point that might be overlooked if the sequence were reversed.

Beyond the problems resulting from different perspectives per se, professional jealousy and perceived territorial rights often serve to generate additional differences to a point where open antagonistic factionalism exists between disciplines. Such factionalism operates at numerous levels, ranging from published criticism to the daily interaction by practitioners working in the field of mental retardation. To some degree the examination of roles and issues in public forums, such as published articles, is more healthy than other approaches and may even be constructive. Obviously the most constructive outcomes may be expected when such an article represents a rational examination of issues (Roos, 1971) rather than an emotionally charged attack that generates a defensive response instead of positive changes.

Dissonance is frequently evident between various disciplines within an organization. Although this phenomenon may be observed in a variety of settings, some of the most visible examples are within professional organizations that deal with mental retardation. One has only to attend regional or national conventions to hear derogatory comments about "the medical contingent," "those institutional people," "this division," or "that division." Such an atmosphere results more in political conflict than constructive improvement and tends to deter substantially from interdisciplinary collaboration.

Beyond the professional organization level, similar factionalism exists openly in state service and political arenas. Agencies are frequently in competition for limited funds with which to carry on their programs. Consequently, lobbying techniques may involve divisive interdisciplinary competition that is aimed at improving the lot of one group by making another appear inadequate. Although such tactics are obviously valuable in terms of agency or disciplinary self-preservation, they often cause people to lose sight of the real reason for existence—service to the retarded.

With the previously noted factionalism existing at various levels, it is of little surprise that some friction also occurs at the practitioner level, the contact point between the service delivery system and the client. The same professional jealousies and perceived territorial rights are operative in daily interactions between the various professionals who are in actual contact with the retarded. The teacher may become angry because the school psychologist does not provide information that is helpful in terms of instruction. The psychologist may derogate the teacher for being unable to understand the psychological report and make the intuitive leap to instructional activities. Examples could be endless, but the point is made. Beyond the differences in the way the retarded individual is viewed—whether from the standpoint of instruction or that of test performance—an overlay of professional antagonism magnifies the problem of inadequate cooperation.

Disciplinary factionalism becomes most blatantly unpalatable when it is discussed in the context of the practitioner. It is here that it becomes most obvious who suffers as a result of an inability to cooperate. However, this is also the level where changes appear to be most evident. The practitioner has greater opportunity to view the unfortunate results of inadequate service than those professionals more removed and serving in other capacities. It is therefore much more difficult to ignore or remain unaware of the crucial necessity of interdisciplinary cooperation and mutual effort.

Facilitating interdisciplinary collaboration

It has been mentioned previously that difficulties with interdisciplinary collaboration are being rectified to some degree. This is obviously a positive change that hopefully will result in vastly improved services to the mentally retarded. Change is progressing slowly, however, and many unnecessary injustices are occurring in the meantime. There is a serious need to accelerate this movement and to promote a more widespread collaboration between disciplines than presently exists. The purpose of this section is the discussion of certain factors that will potentially facilitate interdisciplinary efforts.

There has recently been a serious movement in special education to terminate the labeling of handicapping conditions. Terms such as mental retardation, behavior disorders, and learning disabilities, while convenient for communication, frequently tell very little about the individual child's characteristics or skill level. Likewise, the terms evolve in usage and tend to assume entity status that not only is inappropriate but often results in imprecise application and inaccurate generalizations. Long-standing tradition has also designated disciplines by labels, such as psychology, education, psychiatry, and so on. Disciplinary labels are also extremely convenient for communication and a variety of other purposes. Our contemporary society could not operate without terminology that indicates labels or designates or classifies events and phenomena. Disciplinary labels generate certain difficulties, however. Labels communicate, but they also generate a myriad of connotations concerning what each discipline represents. They frequently also serve to delineate territorial boundaries of operation—territorial rights. Such territorial rights have been noted earlier as a deterrent to effective interdisciplinary collaboration.

It would be impossible to rationally suggest that we suddenly cease to label disciplines. We can, however, view such labels in a different manner than in the past in order to facilitate interdisciplinary effort—in a manner that does not carry such rigid connotations of boundaries. If this type of change occurs, then individuals will have considerably more latitude to operate, broaden their knowledge base, work cooperatively, and ultimately serve the retarded more effectively in an interdisciplinary fashion.

It has previously been suggested that a broadened knowledge base appears to facilitate interdisciplinary collaboration. In retrospect this seems only logical and perhaps simplistic. Without at least some information about another person's profession it is extremely difficult to even communicate let alone effectively collaborate on a task.

Knowledge may be acquired in a variety of fashions. Naturally, we are quite experienced at obtaining information by reading such materials as journals and books. In many cases, however, this approach alone does not provide an adequate foundation to break down interdisciplinary barriers. An additional means of broadening knowledge and perspective is necessary. Personal contact with individuals from other professions serves this purpose very well. In fact, some would maintain that such contact is not only helpful but a prerequisite to facilitating interdisciplinary efforts.

When the topic of interdisciplinary collaboration is raised, people often indicate that a change in attitude is necessary for it to occur. Although most would agree with such a statement, few would be able to specify how this might be accomplished. Attitude is an extremely elusive concept and rather difficult to define. Consequently, it is not at all easy to determine how one knows when an attitude has changed. It is, however, somewhat easier to speak in terms of certain behaviors that need to be altered.

One behavioral change that appears important for interdisciplinary collaboration involves reaction to terminology differences. Frequently there are rather dramatic differences in terminology between professions. Such terminology differences often seem to generate negative visceral reactions, sometimes even openly derogatory remarks, from individuals with different disciplinary perspectives. It is easy to see how such reaction lends itself to friction and antagonism rather than cooperation. Consequently, the individuals involved in an interdisciplinary task need very much to overlook or control reactions to differences in terms. This does not at all mean that one must adopt another's terms, concepts, and approaches. It does, however, imply that value judgments about the appropriateness of the approach of the individual from the other discipline should be minimized. I may not choose to incorporate "ego strength" into my vocabulary or conceptualization, but if that is an important term in your disciplinary perspective, I can understand its meaning and not judge it as inappropriate, simply as "different," terminology. Certainly, acceptance of differentness is a goal of persons working for the benefit of the mentally retarded. Such changes in interactions between professions can result in far less friction and ultimately can promote greater effectiveness in terms of interdisciplinary collaboration.

One of the most crucial points to be made in a chapter on interdisciplinary collaboration involves the purpose of the professional effort to begin with. Often workers in the various disciplines that attend the mentally retarded lose sight of the appropriate focus for their effort—the retarded citizen. Far too much time and attention are devoted to professional self-preservation, sometimes to the detriment of the individuals being served. We frequently begin to focus more on our professional image than on the retarded. Whether the perspective is primarily one of medicine, education, psychology, or any of the many others involved, it is essential to maintain our focus on serving the total individual, for that is our purpose.

STUDY QUESTIONS

1. Mentally retarded individuals were often treated much differently in earlier societies than they are today. How did political, economic, and basic life-style influences impinge on treatment of the retarded during these times? Are some of these influences also operative today? If so, give examples.
2. It has been stated that an interdisciplinary approach to mental retardation is even more vital than with so-called "normal" populations. Why is this so? Couch your discussion in terms of needs at the various stages of the life cycle.
3. A number of difficulties are evident as various disciplines attempt to interact to work on a given problem. What are some of these problems, and how might they be overcome?

REFERENCES

Cranefield, P. F. Historical perspectives. In I. Philips (Ed.), *Prevention and treatment of mental retardation.* New York: Basic Books, Inc., Publishers, 1966.

Drew, C. J. Research on social adjustment and the mentally retarded; functioning and training. *Mental Retardation,* 1971, **9**, 26-29.

Drew, C. J., Freston, C. W., and Logan, D. R. Criteria and reference in evaluation. *Focus on Exceptional Children,* 1972, **4**, 1-10.

Edgerton, R. B. *The cloak of competence: stigma in the lives of the mentally retarded.* Berkeley: University of California Press, 1967.

Edgerton, R. B. Anthropology and mental retardation: a plea for the comparative study of incompetence. In H. J. Prehm, L. A. Hamerlynck, and J. E. Crosson (Eds.), *Behavioral research in mental retardation.* Eugene, Ore.: Rehabilitation Research and Training Center in Mental Retardation, 1968, Pp. 75-87.

Farber, B. Sociological research in mental retardation. In H. J. Prehm, L. A. Hamerlynck, and J. E. Crosson (Eds.), *Behavioral research in mental retardation.* Eugene, Ore.: Rehabilitation Research and Training Center in Mental Retardation, 1968, Pp. 97-109.

Goddard, H. H. *The Kallikak family.* New York: The Macmillan Co., 1913.

Menolascino, F. J. Psychiatry's past, current and future role in mental retardation. In F. J. Menolascino (Ed.), *Psychiatric approaches to mental retardation.* New York: Basic Books, Inc., Publishers, 1970, Pp. 709-744.

Mercer, J. *Labelling the mentally retarded:* clinical and social system perspective on mental retardation. Berkeley: University of California Press, 1973.

Mercer, J. R., and Lewis, J. F., *System of multicultural pluralistic assessment.* New York: The Psychological Corporation, 1977.

Potter, H. W. Mental retardation: the Cinderella of psychiatry. In F. J. Menolascino (Ed.), *Psychiatric aspects of the diagnosis and treatment of mental retardation.* Seattle: Special Child Publications, Inc., 1971, Pp. 14-27.

Roos, P. Misinterpreting criticisms of the medical

model. *Mental Retardation*, 1971, **9**(2), 22-24.

Schreiber, M. (Ed.) *Social work and mental retardation*. New York: The John Day Co., 1970.

Turnbull, H. R., III, and Turnbull, A. P. Deinstitutionalization and the law. *Mental Retardation*, 1975, **13**(2), 14-20.

Wolfensberger, W. with Nirje, B., Olshansky, S., Perske, R., and Roos, P. *The principle of normalization in human service systems*. Ontario, Canada: National Institute on Mental Retardation, 1972.

CHAPTER 3

Theories of intelligence

INTRODUCTION

The fact that individuals differ in a variety of ways has long been recognized. Human differences are concretely manifested by height, weight, skin and hair coloring, physical coordination, sex, and many other distinctive attributes that allow for recognizable differentiation of people. In much more subtle ways we also are able to differentiate people in relation to their creativity, personality, and intelligence to name but a few of the more abstract human factors. All of these traits are of interest, but none has been as controversial as the concept of intelligence. Intelligence has been an intriguing subject for philosophers, psychologists, and lay people for a variety of reasons. In western culture few concepts have been as avidly pursued as has intelligence, both from definitional and measurable dimensions. Indeed, we have been so caught up in quantitative perspectives that we may have difficulty keeping the concept in focus.

One of the perceived problems is perhaps our too rapid development of tests that purport to reflect intelligence and of the simplistic notion that test performance is valid and reliable, without regard to cultural influences. The problem has not been a lack of awareness regarding these other influences. Investigators in all behavioral sciences have pointed out the definitional problems engendered and the influence of behaviors that have not lent themselves to quantification in a direct sense. Our "success" in developing tests is perhaps our own worst enemy, particularly at the expense of neglecting other relevant aspects of intelligence behavior, such as the influence of social and cultural mores, early environmental influences, development, and sexual role expectations.

Intelligence as a phenomenon has been of interest to people for centuries. When people became aware of differences in mental abilities is of little consequence, but it surely antedates recorded history. As the gregarious nature of humans became evident through social groupings, the need to specify skills and competencies of various group members became a priority to facilitate an efficacious division of labor. The need to effectively prepare individuals for group membership became a problem in that it was grossly evident that some were more skilled in some areas than others. As societies developed and became more and more complex, the need to explain individual differences became increasingly important. The development of theories of intelligence parallels society's progress from hunting groups through agrarian communities to industrial metropolitan areas and into the atomic and space age megalopolitan regions.

Intelligence has become an extremely important concept in some cultures. Societies that have moved away from primarily hunting and agricultural pursuits and have instead pursued industrial capabilities require people who possess greater intellectual abilities. Each society emphasizes those areas that best provide for its needs and the group's common welfare. In less industrially advanced societies, skill in hunting, fishing, farming, and so on primarily calls for a sound body, capable of many hours of hard work. In advanced technological societies, machinery has been developed to the extent that physical ability is a declining requirement for employability. To be able to function at a minimal level in a technical society, an education has become more and more a necessity.

The advent of the space age reemphasized the need for the identification of those who have high intellectual ability. Governments of industrial nations have spurred searches and provided concomitant rewards for the intellectually capable through government grants for higher education, merit scholarships, and the promise of exciting, well-paid positions in a variety of areas. Conversely, this emphasis has also brought about an increased attention to those whose intellectual capabilities are limited. Such individuals constitute a concern in technologically advanced societies because they frequently become social liabilities. In less mechanized times those individuals with limited intellectual ability could often make a contribution to the immediate social milieu. As technology has advanced and influenced all spectra of society, the need for unskilled and semiskilled individuals has diminished as machines now more effectively do the work formerly done by individuals with little education. This has not been as great a problem to those who had the requisite intellectual ability but simply lacked the necessary educational training to do more skilled labor. The growth of the public school system in the United States has made an outstanding contribution in helping to provide the academic experiences required. However, for those who cannot profit educationally to the same extent as their more intellectually endowed fellow citizens, the opportunities for status and a fulfilling life have sharply decreased. Any humane society must therefore explore ways and means to reduce the social and economic liability of mentally retarded citizens and at the same time provide educational opportunities commensurate with those individual's intellectual abilities. Since the individual's self-respect often depends on such educational developments, to do less degrades and demeans both the citizens of a society and the society itself.

The need to identify and isolate particular characteristics that are associated with limited mental ability, both from biological and environmental causes, becomes a paramount consideration. As has been inferred, limited intellectual ability has been identified as the central problem. The term intelligence to connote relative intellectual brightness has been a popular abstraction for centuries. Intelligence as a concept has been variously recognized by most cultures as an important factor for group survival, development, and progress, but like most abstractions it has been an elusive, mercurial concept to define. The need to understand, define, and measure this phenomenon remains an important task as we attempt to provide better care for the mentally retarded in our society.

Humankind's attempts to come to grips with intelligence is manifested in the infinite number of theories about its nature. As with other presently unexplainable phenomena, theories play a vital role in assisting us in attempting to delineate and specify the inherent nature or substance of intelligence. It is not a directly observable phenomenon but a will-o'-the-wisp in many respects because of the influence of social values, socioeconomic conditions, and technological advances that tend to affect our perception, both individually and collectively. Therefore, well-delineated theories can assist us in identifying the relevant attributes for further empirical investigations. Theories "... tend to be *both* a tool and a goal" (Marx, 1963). Theories are tools in assisting us in developing researchable hypotheses for empirical investigation and are goals in providing scientists with a way of integrating and ordering existing empirical laws (Marx, 1963).

The following sections attempt to trace the development of theories about intelligence from early times through the present day. The intent is to provide the reader with a historical appreciation for the problems encountered in humankind's attempts to predict intellectual capabilities.

EARLY SPECULATIONS ABOUT INTELLIGENCE

Concern about cognitive abilities and the recognition of individual differences can be traced to the Chinese, who utilized testing to determine capabilities of applicants for civil service positions over 4,000 years ago (Linden and Linden, 1968). The earliest recorded mention of mental retardation is thought to be in the *Therapeutic Papyrus at Thebes* in 1552 BC (Doll, 1962). Plato in *The Republic* recognized the importance of determining individual differences in intelligence. Linden and Linden (1968) also report that "In 413

BC, approximately 7,000 survivors of an ill-fated Athenian army in Sicily were thrown into quarries near Syracuse. For many of them, their lives and release from imprisonment depended upon ability to repeat verses of Euripedes."

Among the Greeks such philosophers as Anaxagoras (c. 528-500 BC), Diogenes (412-323 BC), and Aristotle (384-322 BC) were interested in and concerned with the mind relative to its composition and nature. The Greek physician Hippocrates (460-375 BC) and the Roman Galen (c. 139-200 AD) attempted to provide a more natural, as opposed to a supernatural, explanation of mental abilities and mental phenomena.

The use of achievement examinations in western culture ". . . dates back approximately to the year 1200, when the University of Bologna in Italy held the first oral examination for the Ph.D. degree" (Linden and Linden, 1968). An early concern was the need to identify the mental ability of a person charged with a crime. Sir Anthony Fitz-Herbert (1470-1538) is credited with being the first to provide a working definition that was legally useful and that included developmental, intellectual, and social aspects—giving it a fairly modern ring.

> And he who shall be said to be a sot (i.e., simpleton) and idiot from his birth, is such a person who cannot account or number twenty pence, nor can tell who was his father or mother, nor how old he is, etc., so as it may appear that he hath no understanding, that he know and understand his letters, and do read by teaching or information of another man, then it seemeth he is not a sot nor a natural idiot (Doll, 1972, p. 50).

Swineburne (1560-1623) added the "tests" of ability to ". . . measure a yard of cloth or name the days of the week" (Linden and Linden, 1968) to assist in determining a lawbreaker's mental ability and consequently his responsibility under the law. According to Linden and Linden (1968), the seventeenth century legal criterion for responsibility was: the person charged must have the ". . . level of understanding of a child of 14 years of age."

In earlier times society had difficulty differentiating between retardation and mental illness. John Locke in 1690 provided what is purported to be the first usable differentiation between "idiocy" and "insanity":

> Herein seems to lie the difference between idiots and madmen, that madmen put wrong ideas together and reason from them, but idiots make very few or no propositions and reason scarce at all (Locke, 1690).

There were many who questioned the feasibility of attempting to quantify mental abilities, simply because of the intangible and elusive nature of the concept. Linden and Linden (1968) report that Malebranche (c. 1675) felt that mental ability was not measurable and was later supported by Ploueguet (c. 1763) and Kant (c. 1786). However, others felt that it was possible to apply measures to psychic ability. "Wolff advocated a 'science of psychometry' and Eberhard (c. 1776 and c. 1786) believed that 'a mathematics of the soul' could be devised. Eschenmayer (c. 1822) recognized the possibility of 'psychical' measurements" (Linden and Linden, 1968).

As early as the sixteenth century Juan Huarte, a Spanish physician cited in *Examen du Ingenios* (1575), aptly identified mental abilities when he wrote:

> All the ancient philosophers have found by experience that where nature disposes not a man for knowledge, 'tis in vain for him to labor in the fules of the art. But not one of them has clearly and distinctly declared what that nature is, which renders a man fit for one, and unfit for another science, nor what differences of wit is observed among men, nor what arts and sciences are most suitable to each man in particular, nor by what marks they may be discerned, which is one of the greatest importance (Robuck, 1961).

While Huarte was naturally influenced by the theories of his day, he did pinpoint some of the problems in attempting definitions and subsequent measurement difficulties.

TOWARD A SCIENTIFIC APPROACH

For all intents and purposes, the application of the scientific approach to human behavior began with a group of researchers who in the late eighteenth and early nineteenth centuries began investigating individual differences. Their academic backgrounds represented a variety of scientific disciplines, from astronomy to philosophy. They became interested in differences in individual observations, both between observers reacting to the same phenomenon or event and the difference within an individual over repeated observations. Since observational variations influenced the scientific approach with its demands for accuracy and reliability, many scientists became interested in being able to control and/or account for the now-recognized influence of individual differences. Through the work of Ernst Weber (1795-1878), Gustav Fechner (1801-1887), and Wilhelm Wundt (1832-1920), the application of scientific principles was first utilized in a systematic manner to explore human behavior through investigations of individual differences. Weber's work in the psychophysiological realm spurred Fechner, a contemporary, to expand and provide mathematical formulation to Weber's investigations in *difference limens* (that is, different responses to stimuli). Such investigations inspired others to devote their energies to experimentation with variations in human behavior. The work of Wilhelm Wundt, who was interested in the commonalities of behavior rather than the differences, is important for several reasons. Wundt established a laboratory at the University of Leipzig in which experimentation was carried on under rigid standardized conditions. Wundt's work attracted many of the researchers who were to assume leadership in the mental measurement area.

A contemporary of Wundt's was Sir Francis Galton (1822-1911), whose work in individual differences laid the groundwork for later advances in this area. Galton was interested in heredity, particularly hereditary genius, primarily because of the recurrence of genius in his family. Galton was instrumental in furthering the emerging field of statistics to assist in measuring individual differences. The statistical method of correlation was initially developed by Galton. However, a colleague of his, Karl Pearson (1857-1936), worked out the necessary mathematical formulas. James McKeen Cattell (1860-1944), an American, worked for 3 years with Galton, pursuing their mutual interests in individual differences. Cattell had previously studied with Wundt at Leipzig. Although the Leipzig laboratory was investigating Wundt's primary interest in general laws of human behavior, Cattell requested and received permission to study individual differences. Cattell was an early advocate of mental testing and was at the forefront of attempts to develop predictive measures relative to mental ability and academic achievement.

In France a concern for the mentally deviant prompted work in mental measurement. Jean Esquirol (1772-1840), Jean Itard (1774-1838), and Edouard Seguin (1812-1880) are almost legendary figures in work with the mentally disabled. In 1779 an 11- or 12-year-old boy was found wandering wild and naked in the woods of Aveyron in France. The boy, later named Victor, was brought to Jean Itard at the National Institute for the Deaf and Dumb in Paris. Itard, who had been forewarned that Victor might be an "imbecile," began working with Victor with great enthusiasm. It was not particularly uncommon at this time to find apparent mental defectives who had wandered from their homes and were found again after a few days in the same state as Victor. There were, however, many who felt that these "wild souls" had been lost in infancy and reared by animals. If this were the case, they were viewed as having a lack of normal intelligence since they had been deprived the appropriate sensory input needed for their intellectual development. Etienne Condillac (1715-1780), a French philosopher, had previously advanced a theory that lack of stimulation would produce retarded development. Itard felt that, if the wild boy of Aveyron were exposed to the right kind of sensory input, his intelligence would develop. His goal was to provide Victor with sensory and motor training and the "experience" Victor had supposedly missed. Itard worked with Victor for 5 years in all, keeping detailed records of all of his activities. At the end of this time Itard confessed his failure, since among other things Victor never learned to speak, although he did learn to read simple words and to dress himself.

Itard's "failure" was really a victory because he had amply demonstrated that a rather seriously retarded boy could be greatly improved and brought to a higher level of functioning than anyone had previously imagined. His work gained him the recognition of the French Academy and opened a new field of education.

At about the same time, a French physician, Jean Etienne Esquirol (1772-1840), a colleague of Itard's, differentiated ". . . imbecility from idiocy, and both from insanity" (Doll, 1972). Esquirol further pinpointed lack of language as a primary deficit of the retarded and determined that defective persons *could* often learn unskilled tasks and do elementary reading and writing. Binet and Simon later capitalized on Esquirol's observations that the deficits of retarded people were mainly intellectual and not sensory and that language ability would be a useful diagnostic criterion in developing the standardized intelligence scale.

Edouard Seguin, who had been a student of both Esquirol and Itard, believed that the retarded could be helped. He spent his mature years demonstrating that with patience and determination mentally defective children could be educated. In 1837 Seguin began a school for the mentally retarded to which from all parts of the world ". . . scientists and educators came to marvel at the progress made by the children in the school" (Linden and Linden, 1968). Seguin later moved to the United States (1850) where he was instrumental in work with the mentally retarded and proposed the formation of a national association for a concerted attack on the problem of mental deficiency. This work is presently carried on by the American Association on Mental Deficiency.

In France the need for objective measures in identifying mentally subnormal persons became increasingly important not only to determine responsibility under the law but also to place people in special classes that were becoming prevalent in the late 1800's. Subjective appraisals for placement were increasingly found to be inadequate, and searches for more objective measures to ascertain mental ability were undertaken. Although many scientists interested in human behavior were investigating and attempting such measures, it was Alfred Binet (1857-1911), a Frenchman trained in law and medicine, who became interested in psychology, who along with Theophile Simon (1873-1961) developed the first intelligence test. Primarily because of Binet's interest in intelligence—manifested through his book *The Experimental Study of Intelligence*, published in 1902—the Minister of Public Instruction in 1904 commissioned Binet and Simon to investigate the feasibility of developing a test to assist schools in placing mentally defective children in appropriate classes. In 1905 Binet and Simon published a thirty-item scale, which was felt by the two authors to be only a perfunctory approach to the problem. In 1908 a revision was published in which fifty-nine subtests were grouped over age levels from 3 to 13 years. Binet is credited with being ". . . the first to identify central intelligence as opposed to peripheral disturbances—as the essential problem of the retarded" (Doll, 1962).

Henry Goddard, Director of Research at the Vineland Training School, who was traveling in Europe in 1908, came across the Binet-Simon scales and in 1910 brought out the English translation. Although the scales were refined by several psychologists, it was Lewis Terman who, after many validity checks on American populations, published a test in 1916 based on the original 1908 Binet-Simon Scale of Intelligence. Despite bitter attacks, the Binet Scales revolutionized diagnosis and treatment of the mentally retarded.

Contemporary approaches

As with many other perplexing phenomena, there are about as many ways to define intelligence as there are persons interested and motivated enough to try. While this may be an overstatement, Abraham (1958) reported that 113 different definitions of "the gifted" were found by a student writing a term paper on the subject. Likewise mental retardation, at the other end of the intellectual spectrum, has produced a plethora of definitions. The number of definitions for these two intellectual extremes has probably led many people to think of intelligence in a quantitative sense. Intelligence, however, cannot be considered solely as a linear phenomenon ranging from "more to less" or from "bright to retarded." The complexity of human intelligence dictates that qualitative aspects must also be considered. An appreciation of the many determinants affecting intelligence is necessary if we are ever to fully understand and appreciate this puzzling phenomenon. From genetic selection before and at conception through prenatal, natal, postnatal, and early development, there exists an almost infinite number of variables that can affect the intellectual abilities of the developing human organism. As scientists have grappled with the intelligence concept, two questions have continually emerged: how is intelligence developed, and how can we gain some understanding of its composition in order to make predictions? Both of these questions are not yet completely answered. The first question has been asked from at least the early Greek and possibly Egyptian eras; Plato, in *The Republic*, pursued the second question, with his interest being to identify capable leaders. As science has developed, we have found continued exploration of each question both as parallel and as intertwining aspects of the intelligence dilemma.

DEVELOPMENT OF INTELLIGENCE

The question of how intelligence develops has generated what is most commonly referred to as the "nature-versus-nurture" controversy, which was directly stimulated by the phenomenon of mental retardation. Is intelligence genetically determined with little or no contribution from later environmental conditions and influences, or is intelligence primarily dependent on environmental factors with a limited genetic contribution? Advocates of both positions have been at times exceptionally vociferous in championing their view and lamenting the naiveté of their counterparts. As was indicated in Chapter 2, this controversy has been almost continuous in this country since the turn of the century, with many social and economic implications relative to the way society views and provides for the mentally retarded. However, to compare present discussions with the turn-of-the-century furor or with the repressive actions of Nazi Germany toward the mentally retarded is unrealistic. Out of this controversy has emerged a more reasoned approach, attempting to establish the interrelatedness and interaction of both heredity and environment. It would seem to be an indication of maturity to move from extremes toward a midposition that presumes to recognize and draw from the facts established by both sides of the coin. The dilemma that

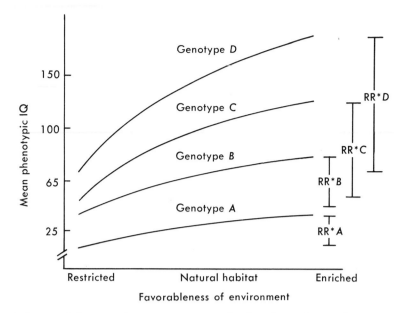

Fig. 3-1. Scheme of the reaction range concept for four hypothesized genotypes. *Note:* Marked deviation from the natural habitat has a low probability of occurrence. RR signifies reaction range in phenotypic IQ. (From Genetic aspects of intelligent behavior by I. Gottesman. In Handbook of mental deficiency, Ellis, N. Copyright 1963, McGraw-Hill. Used with permission of McGraw-Hill Book Company.)

spurs such heated debates is not really whether hereditary factors or environmental conditions play the major role in mental retardation, but the degree of presumed effect. The differentiation between mental retardation and mental deficiency is an example of an attempt, simplistic as it may be, to separate hereditary or endogenous causation (mental deficiency) from environmental or exogenous causation (mental retardation). That such conditions as microcephaly, phenylketonuria, and Tay-Sachs disease are a function of hereditary factors is readily apparent. Similarly, that environmental conditions can affect the level of mental functioning has been repeatedly manifested both through research and observations. It is therefore not actually debatable whether or not genetically induced aspects affect human intelligence or whether or not environmental factors play a significant part in the dynamics of intelligence. Both aspects play a role in that each depends on the other in order for intelligence to be manifested. Dobzhansky (1955) utilized the phrase "range of reaction" to characterize the duality of nature *and* nurture. In this sense the contributions of heredity in setting the limits of intelligence are recognized, and the influence of environmental factors is accounted for in determining the range of intelligence. Gottesman (1963) illustrated this (Fig. 3-1), showing that the inherited traits (genotype) of particular individuals or groups are affected by the environmental factors (phenotype) relative to the favorableness of the environment.

While the interaction between heredity and environment is acceptable to almost all scientists, there remains a controversy about the degree each contributes. It is apparent that, at present at least, we do not have the capability to partition genetic and environmental contributions into percentiles to indicate precise "amounts" of each that contribute to individual performance. However, given similar environmental conditions, it is theoretically possible to estimate the differential contributions of the hereditary aspect. Burt (1955), for example, stated that approximately 90 percent of the difference in intellectual assessments for similar age groups in England results from genetic contributions. This estimate would be considerably higher than most theorists would consider appropriate, given present techniques and sophistication. Since the early part of the twentieth century, there has been a definite trend away from a hereditary primacy toward an extreme environmental position about the cause of retardation.

Probably the most controversial example of the whole nature-versus-nurture debate has been Arthur Jensen's (1969) publication in the *Harvard Educational Review* of an article entitled "How Much Can We Boost IQ and Scholastic Achievement?" This article has generated a host of responses, both for and against, about (1) the dangers inherent in proposing racial intellectual differences, (2) erroneous statements in the article, (3) the extent of academic freedom, and (4) the supposed "weight of evidence" reported by Jensen and others regarding Black intellectual inferiority. Jensen's thesis is that there are two types of learning tasks. Type I refers to "associative learning" tasks, which are of a rote learning nature that requires negligible transformation of the material learned; Type II is learning of a conceptual nature in which transformation of the learned material is requisite for success. In his article Jensen (1969) concludes that Whites possess Type II learning to a greater extent than Blacks. Jensen's topic is not new but certainly has produced the most shock value. In addition to the two learning types described previously, Jensen implied that heredity may have more of an effect than environment;

that as a group Whites score higher on IQ tests than Blacks; and that such projects as Head Start, which are based on environmental enrichment activities, will fail because of the effect of heredity (Rice, 1973). Jensen has not only added fuel to the controversy of nature-versus-nurture but has fanned the flames with the implications relative to "black-versus-white" intellectual capabilities.

MEASUREMENT OF INTELLIGENCE

The question regarding the measurement of intelligence similarly elicits a controversy relative to definition. The way in which intelligence is defined influences the methods utilized in attempting to determine relative degrees of intelligence for prediction purposes. Basically there are two extremes that comprise our theorizing about intelligence. There are those who take a factorial approach, in which the attempt is made to isolate and identify component parts of the intelligence concept, and those who conceptualize intelligence as a holistic construct that is either hypothetical at most or is so intrinsically related to the total personality that it cannot be conceived of as a separate and distinct entity. With variations, most definitions fall between these two extremes.

It is one thing to theorize about the nature of intelligence and another to attempt to measure its integral parts. In order to measure any concept, a decision has to be made regarding the components or aspects that comprise the essentials of the phenomenon under consideration. If, for example, a prospective testmaker believes that intelligence cannot be understood apart from personality, then the subsequent test developed must of necessity include measures of such things as emotions, experiences, physical condition, age, and the myriad of other factors involved in personality development. This would certainly provide a better measurement than we presently have, not only to predict but also to foster intellectual ability and capabilities. The obvious difficulty in this approach is that it is presently impossible to construct such tests that include any and all of the infinite number of factors that would be required. Therefore our present intelligence tests are and can only be measures of limited samples of behavior at a given time in a given place.

The best tests of intelligence presently available cannot and should not be considered as the right way or the only way of measuring the intelligence concept. The difficulty in testmaking lies in what the adaptation and use of such a broad term as intelligence. Intelligence cannot be measured directly. As with any other concept, the primary components of the concept must be identified before any inferences can be made. As Nunnally (1967) points out, the measurable attributes of a concept (in this case, intelligence) must be isolated, evaluated, and subjected to experimental analysis. This is what Binet did, for example, in deciding that judgment was involved in intellectual functioning. The degree to which the testmaker is successfully able to identify *measurable attributes* (or subtests), standardize them, and provide validity and reliability data is the sine qua non of test development. Our present intelligence tests, therefore, are composed of attributes that the testmaker believes are the best measurable aspects of attributes of intelligence presently available. How well a person performs on the attributes (for example, the subtests, such as vocabulary, judgment, analogies, and others) of a test determines how much inference we may make about his relative intelligence.

How well intelligence tests, or any other test for that matter, are able to adequately measure attributes of intelligence has generated considerable debate. In this regard Binet was aware of the shortcomings of his scale when he stressed ". . . the importance of qualitative variables that affect test results, e.g., the persistence and attention of a child while taking a test have an influence upon the score obtained" (Linden and Linden, 1968). The adequacy of a single diagnostic test, much less a single IQ score, has been harshly attacked in recent times (Garcia, 1972; Mercer, 1972; Watson, 1972), especially when minority groups are involved.

As the use of intelligence tests with many different groups has increased over the years, it has become apparent that there are many factors that mitigate against indiscriminate use of tests and quick encapsulation of a person into an IQ score. With a renewed call for consideration of the rights of others, as represented by the civil rights movement, a new consciousness has hopefully been revived. Many of the early psychologists and educators in the mental testing movement in the United States warned against an indiscriminate use of and belief in the sanctity of intelligence and IQ tests. Lightner Witmer was only one of the early twentieth-century psychologists who cautioned that we must recognize ". . . the etiological importance of emotional deprivation, lack of experiential stimulation, functional nervous disease, inadequate or improper nutrition, sensory defects, physical illness and improper discipline" (Doll, 1962).

A good part of our problem can be attributed to expediency. As the applied use of intelligence tests gained in popularity and became more widespread, the concern for theory as a base was, if not negated, at least diminished in importance.

As we approach the 1980's, we find ourselves in the position of having promised too much, yet having neglected important aspects of the intelligence puzzle, such as inter- and intraindividual differences, and having allowed practical considerations to outdistance theoretical speculations.

In order not to get ahead of ourselves and with the above caution clearly in mind, we now need to turn back and look at theory development and its relationship to the testing movement. Most tests have emanated from the factorialists rather than from those who have taken the previously discussed holistic approach for the reasons mentioned earlier. Charles Spearman (1863-1945), who initiated the factorial approach, felt that intelligence could best be expressed through two factors: a general or "g" factor and a specific or "s" factor. He assumed that the "g" factor represented "true intelligence" in that the various tests of intelligence were consistently intercorrelated. Therefore, he hypothesized that a "g" factor was present in all valid tests of intelligence, since it appeared to be an ubiquitious entity. Since the intercorrelations were not perfect between tests, Spearman further hypothesized that an "s" factor was also present, but to a lesser degree than the "g" factor, and resulted from those activities that could be associated with particular situations.

A contemporary of Spearman's, Edward L. Thorndike (1874-1949), however, took a somewhat expanded view in developing a multifactor theory in which he proposed that there were three kinds of intelligence: abstract, concrete, and social. In so doing, Thorndike took issue with Spearman's two-factor theory in that although the intercorrelation of tests was demonstrably high, it was not necessarily attributable only to the "g" factor. The results of a study on transfer of training (Thorndike and Woodworth, 1901) indicated that a student's improvement in one subject did not always bring about a concomitant improvement in another. This study was used by Thorndike to refute Spearman's "g" factorial approach in that it seemed evident that all intellectual traits did not result from one factor. Instead Thorndike believed that intellectual functioning could be divided into three overall factors: (1) abstract intelligence, in which a facility for dealing with verbal and mathematical symbols is manifested; (2) mechanical or concrete intelligence, in which the ability to utilize things in a meaningful way is stressed; and (3) social intelligence, in which the capacity to deal with other persons is paramount. Further, Thorndike believed that intelligence was caused by neural interconnections in the brain and that the number of interconnections was related to the degree of intelligence manifested by a person as exhibited by his performance capabilities.

A considerable debate arose as a result of the apparent disagreement between Spearman and Thorndike. However, by the late 1920's the differences between the two had abated because they were in agreement that "... when a number of variables are correlated, these variables always can be factored into either a general factor and specific factors or into a number of independent factors" (Linden and Linden, 1968) and that more heat than progress was generated as a result of the quasi debates. However, in 1933 Louis L. Thurstone (1887-1955) stirred the embers of Spearman's "g" factor through multiple factor analysis in which group factors could be analyzed. Thurstone (1938) utilized factor analysis to develop his primary mental abilities test in which seven factors were isolated in the belief that they could account for almost all of the correlation between intelligence tests. There were seven factors that appeared to support Thorndike's multifactor theory and to oppose Spearman's "g" factor theory: spatial (S), perceptual (P), number (N), verbal (V), word fluency (W), memory (M), and reasoning (R). In 1940, however, Cyril Burt demonstrated that the supposed difference between Spearman and Thurstone was a result more of different statistical methods than of any substantive difference in theory.

While it is evident that the factorial approach has not, perhaps because of relatively crude measuring devices, provided any conclusive data on what true intelligence is or how to measure it, there have been significant advances in testing. Even though the "debate" remains unsolved, and proponents of multifactor versus single factor are still at loggerheads, albeit presently benign, the importance of the issue remains. Presently, two theorists are at the forefront regarding the makeup of intelligence and subsequent measuring methods: J. P. Guilford and Jean Piaget.

J. P. Guilford and his associates at the University of Southern California have continued the work of Thurstone in utilizing the factor analytic approach relative to identifying the primary factors of intelligence. Guilford has proposed a three-dimensional theoretical model that specifies parameters (operations, products, and contents); incorporates previously identified

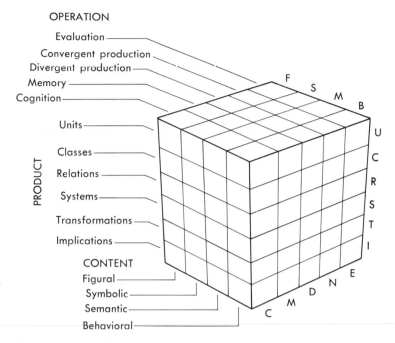

Fig. 3-2. The structure-of-intellect model with three parameters (other parameters may need to be added). (From The nature of human intelligence by J. P. Guilford. Copyright 1967, McGraw-Hill. Used with permission of McGraw-Hill Book Company.)

primary factors; and posits the existence of yet unidentified factors. This model (Fig. 3-2) postulates the existence of 120 possible primary intellectual abilities.

Guilford and his associates believe that human thought processes involved in the *content* division can be subdivided into four major categories: (1) figural (having a visual or tactile form, such as books, trees, houses, clouds, and the like); (2) symbolic (possessing a summarizing quality, such as numbers, musical notes, codes, and the like); (3) semantic (requiring meanings be attached to intangible materials, such as the association of the word pencil with the object pencil); and (4) behavioral (involving essentially nonverbal dimensions, such as perceptions, desires, moods, and so on).

The *product* aspect is currently categorized into six major types or categories, which serve an organizational purpose for the content dimensions of figural, symbolic, and semantic. The subdivisions include: (1) units (the processing of a single item such as a number, letter, or word); (2) classes (the classification of sets of items or information by common properties, such as with figure symbols or semantics); (3) relations (the activity of developing relationships between a product subdivision and a content subdivision or even relationships between relations); (4) systems (an aggregate of interacting parts, such as in sentence diagramming, numerical operations, or social situations); (5) transformations (the more abstract and creative activity of transforming material into different than anticipated results, conclusions, or physical configurations); and (6) implications (the most abstract of the product subdivision, that involves anticipation and making predictions).

The third division, *intellectual operation*, includes the mental processes involved in utilizing the information or contents with which it works. There are five types of operations according to Guilford: (1) cognition (the process of comprehension, knowing, understanding, familiarity, and so on, such as the comprehension of material in a nonthreatening atmosphere that tends to stimulate interest, for example, games, television, and so on); (2) memory (the ability to recall specific information, such as arithmetical steps, telephone numbers, and others; both short- and long-term memory are included in this subdivision); (3) evaluation (mental activities, such as evaluating, judging, comparing, contrasting, decision-making, and others); (4) convergent production or thinking (the process of being able to produce an acceptable response derived, it is assumed, from a large quantity of material); and (5) divergent production or thinking (the process of being able to generalize and produce alternatives based on information possessed or provided).

In the structure of intelligence (SOI) model, as inferred above, the intent and attempt is to be able to identify and provide discrete factors in such a way that they may be distinguishable from one another in order to provide a conceptual understanding of all 120 hypothetical factors individually and collectively. For example, the cell memory-figural-units (MFU) represent the ability to remember figural units, such as being able to recall forms or objects, as in correctly identifying the letter B. The method of factor analysis as represented in the SOI model provides a way of precisely describing missing factors so that further exploratory investigation or research is in large part predetermined (to the extent that the various abilities are isolable, and the necessary instrumentation for precise measurement is available). It is possible that the presently provided SOI model may change in form as research progresses. Indeed, it has been expanded from a previous model (Guilford, 1959) in which only ninety abilities were hypothesized.

Jean Piaget is unique among theorists in that he has approached the problem of intellectual functioning from an entirely different framework. In place of developing various tasks and then evaluating the correctness of the response(s), Piaget has focused on the psychological process that led to the response(s). In addition, he has approached the task developmentally, being primarily concerned with interpreting the development of behavior.

Whereas Guilford was influenced by early work in factor analysis by such psychologists as Spearman, Thorndike, and especially Thurstone, Piaget's early training was in biology and zoology. Piaget's approaches have evolved over the course of more than 50 years of investigations. During this time there have been three distinct phases to his work (Hunt, 1969). In the first stage, he investigated children's language and thought, judgment and reasoning, conception of the world, conception of physical causality, and moral judgments (Hunt, 1969). It was during this phase that Piaget questioned the view that child development resulted completely from environmental influences or was completely genetically caused. His investigations demonstrated that mental growth was not influenced entirely by nature or entirely influenced by nurture but rather by the continual and constant interaction of both aspects. In the second stage, he attempted to observe ". . . the origins of intelligence and reality constructions in his own three infant children" and "revised his method of observation to focus on the child's actions in the course of repeated encounters with objects, persons and situations" (Hunt, 1969). Through such activities, Piaget demonstrated a genius for observations that was continually guided by his theoretical formulations. These observations provided significant evidence for his theories of the development of cognitive structures. In the third phase Piaget and his associates investigated a number of aspects: concrete operations, conservations, relations, preconceptual symbolization, formal operations, sensorimotor stages, probability, perceptions, illusions, logical operations, and so on, all of which emanated from his early theories.

Piaget has postulated a series of intellectual developments in which the order of their appearance is *the* important aspect and not the age at which they appear. Piaget believes that intelligence is an *adaptive* process and is only one special aspect of all biological functioning. The environment places the individual in the position of adapting to it and at the same time in the position of modifying it. The term accommodation is used by Piaget to connote the adaptation of the organism to the environment; he uses the term assimilation in recognition of the organism's adaptation of the environment to fit perceptions. An organism is considered to be adapted when there is *equilibrium* between accommodation and assimilation. Piaget has utilized this biological concept in describing learning activities. For example, a child, when playing, utilizes assimilation (the stick becomes a fishing pole, rifle, or baton; the shoe becomes a car or boat), but when the child is play acting, accommodation becomes predominant (so that he becomes the most feared gunman in the old west, a movie star, or a champion tennis player) in an attempt to initiate the desired model through accommodating ephemeral perceptions. Assimilation and accommodation are complementary and antagonistic functions. Consequently, both aspects create alternate states of disequilibrium until they are gradually resolved into a state of equilibrium. The organism only becomes adapted when accommodation and assimilation are in equilibrium, that is, when there is harmony between the individual and its environment.

Piaget has hypothesized that *mental assimilation* involves the comparing and possible subsequent adjustment of sensory information with the person's present response patterns. *Mental accommodation* is the adapting of the response patterns to the sensory information. The response patterns are referred to by Piaget as *schemas,* which are collections of behavior sequences defined in behavioral terms. For example, once a schema (or strategy) has been worked out to solve an environmental problem, it tends to be repeated in similar situations. Piaget has recognized that developmentally there are various types of assimilation, such as reproductive assimilation, which is the tendency to repeat (practice) schemas in order that they may be integrated and habitual. However, this repetition brings about changes in schemas by the individual in that as they are practiced in a larger and/or slightly different environmental arena, which fosters *a generalization of assimilation,* this in turn creates *recognitory assimilation* in that the organism encounters and recognizes differences. Higher order schemas are developed through *reciprocal assimilation* brought about by combining several schemas that were previously separate. Similarly, accommodation is concurrently taking place as the organism continually revises the existing schemas to better incorporate the complex perceptions.

Piaget has postulated a sequence of developmental periods and substages that are believed to be generally the same for everyone. According to Piaget (1960), maturation and experience influence a child's rate of progress through the following sequences. Also, different cultural and social environments can contribute to differences in the average age of attaining different stages. The four main periods and substages are the following.

1. *Sensorimotor period.* This period is from birth to about 1½ to 2 years of age. In this period the child is involved in a number of behavioral activities leading to a stable imagery. As Hunt (1969) explains, "These kinds of behavior include imitation of models no longer present, solving provlems while looking at them and without motor groping, and following desired objects that are out of sight in a box through a series of hidings in which only the box is visible."

2. *Preoperational period.* The preoperational period is divided into two substages: preconceptual and intuitive.

    a. *Preconceptual substage.* This substage occurs from about 1½ to 2 to about 4 years of age. The development of symbolic thought and language are now manifested, indicating the child's awareness of objects and realization of his relation and interrelation with them. The child is now able to initiate actions and assume the future position of things.

    b. *Intuitive substage.* From about 3 to 7 years of age the child is involved in thinking that is restricted to what is directly perceived. In other words the child enters this stage unable to understand constancy, that is, that the amount of liquid is the same and not less in a bowl rather than a narrow cylinder. By the end of this stage, however, the child is able to recognize other points of view but is not able to generalize to other situations.

3. *Concrete operation period.* This period roughly relates to the ages 7 to 11 years old. During this stage, the child moves toward being able to understand the conservation of quantity, length, and number. He now understands, for example, the constancy of liquid regardless of the size or shape of the container and is able to generalize to other situations. "Piaget interprets this development as an equilibrium between the assimilation of objects and their relations to the subject's actions and the accommodation of the subject's schemata of thinking" (Woodward, 1963).

4. *Abstract operations period.* From approximately 11 years of age onward the child is involved in a continuous refinement of approaches to complex problems. The child engages in reasoning activities that are beyond a concrete operational approach in that now "hypothesizing," from which correct deductions are concluded, is more frequently engaged in and utilized. Verbal

symbolization is now a primary tool utilized in solving problems, providing the developing human organism increasingly abstract concepts that can be manipulated and operationalized.

In the foreword to *Young Children's Thinking* (Almy, 1969), Piaget succinctly points out why traditional learning theories have not had a great impact on education:

> This is the essential conclusion, as far as education is concerned: learning cannot explain development, but the stage of development can in part explain learning. Development follows its own laws, as all of the contemporary biology leads us to believe, and although each stage in the development is accompanied by all sorts of new learning based on experience, this learning is always relative to the developmental period during which it takes place, and to the intellectual structures, whether completely or partially formed, which the subject has at his disposal during this period. In the last analysis, therefore, development accounts for learning much more than the other way around (Piaget, 1966).

Piaget has provided us with a theory of intelligence that is developmental. As the preceding discussion indicates, Piaget sees both a qualitative and a quantitative difference as the person develops. His orientation has been different from other theorists engaged in the area of intelligence and as such has provided us with a different way of looking at children's intellectual growth. "As Flavell (1962) noted at the first Conference on Intellective Development, a psychologist who studies Piaget never again sees children in the same way" (Almy, 1966).

While there is and will be a continuing need to focus on intelligence as a concept, there appears to be a trend away from test development, per se, and toward a reconceptualization of what we know about intelligence and testing. The work of both Guilford and Piaget has to be seen as monumental contributions to our knowledge and understanding. In addition, the contributions of others working from other disciplinary and conceptual frameworks (Cole, Gay, Glick, and Sharp, 1971; Cole and Scribner, 1974; Cromwell, 1976; Merrifield, 1977; and others) have provided and are providing us different perspectives regarding intelligence.

A prime example of an approach utilizing broadened assumptions of intelligence and testing is the work of Jane Mercer and June Lewis (1978). The importance of their work in this context is not theory development per se, but their utilization of a measurement approach that attempts to include advances made in testing along with a recognition of sociocultural influences. While their approach is discussed at some length in Chapter 4, it seems germane to include their conceptual approach in this chapter. Their approach is included here because it is one of the very few attempts to approach diagnosis from a broader intelligence framework. Although there have been many tests that purported to be culture "free" or "fair" or were designed to measure adaptive behavior, either their efficiency has been questionable or their standardization was so limited that the predictive validity and reliability were questionable. Mercer and Lewis (1977) have developed what they refer to as a System of Multicultural Pluralistic Assessment (SOMPA) that requires a view of a child from those different frameworks: medical, social system, and pluralistic. This model, although utilizing extant tests, places considerable emphasis on sociocultural influences on learning ability. We believe that the SOMPA model is exemplary of the growing recognition that traditional testing of intelligence (such as learning ability) has limited uses in a pluralistic society.

SUMMARY

As a concept it is apparent that intelligence has been an elusive abstraction both in a definitional sense and in application. That the theories attempting to explain intelligence have at times been used for other than noble purposes is also apparent. We have followed false leads and utilized the concept of intelligence too often in restrictive rather than in facilitative ways. As in many other areas, we have allowed technological progress to become the "tail that wags the dog." That this is dangerous is by now certainly a recognizable fact. The demand for "quick fix" tests and methodology in all areas, but particularly in education, is real and certainly is needed, but can be a very expensive single avenue to pursue. We pay the price in human terms by responding to every testmakers promise of "the test," "the method," and "the approach" that will satisfy all our educational problems. Indeed, as no less an authority than Buros (1977) has indicated about tests in general, the "most standardized tests are poorly constructed, of questionable or unknown validity, pretentious in their claims, and likely to be misused more often than not" (p. 9). This is not to imply that our efforts in test development have been singularly unproductive, or unimportant. There is, however, the direct implication that when we forget that tests and other measurements are tools, and not ends in themselves, we are being tragically remiss in our role as professional educators. It is a fact that we are a technological society and may have been led at times by our very technical success into seeking the easiest methods to satisfy our problems. In so doing there is a tendency to mask our ignorance by ignoring the critical questions of philosophical use of our assessment instruments. The use of theory is still our most effective avenue in determining needs and programs along with a concomitant but judicious use of tests of intelligence.

In summary, it is evident that there are a multitude of facets that must be considered in theorizing about intelligence and the subsequent devising and revising of intelligence measures. A single framework will no longer suffice, if it ever did. Both multidisciplinary and interdisciplinary approaches must be generated to manage the concept of intelligence as well as the diverse area of mental retardation, which is deeply affected by our perception of relative intelligence. That innumerable persons have been unalterably damaged by premature or expedient conclusions about intelligence is readily apparent. It is our opinion that the seminal work of Piaget and of Cole and colleagues must be a part of future intellectual considerations relative to definitions of intelligence, particularly those implications affecting education.

STUDY QUESTIONS

1. Intelligence has always been a controversial concept. Discuss the problems inherent in trying to define intelligence, particularly the cultural aspects.
2. The relative influence of heredity versus environment on intelligence is now, and has been in the past, a topic of heated debate. Discuss these two viewpoints in relation to one another and support your discussion by references.
3. The measurement of intelligence has been formally attempted since the time of Binet. Discuss the problems incurred by attempting to measure intelligence; include a section on why intelligence can't be measured directly.
4. Compare and contrast the approaches of Guilford and Piaget relative to intelligence.

REFERENCES

Abraham, W. *Common sense about gifted children.* New York: Harper & Row, Publishers, 1958.

Almy, M. with Chittenden, E., and Miller, P. *Young children's thinking: studies of some aspects of Piaget's theory.* New York: Teachers College Press, 1966.

Buros, O. K. Fifty years of testing: some reminiscences, criticisms and suggestions. *Educational Recorder*, 1977, **6**, 9-15.

Burt, C. *The factors of the mind.* London: University of London Press, 1940.

Burt, C. The meaning and assessment of intelligence. *Eugenics Review*, 1955, **47**, 81-91.

Cole, M., Gay, J., Glick, J., and Sharp, D. *The cultural context of learning and thinking.* New York: Basic Books, Inc., Publishers, 1971.

Cole, M., and Scribner, S. *Culture and thought: a psychological introduction.* New York: John Wiley & Sons, Inc., 1974.

Cromwell, R. Ethics, unbrage and the A B C Ds. In M. C. Reynolds (Ed.), Mainstreaming: origins and implications, *Minnesota Educator,* 1976, **2**, 42-47.

Dobzhansky, T. *Evolution, genetics and man.* New York: John Wiley & Sons, Inc., 1955.

Doll, E. E. A historical survey of research and management of mental retardation in the United States. In E. P. Trapp and P. Himelstein (Eds.), *Readings on the exceptional child.* New York: Appleton-Century-Crofts, 1962. P. 50.

Fitz-Herbert, A. *New natura brevium.* Quoted in E. P. Trapp and P. Himelstein (Eds.), *Readings on the exceptional child.* New York: Appleton-Century-Crofts, 1962, P. 23.

Garcia, J. IQ: the conspiracy. *Psychology Today,* 1972, **6**, 40-43, 92, 94.

Goodnow, J. Problems in research on culture and thought. In D. Elkind and J. Flavell (Eds.), *Studies in cognitive development: essays in honor of Jean Piaget.* New York: Oxford University Press, 1969.

Gottesman, I. Genetic aspects of intelligent behavior. In N. Ellis (Ed.), *Handbook of mental deficiency.* New York: McGraw-Hill Book Co., 1963.

Guilford, J. P. Three faces of intellect. *American Psychologist,* 1959, **14**, 469-479.

Guilford, J. P. *The nature of human intelligence.* New York: McGraw-Hill Book Co., 1967.

Hunt, J. McV. The impact and limitations of the giant of developmental psychology. In D. A. Elkind and J. Flavell (Eds.), *Studies in cognitive development.* New York: Oxford University Press, 1969, Pp. 3-66.

Jensen, A. How much can we boost IQ and scholastic achievement? *Harvard Educational Review,* 1969, **39**, 1-123.

Jensen, A. The differences are real. *Psychology Today,* 1973, **7**(7), 80-86.

Linden, K. W., and Linden, J. D. *Modern mental measurement: a historical perspective.* Boston: Houghton-Mifflin Co., 1968.

Marx, M. H. The general nature of theory construction. In M. H. Marx (Ed.), *Theories in contemporary psychology.* New York: The Macmillan Co., 1963.

Mercer, J. R. The IQ: the lethal label. *Psychology Today,* 1972, **6**, 40-43, 92, 94.

Mercer, J. R. and Lewis, J. F. *System of multicultural pluralistic assessment.* New York: The Psychological Corporation, 1977.

Merrifield, P. Guilford and Piaget: an attempt at synthesis. Unpublished manuscript, 1977.

Nunnally, J. C. *Psychometric theory.* New York: McGraw-Hill Book Co., 1967.

Piaget, J. The general problems of the psychobiological development of the child. In J. M. Tanner and B. Inhelder (Eds.), *Discussions on child development.* London: Tavistock Publishers, 1960, Pp. 3-27.

Piaget, J. Foreword. In M. Almy with E. Chittenden and P. Miller, *Young children's thinking.* New York: Teachers College Press, 1966.

Piaget, J. *Six psychological studies.* New York: Random House, Inc., 1967.

Rice, B. The high cost of thinking the unthinkable. *Psychology Today,* 1973, **7**, 88-93.

Robuck, A. A. *A history of psychology and psychiatry.* New York: Philosophical Library, 1961.

Spearman, C. E. "General intelligence" objectively determined and measured. *American Journal of Psychology,* 1904, **15**, 201-293.

Thorndike, E. L., and Woodworth, R. S. The influence of improvement in one mental function upon the efficiency of other functions. *Psychological Review,* 1901, **8**, 247-261, 384-395, 553-564.

Thurstone, L. L. *Theory of multiple factors.* Chicago: University of Chicago Press, 1933.

Thurstone, L. L. Primary mental abilities. *Psychometric Monographs.* Chicago: University of Chicago Press, 1938.

Watson, P. IQ: the racial gap. *Psychology Today,* 1972, **6**, 48-50, 97-98.

Woodward, M. The application of Piaget's theory to research in mental deficiency. In N. Ellis (Ed.), *Handbook of mental deficiency.* New York: McGraw-Hill Book Co., 1963.

ANNOTATED BIBLIOGRAPHY

Cole, M., Gay, J., Glick, J. A., and Sharp, D. W. *The cultural context of learning and thinking.* New York: Basic Books, Inc., 1971.

This book is concerned with the relationship between culture, thinking, and learning. The authors have attempted to incorporate anthropological, linguistic, and psychological approaches in understanding the effect of culture on behavior. It is a most intriguing and readable book that opens new avenues for understanding cognitive processes.

Elkind, D. A., and Flavell, J. (Eds)., *Studies in cog-

nitive development. New York: Oxford University Press, 1969, Pp. 3-66.

This is a collection of essays written by American psychologists relative to their experience and work based on the concepts of Piaget.

Gagne, R. M. *The conditions of learning.* (2nd ed.) New York: Holt, Rinehart and Winston, 1970.

Eight different classes of learning are discussed relative to the conditions necessary for each.

Hunt, J. M. (Ed.) *Human intelligence.* New Brunswick: Transaction Books, 1972.

There is a strong emphasis on social conditions as they relate to intellectual development.

CHAPTER 4

Assessment issues and procedures

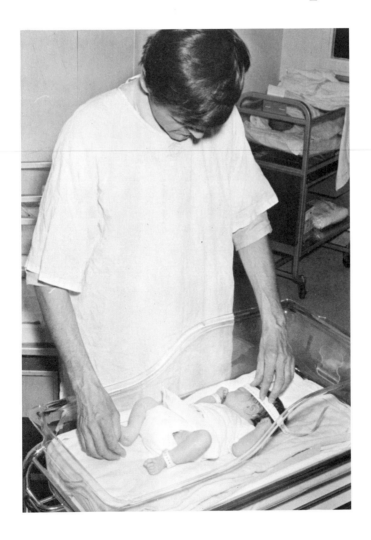

INTRODUCTION

The history of psychological assessment is truly rich and lengthy when compared to other areas of behavioral science. The area within the general field of psychological assessment that has received the most attention is that of intelligence measurement. The work in the measurement of intelligence has been a major force and impetus in psychological assessment. This places the very roots of psychological assessment in the field of mental retardation.

It is commonly accepted that serious efforts aimed at the measurement of intelligence began with the work of Alfred Binet in 1904. Binet was commissioned by school officials in Paris to develop a means by which those children who were "truly dull" could be identified. Although there had been interest in psychological measurement prior to this time, this assignment is generally viewed as an important beginning in the assessment field. The influence of psychological assessment has long since been felt far beyond the area of mental retardation, and the methodology has become increasingly complex, sophisticated, and, some would say, elegant. In certain areas, however, the sophistication may be more superficial than elegant. The purpose of this chapter is to discuss assessment issues, frameworks, and procedures from the perspective of mental retardation. In keeping with the format of this text, assessment will be discussed in terms of the various phases of the developmental life cycle.

ISSUES AND CONCEPTS

As noted before, work in the measurement of intelligence has a very long history. Efforts to evaluate other concepts, such as personality and social development, have been underway for a considerable length of time also. Despite the longevity of such efforts, it seems that much of the work has not been undertaken in a manner that was as thoughtful as might be appropriate or desirable. The development of instrumentation has progressed at an incredible rate—many times at the expense of careful and deliberate conceptualization concerning the purposes and uses of the tests. Drew (1973) criticized such practices as being representative of *"instrumentation fixation* to the near exclusion of attention of questions of 'Why are we testing?'" (p. 324). He noted that "technical precision in psychological assessment has nearly always been far in advance of conceptual precision" (p. 323). Technical precision, in this context, refers to instrument construction and associated technical matters (such as reliability and validity in the classical test theory sense). Conceptual precision refers to considerations pertaining to the underlying purposes for assessment and the utilization of resulting information.

The result of such attention to conceptual issues has been important. Clearly the most rapid progress in terms of sound conceptual development has occurred in the last few years. In fact, the entire evaluation and measurement process is undergoing dramatic reconceptualization. The examination of evaluation and its underlying assumptions represents extremely important progress toward its refinement and value and warrants examination prior to discussing specific assessment procedures.

One of the important conceptual developments in the field of assessment has been the distinction between norm-referenced and criterion-referenced evaluation. This distinction has become rather well known in educational and psychological circles.

Early assessments of intelligence focused on how an individual performed as compared with others. A child's score on a given test was viewed in relation to his agemates or some standard norm. The norms or basis for such a comparison are usually established through research and repeated testing of individuals at various age levels. Similar procedures are used in assessment of factors other than intelligence. Personality measures usually compare an individual's response on certain questions to those of others that have particular personality descriptions. Educational achievement is often measured by the amount of information a child has as demonstrated by correct responses on a variety of test questions. Such performance is then compared with those of other children who are at about the same age or grade level.

This type of assessment, in which the performance of an individual is compared with that of others, is known as norm-referenced evaluation. Reading the term quite literally, the idea is self-explanatory. The interpretation as to how well or how poorly an individual performs is referenced in relation to the scores of others in the form of established norms. *Mental age (MA)* is a concept that is norm referenced and was what Binet and Simon (1908) had in mind in their initial definition of MA, which will receive attention later in this section. Many other areas of assessment, particularly those utilizing standardized tests, are also based on a norm-referenced framework.

This approach has prevailed as the predominant evaluation framework for many years. For the most part, professionals involved in assessment of all types (for example, developmental status, intelligence, personality) have interpreted performance relative to norms. It has served some purposes very well. During the development of assessment as a science, it has been an important foundation for both researchers and practitioners working in all areas related to human behavior. A number of rather serious problems have been generated, however.

As the science of human behavior moved out of its infancy, measurement problems developed that obviously needed attention. Standardized tests provided information that was useful for certain purposes but not very helpful in other areas. Educators, for example, frequently found that scores from norm-referenced evaluation were not very helpful for planning actual teaching. A single score was frequently used for decisions about educational placement, with little or no additional information provided about the child. From such an evaluation the teacher received meager guidance concerning the many activities and specific areas involved in the instructional process. Where to begin in teaching specific math or reading skills was not indicated by a global score or by a psychologist's report. This left the teacher with many practical problems to solve in terms of how to teach the child. There appeared to be no logical link between evaluation and actual instruction.

Similar problems emerged in working with the mentally retarded and other handicapped individuals in terms of social and vocational efforts. Placement, planning, and programming were not facilitated to any great degree by the psychological assessment provided by norm-referenced evaluation. Professionals working in social agencies, such as welfare, employment, and sheltered workshops, soon found that they had to augment such information with their own more specific evaluations. The sheltered workshop director, for example, had to determine what specific skills were present in a retarded client and which skills needed to be taught for the individual to perform productively.

Criterion-referenced evaluation has almost become synonymous with what norm-referenced evaluation is not. An individual's performance is not compared to that of others or to some norm. In addition, criterion-referenced evaluation attempts to assess very specific skill areas individually rather than generating a score based on a composite testing of several skills. Each of these ideas warrants more detailed discussion in order to understand more fully this important evaluation concept.

As noted, criterion-referenced evaluation does not compare the individual's performance to that of others. Tasks are usually arranged in a sequence of increasing difficulty. An individual's performance is viewed in terms of absolute level of performance or the actual number of operations completed.

If a child is being tested on counting skills and is able to progress successfully through counting by two's, but no further, that is the way in which performance is viewed. The child can count by two's with 100 percent accuracy but cannot count by three's. This level of performance would then be referenced in one or both of two ways. First, the evaluator and the teacher (frequently the same person) would ask, "Is this level of proficiency adequate for this child at this time?" The level of proficiency *necessary* for the child is the criterion, hence the term criterion-referenced. If the child needs to have the skill of counting by three's, then the teacher knows exactly what instruction is necessary at this point. As the child progresses or grows older, he or she may be required to perform at a more advanced level of a particular skill, depending on the demands of the environment. This will result in a change in criterion for this skill during the next phase of evaluation and instruction.

The second way that performance or skill level is referenced involves comparison of a given individual's performance in one skill area with performance in other skill areas; for example, a child performs very well in letter recognition but very poorly in sound blending. Performances in such varieties of skill areas are examined, frequently a profile of the child's strengths and deficits is constructed, and instructional effort is specifically pinpointed in view of this profile. In this fashion the second referent for evaluation data remains within a given individual's performance but between skill areas. Usually the measurement involves performance on specific tasks. No inference is made concerning abstract concepts (such as intelligence), and measurement is directly related to specific instruction. This approach has certainly improved the logic and relationship between evaluation and teaching, and promises dramatic changes in the way that education is conceived and carried out.

The past few years have witnessed a theoretical difference of opinion in child assessment. Obviously norm- and criterion-referenced evaluations operate from very different approaches. Proponents of each viewpoint have spent a good deal of time and effort defending their respective positions, often without careful examination of what the other approach had to offer. This is unfortunate because such professional arguing has had very little positive result, and the effort and energy expended probably could have been directed much more productively.

Scrutiny of both frameworks has led some authors to conclude that neither approach in isolation will result in a totally effective evaluation process (Kirk and Kirk, 1971; Drew, Freston, and Logan, 1972).

Criterion-referenced evaluation is very useful for specific instructional programming, a need that was not served by norm-referenced evaluation. It must be kept in mind, however, that ultimately many children will be functioning in a larger world, perhaps even in a regular educational setting on a partial basis. To a great degree, that larger world operates on a competitive basis, with children's performances frequently being viewed in relation to each other. This is a norm-referenced world. In order to maximize the child's probability of success, information must be obtained that will indicate how the child's performance compares to others in this larger world. It would be disastrous to bring a child's skill level from point A to point B (criterion-referenced) and find that point C was necessary for success in a regular educational setting. Thus, those working with the mentally retarded cannot afford to be rigid in using only part of the tools available to them. Since they serve different purposes, both norm- and criterion-referenced evaluation must be utilized in order to work effectively with retarded children. The reader interested in exploring this in more detail will find a discussion in Drew, Freston, and Logan (1972).

Other conceptual developments in the field of evaluation have related directly to the purposes of evaluation. Bloom, Hastings, and Madaus (1971) were responsible for one such development that has received rather widespread interest in recent years. These authors conceived of evaluation in terms of two broad categories: formative and summative. Formative evaluation, in this framework, is thought of as assessment that does not focus on terminal behaviors but rather on those behaviors that represent the "next step" in an instructional program. Viewed in this manner, formative evaluation is frequently an integrated part of the instructional program and is ongoing assessment. Summative evaluation is quite different. It involves assessment of terminal behaviors and might be thought of as an evaluation of a child's performance at the end of a given program. These conceptualizations recently have been combined with those of norm- and criterion-referenced evaluations in terms of functional and comprehensive views of assessment. The "myopic" views of evaluation and psychological assessment seem to be diminishing in favor of more thoughtful approaches to the broad field. This can only be viewed as healthy, if for no other reason than the fact that workers in the field are being more thoughtful and reasoned in their attention to their endeavors.

Further issues that require attention in the area of assessment involve the questions that have been raised regarding discriminatory testing. These questions have surfaced particularly in terms of standardized, norm-referenced testing of minority-group children. Blacks, Chicanos, and American Indians, as well as others, have legitimately asked questions concerning cultural bias and prejudice involved in the construction and use of evaluation instruments. Since the instruments are usually devised by individuals from the cultural majority, there is good reason to think that test items are more representative of that group than others. Likewise, norms more frequently include individuals from the cultural majority than those from minority subgroups. Therefore, when minority children's scores are compared to norms established on other populations, they are quite likely placed at a disadvantage simply because of cultural differences. Efforts to construct instruments that are not culturally biased have been attempted for many years with extremely disappointing results. These efforts have led some to contend that conceptual foundations and uses of norm-referenced evaluation represent more important issues than simply instrumentation (Drew, 1973). Serious attention to this problem is imperative. Professionals working with the retarded cannot afford to wait passively for others to take the lead. Minority children represent a disproportionately large segment of the identified retarded population. The question must be asked, "Are these children present because of cultural bias and prejudice?" If so, what are the implications? Beyond the mere asking of questions, however, rapid movement toward action is crucial.

Although the preceding discussion has been stated primarily in the past tense, the reader should not take this to imply that these problems have evaporated with passing time. Problems involving educational uses and misuses of norm-referenced assessment have only recently been addressed in a serious fashion (Hammill, 1971; Drew, Freston, and Logan, 1972) and even now only by a limited segment of the educational profession, primarily those working with handicapped learners. Norm-referenced evaluation and the complex issues involved in assessment of cultural minorities have only begun to be explored (Drew, 1973; Oakland, 1973; Newland, 1973; Meeker and Meeker, 1973; Bartel, Grill, and Bryen, 1973). Much work remains to be completed, and considerable development in terms of the conceptual underpinnings is yet to come. Even more exciting is the effort by some to combine conceptually firm foundations with the technical precision of advanced instrumentation development (Mercer and Lewis, 1977). The fact remains that advances are evident in the area of evaluation.

Two concepts require at least brief attention. They are not new to the field of psychological assessment, in fact, they have great historical significance and have been particularly prominent in the assessment of intelligence—"mental age" and "intelligence quotient." Both serve as convenient summaries of an individual's performance on tasks that presumably tap behavior that represents intelligence. Both, however, have been subject to similar pitfalls, generated primarily by the ways they have been used.

The concept of mental (MA) was developed by Binet and Simon (1908) as a means of expressing a child's intellectual development. Based on a developmental notion, an MA score represents the average performance of children with chronological ages (CA's) equal to that score. For example, a child who obtains an MA of 5 years and 6 months has performed on the test in a manner that is similar to the average performances of children who are 5 years and 6 months old chronologically (norm-referenced concept). MA has been a useful concept, especially in mental retardation, since it is referenced to average intellectual development at various CA levels. Little sophistication is necessary regarding the measurement of intelligence to grasp the general idea of mental development as expressed in this manner. In particular, MA provides a convenient means of communication with parents and others about retarded children. Most parents, as well as other laypersons, have had opportunities to observe children at various ages. This provides them with behavioral reference points that facilitate an understanding, in a general way, of the capabilities of the retarded individual.

The MA concept has been less useful in other contexts. Since it is a summary score derived from performance on various types of test items, MA is a composite measure that involves several skill areas. The single score provides little information about a given individual's specific skill level, which is why the previous discussion included qualifying statements about understanding mental development *"in a general way."* Two children may obtain the same MA and have very different patterns of skill strengths and deficits. For example, an MA of 7 years might be attained by a child who is chronologically age 5 and by another who is chronologically age 9. These children might be labeled "bright" and "retarded" or a number of other terms, as noted in Chapter 1. Regardless of specific terminology, the same MA may have been attained from very different specific performances. The developmentally advanced child (CA 5) will more frequently succeed in verbal reasoning and abstract items. The slower child (CA 9), on the other hand, will more frequently respond correctly on items of a performance nature or those for which previous learning was quite repetitive. Equivalent MA's do not indicate similar skill capabilities; the usefulness of the concept is limited in terms of teaching, particularly when instruction is pinpointed to skill deficit areas.

The intelligence quotient (IQ) actually came into use somewhat later than MA. Originally the IQ was derived by dividing an individual's MA by the CA and multiplying the result by 100. Thus if a child 6 years old obtained an MA of 6, his IQ would be 100 (6 ÷ 6 = 1 × 100 = 100). This approach to IQ calculation was known as the *ratio IQ*. Certain difficulties developed in the use of the ratio IQ, which prompted its decline beginning about the mid-1940's. Since that time the *deviation IQ* has been used as an alternative to the ratio calculation. This approach uses a statistical computation known as the standard deviation to derive the IQ. Several advantages were afforded by the deviation approach to determining IQ over the ratio calculation. The ratio calculation was quite unstable from age level to age level, making IQ comparison between ages quite difficult. The deviation approach for deriving IQ is a standard score with much more stability along the age continuum. The ratio calculation also became problematical as adulthood was approached. Obviously, as the individual's CA increases and adulthood is approached, there is an apparent leveling or even a decline in measured intelligence even with more items scored correctly. The ratio IQ thus became conceptually less applicable as individuals other than developing children were assessed. Deviation IQ, because it is referenced with a standard score approach, circumvents these difficulties and is conceptually more sound at all ages.

IQ, like MA, is a composite measure derived by performance in a number of skill areas. The problems noted with MA in this regard are likewise presented by IQ. The global score provides an overall assessment of performance but does not indicate specific skill strengths and deficits. This problem may have been more acute with IQ than with MA. Because of the single score and apparent simplicity, users of IQ have tended to forget the component performances of the score and treat it as a unitary concept. Additionally, the score became viewed as somewhat of a sacred and permanent quantity rather than reflection of performance on a variety of tasks. This misconception led to considerable misuse and ultimately a disenchantment with the entire concept.

IQ remains in use today and in many cases the abuses continue. Hopefully, however, it is being used with increasing frequency in a proper perspective of what is actually being assessed. Modification of the idea of IQ plus expansion of evaluation concepts in general appear to have begun movement in the direction of more realistic use of the IQ score.

The preceding discussion has examined some of the issues and conceptual developments in the area of psychological assessment. This examination was, by no means exhaustive, however, it does provide a backdrop for the examination of assessment procedures.

EARLY LIFE

Different assessment procedures are necessary at various stages in the life of a child. This section will examine approaches to evaluation during the early years of life. For purposes of this discussion, early life refers to the period up to about 2 years of age.

Evaluation at this point in the life of children is conducted for at least two interrelated purposes: (1) identification of children who are already retarded in their development and (2) identification of children who have a high probability of being developmentally retarded at a later time. The President's Committee on Mental Retardation noted these purposes as essentially being the two components of what is termed "early screening assessment" (Meier, 1973). Further discussion is necessary for two reasons. First, the idea of screening itself must be examined. Second, the reasons for identification and potential results require additional exploration. Identification cannot stand alone, or it would merely represent identification for its own sake. Such activity without some resulting action would be merely an exercise.

Screening has been likened to a process of size sorting for such items as oranges (Meier, 1973). Oranges might be run across a screen with certain sized holes. These holes would permit those oranges that were of an acceptable size or smaller to fall through. Those that were above the acceptable marketable size would not fall through the screen and thus would be sorted out for other purposes (special gift packages). Those that would fall through would include oranges of a marketable size plus those that were much smaller. In order to complete the analogy, a second screening process might then be used. This second phase would involve a screen with holes that were much smaller than the first. The only oranges that would fall through the second screen would be those that were unmarketable because they were too small (frozen orange juice). This would leave only those oranges that were in the size range that the buying public prefers. Screening for retardation is somewhat like this. Only those who are either now developmentally retarded or who exhibit behaviors that suggest that they will later be retarded are sorted out by early screening.

It is generally agreed that early identification of handicapping conditions is highly important for a variety of reasons. First of all, in certain cases the ultimate impact of a handicapping condition can be reduced substantially if treatment or intervention is implemented early. There is the possibility that certain handicaps may even be prevented if action is taken sufficiently early. This latter assumption is particularly focused on those children who are thought to be "high-risk" in terms of developmental retardation at a time other than infancy. Obviously there are some children for whom neither of these possibilities realistically exists. These are children who are severely retarded, frequently because of birth defect or congenital malformation. Such conditions make identification more easily accomplished, but because of the severity of the problems, positive action is more difficult. In these situations early identification still plays a vital role in terms of future planning, both for the child and for the family.

Despite the importance of early screening assessment in mental retardation, certain problems persist in accomplishing the desired task. One of the serious difficulties in assessing young children involves the accuracy of prediction. The behavioral repertoire of the infant is very much different from that of the child at age 6 or 10. The infant is primarily functioning in a motor skill world. Grasping, rolling over, sitting, and crawling are but a few of the behaviors that are involved in the baby's repertoire. Vocalizations are quite limited and frequently are focused around physiological factors such as hunger, pain, and fatigue. Yet early screening is trying to make some predictive statement about later behaviors that are very different. It is little wonder that prediction is not as accurate as might be desirable. It has long been known that the best predictor of performance on a given task is performance on a sample of that task or on a similar task. For the most part this simply is not possible with an infant.

Although the previous discussion indicates a definite problem area in the assessment of young children, the reader should not take this to mean that no prediction is possible. If this were the case, there would be little reason to even consider early screening. All that is being indicated here is that accuracy is not as great as might be desired. Fortunately for child care workers, developmental status and progress in those psychomotor areas that dominate the world of the infant do predict, even though grossly, later levels of functioning. As noted before, accuracy of prediction at least is much greater with the severely impaired who exhibit clearer signs of impairment earlier. The greatest difficulty is encountered with the mildly handicapped.

Another concern in early screening assessment involves the factors being evaluated during such measurement. More recent research and thinking in this area have changed somewhat the indicators that are assessed in early screening. Meier (1973) reviews research that suggests valuable predictive information is available from assessing environmental factors as well as looking at the actual developmental status of the child. Traditionally such indicators as socioeconomic status and parental education and occupation have been used to differentiate between environments. Other factors have now been shown to be more important in terms of influencing a child's development. Some of these influences include parents' language style, their attitudes concerning achievement, and their general involvement with the young child. Research is just beginning to address these areas and promises important implications for the future.

Early screening has generally been discussed in terms of its positive value for the child, who is faced with the possibility of mental retardation, and for the parents. In a broader societal context, certain ethical issues must be posed. Although social and ethical issues are the major focus of Chapter 14, they warrant brief mention here. One of the negative outcomes that may result from early assessment of a child is some sort of label. Labels and their impact on children have been a serious concern in special education for some time. We share those concerns and find the potential for detrimental influence to be even greater when and if they are attached to a youngster at infancy. Such labeling must be avoided, and child care workers must move to behavior- and skill-oriented descriptions. An additional concern has been mentioned previously but deserves repetition in order to emphasize its importance. Assessment, evaluation, early screening, or whatever it is termed, cannot be justified if the purpose is only identification. During the school years, evaluation must be related to an educationally relevant purpose or action. Such a goal is even more crucial in the early years. Imagine the devastating effect of assessing a young child, placing the stigma of a label, and doing nothing in the form of positive action beyond that. If categorizing or labeling is the only purpose, we cannot support the evaluation process during the early years or at any time in the life of an individual.

Earlier in this chapter the problems involved with evaluation of ethnic groups were mentioned. These same problems are of even greater concern in early assessment. Early screening is very much involved in the societal issues of poverty, race, and environmental quality of life. As we become more skilled in addressing these issues, it is anticipated that not only early childhood assessment but also early childhood education will play an increasingly important role.

Prenatal

Advances in medical science and health care techniques over the past decade have had a significant impact on the field of mental retardation. One area in which dramatic developments have occurred involves assessment and detection of mental retardation on a prenatal basis.

During pregnancy the most common assessment involves routine monitoring of the physical condition of the mother and fetus by the obstetrician or other trained health care personnel. Part of this assessment process includes a detailed record of the mother in terms of family and medical history. In addition to the history, the mother's blood pressure, uterus size, urine status, and other indicators are monitored throughout the pregnancy to assure that there are no symptoms present that would signal danger for the fetus as well as the mother. At this level of examination the mother's physical condition is the primary source of information for assessment. The obstetrician also will examine the fetus by various means, such as fetal heart rate, as the pregnancy proceeds. This ongoing monitoring is crucial to maximize the probability of a healthy baby being born. The mother's diet is frequently altered, and occasionally medication is administered to correct minor deviations from the optimum situation for fetal development. For individuals who do not have access to such health care, a much higher risk is involved in terms of the birth of a defective child. Such higher risks are more frequent among segments of the population that cannot afford adequate health care or for some other reason do not have adequate medical resources available to them.

Ongoing prenatal assessment is generally adequate as long as a healthy mother and fetus are involved. Certain danger signs, however, prompt more extensive evaluation. If the family or medical history suggests that a particular problem may occur (such as an inheritable disorder), routine monitoring of health signs is not sufficient. If the mother's physical condition or that of the fetus progresses in a highly deviant fashion, more extensive evaluation and action are in order. In such cases the evaluation process becomes one of a diagnostic nature aimed at the prenatal assessment of fetal status. This is accomplished by evaluating certain biological and chemical characteristics of the fetus. Diagnostic analyses of this type are not possible with every type of retardation, and work to date has focused on the clinical syndromes that involve genetic metabolic disorders resulting in severe mental retardation.

O'Brien (1971) discusses twenty-seven hereditary disorders for which accurate diagnosis is now possible, including such anomalies as galactosemia, Gaucher's disease, maple syrup urine disease, and Tay-Sachs disease. On an individual basis these disorders occur rarely. Collectively, within an entire society, however, the ability to detect and take action represents a substantial contribution to the field of mental retardation. Perhaps even more significant is the capability of preventing the personal tragedies resulting from the birth of children with such devastating disorders. In most cases parents of these children are forced to watch a progressive deterioration from what appeared to be a healthy normal baby to a helpless individual destined for a vegetative existence or premature death.

Prenatal assessment of the type discussed has not advanced to the point where it is routinely conducted. For the most part the general obstetric monitoring mentioned previously suffices as the first level of screening, similar to the first screening in our orange-sorting analogy. In certain cases, however, metabolic or genetic disorders have a higher probability of occurrence. For these situations recent thinking suggests that the diagnostic type of prenatal evaluation should be routinely conducted. Tay-Sachs disease, for example, is a disorder that is transmitted genetically and is primarily found in individuals of an Ashkenazi Jewish origin. When two individuals with this background plan to have children, it is probably wise always to evaluate the status of the fetus from a prenatal diagnostic standpoint. O'Brien also makes a strong case for such evaluation with all pregnant women over 40 years of age. The maternal age becomes important in terms of the birth of children with mongolism, or Down's syndrome. The detection process for prenatal identification of mongolism is still being refined. As this work progresses, it is quite possible that such diagnostic screening will be recommended even for mothers under 40.

Newborn

A variety of assessment techniques are utilized with the newborn. This represents a crucial period for the child, and clinical assessment at this time is vital. Immediately following completion of the birth process several factors are noted and rated using what is known as the Apgar score. This procedure is completed by delivery room staff at "1 minute and 5 minutes of age, and may be repeated until the infant's condition has stabilized" (Chinn, 1979). Five factors are included in the Apgar scoring: heart rate, respiratory effort, muscle tone, reflex irritability, and color. Each is rated by giving a score of 0, 1, or 2 (0 indicating low or weak, 2 indicating high or strong), and the separate scores are then totaled. Extremely low Apgar scores on the 5-minute measure suggests that there is a potential problem. Chinn (1979) notes that children with a 5-minute score of 3 or below have three times as many neurological problems at age 1 as babies of similar birth weights with Apgar scores of 7 to 10. Apgar scores of 6 or lower are viewed with concern, and infants with such scores are usually monitored more closely for the first several days, and interventions are made as necessary.

Several other assessment procedures are conducted in the medical laboratories at the time the child is born and during the very early part of life. Many of these procedures are aimed at the detection of inherited or congenitally present abnormalities (overlapping some of those that have been discussed under prenatal diagnosis). As with the prenatal evaluation process, a biological-chemical analysis is frequently the means by which such newborn screening is accomplished. Citing earlier work, Meier (1973) lists no less than fourteen different inherited abnormalities that are detectable through analysis of blood specimens alone:

Phenylketonuria*
Maple syrup urine disease*
Tyrosinemia*
Homocystinuria*
Histidinemia*
Valinemia*
Galactosemia transferase or kinase deficiency*

Galactosemia transferase deficiency*
Argininosuccinic aciduria*
Orotic aciduria*
Hereditary angioneurotic edema
Emphysema (adult)
Liver disease (infant)
Sickle cell anemia

Ten of the disorders are treatable, as noted in the above material, in a fashion that will prevent or substantially diminish the developmental problem that would result if the condition were unknown or ignored. These treatable disorders represent over 71 percent of those listed, a substantial proportion that seems to be important evidence supporting such newborn

*Treatable.

screening. One is prompted to wonder why such assessment is not necessarily routine at the present time. Diagnosis can be accomplished, at least on these disorders, from analysis of a dried blood spot, and in each case complete or partial automated analysis is possible. This certainly streamlines the process and permits cost-effective mass screening. Hopefully, future health care services will routinely encompass such newborn evaluation.

Certain other abnormalities are detectable from clinical observation at the newborn stage. Medical examination of such conditions as mongolism and cranial anomalies will indicate the existence of a problem with considerable accuracy. Such effective evaluation, however, involves those conditions that are present and observable either at birth or in the first few days of the infant's life.

Beyond the newborn stage

There is certainly no widespread agreement concerning when one "stage" of development terminates and another begins. In fact it is somewhat misleading to suggest the idea that a *stage* per se is an identifiable, discrete, and existing entity. Even the theoretical concepts of stages are being strongly challenged (Flavell, 1977). Broad usage of terminology such as newborn, infant, and early childhood is fluid at best. In the previous section the term newborn was used to denote the time shortly after birth. The use of this term in such a fashion was not intended to suggest any particular "stage" but was used for convenience in communication. For purposes of the remainder of this discussion, evaluation will be placed in an age context rather than utilizing terms that connote stages.

It has already been noted that certain measurement difficulties are encountered during the period from birth through the first few years of life. This is particularly true when one is attempting to predict later intelligence. Prior to the acquisition of language, the child must be evaluated primarily in terms of sensorimotor development. Since later intelligence measures are heavily weighted by verbal performance items, the prediction difficulty is to be expected. There has, however, been considerable progress in this area of assessment.

A variety of instruments and evaluation procedures have been developed for the assessment of intellectual functioning in young children. The Cattell Infant Intelligence Scale is one of the better-known instruments for evaluation of very young children. Heavily oriented toward sensorimotor assessment, the Cattell Scale is used on children from 2 to about 30 months of age. This scale was designed as a downward extension (age-wise) of the revised Stanford-Binet intelligence test. Research has indicated that the Cattell Scale is useful for predicting intellectual functioning of mentally retarded children who have been referred for examination by physicians. Less accurate prediction has been demonstrated, however, using broader samples of children who have not been referred. This would seem to suggest that the Cattell Infant Intelligence Scale may be useful for screening purposes but is less helpful for general prediction in a non–high-risk population.

Similar to the Cattell Scale in some respects are the Bayley Scales of Infant Development. The Bayley Scales, although somewhat more lengthy to administer, have certain strengths over the Cattell. Initially, the Bayley Scales include test items for the first 2 months after birth, which may be an advantage, depending on the situation. Additionally, there are separate subscales for mental and motor performance. This has obvious appeal from a clinical standpoint but may also be somewhat misleading. Like the Cattell, the Bayley Scales rely heavily on the assessment of sensorimotor performance, since there are little other means of performance evaluation at this age. The two instruments overlap so greatly in terms of what they measure that they have been characterized occasionally as being interchangeable for diagnostic purposes.

More recent research in the assessment of very young children has been conducted by Kagan (1972). Investigating cognitive development from a considerably different framework, this work may provide very valuable results for the early evaluation of intellectual status in the future. Kagan has concentrated on the young child's ability to focus attention on certain stimuli for a sustained period of time. The data suggest that a child proceeds through a series of very different response patterns as early as 30 to 60 days. Additionally, a variety of stimulus conditions appear to be influential at different times, which may well suggest what factors in the infant's environment are important in terms of cognitive development. Although highly speculative at this point, there is the definite impression that different processes of cognitive development are being tapped than that of the sensorimotor performance area, which is predominant in the previously mentioned techniques.

Certainly, other techniques have been developed and are in fact used by many professionals for early assessment of a child's intellectual functioning. Meier, in the 1973 report of the President's Committee on Mental Retardation, discusses seven approaches in addition to those mentioned above, including the Kuhlmann-Binet Scale (birth through 30 months), Griffiths Scale (birth through 4 years), and Revised Gesell Scale (birth through 5 years). The absence of discussion regarding these other efforts should not be interpreted by the reader as implication of lesser worth. The scope of the present text simply does not permit such in-depth examination in any single area. It must be remembered that each facet of behavioral science represents the life work for many professionals. Further inquiry by interested readers may be guided by the annotated bibliography at the end of the chapter.

Although closely related to cognitive development, there has been a separate and distinct effort in the area of early language assessment, at least on a limited basis. The primary work in assessment of language prior to the 3-month age has involved clinical analysis of certain factors in the infant's cry. A review of research by Ostwald, Phibbs, and Fox (1968) included twenty-four studies spanning a period of well over 100 years. Such assessment has not received widespread application and thus far appears to be of limited pragmatic value in terms of early evaluation.

Language assessment after the 3-month age has been addressed in two different procedures, the Playtest (Friedlander, 1971) and the Early Language Assessment Scale (Honig and Caldwell, 1966). The Playtest approach (3 to 12 months) is aimed at the assessment of children's receptive language ability, which Friedlander characterizes as ". . . the effectiveness of their listening to the fine-grained aspects of natural sound and language stimuli (and) . . . their methods of using natural sound input in the integration of their sensory experiences." This evaluation thus goes far beyond the hearing acuity aspect of sound reception. It places the processing of natural sounds as the central issue and also focuses on the young child's receptive abilities in terms of language.

Of particular interest in this area is research comparing children who exhibited substantial impairment in speech development with similar children who did not have such disorders. Television story-telling sequences were shown to the two groups of children. The narration for the story was presented in a natural clear fashion as well as in a totally garbled form to both groups. The group of children who were normal in speech development exhibited a high level of interest and attention to the story with natural narration but not the story with the incomprehensible narration. Those children with speech development problems watched both the natural and the incomprehensible narration sequences with equally high interest and attention. These results would suggest that those children with speech development disorders were not discriminating between the garbled narration and that which was presented in a clear manner. Clearly there is a significant aspect of auditory reception that is operating beyond the mere sound acuity level. Considerable value with regard to early receptive language evaluation may result from this line of work. It is quite possible that developmental retardation, at least in the language area, may be predicted from such assessment. Future research and development in terms of clinical use of these techniques may result in important advances in the evaluation of young children. Certainly the sophisticated instrumentation involved would preclude such assessment on a mass screening basis.

The Early Language Assessment Scale developed by Honig and Caldwell (3 to 48 months) is designed to evaluate both the receptive and expressive language abilities of young children. Operating on a somewhat different basis (and with less involved apparatus) this technique primarily focuses on the young child's response to certain stimuli provided by the examiner. Using this scale, the examiner presents a variety of commands, auditory stimuli of a nonlanguage nature, and certain visual stimuli and imitation items. Depending on the response required, the child's performance is scored on a rating sheet in terms of receptive and expressive language development. Very little training is necessary for administering this evaluation, and language development screening appears to be quite feasible on a rather routine basis. Although widespread utilization is not presently being implemented, this approach appears promising in terms of routine health and well-baby evaluation. Since the primary monitoring at this age is conducted by health care personnel, it would seem that such ongoing assessment might be easily conducted during the early and continuing visits with the pediatrician and office staff.

Evaluation of language development remains an emerging and increasingly important area of interest in terms of early assessment, particularly with respect to developmental mental retardation. As previously noted, evaluation of later mental status relies quite heavily on language and verbal functioning. Undoubtedly, as we become increasingly discrete in our skill description, specific areas of performance level will become more important. Thus language assessment may well be viewed as just that, language skill, rather than representing some abstract and larger concept, such as mental development. Beyond this it is already clear that an area such as language will be more discretely analyzed in terms of component behaviors. As this occurs it is quite likely that our evaluation, screening, and diagnosis efforts will take on a very different description, will increase our predictive ability, and certainly will become more amenable to intervention and modification.

Evaluation of social-emotional development presents a considerable challenge to those working with young children. A variety of instruments have been developed in an effort to effectively assess this area of behavior, and in each case a common problem has been encountered—the reliability of the assessment itself. Of the ten listed in the 1973 report of The President's Committee on Mental Retardation, only three are judged as having both "adequate" reliability and validity. Two of those include the time shortly after birth (Vineland Social Maturity Scale, birth to 18 years; and the functional analysis approach, birth to adult). The third ranges from 1 to 6 years (Quantitative Analysis of Tasks).

The Vineland Social Maturity Scale is constructed with sequentially ordered, age-graded items that cover several content areas. These areas include self-help skills, self-direction, locomotion, occupation, communication, and social relations. This instrument is viewed by its author as designed basically to assess performance and ability of the child in terms of progressing toward independence. Two approaches to data collection are involved, including both an interview of the parent and observation of the child. When the child is not present or available, the information is gathered solely on the basis of interview data. Although this scale has been judged as adequate in terms of both reliability and validity, workers in mental retardation have long believed that better assessment is possible. This has led to recent efforts to design techniques that will either augment or supplant the Vineland Scales.

Also applicable in the very early life of a child is assessment that, for want of a better term, has been labeled a functional analysis approach (Bijou and Peterson, 1970). Although not designed as an instrument per se, this work is founded on the basic principles of applied behavior analysis and is highly relevant to the issues of early childhood assessment. The functional analysis approach to assessment requires direct observation of the child rather than reliance on behavioral description reported by an informant. This observation is conducted for children who are referred because of behavioral or developmental problems and is accomplished in the setting in which the problem occurs. Data are recorded in terms of three categories: behavioral deficits, behavioral excesses, and inappropriate stimulus control. Within these general categories the behavioral description of the child's functioning is very specific, which then permits precise intervention rather than operating from a broad-spectrum antibiotic or "shotgun treatment" approach. This level of specificity represents a definite strength of the functional analysis assessment framework. It does, however, require substantial training in applied behavior analysis. Given such appropriate preparation, the evaluation can be conducted by either professional or paraprofessional staff. An additional strength of functional analysis assessment is the use of direct observation rather than indirect methods such as interviews. Interviews have long been viewed as problematical and have added substantially to the difficulties in reliability and validity of assessment.

Direct observation is also required by the Quantitative Analysis of Tasks developed by White and Kaban (1971). The observer takes a considerably different approach, however, from that in functional analysis. Like functional analysis, the White and Kaban technique involves careful observation of the child's behavior and the environmental stimulus conditions in a natural setting. Unlike functional analysis, the evaluator not only observes but also makes inferences about and describes the child's apparent purpose in terms of the recorded behavior. This interpretation of the child's purpose is then coded and scored in reference to several criteria. The coding of social tasks involves numerous types, including such items as, to gain attention, to avoid attention, to gain approval, to annoy, to maintain social contact, to compete, to provide information. Although the manual is quite specific with regard to coding, the inferences made by the observer are obviously crucial. The strength and reliability of the evaluation (or conversely, the weakness and unreliability) are probably predominantly determined by this factor. This evaluation is viewed as being appropriately administered by trained paraprofessionals. Regardless of who the evaluator is, the soundness, accuracy, and reliability of assessment rest heavily on the judgment and, consequently, the training of the observer.

The discussion thus far has focused on instruments and techniques that assess a child's developmental status in a somewhat limited area. Although the boundaries of performance areas are far from distinct, at least an attempt has been made by many to discretely assess intellectual development, language development, and social-emotional development as well as to consider the early health status and possible presence of inheritable disorders. Assessment, in a somewhat broader framework, has received considerable attention in recent years. This has led to the design of a variety of developmental screening techniques that evaluate several factors simultaneously while still providing specific information in each area. These techniques have witnessed a growth in popularity for several reasons, one certainly being the greater efficiency of using a single instrument to assess several performance areas. The 1973 report of The President's Committee on Mental Retardation discusses six different instruments of the multifactor type: the Rapid Developmental Screening Checklist (designed by the Committee on Children with Handicaps, American Academy of Pediatrics, chaired by Margaret Giannini, 1972); Guide to Normal Milestones of Development (Haynes, 1967); the Developmental Screening Inventory (Knobloch, Pasamanick, and Sherard, 1967); the CCD Developmental Progress Scale (Boyd, 1969); the Denver Developmental Screening Test (Frankenburg and Dodds, 1967); and the Progress Assessment Chart (Gunzberg, 1963). The present text does not permit full examination of each of these instruments; therefore, only selected techniques are discussed. The reader interested in more comprehensive information concerning these instruments should examine either the original sources or the President's Committee Report (Meier, 1973).

One of the more widely used multifactor instruments is the Denver Developmental Screening Test. The instrument is useful from birth to 6 years of age and scores the child's status in four different areas of development: gross motor, fine motor-adaptive, language, and personal-social. Considerable research has been conducted on the Denver scale to determine its reliability and validity of assessment. Results have indicated that both reliability and validity of the Denver scale are considerably stronger than those of most scales. As with so many standardized instruments, however, concern has been expressed about the predictive validity of the Denver scale with minority children.

Similar to the Denver scale in a number of ways is the CCD Developmental Progress Scale. This instrument evaluates the child's developmental status in three areas: motor skills, communication-interpersonal skills, and self-sufficiency skills. The motor skills area actually represents a combination of the two motor areas of the Denver scale. The CCD scale is used from birth to 8 years of age. It has been suggested that the CCD scale is preferable to the Denver for older children, while the Denver is more appropriate for younger children (Meier, 1973). This judgment is based on the concentration of test items in the Denver scale at the younger ages (birth to 18 months) with a substantial decrease in the number of items for ages 4 to 6 years. The CCD scale includes an equal number of items at all levels from birth to 8 years, making this instrument far stronger than the Denver at the age levels above 4 years. In viewing the distribution of test items, either instrument can probably be appropriately used between 2 and 4 years of age.

Both the Denver and CCD scales rely on parent reporting as well as direct observation of the child as sources for developmental status information. Parent reporting has been notoriously problematical throughout the history of measurement and evaluation. The basic difficulty in this area lies with the accuracy of the information provided. Recognizing the possibility of faulty recall, Meier notes that Boyd addresses yet another point that has vital importance in relation to parental reporting in general. It is Boyd's position that in order to obtain accurate reports of the child's typical behavior the phrasing of the question is crucial. Questions must be posed in a manner that elicits behavioral descriptions and not in a fashion that suggests socially appropriate answers. Checklist interviews tend to result in inaccurately high ratings because of the defensive assumption of the parent that the question itself means the child should be able to perform the task. This position would seem to be important with regard to the technique used to gain information from parents. Although the approach requiring a description of typical behavior will not solve all of the problems involved in parent reporting, it certainly appears promising in terms of reducing one source of data contamination.

PRESCHOOL YEARS

It is evident from the preceding discussion that no clear-cut age exists when certain instruments are no longer used and others systematically become appropriate. Certain of the assessment techniques previously examined are used during the years that would be classified as preschool, whereas others are not. Likewise, certain of the evaluation procedures to be discussed in this section extend downward in age to a point that could easily be termed the early years. Techniques that overlap in age ranges will not be discussed again. The purpose of this section is to examine selected evaluation procedures that are used primarily during the years that immediately precede a child's school enrollment.

Intellectual

Perhaps the type of assessment most frequently associated with developmental mental retardation involves the measurement of intelligence. As suggested earlier in this chapter, intelligence has frequently assumed the stature of an existing entity in the minds of many. Actually, intelligence represents an abstract concept that is inferred to exist to some greater or lesser degree depending on an individual's performance on selected tasks. With recent developments in evaluation there has been some conceptual clarification that a particular score on an intelligence test is representative of various performances and that the concept of intelligence, as a general ability, is an inferred rather than a known, observable entity.

Part of the above noted concept of intelligence certainly results from the framework utilized in the development of early instrumentation. Binet's early work was based on the idea that intelligence was a general ability factor. Consequently, his approach involved a mixture of items that aimed at an assessment that represented a composite measure, presumably including performances related to the general ingelligence notion. The revised Stanford-Binet test, the revised version of Binet's earlier work, remains an instrument that generates a composite measure. However, recent use of this instrument in clinical and diagnostic settings has resulted in developments that attempt to isolate the various performances to a greater degree than before (Ferinden, Jacobson, and Kovalinsky, 1970).

The Stanford-Binet is recommended as appropriate for age 2 years through adulthood. Frequently, however, other instruments are used for individuals over 12 years of age because of the administration time required with older people. The Stanford-Binet has frequently been viewed as the standard against which intelligence measurement is compared, but questions may be raised regarding this status. Obviously, the composite nature of its construction presents problems in terms of the pure assessment of discrete skills. This limits its utility with regard to instructionally relevant information. Additionally, the most recent standardization involved a Caucasian population, making cultural bias a substantial potential problem.

Another instrument that is frequently used to assess intelligence with preschool children is the Wechsler Preschool and Primary Scale of Intelligence (commonly termed the WPPSI). The WPPSI is recommended for use with children from ages 4 to 6½ years. Designed somewhat differently from the Binet, the WPPSI is constructed with items that are organized into eleven subtests by content areas. This encourages the use of the instrument as a measure of somewhat more specific skill areas. (Published in 1963, the WPPSI represents a much more recently developed instrument than other Wechsler scales [to be discussed later].) The WPPSI has been used increasingly with the preschool child for whom evaluation of intellectual performance is required. As with most instruments, the WPPSI is not without its problems. In part because of longevity, the WPPSI has considerably less data from a clinical and diagnostic standpoint than either the Binet or other Wechsler scales. Looking to the other end of the intelligence continuum, the WPPSI presents particular difficulties with the very capable child. There appears to be a rather substantial ceiling on the items, which results in inaccurate assessment for these children. It does, however, provide a useful instrument for preschool children who are already suspected of functioning at a rather low level.

Bush and Waugh (1976) discuss the Peabody Picture Vocabulary Test as an instrument for assessing intelligence in preschool children. The Peabody Picture Vocabulary Test (PPVT) is designed as a very quickly administered instrument that can be used with individuals from ages 2½ to 18 years. This instrument involves somewhat different administration procedures than most intelligence tests. The examiner presents a printed page with four numbered pictures and reads a stimulus word. Children being tested then point to the picture they believe best represents the word that was read. Although the PPVT has a rather high correlation with other instruments (notably the Wechsler intelligence scale for children, .70 to .80), it tends to result in scores that are frequently five to ten points higher than those from other instruments. This presents some difficulty in terms of assessment of mildly handicapped individuals. In addition, it has had a somewhat limited clinical use to date, making a large data base unavailable in comparison to other instruments. Also like other instruments, the standardization has been somewhat limited and initially involved only Caucasians, allowing cultural bias problems.

Language

As the child grows older, the assessment of language development and the assessment of intellectual functioning become increasingly blurred, and distinctions between the two areas frequently appear imperceptible. This results from several factors. First, at least in terms of normal language development, the child very rapidly grows in sophistication with regard to language structure. Menyuk (1972) notes that by the time normal children reach 3 to 4 years of age they have use of all of the basic syntactic structures in language. This, then, illustrates the emergence of a very different response mode than was possible when the very young child was operating almost totally as a sensorimotor organism. Likewise, test developers who are working in this age range move very rapidly to take advantage of this new response mode. For the assessment of intellectual status there is a much heavier verbal component as the child's age increases. Thus there is much more of a relationship between language and intellectual assessment as the child grows older.

As evidence of the preceding dilemma, the Peabody Picture Vocabulary Test, one of the instruments discussed previously under intellectual assessment, warrants mention in terms of language assessment. Although the PPVT is formally described as an intelligence test, various professionals view it as being more appropriately conceived as a receptive language measure. In fact some describe it only in terms of receptive language (Lerner, 1976). Because of the nature of the item presentation, such a view appears quite credible. The inference of receptive language evaluation certainly requires the use of a less abstract concept than that of intelligence.

Another instrument that is frequently viewed as assessing language is the Illinois Test of Psycholinguistic Abilities, commonly termed the ITPA (Kirk, McCarthy, and Kirk, 1968). Developed for use with children from about 2½ to 10 years of age, the ITPA is a highly complicated instrument that provides a profile of the child's performance in twelve different subtest areas. The initial usage of the ITPA was primarily with children who were designated as having learning disabilities. However, as concepts of prescriptive education have grown in popularity, it has enjoyed broader application to other populations, including those with developmental retardation. Although there is little doubt that the ITPA is a useful instrument, it is not without problems. It is a cumbersome instrument to use (at least in terms of some subjects) and requires considerable training on the part of the examiner. Additionally, some of the subtests are far from being "pure" in terms of what specific skill is being measured, and depending on the setting, may or may not provide directly relevant instructional information. A third problem with the ITPA involves the standardization population and has particular relevance to the present topic. Only children with IQ scores between 84 and 116 were included in the normative group. This means that a large data base does not exist for many of the retarded children. This does not preclude its use, but the

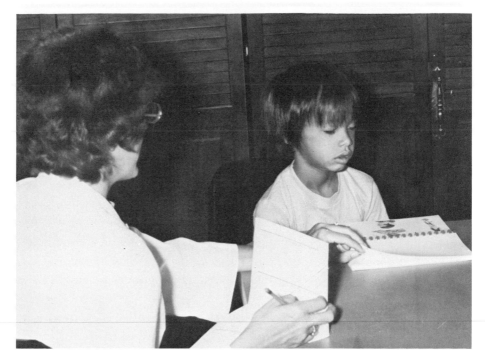

Fig. 4-1. The ITPA is one of several assessment instruments used to determine the existence of learning problems.

existence of such data would certainly provide a clearer picture of the ITPA measurement properties when used with retarded children.

The ITPA has been nearly as useful as a conceptual framework as it has a direct assessment instrument. It has generated a definite change in the way many professionals view children, which has moved many toward the functional analysis of skill level as a way of thinking. This has long been the position taken by those skilled in applied behavior analysis. Certainly a gap remains. Proponents of applied behavior analysis request much more precision in skill definition than is possible by actual application of the ITPA. However, the conceptual change represents a significant impact when viewed in the broader professional perspective of purposes of evaluation.

A variety of other language assessment instruments have been developed with varying degrees of precision and standardization (the Houston Test of Language Development, the Mecham Verbal Language Development Scale, the Utah Test of Language Development). Complete description of all such instruments is far beyond the scope of an introductory text on developmental mental retardation. More appropriate is a brief discussion of an evaluation approach, rather than a particular instrument or technique. Many professionals who are vitally concerned with practical application have viewed assessment as being important only as it relates to intervention or instruction. Such a posture does not place much value on scores unless they represent performance that can be rather precisely related to specific instructional activities that will result in behavior change in terms of skills. As implied in previous discussion, an approach such as this assumes more of the configuration of the specific skill assessment of applied behavior analysis and tends to discount such issues as etiology (except in rare cases, such as a cleft palate that can be rectified by surgery). Consequently, evaluation in this framework frequently becomes an ongoing monitoring system that is built into the instructional program or designed specifically for a given instructional program (Distar Language Program). Such an assessment is very much in line with recent concepts of prescriptive education (in fact, it represents a potent force in the development of such concepts) and is precise in pinpointing instructional effort in areas where it is most needed.

Perceptual motor

Assessment of perceptual motor skills is more commonly an evaluation conducted with children suspected to have learning disabilities than with those thought to be developmentally retarded. Disregarding the theoretical basis that links such an area to specific learning disabilities, perceptual motor functioning is a crucial skill area in terms of many aspects of instruction for retarded children. Without the various visual-motor skills the child is in a difficult position to perform the tasks required in many instructional settings. Consequently a child who is experiencing difficulty in these areas should be assessed in terms of specific level of functioning and should have instructional activities designed in relation to these skills. Therefore a brief discussion of perceptual motor skill assessment appears warranted.

One of the better-known assessment techniques in the perceptual motor area is the Frostig Developmental Test of Visual Perception. This instrument is designed for use with children from about 4 to 8 years of age. Some latitude is obviously available in this age range for children who exhibit developmental retardation to a significant degree. The Frostig can be administered either individually or to groups and assesses five different areas: (1) eye-motor (hand) coordination, (2) figure-ground discrimination, (3) form constancy, (4) position in space, and (5) spatial relations. Frostig has designed specific remediation activities that are coordinated with the evaluation instrument. From her viewpoint, identification of perceptual deficits is crucial in terms of early remediation (kindergarten and first grade) in order to permit appropriate school progress (Frostig and Horne, 1964).

Another device used for assessment in the perceptual-motor area is the Purdue Perceptual-Motor Survey. Although the Purdue was not designed specifically for preschool assessment (norms are based on children between 6 and 10 years old), there is some latitude in the age range. The Purdue is based on a developmental theory that portrays the child as moving through a sequence of learning stages, such as those postulated by Piaget. The survey involves twenty-two items arranged into eleven different subtests. Essentially, the Purdue is designed to tap three major perceptual-motor skill areas: laterality, directionality, and perceptual-motor matching.

Perceptual-motor assessment is also facilitated by use of the Developmental Test of Visual-Motor Integration (VMI). Developed by Beery (1967), this instrument involves a paper and pencil performance by the child in which geometric forms are presented as stimuli to be copied. Although the VMI was designed primarily for use at the preschool and early primary levels, the manual notes that it can be administered to children from 2 to 15 years of age. Basically the VMI was devised to assess the degree to which motor behavior and visual perception are integrated. As with other perceptual-motor evaluation, the purpose is to identify fundamental skill deficits that are essential to performing various academic tasks. These skills then become pinpointed for remedial instruction aimed at preparing the child for basic performance of academic tasks.

The previously discussed assessment devices focus on perceptual-motor skill from a framework of the integration of perceptual functioning and motor performance. These two crucial skill areas must operate in concert in order for many academic tasks to be performed. There are instances, however, in which it is desirable to evaluate the status of one component without the other influencing the assessment. With many instruments this is not possible because, for example, a severe motor problem would substantially reduce the overall performance score. Under these conditions the examiner would not be able to determine how well the child's visual perception is functioning because both visual and motor components are blended in the task.

Colarusso and Hammill (1972) have designed an instrument that circumvents this problem to a great degree, the Motor-Free Visual Perception Test (MVPT). This test presents the child with a series of plates that involve various visual images. The motor response is minimized to a significant degree because the child may only be required to respond with a nod of the head as the examiner points to various components of the drawing. Such an approach represents a very promising assessment technique for situations in which physical disability impairs the motor ability to respond.

Social skill

A variety of evaluation approaches for assessing social skill status were discussed in the section on very young children. In many cases the upper age range extends far beyond the young child, into preschool and elementary years and even beyond. Consequently, only a very brief examination of social skill assessment will be undertaken here.

Adaptive behavior is a concept involving skills that may be generically viewed in the social competence area. As mentioned in Chapter 1, adaptive behavior has become a part of the formal definition for mental retardation of the American Association on Mental Deficiency. This behavior was previously assessed with the Vineland. However, the AAMD has developed an instrument specifically for the evaluation of adaptive and maladaptive behavior, the AAMD Adaptive Behavior Scale (ABS). It was specifically developed for individuals who are either suspected of or are confirmed as being mentally retarded. Despite this purpose, the ABS is described as also being appropriate for individuals who are emotionally maladjusted. This instrument assesses the individual's effectiveness in adapting to the natural and social demands of the environment. Several factors are evaluated, such as self-abusive behavior, destructive behavior, sexually aberrant behavior, independent functioning, time and number concepts, as well as other areas. Scales are available for young children through the adult level, although caution must be exercised in interpreting *scores* per se. Program planning is more appropriately based on a critical analysis of specific skill level in particular areas. This is especially true in light of the fact that institutional populations were utilized heavily during standardization, making *score* interpretation of mildly handicapped individuals even more difficult.

The Cain-Levine Social Competency Scale was specifically developed for assessing trainable mentally retarded children from 5 to 13 years of age. The clinician, however, may find that its usefulness extends beyond the categorical boundaries of the trainable child. Designed as a behavior rating scale, this instrument involves forty-four items divided into four subscale areas: self-help, initiative, social skills, and communication. Administration of the instrument results in an overall score as well as performance scores in each of the four subscale areas. These scores are viewed as being useful for placement and planning of socially oriented training and also for evaluation of the training effectiveness.

ELEMENTARY SCHOOL YEARS

The purpose of this section is to briefly discuss assessment during the elementary school years. The child who is developmentally retarded may be somewhat out of phase with regard to the usual chronological age–formal education sequence. Consequently, the term elementary years is used only as a generic guideline and primarily involves ages 5 to 11 or 12 years. Additionally, the overlapping age ranges for assessment approaches have already become evident in the previous discussion. Certain instruments that were examined in terms of the preschool child extend to and occasionally beyond the age range presently being considered. Such instruments will not be discussed again. Instead, other techniques, which become age-appropriate during this range, will receive primary attention.

Within this section on the elementary years, separate attention will be given to an emerging system of assessment that has been developed by Mercer and Lewis (1977). This system, entitled *System of Multicultural Pluralistic Assessment*, provides for evaluation across several attribute areas and therefore cannot be appropriately discussed under a specific area subheading (such as Intellectual or Achievement).

Intellectual

Several instruments were mentioned previously under intellectual assessment that extended into the 5 to 12 years age range. In addition to these techniques, one of the best-known intelligence tests becomes age-appropriate in this range, the Wechsler Intelligence Scale for Children—revised edition (WISC-R). The WISC-R is recommended for use with children between the ages of 5 and 15 years. This instrument was designed in a somewhat similar fashion as the WPPSI, discussed earlier for younger children. The WISC-R has twelve subtests that are divided into two general areas, verbal and performance measures. Ten of these subtests are used to generate separate scores for verbal and performance dimensions (digit span and maze subtests are not included in the scoring of this revised edition). Like most standardized instruments, the WISC-R is basically a norm-referenced instrument. Used in this fashion the resulting score is a composite IQ that indicates general ability. The revised edition, however, also provides for a profiling of the child's performance in individual subtest areas, which generates more specific information than the composite IQ.

The WISC-R, developed in 1974, has a considerable history and data base as its foundation. Its predecessor, the WISC, was developed in 1949, and over the years generated a vast data base with considerable research, which helped to define the measurement properties of the instrument. Although the recommended age range extends from 5 to 15 years, the WISC-R is not necessarily the preferred instrument for all cases in this range. For general assessment relative to mental retardation, some view the Stanford-Binet as the stronger instrument up to age 8, primarily because of the standardization and clinical use. As data accumulate on the WISC-R it may be found that this preference (which was developed by some clinicians during the period of the WISC) no longer holds. Certainly for children from about 8 to 15 years of age, the WISC-R is more appropriate.

Achievement

Many of the specific areas of assessment previously discussed for earlier age levels remain appropriate during the elementary years. Determination of which areas require evaluation is based on a critical analysis of where the child is encountering difficulty. One assessment area, however, becomes more important in terms of evaluation at the elementary level than was the case during earlier years—that of achievement. A variety of procedures are used for assessing academic achievement during the elementary years, including formal standardized instruments as well as techniques for monitoring progress on a daily basis. Certain strengths and weaknesses are present in each approach, depending on the purpose of the evaluation. This section provides a brief overview of various achievement assessment procedures.

The Wide Range Achievement Test (WRAT) is a general achievement test that assesses a child's performance in three areas: reading (pronunciation and word recognition), spelling, and arithmetic (computation). Constructed with two different levels, the Level I WRAT is used with children from 5 years to 11 years and 11 months of age, whereas Level II is used from 12 years of age to adulthood. The scores are in the form of global achievement scores and are expressed as grade-equivalents and percentiles. This type of score reporting does not provide sufficient detail in terms of specific skill areas to be of much use in determining instructional details. However, the WRAT is generally useful as a screening measure.

Another instrument used to measure achievement is the Peabody Individual Achievement Test (PIAT). The PIAT is designed for use from kindergarten through adulthood. Although the PIAT is also a general achievement measure, it is more useful than the WRAT for instructional purposes. Five subtests are provided, including mathematics, reading recognition, reading comprehension, spelling, and general information. Easily administered, the PIAT results in a profile of the child's performance in the various areas tested. The scores are presented in a variety of forms, including percentiles, age equivalents, grade equivalents, and standard scores, as well as raw scores. Depending on the specific evaluation purpose, the examiner may select any of these score forms as the appropriate method of reporting.

Another set of instruments that is useful for assessing academic achievement is the Metropolitan Achievement Test battery. More appropriately, it should be noted that this is an example of how standardized instrumentation can be utilized in a meaningful fashion with the retarded but in a manner that the test developer may not have conceived. The Metropolitan represents a comprehensive battery made up of several instruments with an extensive *normed* age range. Beyond the readiness scale, which provides a global evaluation (in terms of specific skill level), the primary and advanced batteries include several different areas. These are word knowledge, word analysis (for the younger levels), reading, language, spelling (older levels), math computation, math concepts, math problem solving, and others. The normed areas of evaluation per se are not as important as what can be done with them. When analyzed in terms of the skills required by each item, the Metropolitan can provide a vast amount of information in terms of the level of a child's functioning. This information can then be rather precisely coordinated in terms of specific determination of discrete activities for the child's instructional program. Such an analysis is not possible without considerable information and teacher training in task analysis and precision teaching. However, when such educational expertise is brought to the teaching task, considerable relevance for education of the mentally retarded (as well as others) is evident in instruments like the Metropolitan. More frequently, the data from the Metropolitan are presented in *score summary* form, which may be used for administrative purposes but is certainly less useful from an instructional standpoint.

The achievement instruments discussed thus far have been general achievement measures, with some providing specific skill information. On certain occasions it is necessary to use an instrument that focuses specifically on one content area and provides an in-depth assessment of subskills in that area. Such an instrument is the Keymath Diagnostic Arithmetic Test. Keymath was developed for use with children as young as the preschool level and ranging upward through grade 6 (older in some cases). Both traditional and new math skills are assessed, with fourteen subtests being arranged into three areas: content, operations, and applications. Scores are recorded on a profile, which then serves as a description of strengths and weaknesses for instructional programming. In addition to the profile of specific skills, Keymath may also be scored on a total test-performance basis for use in placement or other administrative decisions.

Achievement assessment that results in only grade- or age-equivalent scores (as well as percentiles and standard scores) is providing norm-referenced information. These same tests may be used in other fashions that essentially become criterion-referenced when a child's performance is not compared with that of other children or with some norm. The more discrete and specific an assessment is, the more potential there is for drawing specific implications for instruction. The greatest relevance for instruction comes from assessment that is built in as an integral part of the instructional program. Such an evaluation-instructional system was mentioned previously under language assessment at the preschool level (such as the Distar Language Program) but certainly warrants rementioning under achievement assessment. Ideally, this type of achievement assessment provides a continuous monitoring of a child's progress in specific skills. The instruction, then, is precisely aimed at the child's level of functioning, which permits a highly efficient interface between evaluation and instruction. There is much to be said for such an approach both in terms of educating those who are developmentally retarded and those who fall into that nebulous area known as "regular" education.

Sompa

A separate subsection is being devoted to the work of Mercer and Lewis (1977) for several reasons. First of all, the *System of Multicultural Pluralistic*

Assessment (SOMPA) provides for assessment in a variety of attribute areas, as noted earlier. Consequently it crosses the conceptual frameworks that have been used to categorize other instrumentation. Additionally, the SOMPA represents an attempt to provide for a comprehensive evaluation, one that strives to overcome some of the conceptual problems and issues presented in the initial part of this chapter. As such it seems to warrant separate discussion and attention.

The SOMPA is designed to be used with children from 5 to 11 years of age. Assessment of the child is extremely comprehensive and views the individual in terms of three broad perspectives: (1) the medical model, (2) the social system model, and (3) the pluralistic model. Six different areas are evaluated within the medical model portion: physical dexterity, weight by height, visual acuity, health history, and the Bender Visual-Motor Gestalt Test. The social system model assesses adaptive behavior and school functioning level (using primarily the WISC-R). The third broad area, the pluralistic model, views the child in terms of "estimated learning potential" and two sociocultural scales (one for the child's own ethnic group and a second based on the school culture). Scoring for all measures is converted to percentile and placed in a profile format. The SOMPA is obviously rather revolutionary in its approach and addresses child functioning in a manner that has not been undertaken previously on any widespread basis. Some professionals are somewhat skeptical with regard to its potential utility because of the massive nature of the evaluation. However, many believe that it will be extremely useful and will circumvent some of the problems that have previously been encountered in assessment procedures.

THE ADOLESCENT AND ADULT YEARS

The adolescent and adult years are only a general reference and could well suggest different specific age ranges when interpreted by different individuals. Assessment in this section generally is referenced in terms of 13 years of age and older. Many of the evaluation techniques previously examined extend well into this age range and therefore will not receive repeated attention.

Intellectual

The instrument that is frequently used in the mid-adolescent and older years is the Wechsler Adult Intelligence Scale (WAIS). The WISC-R, discussed earlier, extends upward into the early adolescent years (5 to 15 years). Similar in design, the WAIS is appropriate for assessment of intellectual functioning above the 15-year age level. The WAIS subscales are the same as the WISC-R with the exception that there are only eleven rather than twelve. The norm group for the WAIS represents a better cross section of individuals including non-Caucasians. As was mentioned in the previous discussion of Wechsler scales, educational interpretations that have been developed from clinical application result in much more information than mere reporting of IQ scores.

Vocational

One area that becomes increasingly relevant as the retarded person grows older involves evaluation of skill level for vocational training and placement. During adolescence and adulthood the retarded individual usually encounters vocational training as a part of the formal educational setting. Of course, the nature of this training (as well as later placement) varies considerably depending on the degree of impairment.

Evaluation in this area, like that previously discussed, must be considered in light of the purpose of such assessment. One purpose of past research on evaluation has involved the prediction of vocational success. A second purpose is the evaluation of training and placement success once the activity is operationally underway. A variety of problems has been encountered in both areas. Gold (1973) presents a comprehensive review of a variety of dimensions in both vocational training and assessment. After discussing several evaluation approaches, including intelligence tests, manual dexterity tests, and work sample tasks, Gold suggests that work samples appear to show the most promise, despite the fact that general efforts to date have been less than satisfying. The work sample assessment is most analogous to evaluation using applied behavior analysis techniques. Such precise analysis of skill level has provided the most practically oriented information in other areas and thus it is not surprising in vocational assessment. The precision is logically generated because the evaluation is conducted in a setting that is natural, to the greatest degree possible. Such a close link between the evaluative procedure and its purpose or referent setting tends to provide the most useful and also the most accurate data. Perhaps the most serious deterrent to more widespread acceptance of this approach is convenience. Work samples, as a test per se, tend to be cumbersome in terms of development and administration. Such techniques are not nearly so inconvenient, however, when they are designed as an integral part of a training program. The logistics of developing a convenient evaluation system rationally related to program activities and to job success remain the challenge of professionals who work in assessment generally and with handicapped individuals in particular.

SUMMARY

This chapter has presented a number of assessment concepts and procedures. Many of the topics and techniques examined have previously been excluded from textbooks and other discussions dealing with the developmentally retarded because they have been deemed inappropriate. Frequently, such exclusion has been based on norm group descriptions or procedures that have traditionally been thought inappropriate for the retarded. Such reasoning does not provide for detailed analysis of the task presented and discrete determination of specific skill levels. A further step that must be noted is the precise relationship between evaluation and subsequent activity (whether it be instructional or vocational performance). Assessment as a science has matured to the point that such a way of thinking is primitive at best. As we noted at the beginning of this chapter, a good many errors have been made in the process of both conceptualizing and developing assessment procedures. Some of these errors are currently being recognized, and our progress in the future might be more thoughtful. As suggested by McFie (1975) the ". . . search for a test of 'brain damage' is destined to be a vain one . . ." and we believe that this type of conclusion is also gaining momentum in a variety of evaluation arenas. Precision prescription in terms of teaching as well as other service areas demands a better performance from the evaluator; it is no longer possible to rest one's case on, or to blame, the instrumentation alone. Hopefully, as the evaluator is expected to perform in a more rational fashion, the retarded will increase performance level, if for no other reason than a refinement of both our conceptualization and techniques.

STUDY QUESTIONS

1. A number of difficulties were found with the calculation of intelligence quotient by the ratio method. What were some of them, and why was the deviation method found preferable?
2. A variety of conceptual developments have been important in the field of assessment during the past years. Among them have been the notions of formative and summative evaluation, and the distinction between norm and criterion referenced

assessment. How do these concepts fit into the evaluation picture, and why were they important?

3. The SOMPA is viewed by some as attending to certain issues and problems that have plagued evaluation professionals for many years. Discuss the broad models involved in the SOMPA, and suggest how you think they may serve to address such problems as discriminatory testing.

REFERENCES

Bartel, N. R., Grill, J. J., and Bryen, D. N. Language characteristics of black children: implications for assessment. *Journal of School Psychology*, 1973, **11**, 351-364.

Beery, K. E. *Developmental Test of Visual-Motor Integration: administration and scoring manual.* Chicago: Follett Publishing Co., 1967.

Bijou, S. W., and Peterson, R. F. The psychological assessment of children: a functional analysis. In P. McReynolds (Ed.), *Advances in psychological assessment.* Vol. 2. Palo Alto: Science and Behavior Books, Inc., 1970, Pp. 63-78.

Binet, A., and Simon, T. Le developpement de l'intelligence chez les enfants. *L'Annee Psychologique*, 1908, **14**, 1-94.

Bloom, B. S., Hastings, J. T., and Madaus, G. F. *Handbook on formative and summative evaluation of student learning,* New York: McGraw-Hill Book Co., 1971.

Boyd, R. D. *CCD Developmental Progress Scale.* Experimental Form, Manual and Direction, 1969.

Bush, W. J., and Waugh, K. W. *Diagnosing learning disabilities.* (2nd ed.) Columbus, Ohio: Charles E. Merrill Publishing Co., 1976.

Chinn, P. L. *Child health maintenance: concepts for family centered care.* (2nd ed.) St. Louis: The C. V. Mosby Co., 1979.

Colarusso, R. P., and Hammill, D. D. *Motor-free Visual Perception Test.* San Rafael, Calif.: Academic Therapy Publications, 1972.

Drew, C. J. Criterion-referenced and norm-referenced assessment of minority group children. *Journal of School Psychology*, 1973, **11**, 323-329.

Drew, C. J., Freston, C. W., and Logan, D. R. Criteria and reference in evaluation. *Focus on Exceptional Children*, 1972, **4**, 1-10.

Ferinden, W., Jacobson, S., and Kovalinsky, T. *Educational interpretation of the Stanford-Binet Intelligence Scale form LM and the Illinois Test of Psycholinguistic Abilities.* Linden, N. J.: Remediation Associates, 1970.

Flavell, J. H. *Cognitive development,* Englewood Cliffs, N. J.: Prentice-Hall, 1977.

Frankenburg, W., and Dodds, J. The Denver Developmental Screening Test, *Journal of Pediatrics*, 1967, **71**, 181-200.

Friedlander, B. Z. Automated evaluation of selective listening in language-impaired and normal infants and young children. *Maternal and Child Health Exchange*, 1971, **1**, 9-12.

Frostig, M., and Horne, D. *The Frostig program for the development of visual perception: teacher's guide.* Chicago: Follett Publishing Co., 1964.

Gold, M. W. Research on the vocational habilitation of the retarded: the present, the future. In N. R. Ellis (Ed.), *International review of research in mental retardation.* Vol. 6. New York: Academic Press, Inc., 1973, Pp. 97-147.

Gunzberg, H. C. *Progress Assessment Chart (P.A.C.) (form I, form II).* London: National Association on Mental Health, 1963.

Hammill, D. D. Evaluating children for instructional purposes. *Academic Therapy*, 1971, **6**, 341-353.

Haynes, U. *A developmental approach to case-finding with special reference to cerebral palsy, mental retardation, and related disorders.* Washington, D.C.: U.S. Government Printing Office, 1967.

Honig, A. S., and Caldwell, B. M. *Early Language Assessment Scale.* Syracuse, N. Y.: Syracuse University Press, 1966.

Kagan, J. Do infants think? *Scientific American*, 1972, 74-82.

Kirk, S., McCarthy, J., and Kirk, W. *Illinois Test of Psycholinguistic Abilities.* (Revised ed.) Examiners manual. Urbana, Ill.: University of Illinois Press, 1968.

Knobloch, H., Pasamanick, B., and Sherard, E. S. A developmental screening inventory. In U. Haynes (Ed.), *A developmental approach to case-finding.* Washington, D.C.: U.S. Government Printing Office, 1967, Pp. 77-85.

Lerner, J. *Children with learning disabilities.* (2nd ed.) New York: Houghton Mifflin Co., 1976.

McFie, J. *Assessment of organic intellectual impairment,* New York: Academic Press, Inc., 1975.

Meeker, M., and Meeker, R. Strategies for assessing intellectual patterns in black, Anglo- and Mexican-American boys—or any other children—and implications for education. *Journal of School Psychology,* 1973, **11,** 341-350.

Meier, J. *Screening and assessment of young children at developmental risk.* Report of the President's Committee on Mental Retardation, Washington, D.C.: U.S. Government Printing Office, DHEW Publication No. (OS) 73-90, 1973.

Menyuk, P. *The development of speech.* New York: Bobbs-Merrill Co., 1972.

Mercer, J. R., and Lewis, J. F. *System of Multicultural Pluralistic Assessment,* New York: The Psychological Corporation, 1977.

Newland, T. E. Assumptions underlying psychological testing. *Journal of School Psychology,* 1973, **11,** 316-322.

Oakland, T. Assessing minority group children: challenges for school psychologists. *Journal of School Psychology,* 1973, **11,** 294-303.

O'Brien, J. S. How we detect mental retardation before birth. *Medical Times,* 1971, **99**(2), 103-108.

Ostwald, P. F., Phibbs, R., and Fox, S. Diagnostic use of infant cry. *Biology of the Neonate,* 1968, **13,** 68-82.

The rapid developmental screening checklist, Committee on Children with Handicaps (M. Giannini, Chairperson), New York: American Academy of Pediatrics, 1972.

White, B. L., and Kaban, B. *Manual for quantitative analysis of tasks of one- to six-year-old children.* Cambridge, Mass.: Harvard University Press, 1971.

ANNOTATED BIBLIOGRAPHY

Drew, C. J., Freston, C. W., and Logan, D. R. Criteria and reference in evaluation. *Focus on Exceptional Children,* 1972, **4,** 1-10.

This article discusses several concepts of evaluation and emphasizes the manner in which assessment should relate to instruction.

Meier, J. *Screening and assessment of young children at developmental risk.* Report of the President's Committee on Mental Retardation, Washington, D. C.: U.S. Government Printing Office, DHEW Publication No. (OS) 73-90, 1973.

This is an extremely comprehensive volume that provides an excellent reference source for assessment in young children.

PART TWO

Early life and preschool years

CHAPTER 5

Basic principles of early development

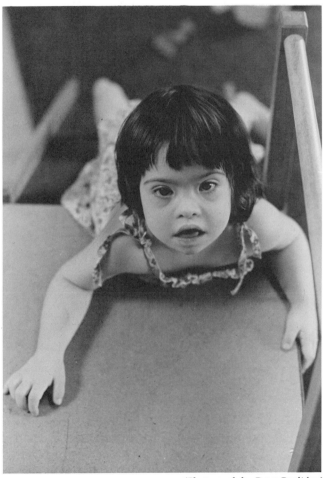

(Photograph by Peter Poulides.)

INTRODUCTION

The study of child development historically has held a very important position in behavioral science disciplines. It has been a fruitful area for both research and application and has represented a field of study essential to full understanding of human behavior. However, recent years have witnessed a number of trends that have served to deemphasize the apparent focus on this most important topic.

Most professionals agree that there has been a recent, dramatic growth in the technological dimensions of education and behavioral science in general. This seems to have occurred in terms of both applied processes and instructional materials. Government funding programs for service, research, and training have appeared that are aimed at the technological (popularly termed "applied") dimensions of education. These movements have "mirrored" what seems to be a public desire for those things that are *practical*. Those who are in high-level policy-making positions are clearly representing a mentality that greatly values activities that produce the greatest product for the expenditure.

Sophistication has increased dramatically in areas of diagnostic evaluation, instructional techniques, and materials design. Such advancements have had definite positive effects on the education of handicapped learners. In fact, the area of education of the handicapped may well be leading the field with regard to technologically related advancements. One of the obvious rewards has been that educators have never been so well supplied with tools to facilitate their efforts. These massive developments and refinements of diagnostic and instructional instrumentation have also presented certain challenges for the student in professional preparation programs, however. The vast amount of information that must be acquired and the number of required skill areas have increased at an astronomical rate. A very practical problem presents itself in this regard. The preparation time allowed to master these skills has seldom been increased in proportion to the amount of material presented.

During the time that the student is acquiring the skills necessary for a specialized sophistication, some critical areas of mastery, such as the study of the human organism itself, are frequently neglected. This tends to result in preparation with tool skills developed to a high degree but a lack of concomitant understanding of the child as a total organism. This chapter, while not intended as a substitute for a basic course in human growth and development, provides an introduction to those principles of early development that have particular relationships to mental retardation. As students progress to more advanced work in various skills, they should master supporting knowledge of the child for whom the tool skills are to be used.

There are other reasons for the particular importance of basic concepts of child development to the study of mental retardation. For many subgroups of the retarded population, developmental considerations are central to their intellectual, physical, and psychological status. From a basic biological standpoint, many of the clinical syndromes are integrally related to human development. Beyond biology, the generic psychological view of the cultural-familial retarded, the largest proportion of mentally retarded children, has long spotlighted child development within the nature-nurture controversy. Thus it seems that an acquaintance with the concepts of child development is essential to the student of mental retardation.

HUMAN DEVELOPMENT: TERMINOLOGY AND CONCEPTS

The discipline of human growth and development has grown in complexity along with advancements in all of its contributing sciences. Information has exploded from biology, embryology, genetics, psychology, and many other areas—all of which has been molded into a body of highly technical knowledge that has unique properties beyond those of the contributing areas. Prior to launching into a discussion of child development it is important to become acquainted with certain basic terminology.

Basic genetic terminology is an important foundation to understanding child development. Genotype is a term used in discussions concerning developmental aspects of the organism related to heredity. Genotype refers to the basic genetic makeup of an individual. Established at conception by the combining of sperm and ovum, the genotype is constant throughout the individual's lifetime. Only rarely does this constancy not hold, as when a mutation or other error in cell division occurs that alters the subsequent course of cell division. The human genotype is not readily accessible for actual inspection, but the phenotype, a term that refers to observable physical traits, may be used to draw inferences about the genotype. Pertaining to both physical and behavioral dimensions of the individual, the phenotype is the observable result of an interaction between the genotype and the environment.

Growth matrix is a common related term used in child development. Growth matrix is also the result of interactions between heredity and environment. Although partially observable (because it includes the phenotype) the growth matrix also includes all of the internal aspects of the child that generate a given response in a particular situation. Growth matrix is more than a simple combination of the phenotype and genotype, however. One distinction is that the genetic concepts are constant, whereas growth matrix changes as interactions occur between the organism and its environment. The growth matrix is a product of that interaction and at the same time determines or regulates subsequent individual response patterns.

Child-development specialists also use the term maturation in a fashion that requires definition. Although a certain amount of difference in use exists, we use the term maturation to signify any instance of development, that is, change in the status or underlying process of a behavioral trait, that takes place in the demonstrable absence of specific practice experience. In the present context one additional restriction is added: the absence of specific *instruction*. It becomes evident from this discussion that maturation is distinguishable from *learning*, which refers to changes associated with specific practice or instruction. In many situations it is difficult to discriminate between changes resulting from maturation and changes resulting from learning. A certain history of maturation and learning and a combination of the two is involved in a child's current developmental status at any given time. This developmental status and its components are very much related to the notion of *readiness*.

A stage of readiness exists when the child is at a point in development (including previous maturation and learning) where he might be expected to profit from a particular situation. An example often spoken of is "reading readiness." From the present standpoint, reading readiness would refer to the point in a child's development at which progress might be expected as a result of exposure to reading experience or instruction. Of course, if the status from either a maturation or previous-learning standpoint were deficient (that is, not adequate to establish readiness), the child would not be expected to progress as a result of a given stimulation. This is not intended to imply that there is some magic formula such as "X amount of maturation plus Y amount of previous learning equals readiness." Although developmental readiness includes both, widely varying amounts and types of each may exist in different children, all of whom have reached a readiness status for some given experience.

A THEORETICAL OVERVIEW

Human development and its various complexities have been topics of interest since the beginning of recorded history. Some of the most prevalent theoretical positions have an extremely lengthy history. Some prescientific explanations of human growth and development, although amusing in retrospect, enjoyed considerable popularity in earlier times.

Preformationist perspective

Those who subscribed to the preformationist theory of human growth and development had many colleagues in the past in terms of shared viewpoints. Preformationism essentially assumed that the human organism is preformed before birth; it proposed that the foundation elements of human behavior are intact from the beginning and do not develop or change from a qualitative standpoint during life. The preformationist thus denied the importance of growth and development except in the sense of quantity, or growing larger. The early homuncular theory of human reproduction exemplifies the preformationist position. This was the contention that a completely formed, tiny person existed in the sperm. This tiny person, termed a homunculus, began to grow in size at conception but did not change in the sense that tissue changes occurred qualitatively, such as in the formation of various organs.

The preformationist position substantially discounted the effects of environmental influences on human development. As suggested by the homuncular theory, the prenatal as well as postnatal environment was viewed as somewhat inconsequential with regard to significant developmental occurrences. Usually the only concessions made to environmental effects involved a mere expansion of existing abilities, drives, and behaviors. Neither new growth nor directional influence of development was thought to be significantly changed from that of the preformed organism.

Predeterministic perspective

The perspective of the predeterministic theorists seems, at first glance, to be based on similar assumptions as preformationism. Although the outcome is essentially the same, there are some significant differences between the two theoretical positions.

Predeterministic positions did not view human development as a simple accentuation of a preformed organism. Instead, the qualitative growth and tissue differentiation played a substantial role in most predeterminism theories. An example of this is found in the doctrine of recapitulation, which was described in great detail by G. Stanley Hall (1904). This notion hypothesized that the development of the child from conception to maturity progressed through all of the evolutionary phases of the human race. Although quite popular for a period around the turn of the century, this theory fell into disfavor primarily because of the absence of objective or observable data to support its sweeping hypotheses.

As noted, the outcome of predeterministic theories was essentially the same as preformationism in that the influence of the environment was thought to be minimal, perhaps limited to minor roles of restricting development. Primary roles of determining growth patterns were viewed as innate or internally regulated. More recently, the disciplines of biology, genetics, and embryology have provided factual knowledge supporting the notion that certain development is primarily regulated internally (for example, prenatal growth, certain infantile behavioral development). Former predeterministic contentions of innate control, however, involved broad applications that have not been supported scientifically.

"Tabula rasa" perspective

Tabula rasa is a term that is used in the present context to refer to approaches that emphasize the prepotency of environmental influences. The term translates to mean "blank slate" and was popularized by John Locke in the seventeenth century. For purposes of this discussion, tabula rasa is used generically to represent positions of extreme environmental impact.

Contrasting with the approaches of preformationism and predeterminism, tabula rasa positions minimize the influence of internal factors (such as heredity) on human development. Environmental influence is viewed as playing a predominant role in determining nearly all aspects of development. The tabula rasa theorist essentially views the human organism as totally plastic and infinitely amenable to molding by the external influences of the environment. Thus an individual's ability is dependent on what is "written" on the blank slate through experience. The weakness of this framework, as with those of preformationism and predeterminism, lies in the extreme to which proponents support their position.

Neither the tabula rasa nor the predeterministic approach to child development has been satisfactory. There is little logical or empirical support for a belief in preformed human functioning at birth. With the exception of very simple reflex responses, there seem to be few human behavioral dimensions that are not influenced in some fashion by the environment. The essential error by the predeterministic proponents was one of excessive discounting of the impact of experience. Tabula rasa theorists caught the pendulum in the opposite extreme position. The assumption that environmental impact is a significant contributor to human growth and development does represent reality, but the tabula rasa theorists were inclined to emphasize the impact of this factor far beyond that which was reasonable.

Interactional perspectives

Difficulties with the preformationist, predeterministic, and tabula rasa perspectives have been discussed briefly in the preceding sections. Current positions concerning the evolution of human development generally subscribe to the notion of an interaction between heredity and environment. Both genetic and environmental factors serve to set limits for growth as well as to selectively influence each other. For example, genetic material determines the actual limits even under the most favorable environment conceivable. Likewise, the environmental contingencies serve to limit the degree to which genetic potential can be fulfilled. Genetic material determines which factors in the environment are more potent by rendering the organism selectively sensitive to some more than others. Similarly, environmental factors, such as cultural or ecological factors, serve to selectively operate on genetic expression by providing selective influences on ability development.

Thus the interactional approach to human growth and development emphasizes analysis of relationships between heredity and environment. This represents a substantial difference from previous positions discussed, in which the prepotence of one over the other was a central assumption. Although other approaches (for example, tabula rasa, predeterminism) may be conceptually simpler, the interaction position seems more reasonably representative of reality.

THE DEVELOPMENTAL PROCESS

Growing support for the interaction approach to human development generated a more intense focus on the developmental process than was previously the case. Researchers and theoreticians alike began to ask questions that were more conducive to testing than were the philosophical positions exemplified by former views. In this section, an examination of various dimensions of the developmental process is presented.

Continuity versus discontinuity of growth

The nature of the developmental process itself has raised a series of interesting questions. At times these questions have become somewhat controversial and have been the subject of considerable debate. One area that has generated considerable discussion involves the continuity or discontinuity of human growth. Essentially the question is whether or not development proceeds in terms of gradual continuous quantitative change or in stages typified by abrupt discontinuous changes in quality.

The discontinuity view of human development was encouraged through theories emphasizing stages. Early developmental stage theories implied that there was little or no overlap of process occurring from one stage to the other, in that each developmental stage is specifically and qualitatively different from the others. The first developmental theorist to dismiss this discontinuity notion was Piaget (1926). Having a background in biology and zoology, Piaget formulated a theory of stages of cognitive development that incorporated the occurrence of immature and mature responses at all developmental levels. Piaget conceived of intelligence as being globally categorized into three developmental periods: (1) the period of sensorimotor intelligence, (2) the period of preparation for and organization of concrete operations, and (3) the period of formal operations (see Chapter 7). Sensorimotor intelligence development is thought to begin at birth and continue for about the first 2 years of life. In the second period, from about 2 to 11 years of age, Piaget views the development of intelligence as involving the essential formation of a conceptual framework that the child uses in interaction with the environment. The third period, from 11 years of age on, is the time when Piaget contends that an individual becomes involved with abstract thought. During this period (formal operations) the person begins to be able to think in terms of hypothetical possibilities as distinguished from the exclusive use of concrete operations, in which cognition depends on a concrete or real object basis. Piaget conceived the total development picture as one of a dynamic interaction, with the organism operating on the environment as well as being molded by it. Piaget's stage theory has come under heavy fire and current thinking places these concepts very much in doubt. Flavell, for example, has stated that he does not believe the stage concept will ". . . figure importantly in future scientific work on cognitive growth" (1977, p. 249).

The continuity position contends that growth is a gradual process rather than a series of abrupt changes followed by periods of less rapid change, or plateaus. A variety of factors can be mentioned as presumably supporting the theory of growth continuity. First, it is well known that both mature and immature responses are made by children at all levels of development. Second, theories embodying the concept of continuity emphasize the testing of hypotheses that are generated from general behavior theories more effectively than do discontinuous stage theories.

Although there have been strong proponents for both the continuity and discontinuity positions, the dispute has somewhat diminished as an issue. Growth and development specialists have progressed beyond the point where polarized thinking prevails. Most theoretically formulated stages are no longer viewed as being precise definitions involving exact ages, behaviors, and response levels. They are more often viewed as convenient approximations, based on averages, which are useful in conceptualizing developmental processes.

Critical periods and developmental vulnerability

Developmental deviancy is a central concern in the field of mental retardation. In view of this, an area of vital importance to those studying mental retardation is the concept of developmental vulnerability. In this context the notion of vulnerability refers to how susceptible the organism is to being injured or altered by a traumatic incident. Traumatic incident is defined broadly to include such occurrences as toxic agents (poisons) and cell division mutations, as well as other deviations from the usual sequence of developmental events.

Research in biology and embryology has provided a great deal of information concerning the manner in which human growth occurs (Timiras, 1972). From the time of conception, a series of complex cell divisions occurs that ultimately results in the highly complicated entity that we call a human. During the early part of this developmental process, the two original cells divide repeatedly from a mass no larger than the end of a sharp pencil lead (at about 14 days) to the ultimate size of a newborn child. Obviously this implies a very dramatic growth process. Cell division occurs extremely rapidly in the first few days after the ovum is fertilized by a sperm. The mass that is to become the fetus does not actually become implanted or attached to the mother's uterus until about 2 weeks after fertilization. In this short period cell division has progressed with considerable speed and has begun a process known as tissue differentiation. Both the speed of cell division and the process of tissue differentiation are important with regard to the vulnerability to trauma.

Tissue differentiation, as noted before, is a process that begins very soon after fertilization. As cell division commences, certain chemical reactions

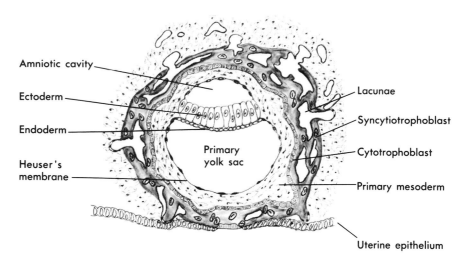

Fig. 5-1. Conceptus at about 12 days, showing cell tissue layers. (From Didio, L. J. A. *Synopsis of anatomy.* St. Louis: The C. V. Mosby Co., 1970.)

occur that generate new cells of different types. These cells in turn multiply, reproducing like cells that distribute themselves to form three different layers of tissue: the ectoderm, the mesoderm, and the endoderm. Fig. 5-1 pictorially represents two of the cell tissue layers—the ectoderm and the endoderm. Although the tissue layers are actually named by virtue of their early developmental position (ectoderm, outer layer; mesoderm, middle layer; endoderm, inner layer), they eventually form distinctly different parts of the organism. For example, parts of the ectoderm become nervous tissue; various types of muscle come from the mesoderm; and so on. During the time that a particular organ or system is being formed, those cells that are generating that system divide very rapidly. There are specific periods when, for instance, the central nervous system is the primary part of the organism that is being developed. During that time, those cells that constitute the central nervous system are dividing more rapidly than other types of cells. It is at this time that the central nervous system is most vulnerable to trauma. If a toxic agent or infection occurs in the mother at this time, there is a high probability that the developing central nervous system (or some particular part of it) will be the most affected.

As suggested by the periods of high vulnerability of tissue development, there are various other critical periods during the prenatal development of a child. These periods are biologically critical for the healthy growth of the fetus. It has long been suspected by some professionals that critical periods also exist after birth. The nature of specific hypotheses has varied considerably in terms of postnatal critical periods. In some cases the "critical periods" of early childhood have been viewed as those times that are *optimal* for the child to learn or experience certain things. Others have conceived the critical period idea in terms of irreversibility. This latter concept holds that, if a child does not acquire certain skills or does not experience certain stimuli at the appropriate time, the development will be altered in some fashion that is not reversible. Under some circumstances the theoretical outcome of either viewpoint is essentially the same. The child, if not taught at the critical time, may not learn given material as well as might be possible.

The critical period concept with respect to very young children has had considerable effect in both research and education. Educational programs, such as that developed by Montessori, have flourished based on an intuitive appeal of the critical period concept. It should be noted, however, that firm research evidence for the concept has been somewhat fragmentary (Ausubel and Sullivan, 1970) and has been vigorously challenged by some researchers (Flavell, 1971, 1977).

PRENATAL DEVELOPMENT

The prenatal period of human development has long been recognized in terms of its importance. As with any unknown or unexplored phenomenon, very early explanations of prenatal development tended to be more philosophical and metaphysical than scientific in orientation. This is certainly evidenced by the prescientific notion of the homunculus described earlier. Contemporary advances in research methods have permitted at least limited glimpses of much of this previously unexplored region. Although much of our current information concerning prenatal development has come from studies with animals, a continually expanding knowledge base is being generated about the human organism. This section presents an overview of the sequence of prenatal development. Such information substantially facilitates a broader understanding of developmental deviations as they relate to mental retardation.

It was noted earlier that early cell division occurs at different rates depending on which portion of the organism is being formed primarily at that time. Beyond these variations in developmental rates there are two important general growth trends that warrant mention. The first is known as the *cephalocaudal* developmental trend, or growth gradient. As the term suggests, the fetus develops more rapidly in the head area (cephalo) first, with maturation in the lower extremities (caudal) or "foot" following. Thus, at nearly all stages of a young child's development the upper regions (and behaviors associated with these regions) are more nearly complete than the lower regions. Dramatically evident prenatally, the cephalocaudal trend also is present after birth. The young child is skilled in a behavior involving the arms prior to a time that a similar skill is developed in the lower extremities. The second general developmental trend is termed the *proximodistal* gradient. This term refers to the fact that the more rapid growth and development occur near the center of the organism (proximo), with extremities (distal) maturing later. This trend is also present both prenatally and during the first few years of infant life.

Very quickly after fertilization occurs, the cell division process commences that ultimately will result in a fully formed human. As noted earlier, it takes about 2 weeks for the dividing cell mass to become attached to the uterus of the mother. Even before this implantation occurs, the cells begin to differentiate. As the ectoderm, mesoderm, and endoderm are initially formed, there remains considerable flexibility in terms of what individual cells within those layers can become. Thus at the 14-day stage a given cell within the mesoderm could still grow into something besides that which is usually formed from the mesoderm. Determination of resulting organs at this point is more a function of layer position than the actual composition of the cell itself. Cell flexibility is lost, however, as growth proceeds. The layers themselves become increasingly differentiated, and as this occurs the individual cells also become more specialized (Arey, 1965). The boxed material summarizes some of the types of structures resulting from growth in the tissue layers.

At the time of implantation the embryo is still very small. Despite all that has gone on, the mass is little more than the mark made by a sharp pencil. The actual estimated size is about that of a ball 2 mm in diameter, and the weight cannot even be estimated (Timiras, 1972). It is difficult for us even to conceive that such a tiny piece of matter is not only living but has already begun to differentiate in anticipation of forming such structures as eyes, brain, and muscles.

After implantation (14 days) activity continues at a very rapid pace. By

Endoderm	Mesoderm	Ectoderm
Epithelium of pharynx, tongue root, auditory tube, tonsils, thyroid	Muscles (all types)	Epidermis, including cutaneous glands, hair, nails, lens
	Cartilage, bone	
	Blood, bone marrow	
Larynx, trachea, lungs	Lymphoid tissue	Epithelium of sense organs, nasal cavity, sinuses
	Epithelium of blood vessels, body cavities	
Digestive tube	Kidney, ureter, gonads, genital ducts	Mouth, including oral glands, enamel
Bladder		
Vagina	Suprarenal cortex	Anal canal
Urethra	Joint cavities	Nervous tissue

*Adapted from Arey (1965).

about the 18- to 24-day point (from the time of fertilization—termed fertilization age) weight is still undeterminable; size, however, has reached the approximate proportions portrayed in Fig. 5-2. Also, at this point blood cells have begun to form, which are much like those that will serve in later life (Chinn, 1979; Arey, 1965).

By the time the embryo has reached the 4-week point (fertilization age) several developments have occurred. Weight is detectable at about .4 g. Fig. 5-2 portrays the approximate size and shape at this point. The circulatory system, in a primitive form, has developed, and the heart structure has begun pulsation (Arey, 1965). The fourth week also sees initial formative stages of other systems, such as trunk muscles and those muscles necessary for respiratory and intestinal functions. Limb buds appear at this time, and the nervous system reaches a point that is crucial with respect to the development of both the sense organs and the area that will later become the spinal cord. Fig. 5-2 illustrates that the tiny embryo has already assumed the curved shape that is usually portrayed in unborn humans. This C shape is primarily generated at the 4-week period by a very rapid lengthening of the neural tube (spinal area), which is not matched by growth on the front or ventral side (Timiras, 1972).

At 6½ weeks fertilization age the embryo has grown and developed to a considerable extent. Fig. 5-2 illustrates the approximate embryonic size and shape at this time. The circulatory system and heart are now more nearly complete. Fig. 5-2 also shows the positioning of the eyes on either side of the

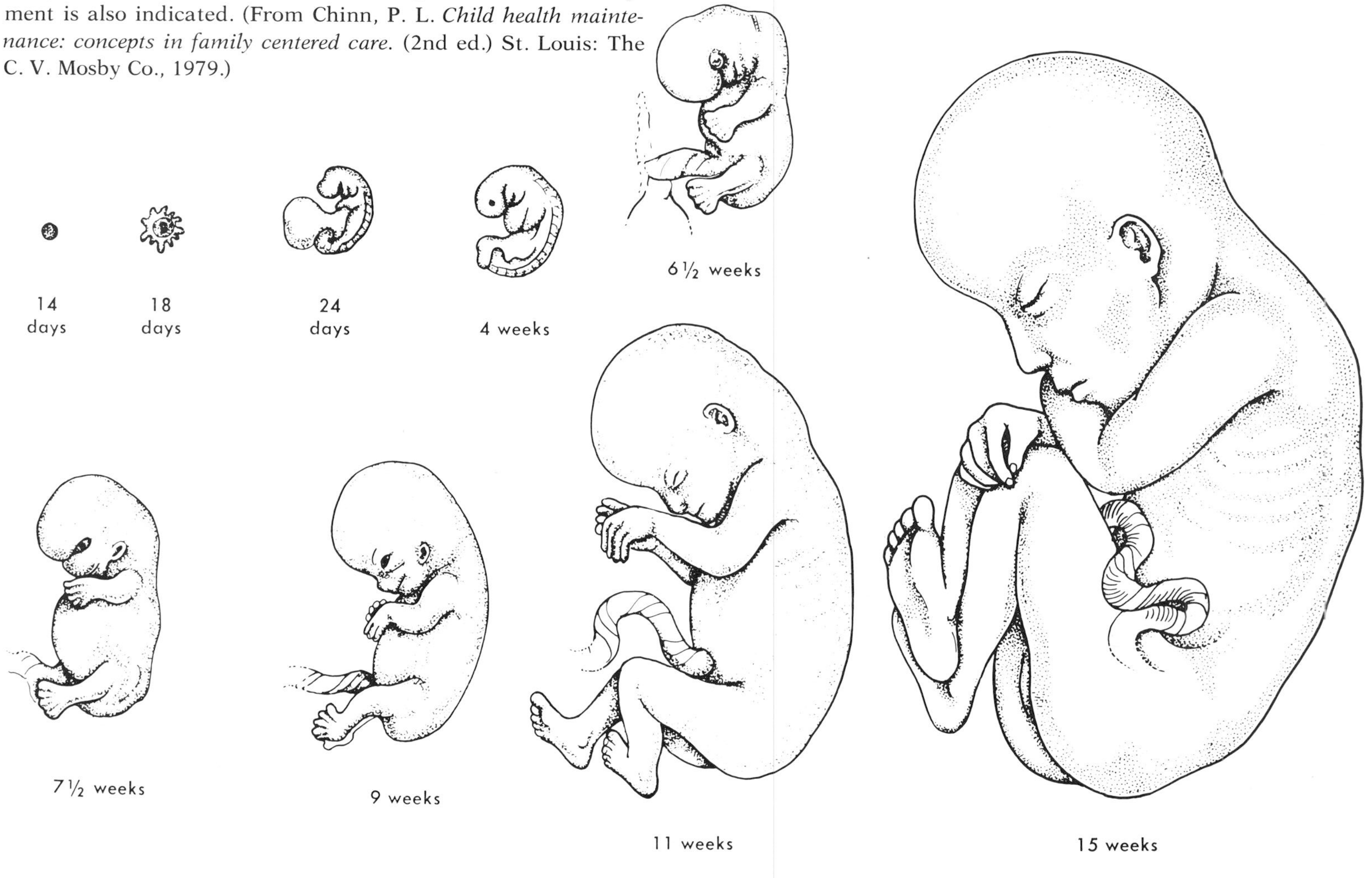

Fig. 5-2. The actual size of human embryos at early stages of development. Comparison of the relative stages of external development is also indicated. (From Chinn, P. L. *Child health maintenance: concepts in family centered care.* (2nd ed.) St. Louis: The C. V. Mosby Co., 1979.)

14 days

18 days

24 days

4 weeks

6½ weeks

7½ weeks

9 weeks

11 weeks

15 weeks

head area. Later these will assume a more frontal position characteristic of the human infant. Lungs and intestinal systems become more developmentally complete, and for the first time a primitive form of the gonad is observable. Differentiation of this tissue has not occurred yet with respect to sex (Arey, 1965).

Fig. 5-2 portrays the embryonic growth at about 7½ weeks fertilization age. At this point the embryo begins to develop openings for waste systems (both urethral and anal). The circulatory system reaches a stage at which heart valves are developed and sensory nerve tissue in the upper region progresses.

As the fertilization age reaches the eighth week, development has reached a stage where the embryo is essentially complete. Beyond this point it is commonly referred to as a *fetus*. There is some difference with regard to when this term is applied. Although most authorities use the eighth week (Arey, 1965; Chinn, 1979), others do not consider the fetal period to begin until the twelfth week (Timiras, 1972). Fig. 5-2 illustrates the size and shape of a fetus at about the ninth week. It is evident that the eyes have begun to assume the frontal position more characteristic of humans. The fetus has noticeably changed its posture. The head region at this point constitutes nearly half of the total mass, and the cerebral cortex has formed.

Particularly crucial growth occurs in the head region during weeks 10 through 12. From about this time through the thirteenth week the palate completes fusion. The forehead is somewhat outsized in comparison to the rest of the head (Fig. 5-2) and at this point contains a brain that is essentially complete from a configuration standpoint. Sex of the fetus may now be determined from inspection of the external organs. The skeleton begins the process of actually becoming bone matter (ossification). Also the vital structures of the eyes are nearly formed (Arey, 1965).

The fetus at this point (12 weeks) has completed one of the most crucial periods in its developmental life span. By no means is the tiny fetus ready to take on the ravages of the outside world, but the primary body structures are formed at this point. In Chapter 6 reference will be made repeatedly to the first trimester of prenatal life. From our discussion of vulnerability and its relationship to tissue growth, it is very easy to see why this period is so vital. Trauma occurring during these first weeks is most likely to injure the essential body structures being formed at this time. The fetus at 12 weeks weighs about 19 g (Timiras, 1972), certainly a long way to go but also considerable

growth since the initiation of growth when the mass was so tiny that assessment of weight was not possible.

During the second trimester of prenatal life (weeks 12 through 24), the
fetus reaches a weight of approximately 600 g. From an appearance standpoint there is no doubt at this point that the fetus is a tiny human. The second
trimester is also the time when the mother first experiences fetal movement.
Bodily proportions have changed somewhat, as illustrated in Fig. 5-2. Internally, several important developments occur during the second trimester.
Various glands mature to the point that metabolic functions are begun. The
lung structures become essentially complete, although not until the third
trimester are they adequate to sustain life. An extremely important function,
called myelinization, begins during the second trimester. Myelinization
refers to the development of a sheath-like material that covers and protects
the nervous system. During the second trimester, development of the myelin
covering begins in the spinal cord area. This process continues during the
third trimester, when the myelinization of higher cortical matter begins.
Completion of the myelin covering of the cerebral cortex is primarily accomplished after birth (Timiras, 1972). The progression of the myelin covering
also relates to the child's vulnerability to trauma, as will be discussed in
Chapter 6.

Development that occurs during the final trimester of prenatal life is
essential for sustaining life outside the sheltered environment of the mother's
body. One of the vital changes involves the final development of the lung
structures. These changes continue right up to the last month of gestation.
The fetus is also growing larger and stronger at a rapid rate. By the time term
is reached at about 40 weeks, the fetus will weigh somewhere around 3,200 g.
Sensory organs continue development, reaching a functional stage at birth.
Thus although the basic structural components have long since been formed,
the third trimester of gestation involves developments that are crucial for
survival.

BIRTH

At the end of the pregnancy, or about 280 days after fertilization, the fetus
leaves the intrauterine environment of the mother's body and begins its life
in the outside world. Despite the vast improvements in delivery techniques
that have occurred over the years, many facets of childbirth are still not well
understood. This section presents a brief overview of the more salient aspects
of this dramatic event.

Preparation for childbirth is not something that can occur at the last moment. Certain changes in the mother's anatomy have been underway since about midpregnancy; these are necessary for the birth to proceed smoothly. The muscle structure of the uterus has been rearranged substantially in order to facilitate fetal expulsion. Another vital change has occurred in the cervix area that is essential to permit passage of the fetus through the birth canal. Fig. 5-3 illustrates an advanced fetus in the uterine environment. In the latter days of pregnancy and during the onset of labor, an expansion occurs in the upper part of the cervical area. By the time the fetus is moving down the birth canal, the cervical muscle structure has expanded to the point where the tiny tubelike structure shown at the bottom of Fig. 5-3 no longer exists. The loosening of the cervix, called effacement, is an important change in the muscle structure that must occur for the fetus to be expelled.

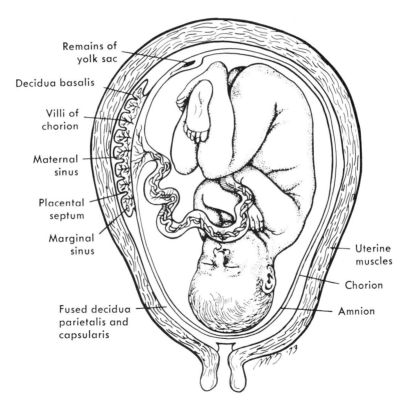

Fig. 5-3. Advanced fetus in uterine environment. (From Chinn, P. L. *Child health maintenance: concepts in family centered care.* (2nd ed.) St. Louis: The C. V. Mosby Co., 1979.)

The exact mechanism that triggers labor remains somewhat speculative. A variety of possibilities have been investigated, including both chemical (hormones) and mechanical (degree of uterine expansion) agents. The usual and desirable fetal position at the onset of labor is that of the head toward the cervix, as illustrated in Fig. 5-3. This is the positioning that occurs in over 80 percent of all childbirth. As the fetus begins to move downward into the birth canal, additional stretching occurs in the pelvic girdle area. Simultaneously, the head of the fetus is molded somewhat by the pressure to facilitate passage through the bony structure of the pelvic girdle. This is why many newborns appear to have strangely shaped heads. Later this misshapen appearance disappears as the head returns to its natural form.

All of this movement is generated by the labor, or muscle contractions of the uterus. At the same time that the fetus is moving downward, there is a counterclockwise rotation occurring. Actually the tiny body is turning to the left (this movement is generated by the uterine muscle action), much as one would unscrew a bolt. Fig. 5-4 presents a series of positions that illustrate this birth process.

Once expelled, the infant is usually followed a few minutes later by the placenta, which has served well in providing oxygen and nourishment and in disposing of waste. Now these functions must be accomplished by the infant. The respiratory tract is immediately cleared of remaining amnionic fluid and mucus, at which point the infant takes over the breathing function. This is the time that most new mothers and fathers remember as the first cry of their newborn. In reality, this crying serves an important function, and if not initiated spontaneously, the physician must provide stimulation. Through crying, the infant's lungs are expanded with air for the first time, providing the circulatory changes that accompany the use of the lungs and loss of the placenta.

The birth process is very complex and involves many different facets that are beyond the scope of this text. Unfortunately, the events of birth do not always proceed smoothly, and difficulties arise that ultimately may result in mental retardation. Some of the problems that can arise are discussed in Chapter 6. The present overview provides a general reference with respect to most normal childbirths.

NEONATAL DEVELOPMENT

The term neonate is often applied to the baby during the first 2 months of life after birth. Beyond that period the terminology is varied and somewhat

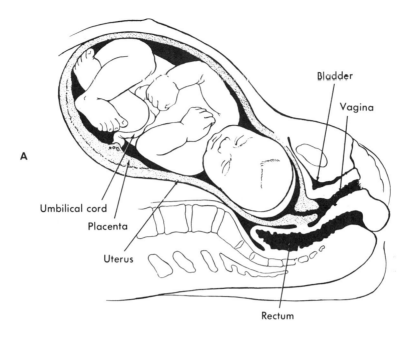

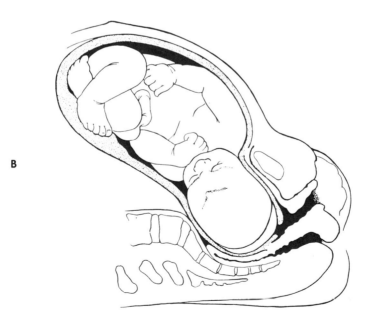

Fig. 5-4. A, Engagement. **B,** Descent with flexion. **C,** Internal rotation. **D,** Extension. **E,** External rotation. **F,** Delivery. **G,** Lateral flexion. (From Iorio, J. *Childbirth: family centered nursing.* (3rd ed.) St. Louis: The C. V. Mosby Co., 1975.)

Continued.

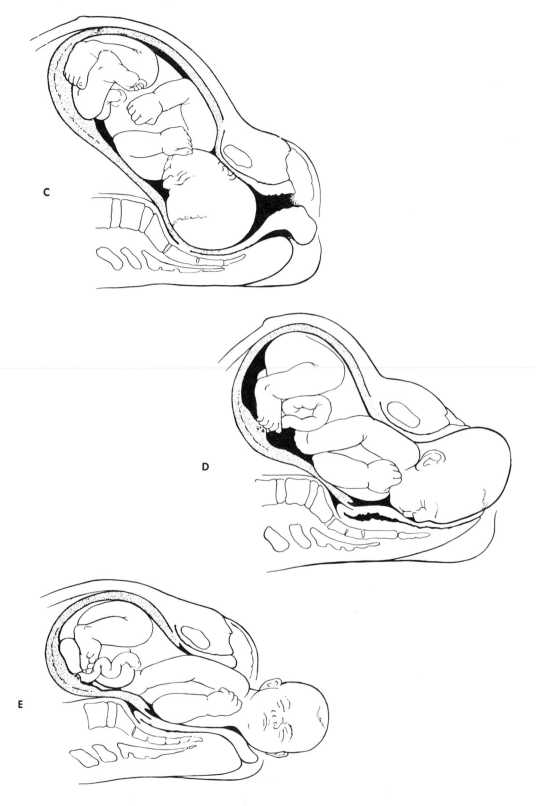

Fig. 5-4, cont'd. For legend see p. 141.

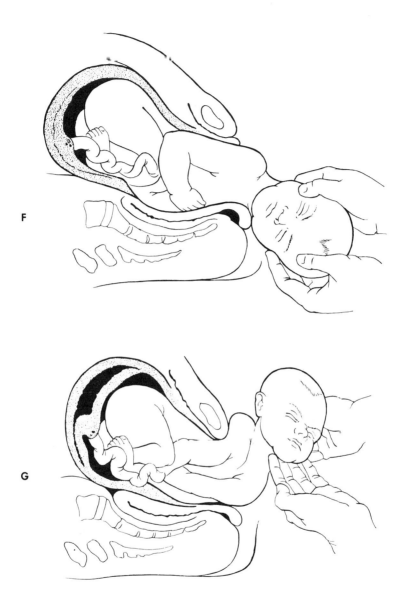

Fig. 5-4, cont'd. For legend see p. 141.

nonspecific. The present section examines early life, with some of the principles applying beyond the neonatal period. Development of the infant and older child is discussed in more detail in subsequent chapters.

The first few weeks of extrauterine life are crucial. Most authorities have viewed the first month as being the most dangerous in the total life span (Timiras, 1972; Chinn, 1979). Many of the developmental functions begun in utero are continuing but without the same protective agents previously available. In addition to physiological changes, the neonate has suddenly become subject to a variety of forces that initiate a more rapid development in psychological and behavioral arenas. As development proceeds, the previous and ongoing physiological changes fuse with changes generated by environmental stimuli (such as learning) to form that integrated complex of responsiveness known as a human being.

From a behavioral standpoint the neonate seems to be little more than a mass of reflex actions. In fact, at this age assessment of reflexes is the primary method of evaluation by health care professionals. The movements seem primarily nonpurposeful and nonspecific and more often than not involve nearly the entire body simultaneously. This movement pattern usually involves gross motor movements often accompanied by verbal output (crying). The frequency and intensity rises between feeding periods and tends to diminish as the hungry neonate becomes satisfied. As noted previously, the cephalocaudal and proximodistal developmental trends remain operative after birth. These are perhaps most dramatically observable in the behavior patterns during the first 2 years of life. More mature responses tend to appear earlier in the areas closest to the brain (for example, eye movement) and progress downward and outward. Thus gross motor movements of the neonate precede control of more distally located movements such as of the fingers. Likewise, infants usually can reach for and grasp objects with considerable precision long before they are able to walk.

Certain physiological changes occur very rapidly during the first period of postnatal life. The central nervous system exhibits a dramatic growth during the first 4 years. This acceleration levels off in later childhood. For example, during this growth period the brain weight increases nearly 400 percent over that at birth. In addition to quantitative changes, the brain matter is rapidly developing convolutions or folds that are vital to later cognitive function (Timiras, 1972).

It was previously noted that a process called myelinization begins prenatally and continues after birth. The progression of this protective sheathing of nerve cells is very rapid during the first 12 months of postnatal life and declines progressively thereafter. The progression of the myelin sheath to some degree follows the course of the primary direction of central nervous system development. At birth the neonate is essentially governed by the lower or subcortical portion of the central nervous system (spinal cord, brainstem). This also represents the first part of the central nervous system to receive the myelin covering. Later, the higher cerebral matter is involved in myelinization and likewise begins to take charge of the child's behavior. The myelin sheath is essentially complete at age 2, although fragmentary myelinization apparently continues through adolescence and perhaps even middle adult life (Timiras, 1972). In our consideration of mental retardation this myelinization process becomes important with regard to possible injury to the central nervous system, as we will see in Chapter 6.

At birth the sensory organs, particularly the eyes and ears, are nearly complete from a structural standpoint. Certain parts of the retina are yet to be completed, but otherwise the basic visual mechanism exists at birth. For the first few weeks the eyes tend to operate somewhat independently rather than as a coordinated pair of organs. By about 6 weeks, however, eye fixation is pretty well coordinated in terms of both eyes functioning together. Visual acuity appears to be imperfect during the neonatal and infant periods. Most probably, the image is primarily one involving somewhat blurred forms, patterns, and shapes.

Auditory perception is apparently intact at birth. The neonate is responsive to a wide variety of auditory stimuli, suggesting that probably the full range of humanly detectable sound is available quite early. Additionally, the neonate seems capable of identifying location of sounds. The development of auditory discrimination abilities has yet to be investigated in any complete sense. It is possible that a portion of the ability to discriminate various sound differences is a learned or acquired skill. Certainly if this is the case, the neonate must grow older in order to have the opportunity to accumulate a background of experience that will permit such learning.

The sense of taste is somewhat more difficult to study in a very young child than some other sensory avenues. There is evidence to indicate that even at the neonatal stage gross taste discriminations are made. Such discrimination, however, is primarily observable in different behavioral reactions to sweetness versus other tastes, such as sourness and bitterness. This sense also appears to improve with experience. The sense of smell is even more difficult to study than that of taste. Consequently very little evidence is available with regard to it in the neonatal period. It does, however, seem that the neonate is responsive to very dramatic or intense odors and that smell sensitivity increases during the infant stage (Chinn, 1979).

It has already been noted that the behavioral repertoire of the newborn is limited. During the first few weeks of postnatal life, verbal output is primarily limited to crying. Crying seems to be mostly associated with discomfort of some sort, although at times the source of discomfort is not evident, as many parents well know. Hunger seems to be a standard stimulus from birth that generates the crying response. Later the young child learns to use crying as a means of communicating in a wide variety of situations that are unpleasurable. Other verbal output (for example, gurgling, cooing, and generating general noise) seems to develop considerably later, often not becoming a significant part of the behavioral repertoire until the infant is several months old.

The sucking response is an important component of neonatal behavior. In addition to its obvious value to the child in terms of feeding, it remains an important early checkpoint of well-being. A weak sucking response serves as a signal of concern. The neonate tends to exhibit the sucking response to a variety of stimuli both in terms of type of stimulus and body part that receives the stimulation. Later the responsivity is reduced on both counts and tends to be elicited primarily in relation to the area around the mouth.

SUMMARY

In a majority of cases, prenatal development, birth, and postnatal development in the first 2 years of life proceed without traumatic incident. Certainly every child is subjected to minor accidents of either a developmental or inflicted nature. Most occurrences, however, are not so serious that they result in a major alteration in the course of developmental progress. In fact, the minor influences that are within the general threshholds of organism tolerance are in part responsible for the individual differences evident in the broad spectrum of normal human behavior. It is important to keep this in mind, particularly as we proceed to Chapter 6 and beyond in the study of mental retardation. To lose this perspective is often detrimental to effective work in the variety of services that must be conceived, developed, and delivered to the mentally retarded.

STUDY QUESTIONS

1. The tabula rasa approach to explain human growth and development differed significantly from both the preformationist and predeterministic positions. Compare

and contrast these three approaches. How do you think their proponents would differ in their explanations of mental retardation?

2. In what manner does the speed of cell reproduction influence vulnerability to trauma that might cause mental retardation? How does this relate to the often noted "first trimester" of pregnancy?

3. Why would you expect a new baby's head and arm movements to be more mature than those of the legs? What other growth gradient is also typical of early development?

REFERENCES

Arey, L. B. *Developmental anatomy: a textbook and laboratory manual of embryology.* Philadelphia: W. B. Saunders Co., 1965.

Ausubel, D. P., and Sullivan, E. V. *Theory and problems of child development.* (2nd ed.) New York: Grune & Stratton, Inc., 1970.

Chinn, P. L. *Child health maintenance: concepts for family centered care.* (2nd ed.) St. Louis: The C. V. Mosby Co., 1979.

Flavell, J. H. Stage-related properties of cognitive development. *Cognitive Psychology,* 1971, **2,** 421-453.

Flavell, J. H. *Cognitive Development.* Englewood Cliffs, N.J.: Prentice-Hall, Inc., 1977.

Hall, G. S. *Adolescence: its psychology and its relation to physiology, anthropology, sociology, sex,* *crime, religion and education.* New York: Appleton-Century-Crofts, 1904.

Piaget, J. *The language and thought of the child.* New York: Harcourt Brace Jovanovich, Inc., 1926.

Timiras, P. S. *Developmental physiology and aging.* New York: The Macmillan Co., 1972.

ANNOTATED BIBLIOGRAPHY

Flavell, J. H. *The developmental psychology of Jean Piaget.* New York: Van Nostrand Reinhold Co., 1963.

This volume represents one of the most complete discussions of Piaget's work available in translated form. An excellent reference for the reader who wishes to explore Piaget's work in depth.

Mental retardation
influences and causation during the prenatal and neonatal periods

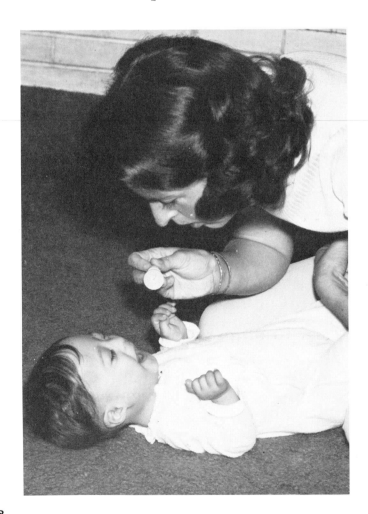

INTRODUCTION

Early life represents a period of human growth and development that warrants considerable attention since it represents such a crucial part of the life cycle of an individual. The organism, prenatally as well as after birth, is essentially at the mercy of the environment and is vulnerable to its impact. Chapter 5 focused on the normal developmental process during early life. This chapter examines the early life period (conception through early infancy) in terms of influences and causes of mental retardation.

Discussion of influences and causation of mental retardation during the prenatal and neonatal periods requires attention to certain physiological conditions and, when possible, treatment of these conditions. Very frequently it is the medical profession that is primarily interacting with the child at risk for mental retardation during this early period. No attempt will be made to present an in-depth examination of the medical aspects of mental retardation. It is our intent to provide readers with an awareness of influences on mental development during this period. Attention will focus on more common conditions of retardation beginning during this period as well as those for which intervention can either prevent retardation or substantially reduce the impact. A variety of developmental and on-going life processes can go awry during this time that may result in reduced intellectual functioning. In fact, the beginning professional occasionally wonders how children can progress through this period at all without involving deviation or abnormality. The vast majority of individuals, however, do develop to a level of functioning that is within the tolerance of society and is considered normal or average.

Maternal and fetal conditions play a central role in the development of the fetus. As expected, a variety of maternal and fetal conditions may also be involved in causing mental retardation during the early life period. The outcomes of these influences may appear as mental retardation that ranges from the profound or severe levels to only mild deviations from the normal. A group of researchers, working primarily at The Johns Hopkins University, have suggested an interesting conceptual framework for viewing the range of disability severity during early life in relation to one another, (Lilienfeld and Pasamanick, 1956). Known as the *continuum of reproductive casualty*, this notion views the mildly handicapped child as being toward the less harsh end of the casualty continuum, whereas the more severely retarded and the stillborn are toward the other end of the continuum. Spontaneous abortion that occurs early in pregnancy may represent the extremely severe end of the continuum, whereas very mild retardation or slight disabilities in basically normal children represent the other extreme. Lilienfeld and his associates contend that this concept is most useful in identifying areas in need of investigation with regard to causation of handicapping conditions during early life. Hopefully such research will continue to identify preventive measures that may be implemented.

EARLY CAUSATION

The first portion of the life cycle is extremely important. Development during the prenatal period and immediately after birth is viewed by many as the most critical in the entire life span. Fortunately most infants enter extrauterine life after a full, successful gestational period, with no complications of labor and delivery and no factors during the first month of life to lead to serious illness or disability. However, when some type of problem does occur in these early months, the family must often adjust to the fact of permanent mental or physical disability. Several conditions are known to place the fetus or infant in a position of high risk for development of serious illness or permanent disability.

The fetus and infant at risk: birth weight and gestational age problems

A variety of problems may occur during the prenatal and neonatal periods. Each of the problems discussed in this section is a condition that places the infant in some sort of risk category. The most prevalent of these disorders are inadequate birth weight and gestational age inadequacy. While these problems do occasionally exist alone, there is more often an accompanying problem of some maternal, genetic, or traumatic condition. The relationship between this and other conditions is mentioned in the following sections.

Infants with problems related to gestational age and birth weight were in the past classified by a simple designation of prematurity based on either birth weight or an estimated gestational age alone. Because of inadequacies encountered with the use of this designation, a classification based on both weight and age has been adopted by many. The graph in Fig. 6-1 indicates both the system of classification and the mortality risk associated with infants in the various classification sectors. The range of birth weight occuring between the tenth and ninetieth percentiles during the twenty-fourth through the forty-sixth weeks of gestation has been plotted. Infants who are

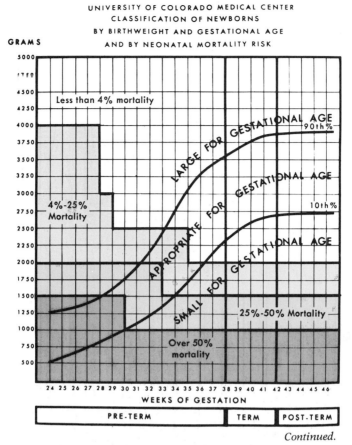

Fig. 6-1. Classification of newborns by birth weight and gestational age and by neonatal mortality risk. (From Battaglia, F. C., and Lubchence, L. O. A practical classification of newborn infants by weight and gestational age. *Journal of Pediatrics,* 1967, **71,** 161.)

born before the thirty-eighth week of gestation are referred to as preterm, those within the thirty-eighth to the forty-second weeks are referred to as term, and those born beyond the forty-second week are referred to as postterm infants. In addition, weight is indicated as "small for gestational age," "appropriate for gestational age," or "large for gestational age." These classifications indicate that both age and weight have been taken into account. In the past, an infant who was about the size of a normal term infant might be mistaken for a term infant while in reality be suffering the disadvantages of the immature, preterm infant. Since it is possible to estimate the maturity of the infant by physical signs of maturation, care for the infant can be more

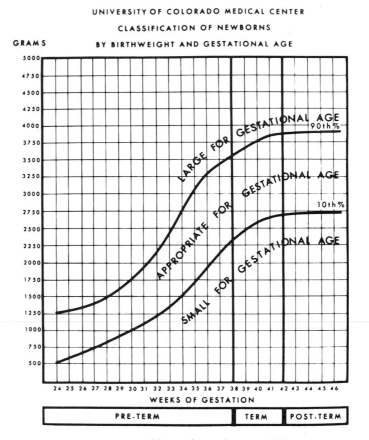

Fig. 6-1, cont'd. For legend see p. 151.

adequately geared to the particular needs that occur according to gestational age. Such improved care has led to a decrease in total neonatal mortality in the United States in recent years, even though the incidence of infants with low birth weight has not changed (Babson, Benson, Pernoll, and Benda, 1978).

Predisposing factors. Several factors have been identified as being related to low birth weight and inappropriate gestational age relationships. Each of the problems discussed in later sections, such as chromosomal aberrations in the infant, maternal-infant interaction problems, and trauma during early pregnancy, can be associated with early termination of pregnancy. However, there are several conditions that appear to lead to early termination of pregnancy and inadequate birth weight.

Table 5. Premature birth rate according to father's occupation*

Occupation	Incidence per 1,000 live births
Farmer	33.8
Professional	49.1
Laborer	71.8
Service worker	78.3
Farm laborer	88.1

*From Kernek, C., Osterud, H., and Anderson, B. Patterns of prematurity in Oregon. *Northwest Medicine,* 1966, **65,** 639.

The age of the mother and the number of previous pregnancies are significant. Very young mothers or mothers over 40, especially those who have had a number of previous pregnancies, tend to have infants who suffer early termination of pregnancy. Socioeconomic factors are known to be intimately related to the incidence of preterm and low gestational weight infants. The father's occupation has been related to profound differences in the incidence of "prematurity" and infant mortality, as indicated in Table 5.

Rates of premature births have also been associated with ethnic group differences, but this factor is probably more related to socioeconomic status than with ethnic differences per se. The percentage of infants born prematurely among white Americans is consistently about half of the percentage born prematurely among nonwhite Americans.

Multiple pregnancies account for a great percentage of infants born with problems associated with gestational age and birth weight. The reasons for this are complex and numerous, including primarily the problems of placental insufficiency leading to fetal malnutrition; this results from ineffective transfer of nutrients across the placenta late in pregnancy. Labor and delivery often commence prior to term, and the infant is usually small for gestational age.

Placental problems are not clearly understood and are often identified as cause of inadequate intrauterine growth when no other cause can be identified. Placental insufficiency implies an impaired exchange between the mother and fetus through the placenta. Several well-defined lesions of the placenta can be definitively associated with fetal and infant disorders, such as occulusion of fetal vessels in the placenta, early separation of the placenta, or a single umbilical artery.

Maternal smoking is another factor that has been associated with inadequate growth during fetal life. Mothers who smoke more than twenty cigarettes a day give birth to growth-retarded (but not necessarily preterm) infants two or three times as often as nonsmoking mothers (Korones, 1976). The reason for this difference has not yet been delineated, and other related factors may be as important as the actual problem of maternal smoking.

Maternal nutrition is another poorly understood factor, but evidence thus far has indicated that this may be a very important factor in relation to fetal outcome. A major portion of families who eat poorly also suffer from socioeconomic limitations and are often influenced by the dietary practices of a subculture. Thus it seems impossible to delineate which of the factors in this complex set of interacting variables have contributed primarily to the occurrence of increased rates of low birth weight and gestational age problems. It is generally known that the pregnant woman has greater nutritional requirements than the woman who is not pregnant. However, the extent to which these increased requirements are a function of the nutritional needs of the fetus are unclear. Maternal malnutrition, which is usually a life-long state of inadequacy, has been implicated as exerting possible damaging influence on the fetus, particularly to the central nervous system. However, such findings are difficult to evaluate and to substantiate because of the inability to examine the direct transfer of nutrients to the fetus and the difficulties in studying the exact nutritional requirements of the fetus itself (Gluck, 1971).

Finally, unwed mothers tend to have greater numbers of preterm infants than do married mothers. A rate of premature births of 93.6 percent was reported for one group of unwed mothers in Oregon in 1966 (Kernek, Osterud, and Anderson, 1966). The reason for this startling increase in prematurity of infants born to unwed mothers is not known, but again several socioeconomic factors may be involved.

Associated problems. Infants at risk, especially those who suffer birth weight and gestational age inadequacies, tend to be susceptible to serious stress after birth. These problems are primarily respiratory and cardiac failure or complications, infection, and nutritional disorders; they may account for many of the sequelae associated with birth weight and gestational age inadequacies rather than the problem of birth weight or gestational age alone.

Respiratory and cardiac failure or complications lead to serious interference with the delivery of oxygen to the tissues. The tissues of the central nervous system are particularly vulnerable, for even though it is known that a newborn can tolerate longer periods of anoxia than can an adult, the continuing lowered level of delivery of oxygen to the tissues interferes with critical tissue development that is occurring during the preterm period. Central nervous tissue cells are still developing until about the forty-second to forty-sixth weeks of gestation, and the tissue depends on an adequate supply of oxygen in order for adequate development to occur. An infant who is born at risk prior to term and who develops such oxygen delivery interference is particularly jeopardized in developing adequate neural tissue. The relationship between such interference and future development has yet to be fully explored, but recent improvements in neonatal care, including prevention of respiratory and cardiac complications and improved care for the infant with these complications, have been made with the anticipation of reducing the serious neurological sequelae of prematurity.

Infection is another serious complication of infants who suffer birth weight or gestational age problems. The fetus and the preterm infant are extremely susceptible to infection from organisms that ordinarily do not cause illness for the older individual, and infants have few physiological mechanisms with which to combat infection. Thus infection that may begin in the skin rapidly progresses to serious types of illness such as pneumonia, septicemia (wide-spread infection of the blood), or meningitis (infection of the central nervous system). Furthermore, the infant does not exhibit the usual signs of infection, such as fever, and detection of the infectious process is difficult or impossible until it has progressed to a serious stage. Infection of the central nervous system leads to particularly serious permanent sequelae, affecting the child's neurological capacity in later life.

Management of nutrition and oxygen intake is another problem of magnitude for infants of low birth weight and inadequate gestational age. Such infants miss the usual optimal nutritional source that is received through the placenta, so they suffer from inadequate intake of basic metabolic nutrients. Of particular importance during the last few months of gestation is the acquisition of glucose, proteins, and oxygen through the placenta, for these materials nourish all growing tissues, particularly those of the central nervous system. Central nervous system tissue depends on each of these nutrients not only for growth and development but also for survival. When an infant is born with fetal malnutrition from placental insufficiency, nutrition to help the child recuperate must be incorporated into the usual care given. Oxygen administration is most complicated for infants of low birth weight or gestational age inadequacy, for transfer of the ambient oxygen across the lung-blood barrier cannot be directly measured, and the infant may be under-oxygenated while receiving large percentages of oxygen or overoxygenated while receiving relatively low concentrations of oxygen. Excessive oxygen delivered to the tissues causes damage to the retina of the eye, with ultimate blindness, a condition known as retrolental fibroplasia.

Psychological and educational sequelae. Precise determination of the psychological and educational sequelae of birth weight and gestational age inadequacies has been extremely difficult. In part these difficulties have been encountered because of the confounding variables of low socioeconomic status and racial minority groups who consistently have a greater ratio of births in this category. Thus, groups that are known to have greater numbers of infants born with gestational age and birth weight problems also are known to have an increased percentage of educational and psychological problems among their young children (Caputo and Mandell, 1970; Eaves, Nuttall, Konoff, and Dunn, 1970; Parmalee and Schulte, 1970). Furthermore, comparison among various investigations is difficult or impossible because of the varying definitions of prematurity, low birth weight, and gestational age classification systems. In addition, the findings of long-term studies, which are necessary in order to determine educational sequelae, are often outdated by the time the data can be collected; for when a prematurely born child reaches 6 years of age or more, the medical and nursing care for current preterm infants has progressed so drastically that there can be little application of the findings for infants born at the time the research findings are reported. For example, 10 years ago little was known about the administration of oxygen to preterm infants for the treatment of lung disorders or prevention of anoxia. Today, great advances have been made in these and other related areas, so that most infants cared for in a high-risk specialty center are treated in such a manner that optimal oxygenation of body tissues is maintained throughout the critical period of instability. It is hoped, therefore, that we now are able to offset the seriously detrimental effects of anoxia, which may have caused many of the psychological and educational sequelae reported for children born in the previous 2 or 3 decades (Babson, Benson, Pernoll, and Benda, 1978; Korones, 1972).

One very interesting investigation on psychological and educational sequelae of prematurely born children was reported in 1973 by Rubin, Rosenblatt, and Balow. The infants were born at the University of Minnesota Hospital between 1960 and 1964, and the factor of socioeconomic status was controlled; the study included only those infants representing the urban population of the North Central United States, with racial background almost exclusively Caucasian. Further, the infants were classified according to both gestational age and birth weight. The major findings of this study led to the conclusion that low birth weight, preterm males, and low birth weight, full-term infants of both sexes constitute "high-risk" groups of children in terms of eventual impairment of school functioning. In particular, the specific findings illustrate many of the problems summarized in this section: (1) low birth weight was associated with a number of abnormal conditions, such as low Apgar scores and elevated bilirubin levels in the neonatal period; (2) birth weight rather than gestational age was the major correlate of neurological, psychological, and educational impairment; (3) low birth weight males and low birth weight full-term children of both sexes had a significantly higher incidence of school problems warranting special school services than did full birth weight, full-term control children; (4) low birth weight children scored lower than full birth weight children on all measures of mental development, language development, school readiness, and academic achievements through 7 years of age; (5) while there were no sex differences among low birth weight children on objective measures of psychological development and academic achievement, males had a higher incidence of school-identified problems than did females; (6) low birth weight and preterm infants did not differ significantly from control subjects on socioeconomic status; (7) at the age of 7, low birth weight children were smaller in stature and had a higher incidence of diagnosed neurological abnormalities than normal birth weight children; and (8) among full birth weight children, there were no differences between those who were preterm and those born at term on any of the psychological or educational variables under investigation (Rubin, Rosenblatt, and Balow, 1973).

Chromosomal aberrations and genetic errors

A number of problems occur, particularly during the prenatal period, as a result of chromosomal and genetic errors. In many cases the mental retardation that results from these difficulties represents the well-known syndrome classes of retardation.

Chromosomal aberrations. Chromosomal aberrations occur when some abnormality emerges in the number of chromosomes or in the configuration of the chromosomes in the body. Fig. 6-2 illustrates a karyotype, or a classifi-

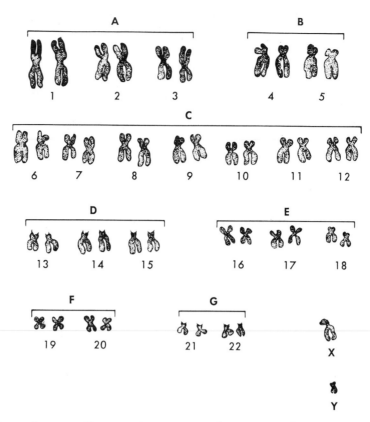

Fig. 6-2. Reproduction of human chromosomes during metaphase. The chromosomes are arranged according to a standard system known as karyotype. This is often provided as a tool in genetic counseling. (From Chinn, P. L. *Child health maintenance: concepts in family centered care.* (2nd ed.) St. Louis: The C. V. Mosby Co., 1979.)

Table 6. Maternal age correlation with incidence of Down's syndrome*

Age of mother	Incidence per 1,000 live births
Less than 20 years	0.5
20-24 years	0.7
25-29 years	0.7
30-34 years	1.1
35-39 years	3.5
40-44 years	10.0
45 and above	16.0

*From Birch, H. G., and Taft, L. T. Mental subnormality and mongolism. In R. E. Cooke, (Ed.), *The biologic basis of pediatric practice.* Copyright 1968, McGraw-Hill Book Co. Used with permission of McGraw-Hill Book Co.

cation of photographed human chromosomes obtained from a blood or skin sample. Such a karyotype is arranged in a standardized manner, and through this technique determinations of the particular chromosomal abnormality causing an abnormal condition can be identified. The karyotype shown in Fig. 6-2 represents a normal chromosomal configuration with 44 autosomal and 2 sex chromosomes. One kind of abnormal condition involves extra chromosomes, such as three chromosomes in position 21 or two or more X or Y chromosomes. Another type of common chromosomal aberration involves abnormally shaped chromosomes, such as an excessively long "arm" on chromosome 15 or another chromosome in the karyotype.

When there is a total of 45 chromosomes present with only a single X sex chromosome, the child has a condition termed Turner's syndrome, or gonadal aplasia. The child is always female, since the Y chromosome conveys maleness to the individual. The gonads are rudimentary, no secondary sex characteristics develop at puberty, and there may or may not be accompanying physical signs such as bowleggedness or webbed neck. It is estimated that approximately 20 percent of individuals with this problem are mentally retarded (Jones and Grumbach, 1968).

Klinefelter's syndrome, which occurs in males, involves two or more X and one or more Y chromosomes in at least some cells. Older maternal age seems to be a predisposing factor to the occurrence of extra X chromosomes in the infant. At puberty the boy may begin to develop secondary sex characteristics typical of the pubescent girl, and the male gonads are often underdeveloped, rendering the individual sterile. Mental retardation occurs frequently, but not invariably (Grumbach, 1968).

Many aberrations occur on the chromosomes occurring in groups A through G, known as the autosomal chromosomes because these contain genetic material that does not involve sexual characteristics. These types of aberrations occur with Down's syndrome and may involve any one of three different chromosomal aberrations. The first type is that of trisomy, or nondisjunction, in which there is an extra chromosome in the G group. This is the most common cause of Down's syndrome, and there is a definite correlation with maternal age, as indicated in Table 6.

A second type of chromosomal aberration that results in Down's syndrome is that of translocation, occurring in 9 percent of affected infants born to mothers under the age of 30 and in 2 percent of affected infants born to mothers over the age of 30. In translocation some of the chromosomal material designated as one of the twenty-first pair of the G group detaches and becomes attached to one of the chromosomes of the fifteenth pair in the D group, causing an extra-long chromosome observed in the karyotype. This type of chromosomal aberration may be inherited, in that a parent is the carrier of the condition, and such an instance can be detected through genetic studies of each parent as well as of the child. When inheritance is not identified, the condition has occurred as a result of a chance instance of chromosomal error.

The third condition resulting in Down's syndrome is mosaicism. In this instance, the cells of the individual's body are identified as mixed, with some reflecting a trisomy condition and others reflecting the normal complement of chromosomes. This error occurs during the very early cell division phases after fertilization, with some cell groups being formed normally prior to the occurrence of the chromosomal error. Such individuals tend to exhibit milder manifestations of the condition, which may reflect the stage of development at which the chromosomal error occurred.

The clinical characteristics of Down's syndrome vary from individual to individual but are similar to the extent that most Down's syndrome individuals resemble one another more than they resemble family members. There is a lateral upward slope of the eyes, protruding tongue because of a small oral cavity, short nose with flat bondage caused by underdevelopment of the nasal bone, flattened head anteriorly and posteriorly, shortness of the fingers, especially the fifth, wide space between the first and second toes, and short, stocky stature. In addition, these children are prone more than the general population to congenital heart defects, respiratory infections, and leukemia. There is almost always mental deficiency, with IQ scores in the moderate to severely retarded ranges. A few individuals have been reported in the normal range, and the effect of early stimulation and education programs may be demonstrated to result in improvement of mental and neurological functioning for some individuals with Down's syndrome (Birch and Taft, 1968).

Genetic errors. Genetic errors are those conditions that occur as a result of inheritance factors involving specific genes. Such disorders are poorly understood, and investigation of these problems is very limited because of the limitations of studying human genetic material. Genetic disorders can be identified because of the ability to study family inheritance patterns, but the problems that exist in identification are great, and the study of these problems is difficult. Such problems cannot be studied in the same manner as the chromosomal disorders, for it is not presently possible to obtain information about the genetic material from study of the chromosomes. Most genetic errors are rare, but a few that result in mental retardation occur with sufficient frequency that diagnostic and treatment approaches have been developed. One example of such a condition is phenylketonuria, which has become one of the most thoroughly studied genetic defects. It occurs about once in every 10,000 live births, and accounts for about 0.5 percent of patients in institutions for the mentally retarded. It is transmitted by an autosomal recessive gene, which has its highest frequency among northern European ethnic groups, but is rare among black and Jewish groups. For affected individuals there is a decrease in the essential enzyme necessary for metabolism of phenylalanine, leading to an accumulation of this product in the serum, cerebrospinal fluid, tissues, and urine. The effect on the central nervous system of this metabolic process is severe, and all untreated individuals become severely mentally retarded within the first few months of life. Elevated phenylalanine in the blood or urine can be detected within a few weeks after consumption of milk, which contains phenylalanine. Thus many states have instituted mandatory screening procedures for all infants in order to be able to institute early treatment measures and to minimize or prevent the serious effects of the untreated condition. In addition to the effect of mental retardation, the child develops some degree of microcephaly and has blond hair, blue eyes, and very sensitive skin.

Influences from maternal-fetal interaction

There are several conditions of abnormal maternal-fetal interactions that lead to serious sequelae for the infant. Infants of diabetic mothers, for example, are always high-risk infants because of excessive birth weight for gestational age, with gestational age often being low. In addition, there is an increased incidence of physical anomalies among infants of diabetic mothers, and the infants are prone to several serious illnesses during the neonatal period, such as lung disorders, seizures, hypoglycemia, and hyperbilirubinemia. Thus the mother's diabetic condition affects the fetus and infant in such a manner that the child is placed at serious risk. The incidence of neurological sequelae is largely dependent on the severity of the maternal diabetes and the neonatal course, including the gestational age and accompanying complications during this period (Babson, Benson, Pernoll, and Benda, 1978).

The problem of maternal-fetal Rh factor incompatibility has a more direct effect on the neurological capacity of the infant. In this instance, the mother has a negative Rh factor, and the infant a positive Rh factor. The mother reacts to the infant's positive factor by developing antibodies that destroy the infant's blood cells, leading to serious consequences during fetal life and during the neonatal period. The infant's condition is known as erythroblastosis fetalis. The higher the level of antibodies in the mother's blood, the more serious the effect on the fetus. In the most severe form, known as fetal hydrops, the fetus begins to develop severe anemia, enlargement of the heart, liver, and spleen, and deterioration of the body tissues. In most instances, the fetus dies during the late second or early third trimester and is stillborn. If the child is born alive, survival during the neonatal period is unlikely. A moderate form of erythroblastosis fetalis, known as icterus gravis, occurs more frequently, for in many instances the infant's delivery is induced prior to term in order to prevent progression of the disease to the more severe form. When this occurs, the infant is placed in a disadvantageous position of being delivered preterm, but the hazards of this condition are in fact less than the hazards of a more severe form of erythroblastosis fetalis. Such an infant, in addition to low gestational age, may also be of low birth weight because of the effect of the condition in utero. The infant is typically anemic and jaundiced and has an enlarged spleen and liver. The high level of bilirubin, which occurs from the metabolism of red blood cells, accounts for the jaundice and for the central nervous system damage that may result. As the bilirubin level rises rapidly, adequate excretion cannot occur, and the molecules enter the skin tissue, resulting in the yellow appearance of jaundice. Subsequently, the bilirubin invades central nervous system tissue and renders a toxic effect, a condition known as kernicterus. The infant's outlook for survival is good if it survives the first week of life, but the possibility of neurological sequelae depends on the severity of hyperbilirubinemia and the accompanying illnesses that may occur during the neonatal period. When the effects of the blood factor incompatibility are minimal, which is usual for the first two or three infants of most Rh-negative mothers, the neonatal problems are minimal, and there are no neurological sequelae (Chinn and Mueller, 1971).

Other trauma during early pregnancy

Trauma can occur to the fetus during the first trimester from a variety of causes, including drug or chemical ingestion and maternal infection. The teratogenic effects of such exposure are poorly understood, but it is known that, while the exact effect of most teratogens is not specified, the timing of exposure to the teratogens probably leads to specific kinds of anomalies. Thus, when a mother contracts rubella during the first trimester, the specific anomalies that occur are probably related more to the timing of exposure than to the specific effects of the virus. Teratogenic effects on the fetus include intrauterine growth retardation, central nervous system infection, microcephaly, congenital heart disease, sensorineural deafness, cataracts and/or glaucoma, and anomalies of the skin. There appears to be a wide range of severity of these conditions, as well as the range of occurrence of each of the conditions known to be possible. Again, the range of severity is probably related to the timing of the infection, as well as the possible individual susceptibility of a particular mother and fetus to the effects of the infection. The infant is likely to have a number of physical, behavioral, and intellectual handicaps (Babson, Benson, Pernoll, and Benda, 1978).

The birth process

As noted earlier, mental retardation may result from a variety of influences that take many specific forms of physical trauma and developmental deviation. The preceding section discussed influences and causes of mental retardation during the prenatal period, from the time of conception to the initiation of the birth process. This section focuses on influences that are operative during the birth process itself.

The birth process has long been characterized as an extremely traumatic event in the life of the human organism. In fact, "birth trauma" has been described as being the basis for a variety of psychological problems in later life. Early proponents of the psychoanalytic school, such as Sigmund Freud, attributed all later life anxiety to the separation shock generated at birth. A variety of other phenomena, such as the content of adult dreams, have been thought at times to reflect the trauma of birth. Although there is little doubt that birth represents a stressful occurrence, recent thinking places much more emphasis on the physical aspects of this stress than on the psychoanalytic orientations.

Chapter 5 outlines briefly the sequence of events that occurs during the birth of a baby. Although the birth process is a stressful time, there is minimal danger if the baby is positioned head first, facing downward, and if the mother's pelvic opening is adequate for the child. This, of course, assumes that fetal development has progressed without mishap to this point. Two general types of problems may result in mental retardation during birth: (1) physical trauma or mechanical injury and (2) anoxia or asphyxia. The first type of problem is nearly self-explanatory. Physical trauma or mechanical injury refers to some occurrence during birth that physically injures or damages the baby in such a way that the mental functioning is impaired. The second general type of problem, anoxia or asphyxia, refers to a situation in which the baby is deprived of an adequate oxygen supply for a long enough period that brain damage occurs, thereby reducing mental functioning. This may be caused by a variety of conditions and will be discussed in more detail. Although the previously noted problems are given different labels and appear to be substantially different, they are frequently interrelated.

It has been mentioned that the danger of birth injury is relatively low if the fetus is positioned correctly. The most favorable fetal position when labor begins is with the head first, facing downward (assuming the mother is lying on her back). Any other fetal position is considered somewhat abnormal and may result in a variety of problems, depending on the individual situation. Both mechanical injury and anoxia may result from abnormal fetal presentation. Some of the more common position abnormalities and resulting problems are discussed briefly.

One rather well-known position abnormality involves a breech presentation of the fetus. Breech presentation occurs when the buttocks present first rather than the head. Fig. 6-3 illustrates a breech presentation and can be compared with the more normal presentation in Fig. 6-4.

Physicians are becoming increasingly reluctant to deliver through the birth canal babies presenting in a breech position. Except when the delivery is conducted by extremely skilled personnel, the danger to the baby is substantial. More and more frequently a baby who is lying breech within the uterus is delivered via cesarean section, which involves surgery and extraction of the baby through the abdomen and wall of the uterus.

There are numerous difficulties encountered in breech birth if delivery is executed through the birth canal. Since the head is presented last, it reaches the pelvic girdle (the bony hip structure of the mother) during the later more advanced stages of labor. Contractions are occurring rather rapidly at this point, and the head does not have an opportunity to proceed through the slower molding processes that are possible in earlier labor. Additionally, molding of the head may occur in an abnormal and damaging fashion since the various solid portions of the skull are receiving pressure in an atypical manner.

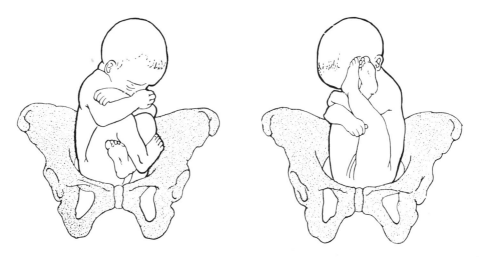

Fig. 6-3. Examples of breech fetal position. (From Iorio, J. *Childbirth: family centered nursing* (3rd ed.) St. Louis: The C. V. Mosby Co., 1975.)

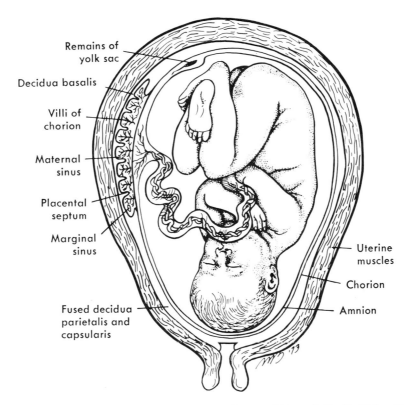

Remains of yolk sac

Decidua basalis

Villi of chorion

Maternal sinus

Placental septum

Marginal sinus

Fused decidua parietalis and capsularis

Uterine muscles

Chorion

Amnion

Fig. 6-4. An example of normal fetal position. (From Chinn, P. L. *Child health maintenance: concepts in family centered care.* (2nd ed.) St. Louis: The C. V. Mosby Co., 1979.)

The abnormal pressure generated by these processes may result in mechanical injury to the brain matter in at least two general ways. Since the skull is still quite soft, there actually may be an injury caused by rapid compression, which crushes a portion of the brain. Such damage is less likely in normal presentation since the skull is molded more gently, permitting protective fluid to absorb the pressure. A second type of injury may occur that may also be viewed as mechanical in nature. The rapid pressure and shifting of cranial bones may be so severe that it damages the circulatory system around the brain. This can result in a hemorrhage within the skull, which in turn damages the brain tissue.

Breech birth may also result in anoxia of the fetus. Since the skull is the last part of the body to be delivered, the baby must depend entirely on the umbilical cord as a source of oxygen until birth is complete. Because of the positioning, the cord is occasionally of insufficient length to remain attached while the head is expelled. If this is the case, the placenta may become partially or completely detached while the head is still in the birth canal. This separation, of course, eliminates the oxygen supply, which may result in a deprivation of oxygen if the delivery is not completed rather quickly. Severe tissue damage may result if the head is not expelled and oxygen supplied through the baby's lungs. This presents a very serious problem if the head becomes lodged in the pelvic girdle, preventing or substantially deterring the progress down the birth canal. Anoxia may also occur even if the cord is sufficiently long to remain attached throughout the delivery. It has been noted previously that the head will present the tightest fit as the baby moves through the pelvic girdle. As the head enters the pelvic girdle, a section of the umbilical cord is necessarily drawn through at the same time. Depending on how tight the skull fits into the bony structure, the cord may become pinched and effectively shut off the supply of oxygen. If the supply is eliminated in this manner for an extended length of time (such as the situation of the lodged skull noted earlier) the anoxic condition will result just as if the cord were cut from the mother.

The previous descriptions represent only a brief look at the difficulties involved in breech delivery and how they may result in damaged tissue and reduced mental functioning. These problems, as well as numerous other variations, are the reasons fewer breech presentations are currently being delivered through the birth canal and the reason delivery by cesarean section is becoming somewhat favored in this situation.

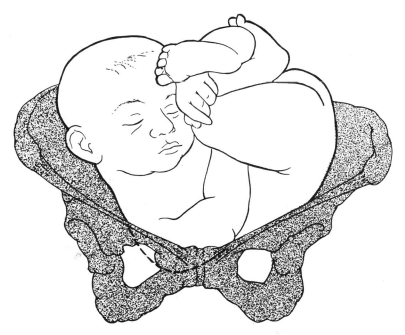

Fig. 6-5. An example of transverse fetal position. (From Iorio, J. *Childbirth: family centered nursing* (3rd ed.) St. Louis: The C. V. Mosby Co., 1975.)

Another abnormal fetal position that presents severe problems is a transverse position, illustrated in Fig. 6-5. The fetus lies across the birth canal rather than longitudinally. All of the injury problems noted with the breech position are potential difficulties with the transverse position, depending on how delivery proceeds. Additionally there are a multitude of other problems that are presented to the attending physician. If it is possible for the physician to rotate the fetus in a safe manner, then delivery through the pelvic birth canal may be attempted. This is particularly true if the baby can be moved into a head-down position that is normal or near normal. If the fetus cannot be rotated into a satisfactory longitudinal position, a cesarean section is performed.

Rotation of the fetus in the uterus presents certain potential dangers. The umbilical cord, as noted earlier, is crucial to the baby's prenatal life. If the cord becomes twisted or pinched severely because of certain changes in fetal position, the oxygen supply may be eliminated, resulting in an anoxic condition or even a stillborn baby, depending on the time without oxygen.

It becomes evident from the foregoing discussion that abnormalities of fetal presentation can cause a variety of difficulties during the birth process. Such difficulties may result in reduced mental functioning because of mechanical injury, anoxia, or both. Abnormal presentation, however, is not the only type of problem that may occur during the birth process. The initial stages of labor are important for several reasons. As the fetus proceeds into the birth canal, the pelvic girdle begins to stretch. With a normally presented fetus, the head is also molded somewhat in order to permit passage through the bony structure. This process occurs during early labor when contractions of the uterus are less intense and less frequent than they are in later labor. Consequently this molding and stretching process occurs, under normal circumstances, without sufficient stress to cause injury to the baby. In order for this to transpire without potentially injurious stress, time becomes an important factor. It requires a certain amount of time for the baby's head to be molded with sufficient gentleness to avoid injury. Delivery of a baby after labor of less than about 2 hours is known as *precipitous birth* and causes considerable concern about the adequacy of time for the processes noted before. Precipitous birth increases the risk of damage to tissue and consequently raises the probability of resulting mental retardation.

Time is also an important factor on the other end of the continuum, when labor is unusually prolonged (24 hours or longer). Certainly most deliveries do not approach 24 hours in length; 7 to 12 hours are average. A variety of conditions may accompany prolonged labor. Under certain circumstances the uterine conditions deprive the fetus of oxygen, which after such a long period of time results in either anoxia or a stillborn fetus. This is particularly a problem if the membranes have ruptured rather early and labor has continued without delivery for a prolonged period. Additionally, if advanced labor continues for a long period of time, the fetal skull is under an unusual amount of pressure. This, of course, raises the possibility of intracranial hemmorrhage. In either case the probability of tissue damage and resulting mental retardation is substantially increased.

This section has reviewed very briefly the influences and causes of mental retardation that occur primarily at birth. A comprehensive examination of this complex process is far beyond the scope of an introductory text. Consequently, we have only given examples of conditions that are most prevalent, more well known, and more easily understood. Even this abbreviated presentation generates a considerable degree of uneasiness in the reader who is still in the initiation stages to the area of mental retardation, but perspective must be maintained. The vast majority of babies are born normally and reach this point in their lives in a fashion that readies them for the challenges of the postnatal world. The challenges of that world during early life remain as discussion points for the remainder of this chapter.

PROFESSIONAL INTERVENTION

We have examined a few conditions that may result in mental retardation. Through various types of professional intervention, mental retardation can be eliminated or at least curtailed in many instances.

Children who are born at high risk because of their inappropriate birth weight or gestational period are frequently predisposed toward mental retardation. As we have seen, problems frequently arise when prenatal care is either inadequate or nonexistent. The inadequacy or lack of availability of prenatal care is often related to lack of financial resources, ignorance, a value system that does not include a high regard for prenatal care, the inefficiency of governmentally sponsored health care plans, or a combination of these factors.

Limitations in financial resources may result in inadequate prenatal dietary intake, lack of necessary drugs and vitamins, and lack of supervision by health care specialists. Many individuals suffer from ignorance regarding the necessity of prenatal care. Others may be informed but have not incorporated quality prenatal care into their value systems and ignore the advice from health care specialists. Governmentally supported health care programs frequently are overburdened and inadequately staffed. Expectant mothers, frustrated by long waits and impersonal care, may become too discouraged to continue seeking prenatal care.

Professional intervention can greatly reduce the incidence of high-risk children. Low-income families lacking the financial resources for adequate prenatal care need to be directed to the proper agencies that can provide governmentally supported health care. In addition these families need to be directed to the various sources necessary to obtain supplemental foods, such as food stamps, surplus food programs, and other types of resources that can improve the diet of the entire family and especially the expectant mother. Information of this type can be provided by social workers, public health nurses, and other individuals working directly with the families. It is imperative that these families be advised how and where to apply for aid. Many agencies require extensive documentation to verify need for financial assistance. These families could be tutored in the skills necessary to complete application forms as well as how to accumulate documentation of financial need. In addition, the heavy case loads of physicians involved in governmentally supported programs could be eased considerably by the utilization of other health care specialists, such as certified nurses and midwives. Postnatal care can also be increased and enhanced by utilizing the growing corps of pediatric nurse practitioners.

Some of the genetic conditions and chromosomal aberrations mentioned can be dealt with effectively through professional intervention. Since the majority of the Down's syndrome cases are of the nondisjunctive, or trisomy, variety, a high percentage of Down's syndrome cases tend to be related to advanced maternal age. Health care specialists and social workers can encourage couples to have their children at an earlier age, preferably prior to maternal age of 35. Older couples might be urged to exercise birth control methods or at least should be informed of the possible consequences of having children at more advanced ages. Young mothers who have children with Down's syndrome should be advised to have a chromosomal analysis to determine if the condition is related to a translocation. If a translocation exists, then the likelihood of a genetic or inherited etiology is high. These parents can be counseled and advised of the risks involved in having other children. Under such conditions sterilization or other forms of birth control may be considered. Parents could also be advised that a biopsy could be performed by drawing a sample of the amnionic fluid during subsequent pregnancies. Should a translocation exist in the fetus, the parents may decide to terminate the pregnancy via therapeutic abortion. The entire issue of abortion is highly controversial and will be discussed at length in terms of social and ethical issues in Chapter 14. Although such alternatives may or may not be acceptable to the counselor, care should be exercised to avoid the imposition of personal values on the parents. They are entitled to know what their alternatives are and the decision regarding the alternatives is rightfully theirs.

Certain disorders such as phenylketonuria (PKU) may be diagnosed early by routine screening. Several states have mandatory legislation requiring the testing of all newborn children. Screening for PKU can be accomplished by the "stick test," which can determine abnormal levels of phenylalanine in the urine. The Guthrie test (Carter, 1975) also determines abnormal presence of phenylalanine through the examination of the blood of the patient.

Prevention of mental retardation frequently can be accomplished through dietary restrictions. At as early an age as possible, the patient is placed on a diet that is essentially free of phenylalanine. Some commercially prepared diets are prepared and marketed under names such as Ketonil and Lofenolac. The earlier a child is placed on the restricted diet, the greater are the chances of avoiding mental retardation. While there is evidence to indicate that a child with PKU may eventually be removed from the restricted diet, the appropriate time is specific to the individual. Thus through early detection and intervention mental retardation can either be avoided or at least the degree can be minimized.

Rh factor incompatibility between mother and fetus can frequently lead to erythroblastosis fetalis and eventually to hyperbilirubinemia, which can cause brain damage and mental retardation. The bilirubin levels can be monitored effectively by periodic testing with a Coombs test or through an amniocentesis, which samples the bilirubin level in the amniotic fluid (Chinn and Mueller, 1971). When the fetus is affected by a high bilirubin content, professional intervention may be in the form of induced labor to deliver the child before the bilirubin level has reached a critical point. There have also been some efforts toward exchange transfusion through a fetal leg extended by surgery. Exchange transfusion immediately after birth has been effective in many instances. One of the most dramatic breakthroughs in medical intervention is the development of the procedure of intrauterine transfusions. Guided by x-rays, a long needle is extended through the abdomen of the mother into the peritoneal cavity in the abdomen of the fetus. Blood of the same type as the mother's is then transfused into the fetus. Since the blood is of the same variety as the mother's, it is compatible and is immune from the antibodies of the mother.

Rh_0 immune globulin (RhoGAM), a desensitizing drug, was introduced to the general public in 1968. Injected into the mother within 72 hours of the birth of the first child, it desensitizes the mother from the antibodies, and she can begin her next pregnancy without the presence of antibodies. The procedure can be continued after the birth of each child and will preclude the development of antibodies, provided it is followed faithfully after each birth. Between the intrauterine transfusions and desensitization through RhoGAM, there should be few incidents of death or mental retardation in the future resulting from Rh factor incompatibility.

As indicated earlier, the first trimester of pregnancy is critical with respect to any type of insult or injury to the fetus. During this period expectant mothers must exercise extreme caution to avoid any exposure to irradiation, which may affect the fetus, or to infectious diseases. Rubella immunization is now available that can and should eliminate the possibility of widespread rubella epidemics. Parents can greatly reduce the possibility of rubella in their homes by immunizing all the children in the family; this also protects the mothers of the future from contracting the disease while pregnant.

Prevention of trauma during the delivery is a major concern of adequate obstetrical management. The primary concerns include maintaining adequate fetal oxygenation during labor and delivery, assuring appropriate delivery if there is a fetus-pelvis size disproportion, and providing adequate observation and care of the infant during the first hour of life. Regional high-risk care centers for mothers recently have been developed to provide a very high level of specialized care for both mothers and infants who are known to be in one of the risk categories described. The effect of these centers has been observed to decrease significantly maternal and infant mortality and morbidity. Thus one of the most important contributions that can be made in prevention is early identification of mothers and infants at risk to allow rapid transfer of these individuals to a specialized center.

STUDY QUESTIONS

1. Smoking and malnutrition have long been identified as factors that influence our health in significant ways. These also may be related to fetal development, and some have suggested that they could be related to mental retardation. Discuss factors such as these involved in prenatal development that appear to be associated with mental retardation. Explain how they may contribute to it.
2. A number of factors contribute to the occurrence of a "high-risk" infant. What are some of them, and how might they appear later in educational and/or psychological sequelae?
3. Both chromosomal aberrations and genetic errors can cause mental retardation. How are these influences different from each other, and with what types of mental retardation are they associated?
4. The idea of birth trauma may be very real in terms of causation of mental retardation, although perhaps not in the manner conceived by the early psychoanalytic school of thought. What are some of the factors involved in the birth process that may result in retardation? How do they operate in such causation?

REFERENCES

Babson, S. G., Benson, R. C., Pernoll, M. L., and Benda, G. I. *Management of high-risk pregnancy and intensive care of the neonate.* (3rd ed.) St. Louis: The C. V. Mosby Co., 1978.

Birch, H. G., and Taft, L. T. Mental subnormality and mongolism. In R. E. Cooke (Ed.), *The biologic basis of pediatric practice.* New York: McGraw-Hill Book Co., 1968, P. 1289.

Caputo, D., and Mandell, W. Consequences of low birth weight. *Developmental Psychology,* 1970, **3,** 363.

Carter, C. H. *Handbook of mental retardation syndromes.* (3rd ed.) Springfield, Ill.: Charles C Thomas, 1975.

Chinn, P. C., and Mueller, J. M. Advances in treatment of Rh negative blood incompatibility of mothers and infants. *Mental Retardation,* 1971, **9,** 12-25.

Eaves, L., Nuttall, J., Konoff, H., and Dunn, H. Developmental and psychological test scores in children of low birth weight. *Pediatrics,* 1970, **45,** 9.

Gluck, L. Appraisal of the fetus and neonate: growth, development, nutrition. In H. Abramson (Ed.), *Symposium on the functional development of the fetus and neonate.* (3rd ed.) St. Louis: The C. V. Mosby Co., 1973, P. 68.

Grumbach, M. M. Anatomic and physiologic considerations (male). In R. E. Cooke (Ed.), *The biologic basis of pediatric practice.* New York: McGraw-Hill Book Co., 1968, P. 1058.

Jones, H. W., Jr., and Grumbach, M. M. Developmental disorders (female). In R. E. Cooke (Ed.), *The biologic basis of pediatric practice.* New York: McGraw-Hill Book Co., 1968, P. 1087.

Kernek, C., Osterud, H., and Anderson, B. Patterns of prematurity in Oregon. *Northwest Medicine,* 1966, **65,** 639.

Korones, S. B. *High-risk newborn infants: the basis for intensive nursing care.* (2nd ed.) St. Louis: The C. V. Mosby Co., 1976.

Lilienfeld, A. M., and Pasamanick, B. The association of maternal and fetal factors with the development of mental deficiency, II: Relationship to maternal age, birth order, previous reproductive loss and degree of mental deficiency. *American Journal of Mental Deficiency,* 1956, **60,** 557-569.

Parmalee, A., and Schulte, F. Developmental testing of preterm and small-for-date infants. *Pediatrics,* 1970, **45,** 21.

Rubin, R. A., Rosenblatt, C., and Balow, B. Psychological and educational sequelae of prematurity. *Pediatrics,* 1973, **52,** 352.

ANNOTATED BIBLIOGRAPHY

Babson, S. G., Benson, R. C., Pernoll, M. L., and Benda, G. A. *Management of high-risk pregnancy and intensive care of the neonate.* (3rd ed.) St. Louis: The C. V. Mosby Co., 1978.

This excellent book provides a comprehensive discussion of each of the major problems affecting the neonate, with accompanying information regarding the mother and pregnancy. The implications for health care are included, with recognition of social and educational requirements in the care of these individuals.

Carter, C. H. *Handbook of mental retardation syndromes.* (3rd ed.) Springfield, Ill.: Charles C Thomas, 1975.

A good reference book with many illustrations. Much of the handbook is drawn from the author's more detailed book, *Medical aspects of mental retardates* (1965), also published by Charles C Thomas.

Gellis, S. S., and Feingold, M. *Atlas of mental retardation syndromes.* Washington, D.C.: U.S. Department of Health, Education and Welfare, 1968.

A well-illustrated (photographs) reference book with a short concise description of various syndromes.

CHAPTER 7

The mentally retarded child during infancy and early childhood

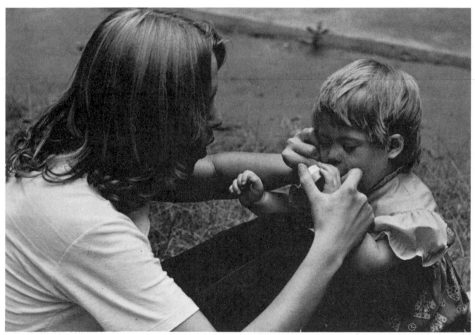

(Photograph by Peter Poulides.)

INTRODUCTION

The importance of development during infancy and early childhood has been mentioned in several sections of this volume. It would be difficult to overemphasize this period since these years are generally thought to be critical with respect to the overall developmental process for all children. Experiences during infancy and early childhood can serve to promote the attainment of optimal development potential or they can deter the fulfillment of this potential. In the former situation, intellectual functioning may be enhanced to such a degree that the child operates in the upper ranges of capability. In the latter the experiences may detract from the developmental process in such a significant manner that permanently lowered functioning may result. The effects of environmental influences during infancy and early childhood are perhaps more lasting and pervasive than during any other phase of the life cycle.

This chapter focuses on development during infancy and the preschool years and those environmental influences that promote or detract from the fulfillment of potential. Four broad areas will be specifically examined: (1) physical development, (2) language development, (3) cognitive development, and (4) psychosocial development. Although these areas are interrelated, they also represent somewhat distinct areas of development that have received considerable attention in terms of research. Consequently they pertain to our consideration of developmental problems. Each of the four areas is critical in one fashion or another to a child's ability to learn, and they seem vulnerable to environmental influence during the early years. Pertinent research will be reviewed in terms of expected traits of development, traits evident in the mentally retarded child, and environmental influence.

PHYSICAL DEVELOPMENT

A number of major body systems may be involved in a discussion of physical development. Those most frequently thought of in terms of a generic conception of physical development include the gastrointestinal, renal, endocrine, skeletal, reproductive, neurological, and muscular systems (Chinn, 1979). Each of these systems has an important function; however, those that are most closely related to the learning process are the neurological and musculoskeletal systems. These two systems are very closely and integrally related from a functional standpoint and are occasionally thought of as one: the neuromotor system. Neurological and motor functions are also influenced by important stimuli and responses provided by the endocrine system. For purposes of this text, we will examine neuromotor development in order to become familiar with the physical dimensions of learning and the influences of the environment on this particular aspect of development.

Neuromotor development

The neurological system includes a number of components that must be considered in an examination of physical development. This system is composed of the brain, spinal cord, and peripheral neurons, including the autonomic system, which is functionally related to the endocrine system. The neurological pathways extend to the muscle and skin tissues and provide for the transmission of neurological sensations from the environment to the central nervous system. These pathways also serve as mediums for neurological control and response between the central nervous system and the muscles that permit movement and vocalizations appropriate to various environmental stimuli. The processes involved in stimulus reception and neurological functioning cannot typically be studied directly. They may, however, be investigated indirectly by observing a variety of performance areas and comparing a given child's functioning with levels that are age appropriate. Neurological development represents a critical dimension of the child's overall development and plays a particular role in the areas of cognitive, language, and psychosocial development. More complete attention will be given to these areas in later portions of this chapter. Initially we will focus directly on the development of the neuromotor system and examine certain physical development conditions that may be detected in mentally retarded children.

Head and brain characteristics. A child's neurological development and capacity are known to be related to head and brain size. It was noted earlier that the brain grows very rapidly during the prenatal period. This rapid growth continues after birth with approximately 90 percent of the adult brain size being attained by the time the child is 2 years of age. Although this growth cannot be directly observed, it can be assessed indirectly by measuring the circumference of the head. Normal circumference ranges have been established for each developmental stage and differ somewhat between the sexes. For example, the mean head circumference for male infants at birth is 34.5 cm and reaches 49 cm by the age of 2. Female infants, on the other hand, have a mean head circumference of 34 cm at birth and reach 48 cm by the age of 2. A deviation of more than plus or minus 2 standard deviations from the expected mean head circumference at any age represents a sufficient variation to warrant concern. If such a condition occurs, the child must receive extensive medical diagnosis to determine if there is a serious pathological condition present that threatens physical health and that may threaten intellectual functioning. An example of such a condition is found in microcephalus where the head circumference exceeds minus 2 standard deviations. (Children with microcephalus also are characterized by several other physical abnormalities and are typically rather severely retarded.) In this condition the child's brain size is limited and abnormalities of brain tissue formation also may be present. Limited brain size, tissue abnormalities, or both may result from a genetic condition or may arise from a condition affecting the skeletal tissue surrounding the brain that arrests the growth of the brain tissue. In either case the functional status of the neurological system is seriously impaired, and mental retardation results.

Other conditions may result in a head circumference that is significantly above the expected mean and may also represent situations of serious concern. Hydrocephalus, for example, is a syndrome that is characterized by an exceptionally large head size while the brain may be inadequately developed or normal, depending on the precise cause of the condition. This difficulty is related to an increase in the amount of cerebrospinal fluid that circulates in the brain cavity and spinal column area. The overabundance of fluid creates an increased pressure on the surrounding structures and, in turn, leads to damage of the brain tissue and ultimate mental retardation, regardless of the initial functional capacity.

Other developments in the brain also are occurring at a rapid rate during the early years. The sulci or convolutions in the lobes of the brain deepen and become more prominent and numerous during this period. These continue to develop throughout life but at a more gradual rate than during the early years. This is thought to reflect processes of learning, memory, and the ability to reason and form conceptualizations. A child who exhibits inadequate neuromotor control and function or who evidences a developmental delay may suffer from some abnormality of form or function of the brain, although such a defect is not typically detectable directly. Some information concerning the size and shape of the brain can be obtained using x-ray procedures, but the primary cause of the child's limited ability to learn, lack of coordination, and speaking difficulty usually cannot be identified with certainty as a defect of the brain tissue itself. Frequently direct evidence of brain abnormality must await autopsy, and even this type of examination can provide only limited information in most cases, such as evidence of identifiable lesions in the brain tissue. There may, however, be indications that the neurological tissue of the nervous system has not been adequately stimulated at an optimal period of development in order to reach an optimal level of functioning—a process that is known to be imperative for development of adequate neuromotor function (Penfield, 1972).

Myelinization. The myelinization process has been previously discussed in Chapter 5. It is commonly accepted that this is an important developmental process, although information about the precise nature of both its function and growth remains inexact. Myelinization involves the development of a protective insulating sheath that surrounds the brain and the neurological pathways. This sheath presumably operates somewhat like insulation on an electrical wire and allows nerve impulses to travel along the nerve pathway rapidly and without diffusion. The newborn has an incomplete myelin sheath, which accounts for nonspecific reactions to stimuli and a lack of motor coordination. Consequently the infant exhibits generalized body movement and crying in response to a painful stimulus to the foot rather than specific withdrawal of the foot and attention to the source of the stimulus with specific vocalizations indicating pain. As with other growth patterns, myelinization proceeds in a cephalocaudal and proximodistal fashion, which provides for this pattern of acquisition of gross motor control prior to acquisition of fine motor control. By the age of 2, a major portion of the myelin sheath is formed, and the child's motor capacity is relatively mature.

Reflexes and voluntary behavior. Reflexive behavior represents a rather primitive human response in comparison to many that are now characteristic of general human functioning. Development of reflex behavior is thought to have evolved out of necessity for protection in a harsh environment prior to the development of sophisticated cognitive skills that provided for ingenuity or voluntary action directed toward protection of the organism. The reflexive behavior of early infancy gradually fades as voluntary control develops through association pathways of the nervous system. Certain reflexes persist throughout life, such as the knee jerk, eye blink, and the reaction of the eye pupil to light. During early childhood, voluntary movement becomes predominant for the child who is neurologically healthy, although involuntary movement on one side of the body may be exhibited as a mirroring of voluntary movement on the opposite side. This involuntary mirroring action is pronounced in children who suffer damage in the central nervous system, but the phenomenon itself does not suggest damage unless it persists beyond the preschool years or is so pronounced that it interferes with the child's voluntary movements. The predominance of the one-sided voluntary function is generally established fully by the age of 4, and the child typically demonstrates a preference for using the right or left hand in performing motor tasks.

Emotions and the central nervous system. The limbic system of the brain is located in the central portion of the tissue and surrounds the hypothalamus. This system functions specifically to mediate the emotional and temperamental dimensions of behavior. Sensations such as pleasure or discomfort and the individual meaning that such experiences develop originate and are stored in this system. Other behaviors known to be related to these areas of functioning include excitement, anger, fear, sleep, and wakefulness. Maturity in these response areas progresses as the young child begins to experience a wider range of environmental stimuli and is able to exercise more self control of behavior as well as control over the behavior of others. The feeling response predominates the early childhood period in terms of determining behavior that indicates that the limbic system is functioning and that associations with voluntary control areas are not fully accomplished. As growth continues and these complex associations mature, the child becomes more effective in disguising and voluntarily controlling the emotional component of behavior (Guyton, 1971).

Sensory organs and cranial nerves. The development and integrity of the cranial nerves and specialized sensory organs also plays an important role in the young child's general functioning status. These maturational processes are essential to the child's ability to receive stimuli from the environment and to integrate them into the perceptual and memory components of the central nervous system. Cranial nerves are distinct nerve pathways that provide for the specialized sensory function and motor performance of the sensory and other essential organs and surrounding muscular structure. These nerves approach functional maturity by the age of 3 and can be tested specifically by assessing the function of the sensory organs. The ears and eyes are particularly crucial in terms of receiving stimuli related to learning. However, other sensory functions, such as smell, taste, touch, and the sense of movement, also are known to be important in providing essential neurological stimulation.

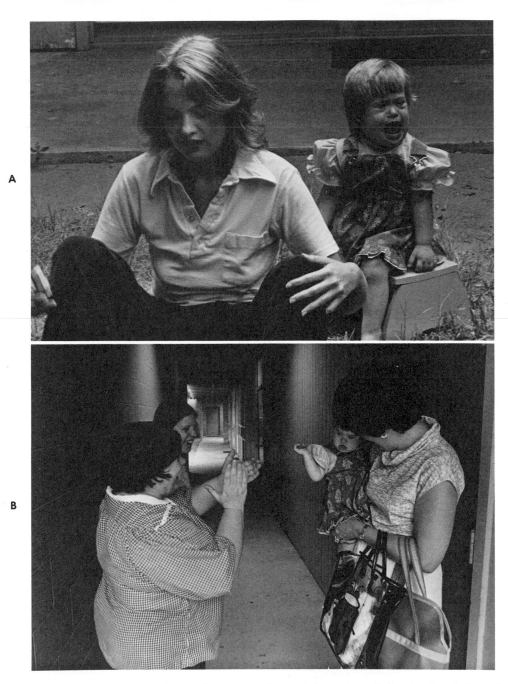

Fig. 7-1. Negative behavior is often ignored, **A,** while positive behavior is reinforced, **B.** (Photograph by Peter Poulides.)

The optimal levels of function for the capacities of taste and smell are attained during infancy. These senses also come under the influence of voluntary control and association with other sensory areas. Consequently a young child is able to, and often will, refuse to taste a particular food that appears unpleasant or about which others have made negative comments. The child is able to respond rather accurately to the sensation that a taste or smell arouses and begins to learn conditioned associations between certain tastes and smells and culturally accepted values. The preferred foods in the child's culture become palatable, and the foods that are not acceptable become displeasing. The role of these sensory capacities in terms of learning problems is not currently understood, but it does appear clear that significant learning stimuli are provided through these channels.

The most critical sense, with regard to the learning process, is often thought to be hearing. Children who have hearing deficits seem to have a greater degree of interference with learning than children with other types of sensory disturbances. This type of observation obviously varies substantially depending on the child and the nature and severity of the deficit. The sense of hearing is dependent on intact tissue structures between the external ear and the cortex of the brain, including the important cranial nerves related to the hearing sensory functions. The functional structures of the ear also are related to the sense of kinesthetic balance and movement.

The infant's hearing apparatus is mature at birth with the exception of two areas that remain to be completed: myelinization of the cortical auditory pathways beyond the midbrain and resorption of the connective tissue surrounding the ossicles of the middle ear. The infant obviously can hear and also can respond differentially to loud noises (by crying) and soft, soothing sounds (by calming and becoming relaxed). The child's reaction to sound at this stage is characteristic of reactions to most stimuli, it is generalized and tends to involve movements of the entire body. Typically these movements are predominantly of a gross motor nature and are nonspecific (that is, they tend to be characterized by a thrashing of the arms, body, and legs or by a generalized calming). As myelinization proceeds, the child begins to exhibit an ability to localize the direction of sound. By the age of 2 to 3 months the child can respond by turning the head responsively in the direction of the sound stimulus.

This discussion should not be interpreted as meaning that the infant has fully developed, adult-like hearing behavior. This does not occur until approximately 7 years of age and involves complex cortical functioning, including the ability to listen, to respond with discrimination, to imitate sounds accurately, and to integrate the meaning of sounds. Identification of hearing deficits during the first year of life is vital in order for maximally effective treatment to be undertaken and optimal learning capacity to be maintained. If a child with a hearing deficiency can be identified at this time and some means of providing auditory stimulation can be instituted, the ability to integrate the meaning of auditory stimuli later in life and to maintain and use these neurological pathways as an avenue for learning is substantially enhanced.

The infant has rather limited visual acuity at birth, although it is fully developed by the age of 6. At birth the infant is only able to differentiate generally between light and dark. The development of visual acuity progresses rather rapidly during the neonatal period, and by the age of 6 months, the infant is generally able to recognize objects and people. The ability to follow movement in the environment also begins to develop during the first months of life, and completely coordinated eye movements should be evident by the sixth month. The preschool child who does not establish the ability to perceive a single object when viewing the item with both eyes (termed the establishment of binocularity) develops a condition known as amblyopia. The existence of such a problem tends to create some unique difficulties with regard to the child's perceptual behavior. Since the condition results in two separate overlapping objects instead of a single unified perception, the child begins to "block" the perception of one eye, which results in the perception of a single object through the preferred eye. The lack of use and stimulation of the unused eye then becomes a problem and results in gradual deterioration of the neural pathways from the eye to the central nervous system. This may result in a permanent loss of function of the eye if it continues to be unused by the child. This phenomenon illustrates and emphasizes the vital role of adequate stimulation in order for neurological tissue to maintain and to develop adequate function.

The integration of incoming visual stimuli with existing neurological functions is an extremely important factor in early learning. By about 2 to 3 years of age the child begins to be able to remember and recall visual images. An interest is displayed in pictures, and the child also begins to be interested in producing geometric shapes and figures. These abilities create a readiness to recognize symbols, or to read, which typically will appear by the time the child is 4 years of age. A further visual discrimination that has important implications for early learning processes is that of color recognition. For the most part, color recognition is well established by the time the child is 5 years of age.

Summary. There are many complex factors that contribute to the advances in development during early childhood. Growth of muscle size, practice of motor skills, continuing organization of associations between established neural pathways, and the establishment of new pathways represent

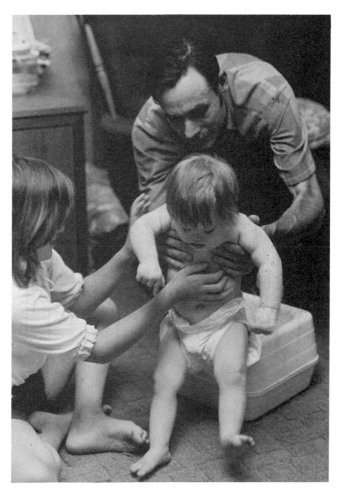

Fig. 7-2. Interaction with all members of the family fosters positive growth of the retarded child. (Photograph by Peter Poulides.)

Table 1. Selected developmental landmarks

	Months							
	1	2	3	4	5	6	7	8
MOTOR								
Sitting				◁		◁	(Supported)	
Walking								
Sucking								
Standing								◁
Crawling							◁	
Creeping								
Bowel control						◁		
Bladder control								
Head: prone		◁ Lifts head ✕						
sitting			◁ Bobs ✕					
PSYCHOSOCIAL								
Smiling				◁Spontaneous✕			Mirror image	
Reacting to others			◁ Follows moving people✕				Discriminates	
Feeding					(Solids)			(Holds)
Socialization		◁						
VERBAL								
Crying								
Cooing			◁		✕			
Babbling, resembles one syllable							◁	Tone
Imitation of word sounds								
Some word understanding (dada, mamma)								
Word repertoire								

	Months															
9	**10**	**11**	**12**	**13**	**14**	**15**	**16**	**17**	**18**	**19**	**20**	**21**	**22**	**23**	**24**

Without support

Supported   Without support

(Utility decreases with use of other feeding means)

Supported   Without support

(Sex differences)

Sustains raised head

Steady

strangers   Waves goodbye

bottle)   Cup   Part. self-feed

Forms primary social relations and emotional attachments

differentiation)

3 to 50 words   50+ begin phrases

only a portion of the developmental process that is underway. In addition, it is during this period that the ability to maintain focal attention emerges, which is a hallmark of the age of early childhood. Incredible gains are evident in cognitive and intellectual function, memory, consciousness, and thought. The role of each of the structures in the nervous system, with regard to the various forms of mental retardation, is not well understood presently. It is apparent, however, that an inadequacy in one dimension of the development of the nervous system is typically accompanied by inadequacies in the system generally. Thus, the child who evidences developmental delays in motor performance during early childhood frequently also exhibits delays in emotional development, language development, and cognitive development since each of these dimensions of performance depends on the general adequacy of the nervous system. Table 1 summarizes selected developmental landmarks during the first 2 years of life in terms of a few motor, psychosocial and verbal developmental features. As noted before, a child observed to be delayed in one area of development is likely also to exhibit signs of delay in other areas. Such a child's behavior generally may be more like that of children who are chronologically younger.

Effects of the environment

A variety of processes involved in development have been discussed and examined. As noted in these discussions, each capability of the child, each function, has an optimal time during the developmental cycle for its appearance and integration into the system as a whole. The child's development of these specific capacities during such periods appears to be vulnerable to disruption that may result in either temporary or permanent problems. Some of these disruptions may occur as a result of environmental influences. The effects of specific environmental conditions or stimuli on the young child are generally recognized to be great, although the exact nature of influences by specific environmental conditions remains poorly understood (Wright, 1971). An early theory developed by Hebb (1949) provides some interesting interpretations of the possible effect of early deprivation or stimulation of the neurological system and the effect of such conditions on later intellectual functioning.

Hebb postulated that the human brain is comprised of two interrelated types of tissue, sensorimotor and associative. It was his view that sensorimotor tissue is primarily determined genetically and provides for the reflexive, sensory, and motor functions of the body. Associative tissue, on the other hand, is partially determined by genetic endowment but must be developed and established through environmental stimulation, mainly occurring during the first 2 years of life. Hebb believed that the nature of this development (of associative functions) would determine the extent of development of future intellectual capacity of the individual. The manner in which this stimulation and development transpires was thought to underlie the higher cognitive functions of the brain. The major portion of the child's behavioral repertoire during the first 2 years is less complex than in later life and is largely supported by the sensorimotor functions of the brain. Consequently it is a wealth of sensorimotor experiences that substantially contribute to the development of associative tissues and functions in the first 2 years. Hebb's theory has not been subject to direct empirical testing and consequently it is not known whether this represents an accurate account of actual neurological development during early life. His theory has, however, stimulated investigation aimed at examining the influence of early environmental experiences. Investigations focusing on the effects of early environmental experience represent an important endeavor in the field of mental retardation and behavioral science in general. Such studies that have supported the importance of early stimuli have not accumulated enough evidence to draw definitive conclusions, although certain trends are beginning to emerge. For example, extreme environmental deprivation, particularly during the early childhood period, appears to be a rather potent influence and one that seems quite unfavorable. Such extreme deprivation has been observed to result in pervasive developmental delays and mental retardation (Zubek, 1969). Perhaps the most dramatic of this evidence involved early observations made on children who had been subjected to accidental conditions or cultural patterns that resulted in extreme deprivation early in life (Mason, 1942; Gesell, 1941).

Considerable evidence has been provided regarding the influence of sensory deprivation during early life in terms of visual stimuli. In large part this information has resulted from studies that involve the restoration of vision after the early developmental period during which the child was blind (Gregory and Wallace, 1963; London, 1960). In this research, individuals of various ages beyond the preschool period received visual stimuli for the first time. This unique source of investigation has mostly been made possible by surgical removal of congenital cataracts and by corneal transplants. After surgery *and* a period of study to learn the meaning of the visual stimuli subjects continued to experience difficulty in pattern discrimination and generalizability. Despite the fact that subjects were able to learn that a particular symbol was a triangle or a square, they had great difficulty perceiving the image as such without relying on ancillary aids to recognition (for example, counting the number of corners). Furthermore, subjects might recognize a geometric shape as being a square when presented on paper but could not recognize the same shape in another format such as a box.

It is difficult to determine the meaning of such extreme evidence for less extreme instances of sensory deprivation that may occur with young children in relatively deprived environments. It seems reasonable to expect that a child who does not have an opportunity to experience and practice certain sensorimotor skills will not have the opportunity to develop such specific motor capacities. However, the effects of such a situation on later development of intellectual functioning remains uncertain. Hebb's position would suggest that a wealth of sensory stimulation during the first 2 years, regardless of the type or nature of such stimulation, would promote favorable development of the cognitive and intellectual skills of the individual. There is some evidence suggesting that the greater the variety of stimuli and the number of situations that promote modification of conceptualization, the more mobile and differentiated the mental structure becomes (Whiteman and Deutsch, 1968). Limited environmental stimulation, a lack of systematic or ordered interpretation and mediation, or limited motivation may bring about stimulus deprivation and, with it, limitations in the development of intelligence.

Research on the effects of deprivation is faced with a number of limitations that prevent a systematic accumulation of data. Ethical considerations regarding the use of human subjects clearly and appropriately prevent the experimental manipulation of stimulus deprivation in a manner that may be harmful to the subjects. Occurrences of natural events that result in environmental deprivation are unsystematic and involve such situational variation that investigation of these instances provides data of only limited value. Studies such as the one on early visual deprivation are rather few in number and have become even more so as a result of advances in medical technology. Because of these serious limitations, many researchers have turned to the study of stimulus enrichment in an effort to gather evidence pertaining to the meaning of environmental sensory stimuli on the development of intellectual functioning. One approach to this type of investigation compares the functioning of young children who have received a natural wealth of sensory stimulation as infants with that of children who received a relative lack of such environmental stimulation. Although the evidence appears to suggest some differential effect, the data are too global to draw definitive conclusions. Such investigations also are not free of difficulties since, in many cases, it is not clear that the presence or relative absence of environmental stimulation is the only influential variable.

A classic study on the effects of early stimulation was reported by Skeels and Dye in 1939. These investigators focused on the influences of stimulation on children under 3 years of age and compared two groups of institutionalized infants placed in two different types of environments. Thirteen infants with IQ scores ranging from 35 to 89 were placed in wards of an institution for retarded children where attendants and older retarded females provided them with a great deal of attention and stimulation. Following a year and a half of this type of treatment, the IQ scores of the children had increased 27.5 points. The comparison group (twelve infants with IQ scores ranging from 50 to 103) remained in the orphanage, where attention and stimulation were minimal. This latter group of children evidenced a drop of 26.2 IQ points during the same period of time. As noted, however, it is not clear in studies such as this whether differences between the two groups are caused by the sensory stimulation itself or other related factors in combination with the stimulation. Additionally, while it seems apparent that stimulation may influence the rate of development, it is not clear whether stimulation is responsible for any lasting effect on the quality of function for normal children.

There have also been investigations undertaken that have attempted experimentally to manipulate sensory stimulation during the first few years of life (White, 1967; Ottinger, Blatchley, and Denenberg, 1969; Greenberg, Uzgiris, and Hunt, 1968). In large part these studies have focused on the influences of visual stimulation during the early months of life and have demonstrated significant effects of controlled stimulation on the rate and quality of specific aspects of development. Once again, whether such effects are lasting or significant with respect to the quality of future intellectual function remains unanswered. Additionally, investigations that experimentally manipulate environmental stimuli are not without some problems. Although fundamentally more sound from a research design standpoint, such studies have raised certain ethical questions relative to the experimental manipulation itself. The concern is focused on the ethical appropriateness of providing stimulation to one group while not providing (thus denying) such treatment to the comparison group or groups. These are difficult questions without easy solutions, but they do represent significant problems in terms of the accumulation of a solid data base.

One notable *long-range* study has been undertaken, and a preliminary report has been presented concerning early and intensive stimulation (Strickland, 1971). Data from this investigation indicate substantial evidence regarding the effectiveness of an early, intensive stimulation program on the development of disadvantaged infants in Milwaukee, Wisconsin. The infants were born to mothers who were assessed as having IQ scores of less than 70. The infants were placed randomly in experimental and control groups. The experimental program of sensory stimulation began in the home shortly after birth, and then the child was brought daily to a center for a regular, planned stimulation program continuing over a period of 5 years. At the conclusion of the study, there was a significant difference in the level of intellectual functioning between the experimental and control groups, with the experimental group of infants estimated to have an average IQ score of 33 points higher than the control group.

As additional research emerges regarding the effects of stimulation of the nervous system during the first 2 years of life, it may be possible to draw more accurate conclusions about the relationship of the development of this system to the nature of intellectual function later in life and to determine the vulnerability of the system to the environment during the first 2 years of life. It appears reasonable at this time to conclude that sensory stimulation may provide some benefit in affecting the rate and perhaps the quality of all developmental traits that depend on the development of the neurological system.

Professional and parental intervention

Major concerns among professionals working with infants and young children include identification of children who begin to display developmental delays, prevention of the occurrence of delays when possible, and assistance to the child and family when a developmental problem is present. Professionals who most often come in contact with children during the infancy and preschool years are health care workers, particularly physicians and public health nurses. These individuals frequently depend on the aid and cooperation of social workers, nutritionists, and dietitians to assist in providing comprehensive services to families who have multiple problems and needs.

Screening represents a very important process in the overall evaluation schema as indicated in Chapter 4. This is particularly crucial in terms of identifying children who may be exhibiting delays in rate and quality of development. The American Academy of Pediatrics has established standards for child health care that recommend monthly screening of all infants during the first 6 months of life, with intervals increasing gradually until the child is seen yearly throughout the preschool period. These health care visits should include an assessment of the child's behavior at home since the last visit, the child's health status, and the child's eating patterns. Additionally, the child's physical systems are evaluated, including the neurological system, in order to determine the adequacy of development, and behavioral observations are recorded to confirm the appearance of behavioral landmarks at each appropriate age. Each visit should also include discussion and guidance sessions with the child's parents related to developmental and health status. Finally, the child is given immunizations to prevent serious contagious disease, and laboratory testing of the blood and urine is undertaken at regular intervals. Developmental guidance should be given to the family in an effort to prevent accidental problems and to alleviate conditions that may lead to problems.

Routine health care, such as that described, is an important means of identifying unexpected developmental problems but becomes even more crucial for the family of the child when a problem has been identified. The child who is mentally retarded or otherwise handicapped and the family need a great deal of support and assistance to meet the challenges of daily care and health maintenance. The health care team is well equipped to provide such assistance.

Prevention of mental retardation has always been a matter that professionals in the field have viewed favorably and have sought to achieve. It is not, however, a subject that can be easily conceptualized or one that is without some controversy (as we will see in Chapter 14). One of the major difficulties in conceptualizing prevention is the field of mental retardation itself. Mental retardation, as a condition, is an extremely heterogeneous phenomenon. It varies greatly in terms of causation, condition severity, environmental circumstances, and professional disciplines attending to the problem. By now it is clear to the reader that mental retardation is a problem with many faces, it is sociocultural, psychological, and biomedical, to name only a few. Given this brief recount of the complex nature of the problem, it is not surprising that prevention, conceptualized in any sort of global fashion, is most difficult. There have, however, been some notable prevention successes if only in a limited way.

The screening and treatment for the enzyme-deficiency disease phenylke-tonuria (see Chapter 6) is a classic example of an instance in which a definitive problem and subsequent treatment can result in prevention of mental retardation. This also represents a situation in which continued assistance for the family from the health care team is critical. The child must be placed on an extremely restricted and expensive diet in order to offset the enzyme deficiency. This may place certain pressures on the family, and maintenance of adequate balanced nutrition for the child and for the entire family may be a serious problem. Additionally, the child's health may be jeopardized in other ways, such as susceptibility to infection.

Well-defined prevention programs, such as that implemented with phe-nylketonuria, are somewhat scarce. However, theories like Hebb's and the results of research such as that described earlier have stimulated considerable interest among health care workers with regard to the identification of families and children who are *at risk* because of inadequate environmental stimulation. Health care workers are often the only professional people who are in contact with such families on any sort of widespread basis. The task of identification of such problems is therefore most logically approached from a health care standpoint if significant impact is to be expected. Nurses and child development specialists have begun to institute programs of environmental stimulation and enrichment in many communities. As the programs develop, research evidence will be forthcoming and hopefully will add to our understanding of the effectiveness of this type of intervention.

Enhanced stimulation is also generating increased interest in terms of intervention beyond the prevention arena. When a child is identified as already being mentally retarded and developmentally disabled, health care workers and child development specialists have often begun infant stimulation programs as a means of assisting the child in developmental progress. As the limited research findings suggest, such intervention in field settings has resulted in rather notable progress. Children whose physical neuromotor development would otherwise be expected to be significantly delayed have shown impressive acceleration of physical development. For example, a child with Down's syndrome is typically delayed by several weeks or months in all aspects of neuromotor development. These delays typically include such areas as sitting, crawling, walking, talking, and feeding.

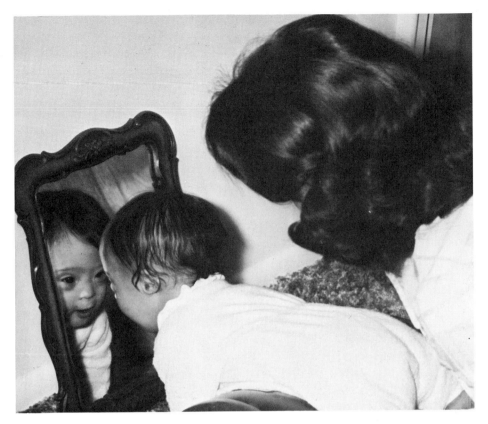

Fig. 7-3. Infant-stimulation programs include a variety of activities involving parents.

Infant stimulation programs focus on systematic, planned stimulation of the infant in all sensory modalities. The desired result of such programming is acceleration of the child's development so that these skills appear at a time more nearly consistent with that expected of normal children of the same chronological age. It is believed that all six perceptual systems must be stimulated. This multiple stimulation may not be undertaken at any single session; for example, one perceptual system at a time may be involved in stimulation instructions that are provided on a given occasion. This is often done to enhance clarity and specificity for the parent who may frequently be involved heavily in program implementation. However, at some point during the program each of the senses are the focus of stimulation, including vision, hearing, touch, kinesthetic movement, smell, and taste. Thus the parent may be instructed to bang a particular kitchen pot with a spoon near the infant, to rattle a toy, and generally to present as many hearing stimuli as possible to attract the infant's attention. As the infant responds, other perceptual systems may be stimulated, and then these same stimuli are repeated but at different distances from the child. Frequently the next step involves engaging the infant in active participation in the stimulation program. As this is undertaken, the child may be encouraged to hold the sound-producing spoon, to move the rattle, to manipulate soft cotton or the hard rock, and so forth.

It should be particularly noted that most children who are born into families with sufficient economic resources receive a wealth of stimulation in all sensory modalities. Such stimulation is a routine part of their environment and results from ordinary interactions and activities of the family. For the most part these infants are wanted and loved; they are held and carried, cuddled, talked to, placed near the activities of the other children and adults in the family, and taken in the car for trips into the community. These all are involved as a natural part of each day's activities. However, many infants are born into environments lacking some or all of these features that are taken for granted by the average middle-class family. The world of these children may have substantially less stimulation than is characterized by that of the middle-class environment. During their early months, they may spend a great deal of time alone, in a room with little color and limited interaction with other people. When they are fed or changed, they may be handled only on a limited basis, and the bottle often may be propped for feeding. Early experiences outside of this meager environment may not exist at all.

Instances of reduced stimulation may also be found in other situations; for example, a relative lack of stimulation may be afforded the child who is born with a significant physical handicap, even if the family is not of limited means. Such a child may be difficult for the family to look at or to interact with and consequently may be excluded from the activities of the family to a considerable extent. This child is not the beautiful baby the family had anticipated and therefore may not be carried into the community to participate in the routine activities of the family.

Establishment of a planned sequence of stimulation programming for these types of situations is one effort to provide an environment for the infant that more closely resembles the richness of experience of most children. It should be emphasized that the justification for such a program does not rest on the valuation of a certain life-style found in "middle" America. Instead it is based on the belief and accumulating evidence that such stimulation is of benefit to the intellectual development of the child. The stimulation programs draw heavily on the environment of the child's home, regardless of socioeconomic level. A family of limited income in a home with modest furnishings can provide interaction patterns and sensory stimulation that are equally significant to those found in a family of greater income.

LANGUAGE DEVELOPMENT

By now it is obvious to the reader that mental retardation may manifest itself in a variety of ways and in a variety of behavioral domains. Perhaps the most serious and obvious deficit that is often evident involves delayed language development. Depending on the specific situation, there may even be a total absence of expressive language. It is quite common for parents and teachers to attribute most, if not all, of the retarded child's learning problems to language deficiencies. Several authorities seem to share this perception or at least highlight the apparent interrelationship between language and intellectual functioning. For example, Berry and Eisenson (1956) note that, "Low intelligence undoubtedly is responsible for many cases of delay in speech, but speech delay is the cause for such apparent low intelligence." Another early statement was presented by Van Riper (1963) who postulated that more intensive language training might well be the key to educating the mentally retarded. He stated:

> It is quite possible that many children appear, or even become, mentally retarded, because they never learn to speak. Thinking, perceiving, remembering, predicting—all of these require the use of symbols. . . . It is true that mental deficiency can cause delayed speech; it is also true that delayed speech can contribute to mental retardation.

Normal language development

The development of language has received some discussion in earlier parts of this book. Reference to Table 1 (pp. 184-185) also provides some limited guidelines to normal developmental landmarks, including certain language and prelanguage behaviors. It is commonly agreed that the normal progression of language development represents an important indicator of general cognitive maturation. Menyuk (1972) summarizes ages at which gross linguistic behaviors appear in normal children in the following manner:

Birth	Crying and making other physiological sounds
1-2 months	Cooing as well as crying
3-6 months	Babbling as well as cooing
9-14 months	Speaking first words as well as babbling
18-24 months	Speaking first sentences as well as words
3-4 years	Using all basic syntactic structures
4-8 years	Articulating correctly all speech sounds in context

This would suggest that, for the normal child, the basic language structure is largely intact somewhere between 4 and 8 years of age. Certainly as maturation continues beyond this point, language facility also tends to grow and expand. Such growth, however, appears largely to represent an embellishment of existing structures.

The processes involved in language development have been the source of considerable theoretical debate. A substantial portion of this debate began in 1957 with the publication of B. F. Skinner's *Verbal Behavior*. It was his contention that verbal behavior is behavior that is reinforced through the mediation of other people who, themselves, must have a prolonged history that has conditioned them in ways of *"precisely"* reinforcing the speaker (Skinner, (1957). Additionally, the mediation of others and the reinforcing consequences are continually important to maintenance of the verbal behavior after initial acquisition. This view of language development is at variance with those of Chomsky (1957) and Lenneberg (1969) who maintain that language is an innate capacity that is species specific to humans and dependent on the maturation of the brain and nervous system.

Lenneberg (1969) appears to be diametrically opposed to Skinner's position and discards learning theory as representing a relevant explanation for language development. His basis for this view is that the onset of language occurs in all children at about the same age in all cultures of the world despite the vast differences between cultures. Lenneberg also notes that language may be impaired by specific lesions in the brain that leave other mental and motor functions intact. He asserts that teaching cannot result in language acquisition unless the individual has the innate biological propensity for language.

Chomsky (1957) takes a position that is somewhat more of a theoretical compromise and recognizes that reinforcement may play some role in language development. However, the role of reinforcement, according to Chomsky, operates along with natural inquisitiveness, casual observation, a strong tendency to imitate, and an extraordinary capacity to generalize, hypothesize, and process information. These latter capacities are viewed as operating in a very complex manner that may be largely innate or may develop through some sort of learning or maturation of the nervous system. From Chomsky's position, *language results from rule-governed processes*, and it is these processes that account for the suddenness and complexity of the child's language development.

The controversy and theoretical debate concerning language development has vastly enriched the basis for consideration of how it occurs. Although it is somewhat unfortunate that so much energy has been expended in controversial debate and theoretical refutation, the value of such thinking should not be overlooked. Each of these theorists have contributed substantially from very different positions, and their hypotheses will surely blend in some fashion in the future as we unravel the processes of normal language development.

Delayed language development

There is little question that language development is commonly delayed or retarded among those who are mentally retarded. Although there are not identifiable language development scales that are specifically aimed at the mentally retarded child, normative language development instrumentation is useful insofar as it helps to identify the extent to which delay or deficiency exists. A variety of language development scales have been constructed over the years. (Lillywhite, 1968; Hedrick and Prather, 1970; Clark, 1973; Murdock and Hartman, 1974). Some of these scales include the phonological (sounds), semantic (meaning), morphological (word forms), and syntactical (word order) skills acquired by normal children. All of these areas of assessment appear important to an evaluation of language development both for children who appear to be progressing normally and those who exhibit delay. For the most part, language development scales focus on the periods from birth to 5 or 10 years of age, which seems appropriate in terms of general child development processes. Such instrumentation, plus that discussed in Chapter 4, provides a significant armory for those attending to language development and particularly to language development that appears delayed or deficient.

It is obvious that delayed language development presents a difficult problem, particularly in our contemporary society. The precise manner in which delayed language relates to reduced intellectual functioning, or mental retardation, is unclear. It is not a characteristic that can be simply analyzed as suggested by the quotations by Berry and Eisenson (1956) and Van Riper (1963). Hass and Hass (1972) draw some analogies that may be enlightening if not accurate. They suggest that the communicative plight of the severely retarded 10-year-old child, who has been institutionalized for several years, might be likened to that of an English-speaking college student in France who finds that school-acquired French does not adequately communicate. They further suggest that such a child might be in somewhat the same position as an anthropologist in a newly discovered primitive culture who also fails to communicate successfully with the people encountered in this culture. Hass and Hass suggest that (1) all the college student must do is master some of the surface features of French, since the semantic representation and basic communication skills are already functional, and (2) the anthropologist may make significant progress based on theoretical background and experience. However, the retarded child may well be faced with a very different problem. Such a child may have to construct the entire experiential organization and content on which linguistic and/or cognitive variations are based. This problem may represent a task that is vastly more complex and difficult than that faced by the college student or anthropologist.

Some efforts have been undertaken that are aimed at rehabilitation of language delay with the mentally retarded. Unfortunately, language rehabilitation efforts with this population in general have lagged for many years because of attitudes and perceptions held by many speech and language specialists, a substantial number of whom have opposed working with the mentally retarded on the grounds that speech and language rehabilitation is almost impossible for these individuals. Such attitudes, although regrettable, are somewhat understandable in view of some of the theoretical formulations concerning language development that have been presented. If the position that language development is "innate" to humans is accepted, many retarded children would have to be rejected for speech and language therapy since language may not appear to be "innate" for them. Other theoretical schemes seem to provide a more optimistic outlook for the mentally retarded; for example, the B. F. Skinner provides a strong theoretical basis for working with children whose language skills fail to develop normally.

It was noted before that some efforts have been underway with regard to language rehabilitation with the mentally retarded. A number of these have been based on Skinner's approach. Several research projects have focused on the establishment of imitative repertoires in retarded children in order to facilitate speech and language development (Baer and Guess, 1971; Baer, Peterson, and Sherman, 1967; Schumaker and Sherman, 1970; Garcia, Guess, and Byrnes, 1973). These investigations have resulted in a number of outcomes that appear promising. Although the details varied between studies, the major conclusions included the following:

1. Imitation apparently can be trained in children who initially did not have significant imitative behavioral repertoires.

2. Imitation combined with differential reinforcement can be used to train for both simple naming or labeling responses as well as generative repertoires of plurality, simple sentences, and verb tense usage.

3. Imitation can be regarded as a particular type of learning set that exemplifies the rule "do as the model does."

4. Language development and consequent behavior that is "rule governed" can be rather directly related to simple training procedures of differential reinforcement and fading, which teach a child to match a series of different behaviors that are modeled.

5. A child with a widely generalized imitative repertoire can be significantly influenced by language models in the environment. Such generalization is essential to the normal acquisition of speech and language.

Some of the results summarized above have prompted the development of programming approaches to language development stimulation that may well alter the course of progress in the mentally retarded child (Sloane and MacAulay, 1968; Schiefelbusch, 1972; McLean, Yoder, and Schiefelbusch, 1972; Gray and Ryan, 1973).

COGNITIVE DEVELOPMENT

The term *cognitive development* generically refers to an individual's developing capacity to formulate mental patterns. Ordinarily, perception refers to sensory experiences received from the environment, whereas cognition is used with respect to the meaning and thought patterns that emerge as a result of combinations of perceptions. Although these definitions vary to some degree, depending on context and the authority consulted, our purpose is served well by these concepts as described. In this section we briefly discuss the work of selected theorists who have given attention to cognitive development and implications for mental retardation.

Theoretical formulations

One individual who has contributed significantly to the theoretical consideration of cognitive development is Jean Piaget. His work has been reviewed in previous chapters and has been noted as being under heavy criticism currently (Flavell, 1977). However, Piaget's theoretical formulations remain worthy of discussion, particularly in the context of cognitive development. Unlike most theorists, Piaget was primarily interested in the functions and structures of intelligent activity rather than the content of intelligence per se. He outlined stages of intelligence development that change both quantitatively and qualitatively throughout the developmental period. It was Piaget's contention that, although different children progress through various stages at different rates, the sequence of progression is always the same. The developmental stages in Piaget's theory are marked by the most recently emerging capability of the child. It is important to remember, however, that behaviors and processes that preceded a given stage continue to occur and may evidence a greater intensity and frequency than the newly emerging function.

Piaget's formulations provide an interesting framework from which to view cognitive development in mentally retarded children. It is speculated that retarded children, particularly those who are only mildly handicapped, progress gradually through Piaget's developmental stages in structural terms, although the rate of progress is somewhat slower than for normal children. This progression is largely demonstrable despite the fact that most retarded individuals do not seem to develop spontaneously beyond the first two periods of sensorimotor and concrete operations. Thus mentally retarded children often appear to possess a cognitive structure somewhat typical of children who are younger in terms of chronological age.

From Piaget's perspective the child's cognitive capacities unfold naturally although the influence of the environment is substantial. It is through adaptation to the environment that the child shapes the exact nature of structures that unfold. A child's readiness to develop the next sequence of intellectual structure is governed largely by the neurological capacity or readiness of the system, whereas the stimulus for actual progression into the next stage is provided by the environment. This view of cognitive development appears to have substantial implication for teaching retarded children since education attempts to present an environment that will stimulate development of maximum potential. For Piaget, conceptualization of an idea precedes verbalization. In other words, children must experience and understand a phenomenon actively in the real world before they are able to put the event into words and demonstrate mastery of the problem. Children who are given opportunities to encounter life experiences appropriate to their stage of cognitive development can be assisted in growth and development of cognitive potential through appropriate environmental stimulation. As we progress in unraveling the complex interactions between system maturation and the environment, we may find that developing cognitive abilities can be more centrally a focus of the teaching process than has been the case in the past (Valett, 1978).

Cognitive development in mentally retarded individuals has been of particular interest to behavioral scientists for many years. In 1944, Inhelder, for example, proposed a system of classifying the retarded according to cognitive development. It was Inhelder's view that severely retarded individuals are fixated at the level of sensorimotor intelligence. This interpretation would suggest that such individuals simply repeat over and over again the innate behaviors that are observed at birth with very little knowledge about the objects with which they interact. Those who advance further within the sensorimotor stage are more closely oriented to the world around them, recognize familiar objects, and demonstrate intentionality in their behavior. They may be able to use trial and error experimentation with objects in their environment in order to produce a novel effect. Assimilation and accommodation may be clearly differentiated, and the individual may actively seek new accommodational experiences. A limited ability to use symbols to represent events that are not directly in the individual's perceptual field may also emerge, as well as the capacity to manipulate and combine these images or symbols. Such abilities may permit the use of rudimentary language and a beginning level of thinking and anticipation of events in the environment. Thus, even though such individuals may be severely handicapped when compared to those of normal intelligence and similar chronological age, they possess certain rather remarkable capacities that provide some potential for interacting with the environment and for learning.

Inhelder's classification scheme viewed the moderately retarded as incapable of progressing beyond the preoperational intuitive subperiod. From this perspective such an individual might evidence some functions similar to a normal child who is about 4 to 7 years old. These functions might include the ability to mentally grasp a complex of distinct and spatiotemporally separate events in succession. Inhelder would envision the moderately retarded as being aware of their own thought processes and able to distinguish truth from fantasy. At this level the cognitive system is thought to be capable of transcending time, space, and reality, and thus the capacity to think of past, present, and future exists at least to a limited degree. The moderately retarded are generally unable to conceptualize any other point of view than their own and thereby remain basically egocentric. Their conceptualization of the symbols used to represent reality remains concrete, and they depend substantially on perceptual experiences to provide mental representation of events. Attention is typically focused on the most immediate, interesting, and compelling attribute of an event, and there is a very limited ability to voluntarily transfer attention to another dimension of the situation. Similarly, the moderately retarded typically cannot mentally reverse an operation or an event in order to examine its components. They also exhibit a very limited capacity to reason logically. Thus, in general, the person functioning at this level of development has many signs of the ability to think and function in a manner much like an older child (for example, using language with reasonable effectiveness, getting along socially, adapting and solving some problems). These abilities are significantly limited, however, and the descriptions by Inhelder and Piaget have contributed to the understanding of cognitive difficulties encountered by individuals in this particular stage of development. The child who is of preschool chronological age and who exhibits some of the linguistic or cognitive behaviors typical of this developmental stage is tolerated well by society. The cognitive "mistakes" of such a child are deemed amusing or something that time will correct. The retarded adult, on the other hand, who functions at the preoperational subperiod, will have similar cognitive traits, but will be tolerated to a much lesser degree. Such a person is socially expected to function at a much more advanced cognitive level, and the limitations frequently become sources of distress to others. More often than not, the abilities that have been developed or can be developed are overlooked.

From Inhelder's perspective the mildly retarded individual may be viewed as being unable to progress beyond the level of concrete operations, and those who previously were classified as borderline retarded may be able to use simpler forms of formal operations when they reach adulthood. The person functioning at this cognitive level is able to move beyond what is expected for the normal preschool-age child and to use well-organized cognitive systems that permit much more effective coping with the environment. One significant development involves overcoming the tendency to stumble into perplexity and contradiction in thought—a characteristic typical of the preschool child. Cognitive operations develop, whereby the individual can engage in an advanced level of logic, establishing concepts and events of reality more systematically.

Implications for professional intervention

The specialist in early childhood education is perhaps the professional who is most intimately concerned with the cognitive development of the preschool child, whether retarded or of normal intelligence. The generic goal of early childhood education is primarily to provide an environment that stimulates maximum social and cognitive development. We have previously examined the important implications of early environmental stimulation for the development of optimal intellectual functioning later in life. As a child

Fig. 7-4. Many communities now provide preschool activities for the young retarded child. (Photograph by Peter Poulides.)

progresses beyond the age of 2, environmental stimulation appears to play a different role in relation to the child's development. During the first 2 years, general stimulation in a wide variety of areas seems to affect the individual's ultimate level of functioning. However, as the child enters the preschool period of 3, 4, and 5 years of age, such general sensory stimulation does not appear highly beneficial in the same manner. Instead, rather specific experiences with particular and focused stimulation seem now to become influential in the child's developmental progress. As expressed in Piaget's notions, conceptualization grows out of reality experiences, and then the child develops the capacity to represent this event symbolically both in thought and in language. The objective of the early childhood education specialist is to provide specific tangible experiences that are consistent with the cognitive capacity of the child and that stimulate the development of the cognitive structures. The initial challenge for the educational specialist working with a mentally retarded preschooler is to understand the level of cognitive development of the child. If, for example, the child is functioning at the sensorimotor stage and is thought to have potential for development into the preoperational thought period, the specialist may direct efforts toward preparing the child for preoperational thinking. This child may be given experiences with a variety of spatial problems, such as physical activities that provide a contrast between objects in the environment and the child and a recognition of how these objects can be manipulated and experienced in a consistent, predictable manner. Through such techniques the education specialist may build a program for the young child that facilitates progression into the next cognitive stage of development.

PSYCHOSOCIAL DEVELOPMENT

It is evident by now that the overall growth and development of the young child involves many different components. Each of these components are essential to the integrated whole with respect to development and are interrelated in a variety of complex fashions. Social-emotional development is one of these vital processes for the young child, regardless of intellectual capacity. The development of social and emotional functioning has pervasive effects on intellectual functioning of the child to the extent that when a child has a serious problem in psychosocial development, there is likely to be an inability to fulfill the intellectual potential that may be present. Thus the development of psychosocial functioning is a central concern for the young

Fig. 7-5. Sharing and peer interaction are important steps in the personal development of the young retarded child. (Photograph by Peter Poulides.)

child. We will explore several theoretical positions that have particular implications for the preschool period of development. Emphasis will be placed on the implications of each theory for the potential intellectual functioning of the child with normal intelligence as well as the preschool-aged, mentally retarded child.

Theoretical formulations

Theoretical formulations in the area of psychosocial development are somewhat different from those we have examined in other behavioral domains. In many cases the topics under discussion represent concepts that are very abstract and have been difficult (some contend impossible) to measure. This does not detract from the importance of considering their development; for, although their conceptualization may be abstract, few would deny that the concepts represent some aspect of reality in terms of behavior.

Development of trust, autonomy, and initiative. E. H. Erickson viewed child development primarily from a psychoanalytic perspective. Erickson hypothesized that infancy is the time in the child's life when the first social achievement is accomplished—that of basic trust. To the extent that the child's parents provide nurturance, familiarity, security, and continuity of experience, the infant is able to develop a basic sense of trust in both the immediate environment and the people in it. The infant's behavior reflects constant testing, experimenting, and exploring of the world in order to discover its predictability, or the extent to which it can be trusted. It was Erickson's notion that when an adequate mothering relationship is not present, the infant develops a sense of mistrust for the environment and the people in it. It was also his contention that such an experience is irrevocable and has an influence on the manner in which all subsequent stages evolve. Clearly all infants experience certain elements of trust and mistrust to some degree. It is the predominance of one over another that seems critical in determining the successful completion of this stage.

The development of autonomy and initiative are involved in Erickson's depiction of emotional development during early childhood. Initially the child undergoes a struggle to attain autonomy and a sense of self and of separateness. As part of this process, the child must overcome the hazards of doubt and shame. The child learns to exercise control over the processes of *having* and *letting go.* The family environment, in turn, offers restraint and freedom in an appropriate balance to permit the young child to experiment without becoming the victim of indiscriminate use of the abilities to hold on and to let go. As this process evolves, the child begins to develop a sense of autonomy, which is ultimately important in terms of further development of independent functioning.

Erickson also conceives of a second stage in early childhood that begins at about the end of the third year. This stage involves the struggle to gain a sense of initiative and to overcome the perils of guilt. The difference between this stage and the establishment of autonomy is likened to the difference between knowing oneself and knowing one's potential. In this process the child develops a sense of conscience, which is the regulatory or control function of the personality. If this function becomes overdeveloped, the individual may have a tendency toward being overly inhibited and even self-destructive with a diminished capacity for creativity and initiative. As with all developmental processes, the desirable outcome is dominance of the positive task accomplishment over the hazards of the stage.

Development of attachment. Attachment behavior is also thought to be an important emotional component of personality with considerable implication for future development. Bowlby (1969) views infancy as the crucial period for the emergence of this behavior. As attachment evolves, the reciprocal behaviors of the mother and other significant individuals are essentially caretaking behaviors. The infant's behavior reflects efforts to maintain proximity to the mother first and then to other members of the family who, in turn, reciprocate the expressed needs for proximity. There are many specific ways in which the older infant maintains proximity, although they seem to emerge in five basic patterns: sucking, clinging, following, crying, and smiling. Some of these behaviors are evident at birth but are manifested as the infant's self-directed attachment behavior at about the age of 4 months. As development progresses, the infant exhibits rather sophisticated goal-directed systems of behavior that maintain proximity to the mother. These systems of behavior usually become apparent between the ages of 9 and 18 months.

Visual and tactile contact are viewed as being crucial for the development of attachment behavior. The nature of visual and tactile interactions provides an important indication of the adequacy of attachment formation. Using mother as a base of security from which to operate, the infant explores the larger world but maintains visual contact during the process. Tactile contact is periodically reestablished, and then exploration continues. When the child becomes frightened, distressed, or uncomfortable for any reason, there is a tendency to establish contact that retains proximity to mother, such as clinging and following. When a serious threat of separation occurs, intense anxiety, anger, and violent distress result. These feelings and behaviors remain strong throughout infancy and are very apparent throughout early childhood, although they begin to lessen in intensity.

Environmental antecedents to self-esteem. There has been considerable interest in developing a better understanding of the influence of environmental factors on emotional and social development. Theoretical formulations concerned with this area typically have not been oriented toward child development, although the implications for infants and young children are substantial. Such theories also highlight the essential aspects of the environment that developmentally oriented theorists also discuss. The eminent therapist Carl Rogers has suggested that individuals need a psychological atmosphere of unconditional positive regard in order to develop to their full potential. This type of atmosphere logically must come from the significant others in one's environment and involves total and unconditional acceptance of the feelings and values of the young child. This does not, however, mean that others must always agree with the child, only accept the feelings and values as real to the child. Evaluative comparisons, rejecting judgments, lack of trust, and harsh punishment lead to the development of underlying doubts of worthiness and competence on the part of the child and may block the development of self-esteem, acceptance, and assurance.

Somewhat more recently, Coopersmith has studied the development of self-esteem and has formulated some theoretical propositions about young children (1967). Coopersmith's work focuses on factors involved in a child's social relationships that lead to optimal development of self-esteem in later life. It appears that children in families that convey to them the feeling that they are significant to the parents tend to develop high levels of self-esteem. Such feelings can be conveyed by parental attention and concern as well as by restrictions imposed regarding behavioral limits. In this type of familial environment the children are made aware of their successes, and they experience frequent success in their efforts toward development and learning. However, children in these types of families are also made aware of situations when success has not occurred and are encouraged to develop behavioral changes needed to achieve success and approval. Additionally, high self-esteem seems to be related to a high level of stimulation, activity, and vigor in the family. Typically there is a high level of communication among members of the family, including differences of opinion, dissent, and disagreement, leading to the development of mutual knowledge and respect.

Implications for intellectual functioning

The discussion presented previously suggests that many of the factors of major concern in psychosocial development are also recognized as important components in intellectual functioning; for example, the role of early stimulation is immediately apparent in both psychosocial and intellectual domains. Personality theorists focus on the crucial relationship of the infant or young child with at least one significant adult who provides necessary care and love for the child. This adult's attention and affection are primarily received by the child through the sensory channels that are so critical in the development of intellectual functioning. Thus it appears that there must be a significant interaction or interdependence between the development of psychosocial and intellectual functions, although the precise nature of this relationship is not currently understood. Children who are victims of the potential restriction of intellectual development through environmental deprivation are also likely to exhibit signs of attenuated emotional development. Such concomitant developmental inadequacies may be evident simply because of missing elements in the vital stimulation of sensory modalities that is required in order for each of these areas to develop properly. Additionally, the child who is unable to develop adequate emotional security, self-esteem, or social relationships with family members and peers is likely to be inhibited in intellectual performance. Whether the inhibiting influence becomes permanent or significant is probably a result of an interaction of a number of factors that have not been investigated sufficiently to draw reliable conclusions. It seems reasonable, however, to state that supporting optimal psychosocial development in early life is likely to have a favorable influence on the child's ability to function intellectually.

There appears to be very little understanding of specific psychosocial development in the mentally retarded infant or preschooler. It does seem that these children evidence developmental lags in the psychosocial features examined, since they remain dependent and relatively immature in social interactions for a prolonged period. It is not clear, however, whether this developmental lag arises from the intimately related neurological bases for both areas of development, or whether there is an environmentally generated psychosocial delay arising from the lack of interaction with significant adults. It seems reasonable to assume that the young retarded child might be expected to exhibit a developmental delay similar to that described cognitively with respect to Piaget's theory. However, all efforts possible should be undertaken to sustain an optimal level of psychosocial development for the retarded child.

Professional intervention

Psychosocial development in the mentally retarded child is no less important than for the child of normal intelligence. Professionals working with retarded children must be as concerned with this area of development as they are with cognitive domains. Such a child may be particularly at risk in terms of adverse environmental influences on emotional development because of unfavorable parental reactions. The family may need assistance from mental health specialists (psychologist, psychiatrist, psychiatric social worker) to facilitate the maintenance of optimal mental health and development for all family members. Particular needs may be evident in the parents as well as the retarded child. Such professionals may provide short-term assistance and intervention during periods of crisis, such as at the time of the child's birth, when the diagnosis of mental retardation is confirmed, or during periods of intense physical, social, or emotional stress in the family. Long-term assistance or intervention may be needed if the family experiences unusual or prolonged stress leading to disorganization of the family unit. It may be difficult for the family to accept such assistance since the emotional integrity of the family unit and the individual members is threatened. Accepting assistance often means recognizing a need that is most difficult to acknowledge and, for many families, represents a weakness or failure, which is shunned and avoided. Friends, health care professionals, or educators need to be alert to signs of a need for mental health intervention and should help the family reach a point of acceptance regarding such assistance.

In many cases the mental retardation is not apparent at birth. Under such circumstances the family often becomes aware of the child's handicap during the first months or years of life. It is not at all uncommon for the family to experience particular stress and crisis as members seek to allay their fears, restore their hopes for the normal, healthy baby they believed to exist, and reach some level of resolution concerning the reality of the situation. The longer the family has lived with the child believing that they had a healthy and normal baby, the more difficult the adjustment when they become aware of the mental retardation. Chapters 8 and 14 discuss further the difficult emotional complexities that families of retarded children experience.

STUDY QUESTIONS

1. Several notable behavioral scientists have postulated theories of language development. In some cases there is a great deal of variation and even disagreement among these theorists. Compare and contrast various theoretical formulations of language development, and suggest how each views the mentally retarded.
2. Both Rogers and Coopersmith have discussed environmental antecedents to the development of self-esteem. Examine these concepts and discuss their similarities and differences. Draw implications for development of self-esteem in the mentally retarded.
3. Early sensory stimulation appears to be important for both emotional and intellectual development. How are these two domains related with respect to the influence of sensory stimulation and development?

REFERENCES

Baer, D. M., and Guess, D. Receptive training of adjectival inflections in mental retardates. *Journal of Applied Behavior Analysis*, 1971, **4**, 129-239.

Baer, D. M., Peterson, R. R., and Sherman, J. A. The development of imitation by reinforcing behavioral similarity to a model. *Journal of the Experimental Analysis of Behavior*, 1967, **10**, 405-416.

Berry, M. F., and Eisenson, J. *Speech disorders: principles and practices of therapy.* New York: Appleton-Century-Crofts, 1956.

Bowlby, J. *Attachment and loss*, Vol. 1. New York: Basic Books, Inc., Publishers, 1969.

Chinn, P. L. *Child health maintenance: concepts in family centered care.* (2nd ed.) St. Louis: The C. V. Mosby Co., 1979.

Chomsky, N. *Syntactic structures.* The Hague: Mouton, 1957.

Clark, P. M. *Communication sequences (language).* Los Angeles: Los Angeles Unified School District, Title III ESEA, P.L. 89-10, 1973.

Coopersmith, S. *The antecedents of self-esteem.* San Francisco: W. H. Freeman and Co., Publishers, 1967.

Erickson, E. H. *Identity, youth and crisis.* New York: W. W. Norton & Co., Inc., 1968.

Flavell, J. *Cognitive development.* Englewood Cliffs, N.J.: Prentice-Hall, Inc., 1977.

Garcia, E., Guess, D., and Byrnes, J. Development of syntax in retarded girls using procedures of imitation, reinforcement and modeling. *Journal of Applied Behavior Analysis*, 1973, **5**, 299-310.

Gesell, A. *Wolf child and human child.* New York: Harper & Row, Publishers, 1941.

Gray, B., and Ryan, B. *A language program for the nonlanguage child.* Champaign, Ill.: Research Press, 1973.

Greenberg, D., Uzgiris, I. C., and Hunt, J. McV. Hastening the development of the blink-response with looking. *Journal of General Psychology*, 1968, **113**, 167-176.

Gregory, R. L., and Wallace, J. G. Recovery from early blindness. *Experimental Psychology Monograph*, 1963, Whole 2, Cambridge, England.

Guyton, A. C. *Textbook of medical physiology.* (4th ed.) Philadelphia: W. B. Saunders, 1971.

Hass, W. A., and Hass, S. K. Syntactic structure and language development in retardates. In R. L. Schiefelbusch (Ed.), *Language of the mentally retarded.* Baltimore: University Park Press, 1972.

Hebb, D. O. *The organization of behavior.* New York: John Wiley & Sons, Inc., 1949.

Hedrick, D. L., and Prather, E. M. *Sequenced inventory of language development.* Seattle: Child Development and Mental Retardation Center, 1970.

Inhelder, B. *Le diagnostic du raisonnement chez les debiles mentaux.* Neuchatel, Switzerland: Delechaux et Niestle, 1944.

Lenneberg, E. H. On explaining language. *Science*, 1969, **164**, 635-643.

Lillywhite, H. Doctor's manual of speech disorders. *Journal of The American Medical Association*, 1968, **167**, 850-851.

London, I. A Russian report on the post-operative newly seeing. *American Journal of Psychology*, 1960, **73**, 478-482.

Mason, M. K. Learning to speak after six and one-half years of silence. *Journal of Speech Disorders*, 1942, **7**, 295-304.

McLean, J. E., Yoder, D. E., and Schiefelbusch, R. L. (Eds.) *Language intervention with the retarded.* Baltimore: University Park Press, 1972.

Menyuk, P. *The development of speech.* Indianapolis: The Bobbs-Merrill Co., Inc., 1972.

Murdock, J. Y., and Hartmann, B. *A language development program: imitative gestures to basic syntactic structures.* Salt Lake City: Word Making Productions, Inc., 1974.

Ottinger, D. R., Blatchley, M. E., and Denenberg, V. Stimulation of human neonates and visual attentiveness. Read before APA, Washington, D.C., 1969.

Penfield, W. The uncommitted cortex, the child's changing brain. In H. W. Bernard and W. C. Huckins (Eds.), *Exploring human development: interdisciplinary readings.* Boston: Allyn & Bacon, Inc., 1972, P. 189.

Rogers, C. R. *Client-centered therapy: its current practice, implications and theory.* Boston: Houghton Mifflin Co., 1951.

Schiefelbusch, R. L. (Ed.) *Language of the mentally retarded.* Baltimore: University Park Press, 1972.

Schumaker, J., and Sherman, J. A. Training generative verb usage by imitation and reinforcement procedures. *Journal of Applied Behavior Analysis*, 1970, **3**, 273-287.

Skeels, H. M., and Dye, H. B. A study of the effects of differential stimulation. *Proceedings of the American Association of Mental Deficiency*, 1939, **44**, 114-136.

Skinner, B. F. *Verbal behavior.* New York: Appleton-Century-Crofts, 1957.

Sloane, H. N., and MacAulay, B. D. (Eds.) *Operant procedures in remedial speech and language training.* Boston: Houghton Mifflin Co., 1968.

Standards of Child Health Care, Council on Pediatric Practice. Evanston, Ill.: American Academy of Pediatrics, 1971.

Strickland, S. P. Can slum children learn? *American Education*, 1971, **7**(6), 3-7.

Valett, R. E. *Developing cognitive abilities: teaching children to think.* St. Louis: The C. V. Mosby Co., 1978.

Van Riper, C. *Speech correction: principles and methods.* (4th ed.) Englewood Cliffs, N.J.: Prentice-Hall, Inc., 1963.

White, B. L. *An experimental approach to the effects of experience on early human behavior.* Read before the Minnesota Symposium on Child Psychology, Minneapolis, 1967.

Whiteman, M., and Deutsch, M. Social disadvantage as related to intellective and language development. In M. Deutsch, I. Katz, and A. R. Jensen (Eds.), *Social class, race, and psychological development.* New York: Holt, Rinehart and Winston, Inc., 1968, P. 86.

Wright, L. The theoretical and research base for a program of early stimulation care and training of premature infants. In J. Hellmuth (Ed.), *Exceptional infant*, Vol. 2. New York: Brunner/Mazel, Inc., 1971.

Zubek, J. P. (Ed.) *Sensory deprivation: fifteen years of research.* New York: Appleton-Century-Crofts, 1969.

ANNOTATED BIBLIOGRAPHY

Chinn, P. L. *Child health maintenance: concepts for family centered care.* (2nd ed.) St. Louis: The C. V. Mosby Co., 1979.

The author provides a comprehensive summary of developmental learning theories and personality theories appropriate to physiology for all ages of childhood and gives information about the health care requirements of all children at different ages of life. Normative growth and development values that can be measured and observed are included, as well as a few standardized tools for such observations.

Hellmuth, J. (Ed.) *Exceptional infant*, Vol. 1. New York: Brunner/Mazel, Inc., 1967.

This book provides a useful compilation of selected articles related to normal development during infancy and studies recently conducted to establish normative information about the period of infancy. Of particular importance is the information related to the role of stimulation during infancy and the selection by R. H. Barsch that outlines a program for prescribed infant stimulation.

Hellmuth, J. (Ed.) *Exceptional infant*, Vol. 2. New York: Brunner/Mazel, 1971.

This volume provides further information related to examination and observation of the infant, particularly abnormal neurological aspects of behavior. Disorders of language and behavior are explored in particular depth.

Schiefelbusch, R. L. (Ed.) *Language of the mentally retarded.* Baltimore: University Park Press, 1972.

This book provides a useful source of information about language development of mentally retarded children, the problems encountered, and therapeutic approaches that may be used.

PART THREE

The retarded child during the school years

CHAPTER 8

The retarded child of elementary school age

(Photograph by Peter Poulides.)

INTRODUCTION

The beginning of elementary school is generally an exciting time for both children and their parents. It is a time to begin learning and to develop new friends and make new associations. Even for the normal child, the beginning of school is filled with many uncertainties as well as anticipations.

The age of 6 is traditionally the time for a child to enter the first grade. For the retarded youngster and his family, this may be the beginning of their difficulties related to mental retardation—for many parents the problems of mental retardation may at this time become a reality.

As previously stated, the majority of our retarded population fall into the educable group. Some children on the lowest end of the continuum will have been diagnosed as retarded prior to the age of 6. A larger percentage of retarded children will enter the first grade without their parents' realization of the academic and other problems that await them.

There may be good reason for many parents to be unsuspecting. Until this period in the child's life, there has probably been little if any emphasis on academics. The maturational lag may be so slight at this time that it may very well slip by unnoticed. For example, when a retarded child with a 70 IQ enters school at the age of 6, developmental lag may be only a year to a year and a half behind many of his normal peers. Compared to borderline-normal children of the same chronological age, the mental age difference may be just a matter of a few months.

With the passage of P. L. 94-142 (1975), we are concerned not only with the educable and the trainable retarded children but with severely and profoundly retarded children. Special educators refer to the first group as educable since these children can usually be educated in the traditional sense of reading, writing, and arithmetic. If developed to their full potential, these children may achieve second-, third-, and fourth-grade levels of performance. Occasionally higher levels of achievement may be attained in certain subjects, such as arithmetic computation. However, if the child consistently scores higher than that which is considered within the educable range on achievement tests, consideration should be given to rediagnosis.

The trainable group, however, lacks the academic ability of the educables. Classroom emphasis is usually placed on social, prevocational and self-help skills. Tool subjects in the past have been limited to reading and writing a few names and words such as warning and directional signs. However, during the late 1960's an emphasis on academics for the trainable mentally retarded began developing momentum in the public schools.

Fig. 8-1. Many skills that other children learn incidentally must be given deliberate attention by the home or school in training the mentally retarded child. (Photograph by Peter Poulides.)

Studies regarding the efficacy of academic programs for the trainable retarded have provided some encouraging results, suggesting that some trainable retarded can profit from academic experiences (Apffel, Kelleher, Lilly, and Richardson, 1975; Bellamy and Buttars, 1975; Richardson, Oestereicher, Bialer, and Minsberg, 1975). Litton, (1978) suggests that while functional academic skills were once considered beyond the capabilities of the trainable child, studies have indicated otherwise. He further suggests that rather than considering academic curriculum based on preconceived stereotyped ideas about their categorical level, educational programming should be based on the child's readiness and capabilities.

TRADITIONAL APPROACHES TO EDUCATING THE RETARDED
Special schools

Special education classes for the mentally retarded have usually followed one of two basic approaches, special schools and self-contained classes. Many if not most of the trainable classes have been located in special schools. These schools operate exclusively for handicapped children and are therefore isolated from the mainstream of education. Proponents of this arrangement argue that special schools provide services for large numbers of retarded children and therefore provide for greater homogeneity in the grouping and programming for children. They also support this type of arrangement because it allows teachers to specialize in their teaching areas. For example, one individual might decide to specialize in art for the retarded, another in physical education, and a third in music. In smaller programs where there are only one or two teachers, these individuals may be required to teach everything from art and home economics to academic subjects.

Special schools also provide for the centralization of supplies, equipment, and special facilities for the retarded. Smaller isolated programs may not be able to justify the purchase of expensive equipment used only occasionally, but the special school may be able to justify the expenditure because of more frequent use by a larger number of classes.

There are, however, large numbers of critics of the special school approach. These individuals contend that while administratively convenient to operate, special schools deprive retarded children of many of their basic rights. First, these schools are quickly identified as being different, being for the retarded. With a stigma attached to such schools, both the children and their parents may suffer. Critics also argue that the real world of society is not naturally segregated, and special schools remove children from the mainstream of society and education, depriving them of valuable experiences.

Self-contained classes

The other traditional approach to providing educational services to the retarded is the special self-contained classroom in the neighborhood school. These classes are utilized most frequently for educable children. However, some school districts may use them for trainable children as well.

To facilitate instruction, educable retarded children are often grouped in several different levels as homogeneously as possible. Groupings usually consider both chronological and mental age. In many cases smaller school districts find it necessary to group more than one level together. While such a practice may preclude desirable homogeneous programming, it is usually better than a total absence of special services.

The educable retarded child, if diagnosed early enough, may begin early childhood classes between ages 3 and 5. Some clinics may provide homebound programming from birth until the child is ready to enter early childhood classes. Preschool classes are usually for children in the chronological age range of 6 to 9 years and a mental age range of 3 to 5 years. The location of this class should be in an elementary school setting, and its activities should be similar to a nursery school program.

Prereadiness concepts and activities such as size, color, and sound discrimination as well as personal and social interaction skills should be emphasized at this level. Between the chronological ages of approximately 9 and 11, and the mental ages of about 5 to 6, the educable child should be in the next level, generally referred to as the primary class. In this class, readiness activities that approximate a kindergarten class are emphasized. These readiness activities are a preparation for the academics the child will face in the next level class. While these children may have mental development that is equivalent to their normal counterparts in kindergarten and while their activities are readiness types, as in many kindergartens, it should be remembered that these children may differ considerably from regular kindergartners. They may be 4 to 5 years older and more experienced, and their physical development may be quite comparable to normal children of the same chronological age.

The third level, most frequently called the intermediate level, is the last class to be situated in an elementary school. The children in this setting are usually about 11 to 13 chronologically or about 6 to 9 mentally. At this level the child is introduced to the basic tool subjects—reading, writing, and arithmetic. While emphasis at this level is on the communicative arts and mathematics, there is much that the special class child can learn at this level in preparation for vocationally oriented training at subsequent levels. At this level the students should become aware of employment opportunities in the community. They should know where people work, particularly those holding jobs suited for special class graduates. They should learn how to travel in the community—bus routes, fares, and transfers—so that they will eventually be able to travel to and from work. How proficient they become in mastering the tool subjects may not necessarily determine vocational success or failure, but may have an important bearing on the type and level jobs for which they may eventually be qualified.

TRENDS TOWARD MAINSTREAMING

With the passage of P. L. 94-142 (discussed in detail in Chapter 13) major emphasis has been toward providing educational programming for the retarded in the least restrictive environment. In some instances for the severely and profoundly retarded the least restrictive environment may be education in an institutional setting or a totally self-contained setting. For the majority of the retarded, however, particularly the mildly retarded, efforts have been made toward mainstreaming them into as much of the regular educational program as is possible. Efforts toward mainstreaming were already in effect in the early 1970's, even prior to the mandate of P. L. 94-142.

Mainstreaming does not merely imply placement in regular classrooms or spending time with nonhandicapped peers. Mainstreaming refers to "temporal, instructional, and social integration of eligible exceptional children with normal peers based on an ongoing, individually determined educational planning and programming process and requires clarification of responsibility among regular and special education administrative, instructional, and supportive personnel" (Kaufman, Gottlieb, Agard and Kukic, 1975).

Many advocates of mainstreaming have emphasized integration at all costs, even the total integration of trainable retarded students into regular education programs. During the earlier years in school, mainstreaming may not be as great a problem as it potentially may be in later years, as developmental differences between retarded students and their normal counterparts become greater. Even integration into "nonacademic classes" can present problems. Educators have at times identified such classes as physical education, home economics, shop, and music as typical nonacademic classes in which the mainstreaming transition can be made with the least amount of difficulty. Yet these educators fail to recognize that in many instances these so called "nonacademic" classes may be highly structured, and in some instances the degree of sophistication required to function in these classes may preclude successful experiences for the retarded. For example, it may be assumed that physical education is nonacademic in nature and, therefore, ideal for mainstreaming. Numerous games and athletic activities, however, are highly structured and require cognitive skills and linguistic understanding that the retarded student may not possess. These activities may also require certain motor skills that either may be lacking or deficient in retarded students in comparison to their counterparts. Thus, while the goal of integration into the mainstream of education may be accomplished, the positive benefits in some instances may be offset by the retarded child's failure to suc-

Fig. 8-2. Learning is often enhanced by children assisting each other.

ceed and the loss of self-respect and confidence from performing poorly before normal peers. Data on social acceptance of EMR students reintegrated into regular classes have consistently indicated that they are sociometrically rejected as potential friends more often than children who remain in regular classes (Goodman, Gottlieb, and Harrison, 1972; Gottlieb and Budoff, 1973; Gottlieb and Davis, 1973).

Hence, the term "least restrictive environment" can be interpreted in many ways. It may well be considered an interpretation that restricts the individual the least and yet allows for a positive educational experience.

It should be noted that properly placed retarded students in mainstreamed situations may profit from such experiences. Budoff and Gottlieb (1976) compared a group of special class EMR children who were assigned randomly to regular classes to a group who were retained in special classes. They found that after 1 school year the mainstreamed students were more internally controlled, expressed more positive attitudes toward school and toward themselves as students, believed others perceived them as more competent, and were more reflective in their behavior than when they were assigned to a special class.

In the effort to provide appropriate educational services for retarded children in the least restrictive environment, a number of options are available. It should be reemphasized that in the selection of the most appropriate instructional arrangements an individualized education program (IEP, as discussed in Chapter 13) must be developed for *each* child to ensure appropriate programming.

The most restrictive programming is probably the institutional setting. While restrictive in comparison to other instructional arrangements, institutional programming may be the most appropriate and viable means of providing educational services for some children.

Cluster and dispersal approaches. Sontag, Burke, and York (1976) suggest that cluster and dispersal approaches may be a consideration in providing services for severely handicapped students. In the cluster approach a large school district or several smaller districts *cluster* students in separate programs. More severely retarded students would probably be clustered with other individuals of various handicapping conditions, such as with multiple handicaps or severe emotional disturbance. Such arrangements have the advantage of being administratively and fiscally feasible to manage.

On the other hand, to some, clustering may be considered another form of institutionalization. Students will, by administrative fiat, be categorically excluded from normalization, or mainstream factors, as they relate to education. The educational community will be deprived of the opportunity of exposure and desensitization to individual differences. The special education students, on the other hand, will be deprived of interaction with other students.

A slightly less restrictive alternative is to *disperse* these special clustered classes throughout the school district. With this arrangement, the students

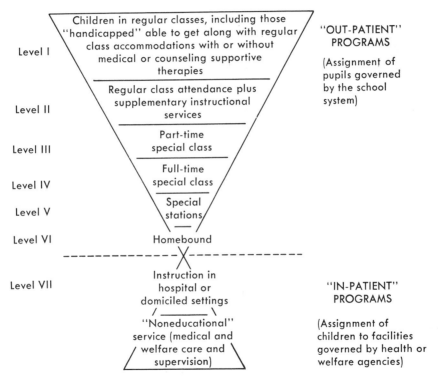

Fig. 8-3. The cascade system of special education service. The tapered design indicates the considerable difference in the numbers involved at the different levels and calls attention to the fact that the system serves as a diagnostic filter. The most specialized facilities are likely to be needed by the fewest children on a long-term basis. This organizational model can be applied to development of special education services for all types of disability. (From Deno, E. Special education as developmental capital. *Exceptional Children*, 1970, **37**, 229-337.)

would be represented in nearly every school, making contact with regular education programs and personnel and "normal" students. Since students may be dispersed into neighborhood schools, transportation may be more convenient than in clustered programs. Problems may develop, however, where neighborhood schools are not physically equipped to accommodate these students.

Educational goals for the more severely and profoundly retarded included physical development. By the time these children reach school they should be able to pull themselves erect, stand partially supported or alone, and eventually develop independent ambulation. Other goals include the establishment of functional independence with subgoals or skills such as self feeding, dressing, toilet use, grooming, motor skills, language development, and socialization (Luckey and Addison, 1976).

A current trend with the passage of P. L. 94-142 and the written IEP's, suggests a movement away from traditional IQ testing toward criterion referenced (as opposed to norm referenced) assessments. This type of assessment would provide a better view of the child's level of functioning. From observation of behavior and criterion referenced testing, educators should be able to determine appropriate educational goals and objectives for each student.

Deno (1970) has suggested a delivery system of services that may be not only more efficient administratively but also may be more fitting to individual needs and differences. Deno's cascade of services assumes that there exists a wide range of abilities and needs among handicapped children. Handicapped children at Level I (Fig. 8-3) are able to function with little if any special support services, while extensive support services are necessary at the lower end of the continuum.

Approaches to mainstreaming

Several types of programming have emerged, which have partially and in some instances totally replaced some of the self-contained models. These approaches, known as resource rooms, cooperative programs, itinerant resource personnel programs, and total integration, are neither completely new to special education nor unique to programs for the mentally retarded. Actually other areas of special education, such as for the visually impaired, have been utilizing resource, itinerant, and cooperative programs for many years. These programs share a common goal—to bring the children back into the regular classroom as much as possible and ultimately into a nearly normal life-style as adults.

The resource room. The resource room reflects a philosophy of sharing of responsibility between regular education and special education for the retarded children in a particular school. This program reflects an effort to integrate children as much as possible into regular education and still provide them with special education support services whenever they are needed.

In the resource program, retarded children are assigned to a regular education teacher (such as third grade, fifth grade) in elementary grades or to a regular education homeroom teacher in the upper grades. These children are primarily in regular education and will participate in as many regularly scheduled activities as possible. Assignments, with possible modifications, will approximate those of all other children. At designated times arranged between the two teachers, the children in the resource programs meet with the special education resource teacher.

The resource room teacher maintains a room within the school building and is a regular member of the school faculty. The special education teacher's function is essentially twofold. The first responsibility is to provide instructional support services to the handicapped child. These services may include orientation to the school for new students, tutorial services, counseling, and, if needed, the development of instructional aids. The second major function for the resource room teacher is to serve as a liaison between the regular classroom teachers and the child. It is the responsibility of the resource room teacher to facilitate understanding between the regular class teachers and the retarded child, to aid the regular class teachers in understanding the needs and the nature of retarded children, and to support the retarded child academically and in areas of personal and social adjustment.

The cooperative program. The cooperative program, like the resource room concept, involves the sharing of responsibility of the retarded child by both regular and special education. The major difference in the two programs rests in the area of primary responsibility. In the resource program, the retarded child is primarily a regular class student with support services from special education. In the cooperative program, the students are assigned to a special education teacher and class, remaining in the same room with the same teacher for a large portion of the day.

The "cooperative" aspect takes place during the remainder of the day when these retarded students are integrated into as many regular education activities as possible. In most instances the retarded child remains in the special classroom for the academically oriented subjects. The integrated classes are typically the less academically oriented ones, such as music, shop, home economics, physical education, art, and driver education. If the cooperative program functions as planned, the student will have the advantage of an unthreatening academic setting along with integration into the social mainstream. It should be noted that in some school district programs that are referred to as resource programs actually function as cooperative programs as we have described them.

The itinerant resource personnel. In the latter part of the 1960's and early 1970's, the Bureau for the Education of the Handicapped of the U.S. Office of Education established a small number of regional resource centers to research the feasibility and viability of itinerant resource programs. The projects have operated under the assumption that, while some handicapped children need extensive special services, there are others who are able to function well in regular classroom settings if the teacher is provided with ancillary services. The ancillary services are provided in the form of itinerant resource personnel who aid the teacher in the diagnosis of educational problems and prescribe or suggest methods and programs to remedy the problems.

The itinerant resource model avoids the traditional categorical approach to special education. While the children are diagnosed, the usual labeling of mentally retarded, learning disabled, and emotionally disturbed are discarded. Instead, attention is focused on the educational problems and methods of remediation.

Total integration. Another option—the one that represents the greatest degree of mainstreaming and the least restrictive environment—is total integration into all phases of the regular educational program. This alternative, like the others, is dependent on the individual needs of each child and the IEP that is developed to promote optimal educational opportunity.

Comments. Administrators and special educators are finding increasing demands placed on them to bring about program changes. Pressure has come not only from parents but also from the courts, which have declared certain organizational and administrative arrangements detrimental to the overall welfare of handicapped children (*Hobson vs. Hansen*, 1967; *Mills vs. Board of Education of the District of Columbia*, 1972).

All programs have advantages and disadvantages. Programs with seeming weaknesses may give better service to children than an organizationally strong program that does not provide adequate personnel or is poorly administered. It is the responsibility of the professionals in the field to provide the best possible programming and personnel to the children rather than mere administrative convenience, which has often been the primary concern (Spicker and Bartel, 1968; Drew, 1971).

The self-contained classroom, as previously pointed out, has often been criticized because it excluded the students from the mainstream of education. This program, however, had and still has its share of supporters. Some research has indicated that social adjustment for the retarded in self-contained classrooms may exceed that of retarded children left in regular education classes (Cassidy and Stanton, 1959). There are indications that retarded children in special classes have less fear of failure than retarded children in regular grades (Jordan and deCharms, 1959). It has also been suggested that children in special classes have a greater opportunity to excel and to become a "star" (Baldwin, 1958). Proponents will also argue that the self-contained class has a teacher who is thoroughly prepared and fully understands the needs and nature of retarded children.

The resource room program can be the answer to some of the criticism of the self-contained classroom. The program provides for the integration of retarded students with their normal counterparts. This program does generate certain criticisms, however. The curriculum for the normal child may not fit the needs of a retarded child. These curricular concerns tend to increase as the child progresses into the upper elementary grades, junior high school, and high school. Learning sentence structure such as nouns, adverbs, and adjectives in a seventh-grade English class may be of questionable value to a retarded adult.

As previously stated, the cooperative program seeks to integrate retarded students into so called nonacademic classes. Yet, as has been noted, many of these classes have activities so highly structured that retarded children may have difficulty functioning. While integration appears to be highly desirable in many instances, caution should be exercised to bring about the goal slowly enough to sensitize and educate regular classroom teachers to the needs and nature of the retarded.

The itinerant resource program has produced some initial benefits for handicapped children. With the itinerant personnel working in the regular classroom, segregation is limited or eliminated. In addition, the categorical designations are avoided, thus limiting the stigmatization.

Which program? There may never be a completely adequate rule of thumb to decide which program is best overall or best for particular types of children. Some programs will adequately fit the needs of some children while neglecting the needs of others. Some children may be so severely retarded or have other handicapping conditions that compound their problems that self-contained classrooms would be the most logical answer. While we may want to set a goal of integration whenever feasible, we should remember that one of the primary goals of special education is to recognize the individual needs and differences of exceptional children and to provide them with the types of programs and services that will foster and nurture optimal growth and development. Therefore, it is our position that all the above-mentioned programs have their merit for specific children. Rather than making gross administrative generalizations, the needs of each child should be assessed individually. Then each child should be placed in the educational setting that will facilitate the delivery of the IEP, which is tailored to the individual needs of each child and which will foster optimal growth.

•   •   •

Cognitive development, learning, personality, emotional developments, motivational problems, and physical and health characteristics of the mentally retarded and related theories will be discussed in the subsequent pages. In most instances, these characteristics and theories are not limited to retarded children of the elementary age. Rather, these characteristics may follow the retarded child throughout life. We have elected to present these concerns in this chapter, however, since it is often at the beginning of the school program that many of these concerns first manifest themselves to the professional working with the retarded individual.

COGNITIVE DEVELOPMENT

In order to understand the cognitive development of the elementary school age child, we again return to the theory of Jean Piaget. Piaget refers to the span of 2 to 7 years as the period of preoperational thought and the span from 7 to 11 years as the period of concrete operations. A few of the younger elementary school age children will be completing the preoperational thought period, and most will be functioning in the concrete operations period.

During the preoperations subperiod, perceptions are the dominant mental activity of the child. At about the age of 7, the child begins to move into a period where perceptions are dominated by intellectual operations, the dominant mental activity of the concrete operations period (Chinn, 1979). The ability to order and relate experiences to an organized whole begin to develop. Rather than being bound to irreversibility as before, the child begins to develop mobility in thought processes and can reverse some mental operations and return to the starting point.

By the age of 4 the child begins becoming less egocentric. By the period of concrete operations the child is able to take into account another person's point of view. Instead of centering on one dimensional property of a situation, the child is able to focus on several properties in sequence and move quickly from one to another.

This period is termed concrete because the child's mental operations still depend on the ability to concretely perceive what has happened. Mental experimentation cannot be performed without dependence on perception. Chinn (1979) states that the basic ability from which concrete operations develop is the ability mentally to form ordering structures, termed groupings and lattices by Piaget. Lattices are a special form of groupings in which the focus is on the connection between two or more objects and the objects that are connected. This allows the child the ability to develop a classification hierarchy system in which he can understand that all humans are animals, but not all animals are human.

Conservation of number begins to appear around the age of 7, conservation of quantity (substance, amount of space occupied by an object) begins to emerge around ages 7 or 8, and conservation of weight begins to emerge around 9 years of age (Chinn, 1979).

During the preoperational period the child's egocentrism is evident in conversations with other children. During this developmental period, conversations with other children the same age will consist of collective monologues. Each child pursues a private, personal conversation regardless of what the other child says. During the concrete operational period, however, these children begin to take into account the other child's point of view and begin to incorporate these views into their own conversations. Thus, more meaningful communication emerges, and the children carry on dialogue, responding directly to what the other has just said (Piaget, 1969; Pulaski, 1971).

The retarded child, however, will be delayed in the development of Piaget's stages. Elementary age educable retarded children will be slower in

Fig. 8-4. Instruction is individualized to the needs of each child.

progressing from the preoperational stage into concrete operations. Delay in development may be as much as 3 to 4 years. Even when the period of concrete operations is reached, only the lower stages may be attained during the elementary school age years, with higher functioning in the period not attained until the adolescent years. Lower functioning retarded children, such as the trainable retarded, may fixate at the preoperational level and may not reach even the most basic stages of the concrete operational period until later adolescence. Severely and profoundly retarded children may fixate at the sensorimotor and preoperational stages and may never develop cognitively into the more advanced periods, regardless of chronological age.

Teachers and professional workers aware of these limitations in cognitive functioning will be able to structure learning experiences commensurate with individual levels of cognitive development.

LEARNING CHARACTERISTICS

When we compare retarded children to normal counterparts of the same chronological age, we find that the very nature of retardation makes retarded children perform more poorly in most intellectual endeavors. Development level must be lower than that of the normal child of the same chronological age, making comparisons of retarded and normal children of the same chronological age difficult to interpret at times. We could begin by assuming that in most instances a retarded child will learn more like a normal child of the same mental age. It is the differences in performance that concern us most in making modifications in learning situations.

Memory

The literature regarding the memory of learned material strongly indicates that ability is related to the type of retention task involved. The short-term memory of the retarded, that is, the ability to recall material over a short period of time, has long been a topic of interest. Early work in the area provided a somewhat confusing picture. Some evidence has suggested that there is no difference in short-term memory performance of the mentally retarded as compared to that of nonretarded individuals (Logan, Prehm, and Drew, 1968; Drew and Prehm, 1970), whereas other researchers obtained results that indicate inferior performance by the retarded (Ellis, 1963; Hermelin and O'Conner, 1964). Probably the most programmatic research on short-term memory has been conducted in the laboratories at the University of Alabama. This work has rather consistently indicated difficulties in short-term memory for the retarded (Ellis, 1970). Smith (1968) indicates that associated with the retarded person's short-term retention difficulties is a high level of distractability by external and irrelevant stimuli. To compensate for the short-term retention deficiencies, Smith suggests that the following procedures be adopted in the classroom:

1. Reduce extraneous environmental stimuli, which tend to distract students and increase stimulus value of the task.

2. Present each component of stimuli clearly and with equivalent stimulus value initially.
3. Begin with simpler tasks, moving to the more complex.
4. Avoid irrelevant materials within the learning task.
5. Label stimuli.
6. Minimize reinforcement to avoid the interfering anticipation of reward.
7. Provide practice in short-term memory activities.
8. Integrate practice material with new subject fields, making use of successful experiences of the child.
9. Dramatize skills involving short-term memory, making them methodologically central to the program.

Studies involving long-term memory of the mentally retarded are even less firm with regard to results than those on short-term memory. Several researchers have obtained results suggesting that on long-term memory tasks retarded and nonretarded subjects do not perform differently (Cantor and Ryan, 1962; Jensen and Rohwer, 1963). Ellis (1963, 1970) has consistently contended that long-term memory is equal between the retarded and the nonretarded although his attention to this area has been secondary to his major research on short-term memory. Other research has indicated that long-term memory performance is inferior for the retarded (Logan, Prehm, and Drew, 1968; Drew and Prehm, 1970). Probably the best summary of the status of long-term memory research with the mentally retarded was provided by Belmont (1966). Although improvements have been evident since 1966, Belmont's serious criticisms are essentially still appropriate concerning the lack of sophistication of research methods. Thus he noted that, because of the primitive research methods, "there is almost no solid evidence either to support or contradict . . ." a retarded person's long-term memory deficit. Smith (1968) suggests that in order to ensure retention in long-term learning situations, we should provide the retarded with opportunities to overlearn material beyond criterion level and also provide them with ample opportunity to utilize the learned material.

Distribution of practice

While many individuals appear to be able to function well by utilizing massed practice, such as cramming for examinations, the literature suggests that distributed practice enhances the learning performance of the retarded when compared to mass practice to a greater extent than it does for normal individuals (Madsen, 1963). Thus the teacher should provide the retarded child with short but frequent practice sessions on day-to-day tasks. Complete mastery of the most elemental concepts would not seem to be a necessary goal for the initial practice sessions: although, perhaps taking more time in number of days, this procedure should result in the teacher having to spend less time overall to teach a particular concept. This procedure would also allow for practice to occur in a variety of situations and contexts and allow for the meaningful introduction of overlearning. This not only should result in an increased rate of acquisition but also should ensure a greater degree of retention.

Learning of concrete versus abstract concepts

The retarded have been observed to be less able to grasp abstract concepts as opposed to concrete concepts when compared to individuals of normal intelligence (Werner, 1948). Therefore the more meaningful and concrete the material, the more apt the retarded child is to learn. The teacher or parent may be advised to teach nothing with inanimate objects if the real living object is available. Likewise it might be said figuratively that we should teach nothing indoors if we can teach the same thing outdoors. The retarded will grasp concepts more readily if the real object is present rather than pictures (Iscoe and Semler, 1964). In other words, rather than reading and looking at pictures of firemen and their equipment, the retarded child may learn faster and to a greater extent if taken on a field trip to a fire station.

Learning set and transfer of learning

Learning set and transfer appear to be interrelated in an individual's ability to solve problems. While learning set refers to an individual's ability to learn how to learn, transfer is generally regarded as the ability to apply learned responses and experiences from previous problems to new problems with similar components. Smith (1968) indicates that retarded children are generally capable of establishing a learning set. He recommends that in order to facilitate the establishment of a learning set retarded children be exposed to a sequential presentation of facts and concepts, mastering easier problems prior to moving on to the more difficult.

The literature on transfer of learning provides several suggestions for working with the mentally retarded. Reviews by Kaufman and Prehm (1966) and Drew and Espeseth (1968) provide greater detail for the student interested in further reading in the area. Several points seem worthy of mention here, however.

1. Age seems to make a difference in the ability to transfer learning for both retarded and nonretarded individuals. Younger children transfer learning with greater ease than do older children.

2. Research also suggests that the retarded individual can transfer learning best when both the initial task and the transfer task are very similar. Emphasizing this even more is the finding by Hirsch and Lowman (1965) that transfer is most effective if a considerable number of the operations involved in the first task can be performed as a unit in the transfer task.

3. Meaningfulness seems very important to the retarded person's ability to transfer, with a more meaningful task being easier to learn initially as well as to transfer to a second setting.

4. Retarded individuals seem to be able to transfer learning more effectively if instructions are more general rather than detailed and specific. This seems to be an opposite trend to that found with nonretarded children who perform better if more detail is involved.

These findings seem to have several implications for working with the retarded in an educational or related setting. Initially it appears that transfer of training ought to be an important consideration in planning a retarded child's early learning. Often such consideration is left unattended until quite late in the curriculum (that is, in prevocational or vocational training). From the second point noted above, it seems that transfer of learning by the retarded will be most effective if the initial learning problem is a simulation of the transfer task. This seems to be an important point when one is involved in planning the activities as well as designing the materials to be used in educating the retarded.

Since meaningfulness seems so important to both the effective learning and transfer of material, this area must receive particular attention by the person working with retarded children. Often the meaning of a given activity is not readily evident. The child may then encounter more difficulty than would be the case if he were aware of how the task will help him. The teacher, and others working with the retarded, may find both learning and transfer facilitated if they make special effort to show the child how the task will be relevant to his later performance, to his life, or even to current interests. This must be done somewhat carefully, however, to avoid the explanation becoming too long and detailed (see the fourth point above). If verbal instructions become too detailed or laboriously specific, the retarded child encounters greater difficulty in transferring learning. Thus the person working with the retarded must be clinically sensitive to finding the most effective level of detail.

Hebb's theory in relationship to learning and the retarded

Hebb (1949) theorized that the human brain generates a complicated network of electrical impulses that travel throughout the central nervous system. Within time and through repeated use and experiences, the system becomes increasingly integrated. Each sensory or perceptual experience lends itself to the eventual development of functional units within the brain called cell assemblies, which "store" these experiences. The cell assemblies through use and experiences evolve into more complex units called phase sequences and eventually to still more complex units called phase cycles. One of the important aspects of the theory is the contention that the various units are built sequentially in lock-step fashion with perceptual and sensational experiences. Benoit (1959) implies that mental retardation is related to faulty development of the network that transmits the electrical impulses.

From all or part of these theories, it would seem imperative that a certain amount of development in the retarded child's system must be attained in order to foster the ability to engage in intellectual functioning, to be able to learn new things. To do this would require increasing exposure to sensational and perceptual events by providing retarded children with a multitude of experiences.

PERSONALITY AND EMOTIONAL DEVELOPMENT

When a mentally retarded child enters school for the first time, he may bring with him emotional problems that have developed during the preschool years, or he may enter school as a reasonably well-adjusted individual. Many retarded children are not recognized as retarded by their families and friends during the preschool years, for they are often able to function quite adequately in their homes and community. When they enter school, academic pressures are levied on them, and their intellectual differences tend to become magnified. Sometimes it appears that school itself may be one of the greatest detriments to some retarded children. In days past, those lacking in academic inclination were often able to depart from academic settings, somehow manage in manual labor or other nonacademic endeavors, and perhaps provide a nonstigmatized and useful service to society. With compulsory school attendance laws and increased emphasis on academic pursuits, the once graceful or at least unnoticed departure from the world of academia has become more formidable for the retarded. Many enter school unaware that they may be different from the rest of the world and unsuspecting of the catastrophe that awaits them. Intellectually inadequate and academically unsophisticated, many of the retarded fail miserably to adjust to the academic world. Their academic problems may be compounded by social development commensurate with their mental age but not with their chronological age. Thus, they may find rejection on two fronts, from the teacher frustrated with their academic limitations and from their normal peers frustrated with their social inadequacies. Failing in their efforts and rejected, the retarded person develops emotional problems.

There appears to be little disagreement with the notion that there is a higher incidence of behavioral disturbances among the retarded population compared to the general population. Studies have indicated that as much as 40 percent of the retarded population may have emotional or personality deviations, compared to about half that percentage for the nonretarded population (Dewan, 1948; Weaver, 1946; Craft, 1959). It appears, however, that the majority of the retarded having emotional difficulties suffer from milder problems, such as personality disorders, with the incidence of true depressive psychosis occurring only rarely (Craft, 1959; Beier, 1964).

Several explanations have been offered for the frequency of emotional disturbances among the retarded. Some believe that the retarded, because of their deficiencies, are subject to a greater number of stresses, frustrations, and conflicts resulting in behavioral disorders. Beier (1964) further states that the most frequently mentioned problems appear to be related to either rejection or overprotection. Many parents consider their children to be an extension of themselves. When a child falls short of parental expectations, as in retardation, the situation may be too ego-damaging for the parents to cope. It is at this point that many problems set in. When a retarded child is born into a family with intellectually limited parents, there may be little if any reaction. If, however, the child is born into other situations, parents may meet the feelings of frustration and failure by rejecting the child, or the parents may have strong feelings of guilt, which may lead them to overprotection.

Because of his limitations, the retarded individual becomes dependent on other individuals for survival (Hirsch, 1959). Because he may have little control of his environment and himself in relation to it, the retarded individual may have difficulty in finding and preserving his identity and his integrity. Frustrated, he may choose to resist, and in doing so he may create problems for himself and others. Sensing futility he may become passive and submissive. Coupled with these feelings of frustration and hopelessness may be feelings of shame and guilt associated with consistent failures.

The retarded individual's emotional adjustment may to a great extent be a function of the public attitude toward retarded children. In a questionnaire administered to 430 adults regarding their attitudes toward retarded children, Gottlieb and Corman (1975) found some revealing attitudes. A large majority of the respondents (88%) expressed an accepting attitude toward retarded children, agreeing that a parent should allow their normal children to play with a mentally retarded child. This acceptance was not, however, accompanied by equally strong support for integrated educational placement. Only 37% agreed that retarded children would learn more if they were integrated into regular classes. Older respondents, parents of school age children, and people with no previous contact with retarded persons tended favor segregation of retarded children in the community. Peterson (1975), investigating the attitudes of nonretarded children toward their EMR peers, found on one of the instruments used that subjects who had contact with EMR peers had more favorable attitudes toward the retarded. Older subjects had more favorable attitudes than younger subjects, and subjects whose parents had attained higher levels of education had more negative attitudes.

It would appear that the studies suggest that attitudes of these groups must be addressed if retarded individuals are to be successfully integrated into society and mainstreamed in education. The development of more positive attitudes is essential for acceptance of the retarded and for development of the retarded individual's positive self-concept.

Freudian theory related to mental retardation

According to Freudian theory, the human mind has three areas of mental activity, the id, the ego, and the superego. Although Freud himself displayed little interest in mental retardation, theorists have described mental retardation as a defect in ego function, which results in the malfunction of the superego. The id is fully developed and functioning (Pearson, 1942). The id is the first to develop in the individual and relates to the basic instincts. Freud himself stated that, "the id stands for untamed passions" (1932). The ego, which is the next to develop, serves as a mediator. As Freud describes it, "the ego stands for reason and circumspection." The last of the three to develop is the superego which, simply described, could be called a conscience.

If the reader accepts Freudian theory as valid, the implications for mental retardation become quite obvious. The basic description of mental retardation is not unlike that of the antisocial personality of sociopathic individuals. The latter have been described as having faulty superego development and as being seemingly devoid of a conscience. They are able to engage in illegal and socially unacceptable behavior without feelings of anxiety, guilt, or remorse (Kisker, 1964). The consequence for the retarded may be drastic. With strong instinctive drives of the id, there is little balance from a conscience or help from a mediating agency such as an ego. If this thesis is correct, it may explain the disproportionately large numbers of retarded individuals who are engaged in antisocial and criminal activities, which will be discussed in Chapter 10.

Related Freudian theory suggests that the retarded individual finds it difficult to utilize the more mature and socially acceptable defense mechanisms. Even non-Freudian theorists generally accept the concept of defense mechanisms. These devices are used regularly by most normal individuals as protection for the ego.

When an individual meets with certain frustrations or defeated plans or hopes, he may take the position that he is incompetent, or he may seek more emotionally satisfying solutions to his dilemma. If he decides that he is incompetent, this, plus repeated insult and injury to the ego, may have severe consequences for the individual and for personality adjustment.

Fortunately most human organisms learn quickly to develop a repertoire of responses or defense mechanisms against the insults to the integrity of the ego. The defense mechanisms begin with very immature and socially unacceptable types of responses, which include repression, regression, denial or lying, and others. Thus the 5-year-old standing next to a broken vase may quickly resort to denial when confronted by his 6-foot tall father with belt in hand. Although the evidence against the child may be overwhelming, he may still resort to denial in order to save both his ego and his hide. Actually, the child may have few alternatives, for he may lack both age and maturity to use more mature and acceptable responses or defense mechanisms.

As the child grows older, his ability to select more appropriate responses increases. The teenager who is jilted by her boyfriend *rationalizes* and decides that she would really prefer to play the field and date more boys. The premedical school student who is turned down for admission into medical school uses the most mature and socially acceptable defense mechanism by *sublimating* and channeling positive effort into his new interest in a position as a pharmaceutical representative.

Freudian theory, as it relates to the use of defense mechanisms, has considerable importance in mental retardation. Retarded individuals, never developing beyond a certain level of intellectual functioning, may never become proficient in the use of mature defense mechanisms. Always behind their normal counterparts in intellectual development, they may be comparably behind in developing an adequate repertoire of responses or defense mechanisms. This may impede both emotional and social adjustment. Thus parents and professionals can greatly assist the retarded child by exercising understanding when observing immature defense mechanisms, and by aiding the retarded person in selecting and developing more mature, socially acceptable responses.

The elementary school years are an extremely critical period in the life of a retarded individual. Personality and emotional development during this period may have a profound bearing on adjustment in later years. Research has indicated that vocational success is more related to personality adjustment than to any other factor (Kolstoe and Frey, 1965). Although emotional problems are prevalent among the retarded, they can be avoided in many cases. Professional and parental intervention in terms of curtailing stressful situations, counseling both the retarded and their families, providing psychotherapy, and offering old-fashioned understanding and concern can go a long way in developing a well-adjusted, stable retarded adult.

Motivational problems

Professionals and most parents of retarded children have accepted the fact that individuals with normal intelligence, when compared to their mentally retarded counterparts, will excel in nearly all dimensions of human behavior. We have seen, however, remarkable evidences of retarded individuals' ability to achieve. When motivated and producing at optimal levels, the retarded are often able to maintain competitive employment positions and become a useful and integral part of society.

Self-actualization. With a goal of useful integrated functioning in mind, many parents and professionals have sought to bring about maximum realization of the potential within the retarded. Maslow (1954) has emphasized the natural and sequential development of the individual through basic stages of needs until he progresses to higher levels of motives and organization. The eventual goal for the individual is self-actualization, which reflects the developmental stage of maximum potential. Typically we think of limited numbers of individuals who have reached self-actualization. Individuals such as Albert Schweitzer, humanitarian, physician, theologian, and accomplished musician, and Leonardo da Vinci, artist and inventor, are sometimes mentioned as possible self-actualized individuals. Little consideration has been given to the retarded as self-actualized individuals.

Kolstoe and Frey (1965) have discussed the possibility of self-actualization among the retarded, but only after they have progressed through the basic stages of needs or prepotency of needs. Maslow (1954) conceives of the five levels of needs arranged in a sequence from "lower needs" to "higher needs":

1. Physiological needs; e.g., to satisfy hunger, thirst
2. Safety needs; e.g., to maintain security, order, stability
3. Belongingness and love needs; e.g., to receive affection, identification
4. Esteem needs; e.g., to experience prestige, success, self-respect
5. Self-actualization needs

The prepotency of needs has important implications for parents and professionals (such as the special education teacher or rehabilitation counselor) who work with the retarded. The retarded child of elementary school age may have very real physiological needs. Some may come to school with severe nutritional deficiencies. These may vary from improper diet to insufficient intake. Many come hungry because of lack of food, tired because of lack of sleep and rest, cold because of lack of adequate clothing, or in physical discomfort because of lack of medical or dental attention. The observant teacher can identify these problems and make sure that proper attention is given to them. A bowl of milk and cereal before the start of school may be sufficient to turn the child's mind away from a growling stomach to a math lesson. Likewise, providing for a child's clothing and medical and dental needs can change his perceptions of what is immediately important to him. Chinn (1973) found a relationship between health problems and academic and social problems in the classroom.

The professional can provide for many of the safety needs of a retarded child. If the teacher notices that the child has been physically abused, this should be reported immediately to the proper authorities. While some schools may be justly criticized for their rigidity, others may provide the order and stability that may be lacking in the homes of some children. The security of knowing that for 5 days a week he can expect a warm meal during the noon hour and a certain amount of order within the day may be vital to the life and development of a retarded child.

Nearly every child wants to be identified in a special way with someone or something. Except in unusual circumstances, most children need affection and a sense of belonging to a group or an individual. For retarded children, lacking in social skills, this need may be difficult to fulfill. The special education teacher can in many instances facilitate group acceptance. Even if this cannot be accomplished immediately, the teacher can provide a sense of belongingness if he himself can accept the child as he is, as an individual worthy of his concern and affection.

The retarded child may never progress beyond belongingness and love needs. Prestige, success, and self-respect, which fulfill the esteem needs, may be formidable goals for the retarded. If the parent and professional will look hard enough, somewhere, buried amidst all the disabilities of the most lacking child in the classroom is hiding some ability to do something as well as if not better than the rest of the children in the class. By capitalizing on this ability and drawing attention to it, respect by peers in the classroom may be attained. Even if this cannot be achieved, the self-respect that comes with worthy accomplishment may suffice to meet this basic need.

When the first four basic needs have been met, the retarded individual may then look toward the final goal of self-actualization. While he may never be able to match the accomplishments of his normal peers, the retarded individual may find considerable satisfaction and contentment in being the best at whatever he is capable of doing, being well liked by his peers, and contributing to a better life for himself and his family.

Social learning theory. We have already discussed the problems and frustrations associated with failure among the retarded. Rotter (1954), in his social learning theory, and Cromwell (1959, 1961, 1963) have theorized that individuals fall into one of two categories: success-striving or failure-avoiding. The theory closely examines an individual's reinforcement expectancy. Success-striving individuals are basically successful individuals whose success continually reinforces them. They soon come to expect success and thus enter each new situation anticipating a successful experience, put forth the necessary effort, and are as usual successful. The failure-avoiding individual is more oriented toward failing experiences. Rather than expecting success he is primarily concerned with avoiding another failing experience. With his pessimistic attitude, he will probably not be able to accomplish his goal, further reinforcing his expectancy orientation.

Most retarded individuals obviously fall into the latter category. With an expectancy of failure, there is little wonder that it is difficult to motivate many retarded children to embark on new activities.

Recent research has indicated that the expectancy may in fact alter the retarded person's response to positive reinforcement (Welch and Drew, 1972). This may mean that a lot of what we know about rewards may be somewhat different in light of the retarded person's failure expectancy. Until more clear evidence is available, we may find more consistent success by structuring the situation than depending entirely on rewards. As teachers, vocational rehabilitation counselors, and parents, we may attempt to provide retarded children with successful experiences by structuring the situation in a manner that success is almost assured at first. As the retarded individual builds a backlog of successful experiences, we can progressively place him into more challenging and competitive situations and experiences. For instance, a vocational rehabilitation counselor may place the retarded trainee in a comparatively easy vocational training experience at first, where he may have a 90 to 100 percent chance of succeeding. In other words, he would almost have to work at failing in order to do so at this point. As he succeeds in his assigned tasks, he is placed in progressively more difficult assignments until he is placed in training situations where he has a 50-50 percent chance of success or failure. If he works hard and puts forth the effort, he will succeed. If he puts forth insufficient effort, he will fail.

We are theorizing that by placing the retarded person in progressively more difficult situations after a series of successful experiences, we have helped to alter his expectancy from one of failure to success. We are assuming that he will like success and will continue to seek it once he has had adequate exposure in this direction. We should be concerned with a possible failure when he reaches a point where he is in a relatively competitive situation. Assuming that he has had a backlog of successful experiences to make him more oriented toward success-striving, we may theorize that in spite of his previous failing experience the parent or vocational rehabilitation counselor can give him positive, realistic counsel. In most cases he can be helped to accept the fact that everyone faces setbacks, but on the next experience he can put forth a superior effort to ensure success.

Rigidity. In 1935 Lewin in his field theory postulated that the mentally retarded, when compared to normal individuals of the same mental age, were more rigid in their functioning. The rigidity concept may be described as firm or rigid boundaries between different areas of one's life space. The boundaries of a younger individual are fluid in the sense that it is easier to move from one area of one's life space to another. As we become older, we become increasingly more rigid and it becomes more difficult to alter our activities. Kounin (1941) attempted to find support for the rigidity notion by administering a concept-switching task to a group of institutionalized mentally retarded children and comparing them to children of normal intelligence of the same mental age. Keeping track of the number of attempts until the subjects were able to switch concepts or reach criterion, Kounin concluded that the retarded group was significantly more rigid, thus finding support for Lewin's theory.

Zigler, Hodgen, and Stevenson (1958) took issue with Kounin's findings, theorizing that there were two important variables that Kounin did not consider. In their social deprivation hypothesis, Zigler, Hodgen, and Stevenson postulated that the institutionalized retarded, because they were deprived of adequate adult interaction, would prolong activity as long as possible in order to maintain this interaction. Providing a group of institutionalized retarded children with a satiation task and comparing them with normal school children of the same mental age, Zigler, Hodgen, and Stevenson found that the normal children tended to terminate activity after a certain period of time, while the retarded children prolonged the activity and tended to wait for cues from the examiner before terminating. The result of this study suggested that Kounin's retarded subjects may have been less successful on the concept-switching task in order to prolong activity with the examiner.

In a motivational hypothesis, Zigler postulated that, if faced with a concept switching task, the retarded could function as well as the normal children of the same mental age if proper incentives were offered. In another study Zigler and deLaney (1962) used the identical concept-switching task that Kounin had used in 1941. This time, however, they divided the normal group into social classes of middle-class and lower-class and compared them to an institutionalized retarded group of the same mental age. He also introduced the motivational variable by providing two reward situations. An intangible reward of praise was offered as a reinforcer whenever a correct response was elicited. A tangible reward consisted of a choice of several 25¢ items such as toy watches and harmonicas given to the children whenever they responded correctly. In comparing the retarded, middle-class normal, and lower-class normal children under the intangible reward condition, Zigler found that the retarded and lower-class normal children took significantly more trials to complete the task than did the middle-class normal children. Under the tangible reward condition, however, there were no significant differences between any of the groups. As a matter of fact, the retarded and lower-class normal children's lower score under the tangible reward condition equaled the lower score of the middle-class normal children under the intangible reward condition.

As an explanation, we might surmise that middle-class children function well under intangible reward conditions because they are sufficient in their material possessions whereas the institutionalized retarded and the lower-class normal children are more materially deprived and therefore do not function as well with praise as a reinforcer. Under the tangible reward condition, the retarded and the lower-class normal children had adequate incentives and as a result equaled best performance of the middle-class normal children.

The work of Zigler and deLaney has not only cast doubt on the rigidity theories but has pointed out to individuals working with the retarded the necessity of providing the proper types of reinforcers and incentives in order to motivate optimal performance. Thus, providing a smiling face on a retarded child's worksheet in order to reward good work may not be an adequate reinforcer for some children. These children may be turned on by something more tangible or fitting to their individual needs. Strong evidence for the power of individualized rewards has been obtained by Heber (1959). He permitted his subjects to indicate their own preference for reinforcers, which thereafter were used to reward performance. His results suggest that this is a very useful technique which may be quite functional in a classroom.

PHYSICAL AND HEALTH CHARACTERISTICS
Physical defects

While the majority of retarded children have few observable deficiencies in their physical characteristics, there appears to be a direct correlation to the degree of retardation and the degree of physical defect. Among the educable group, which constitutes the majority of retarded children in special classes, we find few clinical types of retarded children. To be classified as a clinical type, a retarded child must possess anatomical, physiognomical, and pathological characteristics sufficiently pronounced to enable them to be placed in a readily identifiable group. The anatomical characteristics refer to the bodily characteristics, the physiognomical refer to facial characteristics, and the pathological refers to the disease process. Among the trainable, however, we find an increased number of clinical types of children, such as those with Down's syndrome. As we progress into the custodial range, we find an even higher percentage of clinical types and physical defects.

Early studies have generally been supported by more recent ones that suggest that the mentally retarded as compared to normal children are generally deficient in physical characteristics of height and weight (Fishler, Share, and Koch, 1964; Flory, 1936; Mosier, Grossman, and Dingman, 1965). Flory's study indicates that not only is the average growth rate slower among retarded children, but their period of growth is extended.

The survey of the literature suggests a preponderance of sensory defects among retarded children. In an audiometric study of retarded residents in an institution, Matthews (1951) found that approximately one-third of the group had subnormal hearing and approximately one-half of the subjects had some hearing deficit. Kempf and Collins (1929) found a higher percentage of defects in visual acuity in dull children as opposed to those of normal intelligence. O'Conner (1957) found a higher incidence of color blindness among moderately retarded males. The incidence among the higher grade male retarded was average, however.

The literature generally indicates that the retarded are inferior to their normal counterparts with respect to their motor proficiency (Tizard, O'Conner, and Crawford, 1950; Cantor and Stacey, 1951). Francis and Rarick (1960) suggest that mental retardation need not cause motor retardation. Motor deficiencies among the retarded may be more a function of deprivation in learning and practice opportunities rather than the retardation itself.

Health problems

Kirk (1972) suggests that the mentally retarded often come from "substandard" homes where little attention is given to sanitation and health matters. Many of these homes must depend on governmentally supported medical care. For others, health services may be minimal or nonexistent. Thus many of the community's health problems tend to originate at the socioeconomic level at which the retarded tend to function.

The literature strongly suggests that the retarded are deficient in their physical characteristics and have greater amounts of sensory defects, motor deficiencies, and health problems. The implications for those working with the retarded are rather obvious. First, it would appear to be imperative that adequate screening for sensory defects be provided for retarded children. If defects are found, the children should be fitted with visual or auditory correctional devices if possible, or surgery should be made available if warranted. If neither is possible, teachers should be advised to place the sensory impaired child in preferential seating assignments to minimize the problem.

The health and sanitation problems are often difficult to overcome. Many of the retarded exist in a way of life that is accepted for their particular subculture. They may feel little if any need to change their life-style. Refinements in health delivery services to make medical and nursing services more readily accessible are necessary. This should include not only services to expectant mothers and the ill, but preventive medicine and educational services by both public health and social service workers. The remediation of inferior and substandard housing, which promotes health hazards, needs priority consideration as one of the more popular and publicized social issues. Unfortunately, needs of a minority population and social conscience along with adequate funds do not often coincide. We as professionals must therefore teach the retarded to protect themselves from potential hazards and to become resourceful enough to find the best medical services available to them.

Physical education and recreation for the retarded

Francis and Rarick (1960), as previously discussed, suggested that motor deficiencies may be related to lack of opportunities rather than to mental retardation itself. We may speculate that many other physical deficiencies, such as height and weight, may be related to factors other than retardation. Since many retarded persons come from lower socioeconomic backgrounds, such factors as dietary deficiency, may have relevance to our concerns. Again, education may provide some of the solutions. Adequate pre- and postnatal care and parental education are necessary. We may also be concerned with the lack of opportunity for the retarded to participate in physical education programs. Brace (1966) had only a 37 percent response out of 4,022 question-naires from a nationwide survey regarding physical education for the mentally retarded. Of those responding, 40 percent had physical education programs in which the retarded were integrated with normal children, 40 percent were segregated, and 15 percent had no formal physical education programs for the mentally retarded. Since only 37 percent responded, there appears to be some likelihood that many of the remaining 63 percent of the nonresponding programs had no physical education provisions for the retarded.

The results from a survey by Rarick, Widdop, and Broadhead (1967), who investigated 315 schools in 21 states, were slightly more encouraging. Fifty-four percent responded affirmatively with respect to provisions for the retarded. However, the time allotted for physical education was judged inadequate by the researchers; the maximum time for weekly activity ranged from only 30 to 45 minutes.

Recreational provisions for the retarded have fared no better than physical education in past years. Kelly (1964) estimated that only 1 in 100 recreational agencies provided for the retarded. Thompson (1965) found that only 427 out of 2,000 communities surveyed had recreational facilities for the retarded. Today the picture for physical education and recreation for the retarded is much more encouraging. Some agencies and communities surveyed in the above studies were in the process of initiating new programs for the retarded at the time of the survey and have undoubtedly since started them. Colleges and universities have started new programs in physical education, recreation, and therapeutic recreation to prepare individuals to work with the handicapped. Other programs such as the Special Olympics sponsored by the Joseph P. Kennedy Foundation have provided for competition for the retarded in athletic events among themselves.

Results of physical education and recreation programs are not only promising but also are intriguing. Oliver (1958) and Corder (1966) found substantial gains in motor performance within weeks of the initiation of rigorous physical activity programs. Oliver found not only gains in physical fitness, but improved personal and social characteristics, which possibly may be attributable to the physical fitness program. Corder (1966), in an attempt to relate physical activity to intelligence, found what appeared to be an increase in IQ level following a physical activity program.

The average American spends 36 to 39 hours a week working. It has been

Fig. 8-5. The school-aged child often needs assistance in developing physical education skills.

estimated that by the year 2000, Americans will be spending only 32 hours a week in work activity (Bucher and Bucher, 1974). Not all persons can enjoy commercial recreation; however, Staley and Miller (1972) suggest that often those having the most leisure time are least able to cope with it. Frustrated with the inability to find legitimate forms of leisure expression, individuals may adopt deviant solutions to this problem. The amount of free time has in some instances led to increased social pathology in the form of crime and violence (Murphy, 1975).

Verhoven (1975) suggests that because the handicapped have fewer employment opportunities, enforced leisure is even a greater problem for them

Fig. 8-6. Television is often the major source of recreation for the retarded. (Photograph by Peter Poulides.)

than for their nonhandicapped peers. The need for leisure education for this segment of the population is critical because of the fact that handicapped persons have a disproportionately large amount of leisure time.

P. L. 94-142 specifically lists recreational services under related services that each child is to receive. This includes assessment of leisure function and provision of therapeutic recreational services, recreational programs through schools and community agencies, and leisure education.

Without minimizing the importance of psychomotor contributions of recreational activities, Wright (1974) suggests that perhaps the greatest value of these activities may be in their contributions to the emotional, psychological, and affective development of these children. Thus, Bracky (1971) suggests that recreational activities may enable a child to perceive himself as successful for the first time.

We have already indicated that a greater number of professionals specializing in physical education and recreation for the handicapped are entering these fields. The responsibility of providing for the physical activity needs of the retarded should not rest solely with these professionals. Special education teachers should acquaint themselves with programs that can provide such benefits for their children. Parents should provide as many opportunities for physical and recreational fulfillments as possible. Finally, concerned individuals can volunteer their time to help provide the retarded with the fuller and richer life to which they are entitled.

STUDY QUESTIONS

1. Explain what mainstreaming is and discuss its advantages and disadvantages.
2. Compare the traditional approaches to educating retarded children to the emerging trends in educating the mentally retarded.
3. What are the implications of the level of cognitive development of retarded elementary school age children for educators?
4. How do mentally retarded children compare to normal children with regard to memory?
5. How do the retarded function with regard to learning set and transfer of learning?
6. How do the retarded compare to the normal with regard to emotional adjustment? Why do the retarded use immature defense mechanisms?
7. How does Maslow's theory of self-actualization relate to the mentally retarded?
8. How does Potter's Social Learning Theory relate to the retarded?
9. What did Zigler and his associates find in the research regarding rigidity among the mentally retarded?
10. Why is leisure education an important aspect of curriculum for the retarded?

REFERENCES

Apffel, J. A., Kelleher, J., Lilly, M. S., and Richardson, R. Developmental reading for moderately retarded children. *Education and Training of the Mentally Retarded*, 1975, **10**(4), 229-235.

Baldwin, W. D. The social position of the educable mentally retarded in the regular grades in the public schools. *Exceptional Children*, 1958, **25**, 106, 108.

Beier, D. C. Behavioral disturbances in the mentally retarded. In H. A. Stevens and R. Heber (Eds.), *Mental retardation*. Chicago: The University of Chicago Press, 1964, Pp. 454-482.

Bellamy, T., and Buttars, K. L. Teaching trainable level retarded students to count money: toward personal independence through academic instruction. *Education and Training of the Mentally Retarded*, 1975, **10**(1), 18-26.

Belmont, J. M. Long-term memory in mental retardation. *International Review of Research in Mental Retardation*, 1966, **1**, 219-255.

Benoit, E. P. Toward a new definition of mental retardation. *American Journal of Mental Deficiency*, 1959, **63**, 559-564.

Brace, D. K. *Physical education and recreation for mentally retarded pupils in public schools.* Unpublished study. Washington, D.C.: American Alliance of Health, Physical Education and Recreation, 1966.

Brackey, L. How our flowers grow. In *The Best of Challenge*, Washington, D.C.: American Alliance of Health, Physical Education and Recreation, 1971.

Bucher, C. A., and Bucher, R. D. *Recreation for Today's Society.* Englewood Cliffs, N.J.: Prentice Hall, Inc., 1974.

Budoff, M., and Gottlieb, J. Special-class EMR

children mainstreamed: a study of an aptitude (learning potential) X Treatment Interaction, *American Journal on Mental Deficiency*, 1976, **81**(1), 1-11.

Cantor, G. N., and Ryan, T. J. Retention of verbal paired-associates in normals and retardates. *American Journal of Mental Deficiency*, 1962, **66**, 861-865.

Cantor, G. N., and Stacey, W. L. Manipulative dexterity in mental defectives. *American Journal of Mental Deficiency*, 1951, **56**, 401-410.

Cassidy, V. M., and Stanton, J. E. *An investigation of factors involved in educational placement of mentally retarded children: a study of differences between children in special and regular classes in Ohio.* U.S. Office of Education Cooperative Research Program, Project no. 043, Columbus, Ohio: Ohio State University, 1959.

Chinn, P. L. A relationship between health and school problems: a nursing assessment. *Journal of School Health*, 1973, **43**(2), 85-92.

Chinn, P. L. *Child health maintenance: concept in family centered care.* (2nd ed.) St. Louis: The C. V. Mosby Co., 1979.

Corder, W. O. Effects of physical education on the intellectual, physical and social development of educable mentally retarded boys. *Exceptional Children*, 1966, **32**, 357-364.

Craft, M. Mental disorder in the defective: a psychiatric survey among inpatients. *American Journal of Mental Deficiency*, 1959, **63**, 829-834.

Cromwell, R. L. A methodological approach to personality research in mental retardation. *American Journal of Mental Deficiency*, 1959, **64**, 330-340.

Cromwell, R. L. Selected aspects of personality development in mentally retarded children. *Exceptional Children*, 1961, **28**, 44-51.

Cromwell, R. L. (Ed.) *Abstracts of Peabody studies in mental retardation*, vols. 1 and 2. Nashville: George Peabody College for Teachers, 1961, 1963.

Deno, E., Special education as developmental capital. *Exceptional Children.* 1970, **37**, 229-237.

Dewan, J. G. Intelligence and emotional stability. *American Journal of Psychiatry.* 1948, **704**, 548-554.

Drew, C. J. Research on social adjustment and the mentally retarded: functioning and training. *Mental Retardation*, 1971, **9**, 26-29.

Drew, C. J., and Espeseth, V. K. Transfer of train-

ing in the mentally retarded: a review. *Exceptional Children*, 1969, **35**, 129-132.

Drew, C. J., and Prehm, H. J. Retention in retarded and nonretarded children as a function of direction of recall and material associative strength. *American Journal of Mental Deficiency*, 1970, **75**, 349-353.

Ellis, N. R. The stimulus trace and behavioral inadequacy. In N. R. Ellis (Ed.), *Handbook of mental deficiency.* New York: McGraw-Hill Book Co., 1963, Pp. 134-158.

Ellis, N. R. Memory processes in retardates and normals. In N. R. Ellis (Ed.), *International review of research in mental retardation*, vol. 4. New York: Academic Press, Inc., 1970, Pp. 1-32.

Fishler, K., Share, J., and Koch, R. Adaptation of Gesell Developmental Scales for evaluation of development in children with Down's syndrome (mongolism). *American Journal of Mental Deficiency*, 1964, **68**:642-646.

Flory, D. D. The physical growth of mentally deficient boys. *Monographs of the Society for Research in Child Development*, 1936, **1**(6).

Francis, R. J., and Rarick, G. L. *Motor characteristics of the mentally retarded.* Cooperative Research Monograph, no. 1, Washington, D.C.: U.S. Department of Health, Education and Welfare, 1960.

Freud, S. The anatomy of mental personality (1932). In *Great Books of the Western World.* Chicago: University of Chicago Press, 1952, Pp. 830-840.

Goodman, H., Gottlieb, J., and Harrison, R. H. Social acceptance of EMR's integrated into non-graded elementary school. *American Journal of Mental Deficiency*, 1972, **76**, 412-417.

Gottlieb, J., and Budoff, M. Social acceptability of retarded children in non-graded schools differing in architecture. *American Journal of Mental Deficiency*, 1973, **78**, 15-19.

Gottlieb, J., and Corman, L. Public attitudes toward mentally retarded children. *American Journal of Mental Deficiency*, 1975, **80**(1), 72-80.

Gottlieb, J., and Davis, J. E. Social acceptance of EMR's during overt behavioral interaction. *American Journal of Mental Deficiency*, 1973, **78**, 141-143.

Hebb, D. O. *The organization of behavior.* New York: John Wiley & Sons, Inc., 1949.

Heber, R. F. Motor task performances of high grade mentally retarded males as a function of the magnitude of the incentive. *American Journal of Mental Deficiency,* 1959, **63,** 667-671.

Hermelin, B., and O'Connor, N. Short-term memory in normal and sub-normal children. *American Journal of Mental Deficiency,* 1964, **69,** 121-125.

Hirsch, E. A. The adaptive significance of commonly described behavior of the mentally retarded. *American Journal of Mental Deficiency,* 1959, **63,** 639-646.

Hirsch, W., and Lowman, C. L. Motor skill transfer by trainable mentally retarded. *Research Relating to Children,* 1965, **19,** 82.

Hobson vs. Hansen. *Abolition of track system.* Washington, D.C., 1967.

Iscoe, I., and Semler, I. J. Paired associates learning in normal and mentally retarded children as a function of four experimental conditions. *Journal of Comparative and Physiological Psychology,* 1964, **57,** 387-392.

Jensen, A. R., and Rohwer, W. D., Jr. The effect of verbal mediation on the learning and retention of paired associates by retarded adults. *American Journal of Mental Deficiency,* 1963, **68,** 80-84.

Jordan, T. E., and deCharms, R. The achievement motive in normal and mentally retarded children. *American Journal of Mental Deficiency,* 1959, **64,** 80-84.

Kaufman, M. E., and Prehm, H. J. A review of research on learning sets and transfer of training in mental defectives. In N. R. Ellis (Ed.), *International review of research in mental retardation,* vol. 2. New York: Academic Press, Inc., 1966, Pp. 123-149.

Kauffman, M. J., Gottlieb, J., Agard, J. A., and Kukic, M. B. Mainstreaming toward and application concept. *Focus on Exceptional Children,* 1975, **7,** 1-12.

Kelly, F. P. Recreational services for the retarded—an urgent need. *Recreation in Treatment Centers,* 1964, **3,** 12-15.

Kempf, G. A., and Collins, S. S. A study of the relation between mental and physical status in two counties in Illinois, *Public Health Report, U.S. Public Health Service,* 1929, **44**(2), 1743-1784.

Kirk, S. A. *Educating exceptional children.* Boston: Houghton-Mifflin Co., 1972.

Kisker, G. W. *The disorganized personality.* New York: McGraw-Hill Book Co., 1964, Pp. 230-232.

Kolstoe, O. P., and Frey, R. *A high school work-study program for the mentally subnormal student.* Carbondale, Ill.: Southern Illinois University Press, 1965.

Kounin, J. S. Experimental studies of rigidity. I. The measurement of rigidity in normal and feebleminded persons. *Character and Personality,* 1941, **9,** 251-273.

Lewin, K. *A dynamic theory of personality.* New York: McGraw-Hill Book Co., 1935.

Litton, F. W. *Education of the trainable mentally retarded:* curriculum, methods, materials. St. Louis: The C. V. Mosby Co., 1978.

Logan, D. R., Prehm, H. J., and Drew, C. J. Effects of unidirectional training on bidirectional recall in retarded and non-retarded subjects. *American Journal of Mental Deficiency,* 1968, **73,** 493-495.

Luckey, R. E., and Addison, M. R. The profoundly retarded: a new challenge for public education. In R. M. Anderson and J. G. Greer (Eds.), *Educating the severely and profoundly retarded.* Baltimore: University Park Press, 1976.

Madsen, M. C. Distribution of practice and level of intelligence. *Psychological Reports,* 1963, **13,** 39.

Maslow, A. H. *Motivation and personality.* New York: Harper & Row, Publishers, 1954.

Matthews, J. Speech problems of the mentally retarded. In L. E. Travis (Ed.), *Handbook of speech pathology.* New York: Appleton-Century-Crofts, 1951.

Mills vs. Board of Education, Civil Action No. 1939-71. Washington, D.C., 1972.

Mossier, H. D., Grossman, H. J., and Dingman, H. F. Physical growth in mental defectives. *Pediatrics,* 1965, **36,** 465-519.

Murphy, J. F. *Recreation and leisure service,* Dubuque, Iowa: William C. Brown Co., Publishers, 1975.

O'Conner, N. Imbecility and color blindness. *American Journal of Mental Deficiency,* 1957, **62,** 83-87.

Oliver, J. M. The effects of physical conditioning exercises and activities on the mental characteristics of educationally subnormal boys. *British Journal of Educational Psychology,* 1958, **28,** 155.

Paterson, D. G. *Physique and intellect.* Watkins Glen, N.Y.: Century House, Inc., 1930.

Pearson, G. H. J. The psychology of mental defect. *The Nervous Child,* 1942, **2,** 9-20.

Peterson, G. Factors related to the attitudes of non-retarded children toward their EMR peers. *American Journal of Mental Deficiency*, 1975, **79**(4), 412-416.

Piaget, J. *The theory of stages in cognitive development*, New York: McGraw-Hill Book Co., 1969.

Pulaski, M. A. *Understanding Piaget—an introduction to children's cognitive development*. New York: Harper & Row, Publishers, 1971.

Rarick, G. L., Widdop, J. J., and Broadhead, G. D. *The motor performance and physical fitness of educable mentally retarded children*. Madison, Wis.: University of Wisconsin Press, 1967.

Richardson, E., Oestereicher, M. H., Bialer, I., and Minsberg, B. Teaching beginning reading skills to retarded children in community classrooms: a programmatic case study. *Mental Retardation*, 1975, **13**(1), 11-15.

Rotter, J. B. *Social learning and clinical psychology*. Englewood Cliffs, N.J.: Prentice-Hall, Inc., 1954.

Smith, R. *Clinical teaching: methods of instruction for the retarded*. New York: McGraw-Hill Book Co., 1968.

Sontag, E., Burke, P., and York, R. Considerations in serving the severely handicapped in public schools. In R. M. Anderson and J. G. Greer (Eds.), *Educating the severely and profoundly retarded*. Baltimore: University Park Press, 1976.

Spicker, H. H., and Bartel, N. R. The mentally retarded. In G. O. Johnson and H. D. Blank (Eds.), *Exceptional children research review*. Washington, D.C.: Council for Exceptional Children, 1968, Pp. 38-109.

Staley, E., and Miller, N. P. *Leisure and the quality of life: a new ethic for 1970's and beyond*. Washington, D.C.: American Alliance for Health, Physical Education and Recreation, 1972.

Thompson, M. National survey of community recreation services to the mentally retarded and physically handicapped. *Recreation*, 1965, **58**(4), 191-192.

Tizard, J., O'Conner, H., and Crawford, J. M. The abilities of adolescent and adult high-grade male defectives. *Journal of Mental Science*, 1950, **96**, 889-907.

Verhoven, P. J. *A proposal for the development and pilot testing of a leisure education program model in select school systems*. Washington: National Recreation and Park Association, 1975.

Weaver, T. R. The incidence of maladjustment among mental defectives in military environment. *American Journal of Mental Deficiency*. 1946, **51**, 238-246.

Welch, R. F., and Drew, C. J. Reward anticipation and performance expectancy on the learning rate of EMR adolescents. *American Journal of Mental Deficiency*, 1972, **77**, 291-295.

Werner, H. *Comparative psychology of mental development*. New York: International Universities Press, 1948.

Wright, B. Success breeds success. In *The Best of Challenge*, vol. 2, Washington, D.C.: American Alliance of Health, Physical Education and Recreation.

Zigler, E., and deLaney, J. Concept-switching in middle class, lower class, and retarded children. *Journal of Abnormal and Social Psychology*, 1962, **65**, 267-268.

Zigler, E., Hodgen, L., and Stevenson, H. The effect of support and non-support on the performance of normal and feeble-minded children. *Journal of Personality*, 1958, **26**, 106-122.

ANNOTATED BIBLIOGRAPHY

Arnheim, D. D., Auxter, D., and Crowe, W. C. *Principles and methods of adapted physical education and recreation*. (3rd ed.) St Louis: The C. V. Mosby Co., 1977.

A basic text of principles and methods of adaptive physical education and therapeutic recreation.

Audio-visual guide: physical education and recreation for the mentally retarded. Washington, D.C.: American Alliance for Health, Physical Education and Recreation, 1968.

A fine guide to films, slides, records, and tapes pertaining to physical education and recreation for the mentally retarded.

Beier, D. C. Behavioral disturbances in the mentally retarded. In H. A. Stevens and R. Heber (Eds.), *Mental retardation*. Chicago: University of Chicago Press, 1964.

A review of the nature, incidence, and causes of behavioral disturbances as they relate to mental retardation. An excellent review, but somewhat dated.

Denny, M. R. Research in learning and performance. In H. A. Stevens and R. Heber (Eds.), *Mental retardation*. Chicago: University of Chicago Press, 1964.

A review of research pertaining to learning and related

performance characteristics of the mentally retarded. Somewhat dated, but excellent.

Heber, R. Personality. In H. A. Stevens and R. Heber (Eds.), *Mental retardation.* Chicago: University of Chicago Press, 1964.

A review of research related to personality characteristics of the mentally retarded. Somewhat dated, but excellent.

Leisure Information Service, *A systems model for developing a leisure education program for handicapped children and youth (K-12)*, Washington, D.C.: Hawkins and Associates, 1976.

Provides rationale, relevant research, and suggested leisure curriculum for the handicapped.

CHAPTER 9

The retarded adolescent

(Photograph by Peter Poulides.)

INTRODUCTION

Adolescence is perhaps one of the most challenging times in the life of an individual and his family. Chinn (1979) suggests that the child becomes a young adult and is suspended for several long years between childhood and adulthood. During this period the individual is neither a child nor an adult. Confusion and dissonance are compounded by society's reaction to the adolescent—confused and ambivalent.

This period of life may be conceptualized as one during which emancipation from the primary family unit or from one's parents is the central task concerning the young person (Chinn, 1979). It is a difficult period of transition, for the adolescent is desperately attempting to be free from the role of a child. However, he may not be fully equipped to assume the responsibilities of adulthood.

This may be a difficult time for those of normal intellectual abilities; the retarded adolescent's problems are often intensified. Many retarded adolescents have the physical attributes of a normal adolescent or even an adult. Yet they do not in most instances possess the capabilities to cope with either the demands of their environment or their own desires for emancipation from childhood. They are faced with the awesome responsibility of preparing for vocational competence as well as developing the social and emotional characteristics that will provide them with acceptance in society.

Hurlock (1964) indicates that sexual maturity begins at approximately age 13 for girls and age 14 for boys. She states that the major developmental task of adolescence is the preparation for adulthood. Early adolescence (to age 17) is marked by increasing independence from guidance and control. The later adolescent period places emphasis on preparation for life as an adult.

Adults frequently have stereotyped responses to adolescence. One such viewpoint characterizes the adolescent as a maladjusted individual (Anthony, 1970). Adults in our culture have learned to anticipate a state of extreme disequilibrium and anticipate a period of "storm and stress." While there are adolescents who fit this stereotype, such a description need not be applicable to the majority (Anthony, 1970; Chinn, 1979). Chinn states that social attitudes and cultural definitions of the role of the adolescent have created a number of circumstances that cause this period of life to be what it is in our Western culture.

For the purposes of our discussion of adolescence as it relates to mental retardation, we shall delimit this period as the age of 13 through the end of formal public school education, when the individual is eligible for sheltered or competitive employment. This upper limit may vary from ages 18 to 21.

The purpose of this chapter is to consider the educational programs that have been developed for the mentally retarded to prepare them for some degree of vocational competence. We shall also explore the social and emotional adjustment problems that develop during this time and the various means of facilitating positive adjustment.

EDUCATIONAL SETTINGS

As discussed in Chapter 8, there are both traditional educational settings for the retarded and those that are newly emerging, such as resource rooms, cooperative programs, and itinerant resource personnel. The educational settings for the mentally retarded adolescent are essentially the same. It should be noted, however, that while the structure of the classes and the settings may be similar, the programs and general curricula vary considerably.

As previously stated in Chapter 8 (and discussed in detail in Chapter 13), P. L. 94-142 requires all states to provide free and appropriate education for all children by 1980. A major thrust of this legislation is directed toward the severely and profoundly handicapped as well as the multiply handicapped. The law provides for an education in the least restrictive environment for the child.

Each child is to be dealt with individually. Thus, in some instances, a severely retarded adolescent may be integrated into some form of public school education. While it is conceivable that in some instances a few of these individuals will receive some form of career and vocational training for competitive employment, it is more likely that such training will be geared toward sheltered workshop settings.

Others, particularly the profoundly and lower-level severely retarded, may receive their educational training in institutional as well as public school settings with less orientation toward career-vocational education and more emphasis toward self-help skills. It is important to reemphasize that where education is feasible, individualized education programs (IEP) will be developed and tailored to the individual needs and differences of each child. Undoubtedly, the law will be tested and challenged in the days to come. Many debates will surely take place regarding the interpretation of what education is and when it is feasible for some individuals.

The trainable

As the trainable retarded reach the adolescent period, they represent a unique concern for professionals and parents. These individuals like the severely/profoundly retarded have in the past been ignored by educational programs. In more recent years, however, programming for the trainable retarded has developed as a result of parental pressure, court action, and increasing awareness of professional responsibilities. Programming varies because there are differing philosophical orientations with respect to the kind of preparation necessary as well as differences in the objectives of educational programming.

It would appear that while there are a number of specific possibilities in terms of adolescent trainable programs, these may be characterized as two general types. The first type emphasizes personal, social, and self-help skills to prepare the individual to function adequately in the home. The second type places a greater emphasis on vocational preparation; many schools in recent years have developed their own sheltered workshops. The students may work exclusively in the workshop setting or may participate in some sort of combination program in which periods of time are spent both in the classroom and in the workshop.

Follow-up studies on trainable retarded persons in the community indicate that the majority of trainable adults have a relatively comfortable existence at home with few working and nearly all dependent on their families in some manner (Saenger, 1957). Such findings lead to questions regarding the efficacy of special classes for the trainable. If the objective of these classes is to prepare the retarded for a relatively comfortable and useful existence within the home, without employment, the emphasis on self-help skills appears to be appropriate. If the objective is employment, then a greater emphasis on vocational training appears to be a needed component in the curriculum.

The educable

In Chapter 8 we discussed the various educational settings for educable children in self-contained classrooms in the elementary schools. At the secondary level there are two basic programs: the prevocational at the junior high school and the vocational at the high school.

In recent years considerable attention has been given toward the career and vocational education of the mentally retarded. While it could be appropriate to suggest that career and vocational education really begins when the child enters school, the major emphasis is during the adolescent years and continuing into adulthood. Efforts toward the development of specific curricula have been advanced by numerous individuals (Kolstoe and Frey, 1965; Kolstoe, 1976; Brolin, 1976). A social and prevocational information battery measuring social and prevocational awareness has been developed at the University of Oregon by Halpern and his associates (Halpern and others, 1975). This battery used with approximately 1,000 educable retarded adolescents in Oregon has considerable promise for screening pupils, monitoring pupil progress, and evaluating programs.

Section 504 of the Rehabilitation Act of 1973 provides new civil rights mandates for the handicapped. The regulations of the Rehabilitation Act were signed by Joseph Califano, Secretary of the Department of Health, Education and Welfare on April 28, 1977. In signing the regulations, Secretary Califano stated, "The 504 Regulation attacks the discrimination, the demeaning practices and injustices that have afflicted the nation's handicapped citizens . . . It will usher in a new era of equality for handicapped individuals in which unfair barriers to self-sufficiency and decent treatment will begin to fall before the force of the law."

Subsection 84.11 states that, "No qualified handicapped person shall, on the basis of handicap, be subjected to discrimination in employment under any program or activity to which this part applies." Discrimination is prohibited in:

1. Recruitment, advertising, and the processing of applications
2. Hiring, alterations in job status, rehiring
3. Rates of pay and other forms of compensation
4. Job assignments and classifications, lines of progression, and seniority
5. Leaves of absences and sick leave
6. Fringe benefits
7. Selection and financial support for training, conferences, and other job-related activities
8. Employer-approved activities, including social and recreational programs

The signing of these regulations does not mean that the negative attitudes that have long been in existence toward the handicapped will by any means change immediately. This, however, is a first step toward opening new vocational doors for the handicapped in general and, for our purposes, the retarded specifically. It makes career and vocational education for the retarded even more important than ever. Section 503 of the same Rehabilitation Act of 1973 emphasizes the regulations for affirmative action to employ the handicapped. Thus, if the retarded are properly educated and are able to perform competitively for jobs, the federal government now stands behind these individuals both in promoting affirmative action in their employment as well as prohibiting any discrimination in their hiring. Hopefully, this will open doors of employment that previously have been shut to the retarded. It is, however, critical to reemphasize that the retarded be educated and trained as competent employees. While the new laws facilitate employment of the handicapped, they do not obligate an employer to employ nor retain those who cannot demonstrate competence.

The prevocational level. Between the ages of 13 and 15, educable children are frequently placed in self-contained classrooms designated as prevocational classes. These individuals usually range in mental ages from 7 to about 11 years. As some come close to reaching maximum development in their mental age at this level, there will be some mental age overlap with the intermediate group discussed in Chapter 8. In this class, located in a junior high school setting, students are introduced to occupational information that should provide an introduction to the vocational opportunities within the community. This vocational introduction can be accomplished by the use of films, filmstrips, guest speakers, and field trips.

In order to facilitate vocational adjustment, this class usually places a great emphasis on social and personal relationships as they relate to vocational proficiency. In addition, an emphasis is often placed on home living skills that will facilitate eventual independent living. Tool subjects (reading, writing, and arithmetic) should continue, with an orientation toward vocational and other real-life situations.

As this level, vocational training in the school setting is often introduced. Campus work, such as cafeteria workers, office messengers, custodian's assistants, and library assistants, often provides excellent experience. Such training stations should be selected with careful consideration of the qualifications of the individuals who will be supervising the students. Certainly the supervisors should be acquainted with the nature and needs of the mentally retarded. The placements tend to be somewhat sheltered so that the students can learn without anxiety and can profit from their mistakes. The special education teacher functions as a liaison between the students and the various work supervisors.

The teacher and supervisors can serve as evaluators. Together they can evaluate the students' abilities and can identify specific deficiencies and areas of concern. These evaluations will aid the staff in determining readiness for the vocational level and the varieties of experiences most appropriate at the next level.

The vocational level. By the age of 16, the majority of the educable students are ready for vocational level classes. At this level the students move from the junior high school setting to the high school. By the time they reach this level, they should have had sufficient experiences at the prevocational level to facilitate adjustment within the vocational class. The self-contained educable class may or may not be conducted in conjunction with a work-study program. As the name implies, work-study programs provide the student with integrated work and study experiences. For a portion of the day the student spends time in the classroom, increasing tool subject skills that will facilitate independent adult living. During the remainder of the day the student leaves the campus and receives training in an on-the-job training facility somewhere in the community. These facilities may range from sheltered workshops to competitive employment settings, such as service stations. The kind of placement will be dependent on the student's aptitude, ability, and readiness. At the end of 3 to 4 years, most schools have provisions for a high school diploma. The student is then released from school and placed in some form of gainful employment.

Attempts to determine the efficacy of work-study programs have been made by Howe (1967) and Chaffin, Smith, and Haring (1967). In these two separate studies experimental groups having the benefit of work-study programs were compared to more traditional self-contained classes without the work-study component.

In Howe's study, the postschool adjustment was evaluated. No significant differences could be determined in either group in terms of overall adult adjustment. The group educated in the traditional special education program achieved as well in the adult community as the group with work-study experience. While nothing was found to indicate that a work-study program is detrimental to later adjustment, the findings of this study suggest that not all educable mentally retarded students in vocational level classes need off-campus placement as part of their training program.

In a similar study by Chaffin, Smith, and Haring (1967), thirty students who participated in work-study programs in educable classes were compared with a control group who were also in educable classes but did not

Fig. 9-1. In a work-study program the student spends a portion of the day in a work setting and combines this with classroom activities. (Photograph by Peter Poulides.)

receive the work experiences. The experimental group with the work experience excelled in all differences measured. The experimental group missed fewer days while enrolled, dropped out of school less frequently, and were employed more often. The study also found that after leaving school 95 percent of the experimental graduates were employed, as contrasted to 70 percent of the control graduates.

The findings of the two studies do not appear to be consistent. One study suggests that work-study programs are advantageous to educable students, while the other suggests no particular benefit. An important variable, which always needs to be considered in such studies, but which cannot always be assessed accurately, is that of competence of the professional individuals working in various capacities during the training period. Training and educational programs for the retarded that are sound in terms of curriculum can be effective only if the professionals employed are competent in their work. This statement in no way reflects our opinions of the competence of the professionals working with the retarded subjects in either of the above-men-

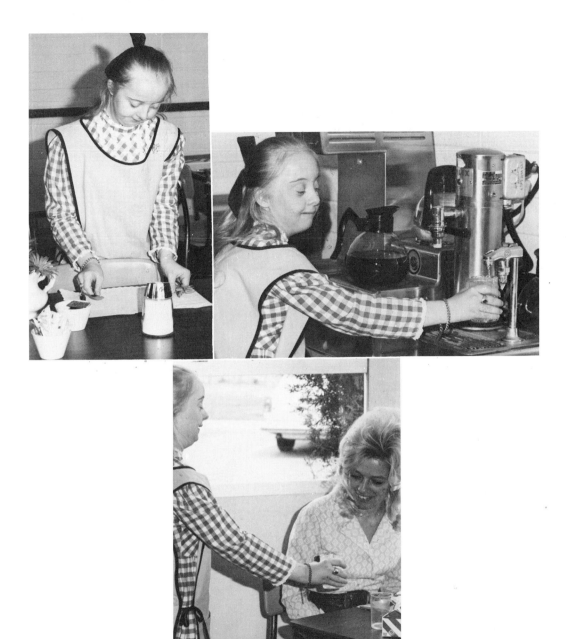

Fig. 9-2. In a sheltered workshop setting a trainable student can learn basic skills that will enhance the possibility of eventual employment (From Chinn, P. L. *Child health maintenance: concepts in family centered care.* (2nd. ed.) St. Louis: The C. V. Mosby Co., 1979.

tioned studies. Rather, we are drawing attention to the importance of carefully assessing all possible variables in any research that may have a bearing on the findings. In the two above-mentioned studies, many different individuals may have had an effect on the outcome of the research. Students are very much affected by the teachers and the quality of vocational preparation prior to the actual work experience. Vocational rehabilitation counselors also have a prime role in the development of student competencies. Likewise the employers providing the work training are an integral part of the rehabilitation process. Finally, the attitudes that parents reflect may affect the performance of their children. Considering the Chaffin, Smith, and Haring (1967) study, we may conclude that the preparation of retarded students for effective and competitive functioning in an adult society can be facilitated by a concerted team effort, including work experience in the real world.

In any case, regardless of program biases, the curriculum for the educable retarded at the high school level appears to have moved in recent years in the direction of work-study or some type of vocational experience. At the time these students reach a vocational level class, they usually become eligible for assistance through vocational rehabilitation. If the individual meets eligibility requirements, a number of services become available that can enhance his chances of becoming vocationally competent. To be eligible for vocational rehabilitation services in most states an individual must: (1) have a disability, (2) have a disability that represents a vocational handicap, or (3) represent reasonable feasibility for rehabilitation.

In the past, rehabilitation counselors working under rigid case closure quotas were hesitant to certify and accept as clients retarded individuals who were considered difficult to rehabilitate (Chinn, 1968). In most states, quotas for rehabilitation counselors working with the retarded have now either been eliminated or modified to realistic levels. In many instances, the counselors come into the public schools and work closely with the special education teacher. Basically, the responsibilities of the vocational rehabilitation counselor working with retarded students are as follows:

1. Certify all trainees for vocational rehabilitation services.
2. Consult with school officials on training arrangements within participating school districts.
3. Provide vocational rehabilitation services for the individual trainees when extended services are needed (for example, psychotherapy, surgery, and so on).

4. Evaluate public school records pertaining to those individuals referred for rehabilitation services.
5. Initiate and conduct joint conferences with the work-study teachers.
6. Approve all job training. Evaluate training facilities, make training arrangements and agreements, and consult with the trainee and work-study teacher.
7. Approve all expenditures for client services.
8. Approve all individual vocational rehabilitation plans for clients accepted for vocational rehabilitation services.
9. Maintain individual case records of the vocational rehabilitation clients.

In addition to providing the above services, vocational rehabilitation counselors can instigate other traditional rehabilitation services, such as the fitting of prosthetic devices, the provision of corrective surgery, and the payment of training fees. Rehabilitation counselors can also provide another important service by issuing subminimum wage exemption certificates when deemed necessary. Many employers who are interested in hiring handicapped individuals are hesitant to do so when the worker's production level does not meet the criterion set for other employees, and minimum wage restrictions are nevertheless imposed. Under such circumstances, the vocational rehabilitation counselor can issue a subminimum wage exemption certificate that will allow for payment of wages commensurate with the level of productivity.

WORK EXPERIENCES. The nature of the work experiences will vary somewhat according to the philosophy of each particular program. Some programs begin work experiences within the school setting and eventually work the student into community settings. Other programs may begin the experiences in the community immediately. The nature of the experience with respect to difficulty and the actual type of assignment is usually dependent on the needs and the nature of each student. Before placements are made, each student is carefully evaluated with respect to ability and interests. During the years spent in the vocational level class, the student may have an opportunity to work in a variety of settings to maximize exposure to different types of vocational experiences that may be encountered; this may allow the student to find the permanent placement he would like at the completion of school. The primary purpose of the work experience, however, is not to develop specific vocational skills, but rather to enable the student to develop the work habits and interpersonal skills necessary to acquire and maintain any job. If in the course of training, specific skills are acquired, these naturally could be helpful in obtaining specific jobs at the end of school. But specific skill competencies should not be emphasized at the expense of the affective dimensions of vocational behavior.

PROBLEMS RELATED TO WORK EXPERIENCE. The professional working with retarded adolescents in work-experience programs frequently encounters problems that may hinder and even preclude the development of effective programming for the student. As discussed in earlier chapters, the majority of the retarded come from lower socioeconomic backgrounds. Work-related motivational problems sometimes develop when the student's family has existed for a number of years, if not generations, on public assistance. Difficulties may arise when the student in training or his parents come to the realization that employment following school may take the form of a relatively low-paying job. When remuneration is low, there may be little incentive to work unless other work values have been emphasized.

We do not intend to imply that public assistance is an adequate alternative to work; rather, attention is being directed to the fact that the vocational level of retarded individuals is frequently on the lower end of the continuum. Perhaps the problem is primarily attributable to the limited vocational capacities of the retarded. In some instances, however, we may view the problem as an indictment of the lack of imagination and resourcefulness of professionals involved in the training and placement of retarded individuals. Too frequently handicapped individuals are vocationally stereotyped. The blind, at least in the past, have been stereotyped into vocations such as piano technicians and chair caners, paraplegics into positions as watchmakers and accountants. Retarded individuals are often ushered into positions as dishwashers and janitors. While these occupations may be personally satisfying and rewarding to some handicapped individuals, they too frequently represent the lack of consideration for the individual's interest and aptitude. The limitations of each individual must be considered but training programs and vocational placements that consider only administrative convenience are inexcusable. Researchers such as Howe (1967) have found some retarded individuals employed in positions paying well over the national mean.

Creativity and imagination can provide a wider variety of occupations suitable for the handicapped. At a conference on vocational preparation for the mentally retarded Kidd (1969) provided an example of such imaginative vocational placement for the trainable retarded. A business that raised and packaged worms for fishing considered hiring trainable retarded individuals to count and package the worms. As might be expected, the retarded were unable to count accurately. To overcome this obstacle, a box of pennies of the exact amount of worms to be counted was placed on one side of the individual along with an empty container. On the other side of the individual was a large container of worms and the containers to be filled. With each penny that was picked up and placed in the empty container, a worm was picked up with the other hand and placed in the packaging container. When the pennies were gone, an accurate number of worms were placed in the container for sale. The entire process was repeated continually. While the example appears to be a simple story, it points out how ingenuity can create jobs we would not ordinarily consider possible for the retarded.

Another problem affecting work experiences is the sometimes inappropriate self-concept some retarded people have regarding their abilities (Ringness, 1961). Some retarded individuals tend to set vocational goals for themselves that cannot be realized. Some of the problems are created by parents themselves, who set inappropriate expectations for their children. Often these vocational expectations carry with them educational requirements beyond the capabilities of the student. These unrealistic expectations appear to be incompatible with Rotter's social learning theory discussed in Chapter 8. However, whether the student is fantasizing or really believes that he possesses greater capabilities than he has, problems do develop when the student considers the work to which he has been assigned to be demeaning. In situations of this nature the task for parents, teachers, and counselors is difficult. They must endeavor to help the retarded individual to realize his limitations, but at the same time they must not jeopardize the fragile self-concept of most retarded persons. The task then is to help the student to rechannel unrealistic vocational choices for those that are functional and still satisfying to the individual. The student aspiring to become a nurse may be led into a nurses' aide position, while the aspiring airline hopeful is led into a position in the airline industry loading baggage or maintaining aircraft. Effort should be directed toward finding acceptable alternatives without the loss of personal dignity.

Career education. Brolin, (1976, 1977) suggests that while the work-study programs instituted in the 1960's were a marked improvement over exclusively academically oriented curricula as far as the vocational outcomes were concerned, the academic and work-study combinations are still not enough to assure community adjustment for the retarded. Career education holds promise in this area by emphasizing the development of daily living, personal-social and occupational skills for career development. Brolin further suggests that career education must be life centered, which includes preparation in life roles, such as student, homemaker, consumer, citizen, parent, and worker. Brolin further suggests that career education is a unified approach to education for life beginning with early childhood education and continuing throughout the adult years.

Brolin further suggests that career education is a total educational concept that systematically coordinates all school, family, and community components, thus facilitating the individual's potential for economic, social, and personal fulfillment. The U.S. Office of Education (1975) defines career education as the "totality of experiences through which one learns about and prepares to engage in work as part of her or his way of living."

The U.S. Office of Education (1975) developed learner outcome goals for persons leaving the formal educational system at the completion of specified levels of education. D'Alonzo (1977) suggests that the following goals are commensurate with those traditionally advocated by special educators involved with the education and training of the mentally retarded and must be individualized to meet the developmental needs of mentally retarded individuals:

1. Competent in the basic academic skills required for adaptability in our rapidly changing society
2. Equipped with good work habits
3. Capable of choosing and have chosen a personally meaningful set of work values that foster a desire to work
4. Equipped with career decision-making, job-hunting, and job-getting skills
5. Equipped with vocational personal skills at a level that will allow them to gain entry into and attain a degree of success in the occupational society
6. Equipped with career decisions based on the widest possible set of data concerning themselves and their educational-vocational opportunities
7. Aware of means available to them for continuing and recurrent education once they have left the formal system of schooling

8. Successful in a paid occupation, in further education, or in a vocation consistent with their current career education

9. Successful in incorporating work values into their total personal value structure in such a way that they are able to choose what is for them a desirable life-style.

D'Alonzo suggests that at the present time most elementary and middle school curricula fail to provide those learning experiences that have a direct relationship to career or prevocational development. The lack of these experiences at earlier levels creates a problem for those attempting to develop career education skills at the secondary level. A second problem that D'Alonzo draws attention to is the lack of programming for retarded children functioning below the educable level. Trainable children, he suggests, are not processed through programs to prepare them for careers in the community outside of sheltered placement.

COGNITIVE DEVELOPMENT

The typical adolescent functions in what Piaget has identified as the period of formal operations. This period usually begins at the age of 11 years. The critical aspect of this period is the individual's ability to begin with the theoretical or hypothetical rather than the real (Flavell, 1963; Chinn, 1979) and to think beyond the present and to consider things that do not exist but that might be. Chinn further states that the term "formal" is used by Piaget to represent the fact that the child at this stage of cognitive development centers on the "form" thought, objects, and experiences rather than exact content. In contrast, the child who functions in the period of concrete operations responds to things about him in various ways for organizing and ordering, but always in relation to what is reality and what is readily available through perceptions. While the child who enters the period of formal operations may begin to use more mature thought patterns, there are times when concrete operations may still be used to a significant degree (Chinn, 1979).

In contrast to their normal peers, only a few retarded adolescents reach and function in the period of formal operations. Those who are capable of functioning in formal operational thought are the higher-functioning mildly retarded, and most likely they will function only at beginning stages of this period. It is unlikely that the retarded adolescent or even adult will develop a mental age beyond 12 years; therefore, much of the functioning of the mildly retarded or educable adolescents will be at the concrete operations period, while severely and moderately retarded adolescents are likely to function in the period of preoperational thought. It is likely that some may fixate at this level even in adulthood. A few of the profoundly retarded may not be able to function above the period of sensorimotor intelligence.

Understanding the level of cognitive functioning of the adolescent retarded can be extremely useful for both professional workers and parents. By recognizing the individual's abilities as well as limitations, learning and training activities appropriate to the individual level of cognitive level can be designed. Unrealistic goals and expectations can be avoided. It has been noted in earlier chapters that Piaget's stage formulations have been the object of serious criticism recently (Flavell, 1977). They are, however, helpful in terms of conceptualizing behaviors evident at various stages of human development.

SOCIAL AND EMOTIONAL ADJUSTMENT

Chinn (1979) suggests that because the young adolescent is neither child nor adult and often lacks understanding from adults, the peer group becomes paramount in importance. The peer group may provide understanding from others who are experiencing the same transition pains. Chinn further suggests that because the adolescent may be unable to relate to the world as an individual, the achievement of satisfying intense peer group relationships may facilitate the transition required.

Life and adjustment for retarded adolescents may be even more complex and difficult than for their normal counterparts. Difficulties in establishing peer group relationships, perhaps because of rejection by normal peers or lack of sophistication and maturity in developing meaningful relationships with retarded adolescent peers accentuate the frustrations.

Discrepancies in chronological and mental ages

As the retarded individual grows older, the discrepancy between chronological and mental age becomes even greater. As discussed in the previous chapter, at the age of 6 the child with a 75 IQ has a mental age of approximately 4½, only a year and a half behind his normal peers. The 6-year-old with an IQ of 50 may have a mental age of 3, representing a 3-year gap between him and his normal counterparts. At the age of 16, however, the adolescent with a 75 IQ may have a mental age of 12. Thus the distance over the 10-year period has increased from 1½ years to 4 years. For the

16-year-old adolescent with a 50 IQ it has become even more dramatic—the discrepancy over the 10-year period has changed from approximately 3 years to 8 years.

From this widening gulf may come a host of problems. Childhood friends who were once willing to share their time and activities with the 6-year-old retarded neighbor may find that their 16-year-old former friend is too deficient and unsophisticated in interests and social skills to be included in peer group activities. When the retarded adolescent is the only retarded individual in the same age range in the neighborhood, the problem may be intensified, for there is little if any opportunity for peer group interaction. This type of social isolation and rejection can frequently lead to emotional stress, which in turn may result in behavior that makes the individual even more socially unacceptable.

When we discussed Maslow's theory of prepotency of needs (Maslow, 1954) earlier, we alluded to the need for acceptance or belonging. If acceptance cannot be obtained through socially acceptable means, the retarded adolescent may resort to seeking acceptance in socially maladjusted or delinquent groups. If the retarded individual is able to meet minimal group requirements and expectations, full acceptance may be a possibility. If, however, the retarded individual is unable to meet group standards, then acceptance may be on a partial or conditional basis. The group may accept the retarded to do their "dirty work" or to assume the responsibility for less desirable group functions. Under such conditions the retarded may be misused and may operate under the false illusion of being a fully accepted member.

In order to minimize the likelihood of acceptance being sought in socially maladjusted groups, parents, teachers, and other professionals must work toward providing necessary recognition of all positive efforts on the part of retarded adolescents. If these adolescents can gain recognition in this manner, the need to engage in socially unacceptable attention-getting behavior may be avoided. By providing a place of acceptance and by facilitating peer acceptance, families and professionals can help the retarded adolescent avoid a considerable amount of social deviancy.

Personal appearance and grooming

An area of concern that may be directly related to social development with retarded adolescents is the area of personal appearance and grooming. By the time children reach the period of adolescence, many become acutely aware of the relationship of their personal appearance to their sex role expectations. At this time many adolescents develop heterosexual interests and are thus concerned with enhancing themselves by making positive impressions on peers of the opposite sex. Adolescents typically conform to peer opinions, activities, and appearances (Horrocks, 1969; Group for the Advancement of Psychiatry, 1968). Girls become increasingly more interested in the use of cosmetics and more fashionable hair styles and clothing. They are also concerned with their height and weight. Likewise, boys are concerned with clothing, hair styles, and their physical attributes as compared to their peers.

Many retarded adolescents lack the financial resources and/or the necessary skills and sophistication needed to groom themselves adequately. While normal adolescents learn from peers or siblings the methods of hair styling, use of cosmetics, and coordination of clothing styles, the retarded frequently have little if any help. They may be unable to learn from observing the examples set by others and experimenting on their own.

Puberty frequently brings about acne problems. This condition frequently causes emotional scarring that may be far more significant and permanent than the physical scarring that occurs (Reisner, 1973). Normal adolescents have the advantage of being able to read and ask questions. Some have access to a dermatologist to help protect their cosmetic appearance. The retarded may have difficulty in locating necessary help. Many lack the financial resources to receive treatment from a dermatologist. Unable to groom themselves adequately and maintain an acceptable cosmetic appearance, retarded adolescent's may find social acceptance nearly impossible.

Unfortunately, some parents of retarded children make the assumption that, because of a retarded child's intellectual limitations, physical appearance is of little consequence. Yet most retarded children strive constantly to be as much like their normal peers as possible. They want nothing to draw any attention to the fact that they are somewhat different from other children. Adverse physical appearance does draw attention and hinders if not precludes social acceptance. Parents and teachers must be aware that how an individual looks usually has a bearing on self-concept. Thus programs and curricula must include this important area in the education of retarded adolescents.

Parents at times lack the ability to teach their retarded children adequate grooming skills. In such situations, the responsibility may fall heavily on the schools. The manner in which the students are taught may take several different forms. Positive discussions in class are a possible means. Guest speakers from clothing stores can usually be brought into the schools or the students taken to the stores for a demonstration. Likewise, the people in cosmetic sales are usually very cooperative and will often teach and demonstrate the proper use of cosmetics for the girls. If a dermatologist is not available, then the school nurse should be able to provide the necessary information on the care of skin and treatment of acne problems. Beauty colleges that train cosmetologists are frequently willing to provide their services to teach the retarded students how to shampoo and care for their hair.

Even if the students are able to learn how to properly groom themselves, the problem of financial resources at times presents an obstacle to the mentally retarded. Many come from lower socioeconomic backgrounds in which resources are insufficient to purchase the necessary clothing and supplies. There are several alternatives to working through this problem. First, the students can learn to make their own clothing. Even the boys can learn how to sew, to repair and make clothing. This can be taught by the teacher, or perhaps through a cooperative arrangement with the home economics teacher. This process can provide clothing at a substantially lower cost as well as develop a leisure-time activity for the retarded. Other benefits can be derived from the making of their own clothing. There is usually a certain amount of pride that evolves out of creating and making something of value. There is also the benefit of learning to measure and to follow directions, which sewing requires.

Another alternative to the teaching of sewing is for the teacher to find suitable used clothing. Often there is good clothing that may be new or in nearly new condition but that is no longer useful to some individuals. Clothing stores may also be willing to donate clothing they are unable to sell or make use of. If the clothing is given to the students in a tackful manner, rather than as a useless castoff, it may serve a very useful function. It should also be noted that more casual modes of dress for youth have been generated by the social liberation movement. The use of used clothing has become more acceptable and, in some instances, even a status symbol among normal adolescents.

Dating and social activities

One of the greatest needs for the retarded adolescent—one that is often not fulfilled—is the need for social outlets. Lacking the necessary social sophistication gained by normal children through observation, many retarded adolescents are unable to plan and successfully carry out social activity. Their social problems include several facets, such as transportation, planning parties, asking for and accepting dates, behavior on dates, and financing their social activities.

Transportation is a problem for many teenagers. Some are unable to drive because they are not old enough or because they lack access to an automobile. If the retarded adolescent is unable to drive because of age, or inability to pass driver's training, instruction in the use of public transportation can be provided by parents and teachers. The ability to utilize public transportation may be important not only for social but for vocational reasons as well. If public transportation is not available, then transportation must be provided by parents, teachers, or volunteers, such as youth groups belonging to the National Association for Retarded Citizens. For those young people able to profit from driver's education and successfully fulfill state requirements, it should be made available in the public schools when legal age is reached. Driver's education is a debatable issue for the retarded. It can be argued that only the most capable of the educable students should be encouraged to drive. These would include those who possess the coordination and the ability to think critically in emergencies. We are in complete harmony with this position. There are more than enough incompetent drivers with normal intelligence on the highways, and there is no justification for increasing hazards by adding incompetent retarded individuals. We do share the concern, however, that there will always be a significant number of retarded individuals who will drive even if they lack both competence and licensure. Because of these individuals, some professionals see the need for all educable adolescents to be exposed to drivers' education. While there appears to be some risk that the drivers' education exposure may serve as an incentive to the less able, if the course were taught properly it could help many to realize their limitations and to understand the consequences of driving without the necessary competence or a license.

Many retarded adolescents have only limited financial resources for dating expenses. While traditional patterns of social behavior require the male to bear the expenses for dates, it would not seem inappropriate in these days of liberation from many traditional sex roles for both individuals to share the cost of a day's or evening's activity. It would also be appropriate for parents and professionals to draw attention to and encourage the many activities available in most communities that are both pleasurable and available without cost or for a nominal amount. Since the retarded themselves may not be capable of taking the initiative for planning social activities, the responsibilities rest with volunteer groups, local associations for the retarded, and parents to provide social activities. Many social functions can be planned at school with the aid of the teacher. If an institution of higher learning is in proximity, special education and recreation therapy majors might be available to assist in planning and supervising these social functions.

Proper social behavior and personal interaction skills should begin early in the home and in school and should continue throughout the school years. Most retarded adolescents are eager to learn, as they would like to be as much like their normal peers as possible. They would prefer to avoid any behavioral patterns that draw attention to their limitations.

Retarded adolescents who are eager to show their affection for others of the opposite sex lack the skills to do so in socially acceptable ways. Many try to emulate what they have seen on the television or movie screen or what they have heard their peers discussing. Unfortunately, many are unable to distinguish reality from fantasy. They are frequently unable to "read" their environment to determine what is really acceptable and what is not. It is the responsibility of both parents and professionals to help the retarded child as he develops through adolescence and adulthood to learn acceptable behavioral patterns that are pleasing to himself and others.

PHYSICAL DEVELOPMENT

In Chapter 8 physical and health characteristics of the mentally retarded child were discussed. Most of these characteristics are applicable to the retarded adolescent as well. In this section we shall examine some of the characteristics and research findings that are directly related to the retarded adolescent.

Puberty begins approximately at the same time as adolescence. During this period gross physiological changes occur. The retarded adolescents' ability to cope with these changes may have a direct relationship to their ability to adjust to the demands of their environment.

Physical problems

In Chapter 8 we noted that there are strong suggestions that the retarded have both health and physical deficiencies; one of the primary needs listed in

Maslow's prepotency of needs were the physiological needs. Thus, if we are to be concerned with ultimate self-actualization among retarded adolescents, we must address ourselves to their physiological needs first.

Hammer and Barnard (1966) examined the nutritional health, dental health, and physical defects of a group of forty-four retarded adolescents, consisting of twenty-six boys and eighteen girls. They found that diets for the group were generally high in carbohydrates and low or marginal in iron and ascorbic acid. Parents typically reinforced good behavior with candy and desserts. Two out of the forty-four were obese.

A dental hygienist assessed the dental health of the Hammer and Barnard subjects. The overall dental condition of the group was considered poor. Problems tended to be related to inadequate care and lack of instruction regarding tooth brushing. Only a limited number of the group had received routine dental examinations, and few had received any type of restorative treatment. Neglect was attributed to inadequate dental facilities, unavailability of dentists, and insufficient financial resources to meet the cost of dental care.

Physical defects and/or signs of central nervous system dysfunction were found in thirty-one (70 percent) of the Hammer and Barnard subjects. Defects identified were minimal brain damage (15), seizure disorders (7), growth retardation (5), visual defects (4), and cerebral palsy (3). While these findings were the results of only one study and may not be typical of most retarded adolescent groups, there is a distinct need for professionals in the health care fields to monitor the physical conditions of retarded adolescents. Because of the lower socioeconomic status of many retarded individuals, routine physical and dental examinations may be minimal or nonexistent. Teachers and public health nurses can provide important instruction to the retarded individual and his family in dietary management and general health care procedures including dental care. Social workers and health care specialists should be particularly concerned with health delivery service to those unable to afford routine private examination and treatment.

While the present social liberation movement has focused much attention on restructuring traditional masculine-feminine roles, many of the stereotype roles persist, especially in the lower socioeconomic levels. Social pressure is exerted on adolescent boys and girls to conform to the roles. Thus retarded boys who are physically inadequate either in size or motor development may be pressured to participate in athletic activities. Rejection by peers and even their fathers may result. Such conditions frequently contribute to the already devalued self-concept.

As previously discussed, the retarded tend to be somewhat immature in physical stature and deficient in motor development (Abernathy, 1936; Malpass, 1963; Rarick, 1976). Kolstoe (1970) suggests that the retarded on the average are 10 percent below their normal counterparts in motor proficiency. Thus the retarded adolescent may be at a distinct disadvantage in competitive athletics. In many instances he may be physically deficient as well as having intellectual limitations that preclude the mastery of necessary rules that many highly structured activities require. Thus, the inability of the retarded adolescent male to meet traditional masculine expectations with regard to physical activities may be extremely ego-damaging.

Physiological changes related to puberty

During the early adolescent period there is a significant surge in growth and development. These changes include physiologic and behavioral changes, including the attainment of sexual function (Chinn, 1979). When these physical changes begin to occur, estrogen, progesterone, and testosterone production levels also increase. These hormones are essential for secondary sex characteristics, (such as broadening of the shoulders and increased muscle mass for boys and widening of the hips for girls). Changes occur in reproductive systems as well as in distribution of body hair and adipose tissue. The rate and the time of these changes are variable: girls begin puberty changes generally between the ages of 10 and 14; boys are usually later in adolescent developmental changes, which tend to occur between 12 and 16 (Timiras, 1972).

The beginning of reproductive capabilities is evident with the beginning of menstruation for girls and seminal emission for boys. Menstruation is usually irregular and is usually not accompanied by ovulation for several months. Likewise in boys, mature sexual capabilities may not occur for several months after the first indications of development (Chinn, 1979).

Unless retarded adolescents are prepared for the gross physiological changes brought about by puberty, they may come as traumatic experiences. The adolescent retarded girl who has not been prepared for menstruation may find her initial experience frightening and may be too embarrassed to seek help. The responsibility for providing sex education has been a widely debated issue. While some individuals feel that sex education belongs in the school, other individuals and some school boards contend that sex education is the responsibility of the home or the church. Rauh, Johnson, and Burket (1973) contend that, next to school tax levies, sex education is probably the most controversial subject confronting American public schools today. Several school districts that have developed sophisticated, sequential sex education programs have given them up because of public pressure.

It would be fine if either the school, the home, or the church would assume the responsibility for sex education. Unfortunately, in many instances no one is willing to assume this responsibility. Teachers are hesitant to do so without authorization. Thus peers are the only source from which the young people can obtain any information, and this is often distorted or highly inaccurate. This problem is not unique to the retarded—it relates to children in regular classes as well. The problem for the retarded is even greater, however, because their accessibility to accurate information may be even more remote. The normal adolescent can seek and find information in a library. The retarded adolescent may not be able to read or comprehend the written information even if it is made available.

Brody (1978), reporting the results of a national survey, suggests that many teenagers are sexually active. The survey indicates that each year 680,000 premarital pregnancies are avoided because sexually active teenagers use birth control devices. The survey further reports, however, that 313,000 additional pregnancies could be prevented if all those who did not want to become pregnant used contraceptives consistently. The survey showed that 41 percent of teenagers had sexual intercourse before marriage. Among the reasons why teenagers did not use contraceptives was the failure to appreciate the risk of pregnancy and embarrassment or lack of knowledge about where to get birth control services. This particular report makes no specific mention of retarded adolescents. If, however, some sexually active normal teenagers are failing to obtain adequate birth control services, it is reasonable to assume that retarded teenagers will have as much, if not greater, difficulty as their normal counterparts.

Parents tend to have difficulty discussing their child's sexual maturation with their pediatrician. Even though they may recognize the need for information in order to deal effectively with their child, they are reluctant to ask questions. It is not until the natural course of physical development forces the issue of sex education into the open that many parents of the retarded seek counsel (Fischer and Krajicek, 1974). In Hammer and Barnard's study of retarded adolescents (1966), sexual behavior appeared to be one of the greatest concerns of parents. The parents generally considered themselves ill prepared to provide adequate sex education and even considered institutionalization as the only means of avoiding pregnancies and sexual deviancy. It is interesting to note that professional observers did not perceive the problem to be of the magnitude that the parents did.

Fischer and Krajicek (1974) suggest that a retarded child's general attitude toward accepting himself as a sexual being will tend to reflect the attitude of important adults in his environment. If they are comfortable with all facets of themselves, the child will be also. They suggest that the common advice that adults should answer only those specific questions that the child asks about sex is not generally applicable to the retarded. Retarded children, particularly the more limited, tend to have inadequate verbal skills. Adults must therefore take the initiative with matters related to sex education. Success in dealing with the retarded in sex education depends greatly on the adults' willingness to "give the child permission" to ask questions or to "wonder" about sexually related matters. Cultural implications that sex is something dirty and should not be discussed tend to restrict adequate parent-child interactions.

While our Puritan heritage has imposed restrictions that influence the official attitude of society, there appears to be points of view in our culture that are diametrically opposed to one another with regard to sexual permissiveness. There is little doubt that sexual activity among adolescents is on the increase (Christensen and Gregg, 1970; Luckey and Nass, 1969; Zelnik and Kantner, 1972). Related to the increase of sexual activity among adolescents is the increasing incidence of veneral disease (Blount, Darrow, and Johnson, 1973). It can be assumed that with or without the approval of society adolescents, including the retarded, will continue to engage in sexual activity. Unless they receive adequate sex education, both unwanted pregnancies and venereal diseases are inevitable. While school boards, parents, and the public argue over the responsibility of sex education, many retarded adolescents continue in their ignorance, victims of our indecision.

Adolescence is a time when the individual is in a "marginal" status in relationship to childhood and adulthood in that he does not appropriately belong to either group. The attitudes, ideologies, and styles of living of childhood and adulthood are in conflict with one another, and the adolescent is caught in the middle of the conflict. Adolescence can be a time of fun, a time of increased freedom, a time of increased responsibility, a difficult and trying time for the normal as well as the retarded adolescent. However, the stereotyped problems of adolescence can at least be minimized and may be avoided entirely. With a team effort among the adolescent himself, parents, professionals, and volunteers, this time in the life of a retarded individual can be both rewarding and self-fulfilling.

STUDY QUESTIONS

1. How has Section 504 of the Rehabilitation Act of 1973 affected the mentally retarded?
2. What have the research studies found regarding the efficacy of work-study programs?
3. What is career education?
4. How does the retarded adolescent compare to normal counterparts with regard to cognitive development?
5. How do retarded adolescents compare physically to their normal counterparts?

REFERENCES

Abernathy, E. M. Relationship between mental and physical growth. *Monographs of the Society for Research in Child Development*, 1936, **1**(7).

Anthony, E. J. The reactions of parents to adolescents and to their behavior. In E. J. Anthony and T. Benedek (Eds.), *Parenthood, its psychology and psychopathology*. Boston: Little, Brown and Co., 1970.

Blount, J. H., Darrow, W. W., and Johnson, R. E. Veneral disease in adolescents. *Pediatric Clinics of North America*, 1973, **20**, 1021-1034.

Brody, J. E. Sexually active teenagers use contraceptives effectively. *Dallas Morning News*, June 9, 1978.

Brolin, D. E. *Vocational preparation of retarded citizens*. Columbus, Ohio: Charles E. Merrill Publishing Co., 1976.

Brolin, D. E. Career development: a national priority. *Education and Training of the Mentally Retarded*, 1977, **12**(27), 154-156.

Chaffin, J. D., Smith, J. O., and Haring, N. *Selected demonstration for the vocational training of mentally retarded youth in public high schools*. Kansas City: U.S. Department of Health, Education and Welfare, Vocational Rehabilitation Administration, Division of Research Grants and Demonstrations, Sept., 1967.

Chinn, P. C. Habilitation of the educable mentally retarded through high school work-study programs. In H. Love (Ed.), *Educating the men-* *tally retarded*. Berkeley: McCutchan Publishing Corp., 1968.

Chinn, P. L. *Child health maintenance: concepts for family centered care*. St Louis: The C. V. Mosby Co., 1979.

Christensen, H. T., and Gregg, C. F. Changing sex norms in America and Scandinavia. *Journal of Marriage and the Family*, 1970, **32**, 616-627.

D'Alonzo, B. J. Trends and issues in career education for the mentally retarded. *Education and training of the mentally retarded*, 1977, **12**(2), 156-158.

Fischer, H. L., and Krajicek, M. J. Sexual development of the moderately retarded child. *Clinical Pediatrics*, 1974, **13**(1), 79-83.

Flavell, J. H. *The developmental psychology of Jean Piaget*. New York: Van Nostrand Reinhold Co., 1963.

Flavell, J. H. *Cognitive development*, Englewood Cliffs, N.J.: Prentice-Hall, 1977.

Group for the Advancement of Psychiatry, *Normal adolescence*. New York: Charles Scribner's Sons, 1968.

Halpern A. S., Raffeld, P., Irvin, L. and Link, R. Measuring social and pre-vocational awareness in mildly retarded adolescents. *American Journal of Mental Deficiency*, 1975, **80**(1), 81-89.

Hammer, S. L., and Bernard, K. E. The mentally retarded adolescent. *Pediatrics*, 1966, **38**(5), 845-857.

Horrocks, J. E. *The psychology of adolescence: behavior and development.* Boston: Houghton-Mifflin Co., 1969.

Howe, C. D. *A comparison of mentally retarded high school students in work-study versus traditional programs.* Long Beach, Calif.: U.S. Department of Health, Education and Welfare, Office of Education, Bureau of Education for the Handicapped, Sept., 1967.

Hurlock, E. B. *Child development.* New York: McGraw-Hill Book Co., 1964.

Kidd, J. W. Address at the National Conference on Vocational Education of the Handicapped, Pittsburgh, Feb., 1969.

Kolstoe, O. P. *Teaching educable mentally retarded children.* New York: Holt, Rinehart, and Winston, 1970.

Luckey, E. B., and Nass, G. D. A comparison of sexual attitudes and behavior in an international sample. *Journal of Marriage and the Family,* 1969, **31,** 364-379.

Malpass, L. F. Motor skills in mental deficiency. In N. R. Ellis (Ed.), Handbook of mental deficiency. New York: McGraw-Hill Book Co., 1963.

Maslow, A. H. *Motivation and personality,* New York: Harper & Row, Publishers, 1954.

Rarick, G. L. Stability performance of educable mentally retarded and normal children. Research Quarterly, **47**(4): 619-623.

Rauh, J. L., Johnson, L. B., and Burket, R. L. The reproductive adolescent. In D. C. Garrell (Ed.), *Pediatric clinics of North America,* 1973, **20,** 1005-1020.

Reisner, R. M. Acne vulgaris. In D. C. Garrell (Ed.), *Pediatric Clinics of North America,* 1973, **20,**851-864.

Ringness, T. A. Self-concept of children of low, average, and high intelligence. *American Journal of Mental Deficiency,* 1961, **65,** 453-462.

Saenger, G. *The adjustment of severely retarded adults in the community.* Albany, N.Y.: Interdepartmental Health Resources Board, 1957.

Timiras, P. S. *Developmental physiology and aging,* New York: The McMillan Co., 1972.

U.S. Department of Health, Education and Welfare, Office of Education, Office of Career Education. *An Introduction to Career Education.* Washington, D.C.: U.S. Printing Office, 1975.

Zelnik, M., and Kanter, J. F. The probability of pre-marital intercourse. *Social Science Research,* 1972, **1,** 335-341.

ANNOTATED BIBLIOGRAPHY

Brolin, D. E. *Vocational preparation of retarded citizens.* Columbus, Ohio: Charles E. Merrill Publishing Co., 1976.

Provides a basic background regarding mental retardation and vocational adjustment of the mentally retarded as well as specific techniques of vocational preparation and program models and evaluations.

Gendel, E. S. *Sex education of the mentally retarded in the home.* Arlington, Tex.: The National Association for Retarded Citizens, 1968.

A short, helpful pamphlet on sex education for the retarded. This organization has many helpful publications for parents and professionals working with the retarded. (Their address is in the Appendix.)

Kolstoe, O. P., and Frey, R. *A high school work-study program for the mentally subnormal student.* Carbondale, Ill.: Southern Illinois University Press, 1965.

An easy-to-read book dealing with the nature and needs of the retarded adolescent and educational and rehabilitation programming.

Pattullo, H. *Puberty in the girl who is retarded.* Arlington, Tex.: National Association for Retarded Citizens, 1969.

A helpful booklet designed to help mothers of mentally retarded girls cope with some of the problems of puberty. Section headings include "What about heterosexual behavior?" and "Should my daughter marry?"

PART FOUR

The retarded adult

CHAPTER 10

The retarded adult

INTRODUCTION

The scientific study of the life cycle is a relatively new phenomenon. Scientists have tended to devote most of their attention to development during childhood, because it progresses so rapidly, is so readily distinguishable into stages, and is so clearly significant for later life (Bradbury, 1975). Thus, while adulthood constitutes the major portion of an individual's life, it has received comparatively little attention in the available literature.

Finding a definition that is suitable for all cultures or situations may be a difficult, if not impossible, task. Webster's New Collegiate Dictionary (1975) defines "adult" as "fully developed and mature; grown-up . . . a human being after an age (as 21) specified by law."

Various cultures and religious groups may have their own definition or criteria for an individual reaching adulthood. Jewish males celebrate their Bar Mitzvahs at 13. This signifies their admission into the adult religious community. Puberty, the biological coming of age, is observed as a social coming of age by many religious communities and traditional societies (Bradbury, 1975).

Adulthood generally marks a period in the life of an individual in which a transition has been made from a life of relative dependence to one of increasing independence and responsibility. Agreement among the various professions tends to be lacking as to when adulthood formally takes place. From a legal standpoint, an individual becomes an adult upon reaching a specific age. Legal age for adulthood varies from 18 years in some states to 21 years in others. Thus an individual may be instantaneously transformed from adolescent to adult on a specified birthday. An individual may also be transformed from adolescent to adult or vice-versa in a matter of minutes by crossing from one state to another.

Public school officials have tended to view either the completion of a high school program or exclusion from school because of age (often 21) as the point at which the school's responsibility ends, and presumably the individual has reached some semblance of adulthood. Professionals in the health sciences tend to equate specific levels of physical development with adulthood. Such a criterion would perhaps preclude those with certain physiological deviances regardless of their intellectual or social competencies. Adding to the frustrating lack of uniformity in criteria is a behavioral science view that emphasizes specific behavioral patterns to meet adulthood standards.

For the purpose of this text we shall utilize a legal age criterion to define adulthood. The mentally retarded adults we shall be discussing are those individuals who have reached their eighteenth birthday. Were we to use some of the other criteria, some retarded individuals might be permanently excluded from adulthood.

Retarded adults exist as a paradox. They have achieved the status of adulthood because they have lived long enough to deserve the distinction. Yet they are seldom able to attain a level of total independence; they lack the intellectual skills to meet typical high school graduation requirements and may lack many behavioral characteristics considered by some as essential for adequate adult functioning.

Many educable and some trainable retarded individuals endure the frustrations of a mentally retarded's childhood and adolescence with the hope and expectation that adulthood will bring an emancipation from the many problems associated with school, failure, and rejection. While academic pressures and certain intellectual demands tend to subside on completion of school, other demands find their way into the life of a retarded adult. What are the expectations for an adult in our society? An adult works, earns money, and buys the necessities of life and as many of the pleasures as can be afforded. An adult socializes, often marries, has children, and tries to live as productively and happily as possible. The retarded adult often is unable to find or hold a job. Even if jobs are available, the wages may be so low that even the necessities of life may be out of grasp. What if the retarded adult has no one to socialize with, no one to love or to be loved by? What if the retarded adult must become dependent on parents for mere existence and the parents become too old to help or they die? There are many "what ifs" for the retarded adult; the ego-damaging frustrations of earlier life are exchanged for newer and sometimes harsher ones.

One needs to spend only a few hours examining the available literature to realize the paucity of research and writings that have been generated on the subject of the retarded adult. Concern for needs of the retarded has been relatively slow in developing in comparison to concern for other handicapping conditions, such as blindness and hearing impairment. Because of the tardiness in providing programs for the retarded, research and programming have tended to focus on retarded children, since it is in the schools and in the earliest years of life that the deficiencies of the mentally retarded tend to be more evident. It is interesting to note that it was not until 1973 that the National Association for Retarded Children appropriately changed its name to the National Association for Retarded Citizens. While long campaigning for the rights of all retarded individuals, the change is indicative of a growing recognition of the need to emphasize programming at all stages of life. We have no quarrel with the emphasis on retarded children and youth. We are concerned, however, with the seeming lack of programming for retarded adults, with the possible exception of vocational training and placement. A retarded individual will live three times more years as an adult than as a child and adolescent if an average life expectancy level is reached. It would seem only appropriate, therefore, for us to devote some time to the needs and nature of retarded adults.

In the subsequent pages of this chapter we shall examine how retarded adults have adjusted in society. We shall examine vocational programs as well as some of the emerging programs that provide for the needs of this segment of the retarded population. We shall also recommend what we believe are needed programs for the retarded adult.

STUDIES OF THE RETARDED ADULT IN THE COMMUNITY

The literature concerning follow-up studies of retarded individuals dates back to 1919, when Fernald conducted the first study of this nature recorded in the literature. In this section we shall not attempt a comprehensive review of this subject. Rather, we shall present a representative group of studies to provide the reader with some understanding of the nature of adjustment patterns of retarded individuals in the community. Some of the earlier studies may tend to have methodological weaknesses. They are presented in spite of any weaknesses, for they represent early attempts to provide us with information in this area and are considered classical studies in the field of mental retardation.

The study by Fernald (1919) involved individuals discharged from the Waverly Institution over a 25-year period. It is important to note that nearly all the subjects in the study were released under protest by the staff. It may therefore be assumed that preparation for release may be questionable in both a qualitative and quantitative sense.

Of the 1,537 individuals released by the institution during the period of the study, postinstitutional information was available on only 646, or less than half the original subjects. Fernald found that 612 were in other institutions for the retarded, while 279 could not be located. Of the 646 available subjects, 176 were females and 470 were males. Many of the female subjects appeared to make a satisfactory adjustment to community living. Of the 90 females who were located in the community, 11 were married and were housewives, 8 were self-supporting and independent, 20 worked at home, and 13 were living totally dependent at their parents' home. Thirty-eight of the female subjects had negative or antisocial records. Four of these had been committed to correctional institutions.

The male subjects appeared to make a better adjustment to community life than their female counterparts. Twenty-eight were self-supporting and living independently; 86 were employed and living at home; 77 worked at home; and 59 lived dependently at home with their families. The majority of the dependent group were lower grade retarded, while those holding jobs tended to come from higher functioning levels.

Three studies comparing the community adjustment of mentally retarded individuals to control groups of nonretarded individuals are frequently mentioned in the literature. These include the studies of Fairbanks in Baltimore (1931), Baller in Lincoln, Nebraska (1935), and Kennedy in Connecticut (1948). Fairbanks and Kennedy conducted their studies during periods when economic conditions were generally favorable, as were general employment conditions. Baller's study was conducted during a period of severe depression. When economic conditions are poor, the mentally retarded are frequently among those most severely affected. Employers may consider them the most dispensible of their employees, thus they are often the first to be laid off. This is particularly evident in Baller's study—only 20 percent of the retarded subjects were gainfully employed, as opposed to 50 percent of the controls (normal subjects). In Fairbanks' and Kennedy's studies, however, the retarded compared very favorably with the controls with respect to gainful employment.

In all three studies the marital status of the retarded appeared to be somewhat comparable to the control. Home ownership as reported by Fairbanks and Kennedy also appeared comparable. The retarded subjects in all three studies showed a higher evidence of dependency and relief by either family or agencies. The retarded in the three groups had more involvement with the police, the Baller group showing the highest incidence with nearly 43 percent of the retarded having some record of arrest as opposed to slightly over 10 percent of the controls. This higher incidence may also be attributable to the general economic conditions during the time of the study.

The three classical studies suggest that the majority of retarded subjects were able to make acceptable adjustments to community life. The studies also suggested that the majority tend to be occupied in the semiskilled and unskilled jobs. Economic conditions as well as the type of community may have some effect on their ability to adjust. Follow-up studies of the subjects in these studies suggest that even in later years, community adjustment of these individuals can be considered typically successful (Baller, Charles, and Miller, 1966; Kennedy, 1966).

Edgerton (1967) examined the posthospital lives of a number of individuals released from Pacific State Hospital, a California residential institution. The subjects of Edgerton's study were mildly retarded individuals who had had the benefit of vocational rehabilitation training programs both in the hospital and in the community. These individuals were considered among the more intellectually, socially, and emotionally capable within the institution.

Between 1949 and 1958, 110 individuals were released from Pacific State after successfully graduating from the vocational rehabilitation program. These individuals were released without any reservations or restrictions on their freedom. They were allowed to conduct their lives freely as any other citizen in the community. There were no guardians appointed, and they were essentially free from influence of parents, relatives, and the institution.

Edgerton's subjects ranged in age from 20 to 75, with a mean age of 35. The group was evenly comprised of men and women. Of this group, 81 were Caucasian, 22 were Mexican-American, 5 were black, 1 was American Indian, and 1 was Asian-American. The mean IQ of the group was 64. Fifty-three of these 110 individuals were found to be living within a 50-mile radius and became subjects of Edgerton's intensive and prolonged study. Interviews were conducted with the subjects, their friends, neighbors, relatives, and employers.

As a group, Edgerton found his subjects generally living comfortably, with most of them married and enjoying various leisure activities. By and large their existence was rather inconspicuous. They could not be considered model citizens. Neither were they a burden on society. Only two attended church or professed any religious beliefs; none had ever voted or taken part in community affairs. On the other hand, they were rarely in any sort of trouble that would lead to civil or criminal complaint. They used alcohol sparingly, and only three had ever used narcotics. Thus, to the casual observer their lives and existence would appear to be ordinary or inconspicuous.

Edgerton suggests that one of the greatest problems faced by this group is the stigma of the label of mental retardation. These individuals could not and would not accept the "fact" that they were or had ever been mentally retarded. To do so would tend to be humiliating and would devaluate their feelings of self-worth. Thus, much of their effort was in the direction of attempting to convince others as well as themselves that they were "normal" individuals. Many attribute their relative incompetence to the years spent in the institution, locked up and deprived of knowledge and experience required by society for competent living and functioning.

It is also interesting to note that, with the exception of three subjects, each individual had acquired the assistance of one or more individuals of normal intelligence to enable them to cope with the daily demands of life. Edgerton concluded that the assistance of these benefactors, usually unseen or unnoticed by others, provided these subjects with sufficient assistance to maintain a satisfactory degree of social competence and self-esteem.

Edgerton's 1967 study was conducted after the subjects had been living in the community for an average of 6 years. In a follow-up study Edgerton and Bercovici (1976) examined the lives of many of the same individuals 12 years later to determine what effect the passage of time had on their community adaptation. The same type of information sought in Edgerton's earlier study was also the major focus of interviews and observations; quality of residential environment, aspects of making a living, sex, marriage, and reproduction, use of leisure time, reliance on benefactors, and concern with stigma and passing as a normal individual.

Edgerton's original group of 48 consisted of 20 men and 28 women. Efforts to locate the original 48 members of the study included traveling beyond the 50-mile radius that was placed as a limitation in the original study. Despite these efforts, Edgerton and Bercovici were able to gather adequate information from only 30 individuals, 15 men and 15 women.

Three raters utilized the available information on the 30 subjects and placed them into one of three categories to compare their relative adjustment to that of the 1967 study: better, worse, the same. Judgments were made relative to the individual's age, sex, marital status, and ethnicity. The adjustment of 8 individuals (3 men and 5 women) was rated better, 12 individuals (5 men and 7 women) rated the same, and the remaining 10 (7 men and 3 women) rated worse.

Prior to the initiation of the follow-up study, Edgerton attempted to predict who among the original 48 subjects would improve, who would remain stable, and who would decline in level of community adaptation. After the study was completed, it was discovered that the predictions were correct less than half the time. Even when predictions were correct, they were often correct for the wrong reasons. Even with the advantage of studying community adaptation for 6 years prior to making the prediction, accurate predictions were, at best, difficult.

It may be of interest to note that during the 12-year period between the two studies, 4 of the female subjects lost their husbands through death or divorce. Three had been heavily dependent on their spouses. For this reason a substantial decline in community adaptation might have been predicted. Instead, all 4, with welfare assistance, had achieved a higher level of adaptation and were judged not only more competent but also more satisfied than before. Edgerton and Bercovici suggest that marriage to a normal man may place the woman in a role relationship that reduces her displayed competence.

In Edgerton's 1967 study, a primary concern of the subjects was in dealing with the stigmas of having been institutionalized and being labeled as mentally retarded. They devoted much effort to denying the correctness of this label and in passing as nonretarded. In the follow-up study 12 years later, the concern for passing and stigma was far less evident. Only 5 individuals seemed particularly concerned in this area. Three (2 women and 1 man) had married normal individuals and were cautious not to expose their past institutionalization. In summary, in the initial study the lives of the subjects were dominated by their concern regarding stigma. Twelve years later, in the follow-up study, stigma was a relatively unimportant concern for 25 of the 30 subjects. While labeling may have an initial deleterious effect on retarded individuals, its effect need not be permanent.

In the initial 1967 study, Edgerton's subjects, we may recall, were highly dependent on benefactors who provided vital assistance with life crises as well as with more routine aspects of everyday life. In some instances, these benefactors assisted in coping with stigma and in passing as nonretarded. In the 1976 follow-up study, however, Edgerton and Bercovici found that these benefactors played a less significant role in all these aspects. Edgerton's staff concluded that 16 of the group were less dependent on their benefactors and 11 were dependent to the same degree. None were considered more dependent (the remaining 3 subjects had died). In summary, dependence on benefactors lessened over time. This may have been the result of a lesser degree of need for these benefactors or the lessening availability of them. Edgerton and Bercovici conclude that the reduced stigma may have helped to lessen the need for benefactors, and the additional 12 years of experience in community living may have lessened the need for assistance.

Vocational success has often been listed as a major criterion for community adjustment and as an important ingredient of normalization (Wolfensberger, 1972; Olshansky, 1972). In Edgerton's earlier study (1967) all subjects had been employed as a criterion for discharge from the institution. Six years after their discharge, only 21 of the 48 were employed full time; 6 were unemployed; and 21 were married to someone who was employed, and of this latter group, only 3 were employed part time.

In Edgerton and Bercovici's follow-up study (1976), three of the men had died and one was terminally ill. Seven individuals were single and unemployed, 5 of these were receiving welfare payments, while the other 2 had no source of income. Nine women and 1 man were supported by their spouses. One woman was married and working part time. Only eight individuals (7 men and 1 woman) were employed full time and had been for most of the time since release from the institution. Of this group, 6 were receiving wages that were identical or only slightly above what they had received when they were first employed. Considering the increased cost of living over this period, even though these individuals had been able to maintain employment, they had suffered a decline in their status. It is apparent that these subjects had declined in this area of community adjustment since they were first investigated by Edgerton.

Edgerton and Bercovici, however, suggest that the situation may not be as bad as it may appear. For the women, marriage was a more important goal than employment, and over half the women had achieved this primary goal. Excluding the 4 men who were deceased or dying, 7 of the 11 men had maintained continuing employment. Attitudes had also changed among the subjects in the passage of time. Edgerton and Bercovici found that work, for most, was no longer fundamental to their self-esteem. Those receiving welfare made no apologies for doing so and expressed no eagerness to return to work. There are other factors worthy of consideration. During the original study (1969), employment was more readily available. Welfare eligibility, at the time of the follow-up study, was more easily attained. It also should be pointed out that the average age of the subjects during the follow-up study was 47, an age that may not be particularly favorable in the unskilled labor market. Another important variable that would likely affect employability was the declining physical health of the group. While in generally good health at the time of the original study, the follow-up study 12 years later found only 14 of the 30 subjects in good health. Three were deceased, 1 was terminally ill, and 9 had disabling ailments. For these individuals, welfare income was a satisfactory alternative (1976).

While Edgerton and his associates (1976) rated the life circumstances for the total group slightly worse as compared to their status in the earlier study, it is interesting to note that in general the subjects themselves considered their circumstances to be happier. Omitting the 4 subjects who were deceased or terminally ill, 12 said they were happier, 7 said things were about the same, and 6 said they were less happy; 1 was not sure. It may be important to note that of the 12 who said they were happier, only 3 were employed. One who was employed said he was less happy. The majority of these individuals considered themselves happier, and their happiness apparently was not necessarily a function of vocational success. Rather, happiness may be more a function of being more "normal" and in periods of high unemployment, many "normal" individuals may not be working. This study by Edgerton and Bercovici suggests that the majority of these 30 individuals learned to function without work quite adequately. These findings may suggest that in periods of high unemployment attempts to normalize the mildly retarded individual by maintaining a commitment toward a work ethic may be counterproductive to their adjustment.

We noted in Chapter 8 that many retarded children are not identified until they begin school, and their intellectual limitations become apparent because they are unable to function well in academic areas. In order to be placed in most special education programs a retarded child must be properly diagnosed, identified, and labeled. The labeling process enables many children to be programmed into classes that can best meet their needs. However, the stigmatization often present in the school and in adult life, as Edgerton suggests, can create increased burdens. Once they leave the school setting, many of the academic and intellectual tasks that identify them as deviant are minimized or cease to exist. Thus, for many borderline and mildly retarded individuals it is possible for them to integrate themselves reasonably well into the community as ordinary citizens. However, if the mental retardation labeling follows them from school on through an occupational placement, successful integration may be jeopardized.

Howe (1967) investigated the postschool adjustment of educable mentally retarded students who had either graduated from or had voluntarily withdrawn from senior high schools in the Long Beach Unified School District between September, 1961, and June, 1964. All subjects were enrolled for a minimum of two semesters. Of the 81 original subjects, Howe was able to locate and interview 68 (84 percent) when the follow-up study was conducted 2 to 4 years after the subjects left school.

Howe attempted to determine overall adult adjustment by examining: (1) weekly wage, (2) continuity of employment, (3) ability to travel independently, (4) degree of self-support, (5) ability to conform to laws, and (6) material possessions. In each of the six categories each subject was rated on a five-point scale. A computer program was developed to calculate the scores from the six areas and to determine overall adjustment. An analysis of the data found 30.9 percent making a poor overall adjustment, 30.9 percent making an average adjustment, and 38.2 percent making a good adjustment. On the 1 to 5 scale a score of 1 was considered poor, 3 was average, and 4 was good. Nearly 70 percent of the subjects were able to make at least an average adjustment (by Howe's standards) to adult life.

In examining weekly wages, for example, the 51 male subjects earned an average of $85.40 per week (on a scale from $0 to $425). It is interesting to note that the mean wages of minority subjects compared very favorably with white counterparts. The mean for white males was $84.98 per week, while the means for black and Mexican-American (Chicano) males were $83.89 and $92.78 per week, respectively. All 13 minority males were employed, as compared to an unemployment rate of 18.4 percent for the 38 white male subjects.

Approximately 35 percent of the males and slightly less than 50 percent of the female subjects had married. There were no divorces at the time of the study, although one woman had been deserted by her husband. It was interesting to note that only 1 of the 26 married subjects had wed another person known to be retarded. The school records of nearly all the spouses were examined. With the exception of only one, test score data indicated that the spouses were not eligible for classes for the mentally retarded. Howe noted that a part of the school curriculum stressed the risks involved in marrying another person with limited academic ability. The curriculum emphasized the advantage of one person in the family having higher level skills in reading, money management, and so on. Another part of the curriculum emphasized integration in elective classes and integration in social functions. Howe suggests that these two factors in the curriculum may have contributed to marriage choices.

A second follow-up study of graduates from special education EMR classes 2 to 4 years after the completion of school in Kansas City was conducted by Chaffin and his associates (1971). These graduates were divided into two groups. An experimental group consisted of EMR students who had participated in special education classes with work-study programs.

A comparison group consisted of subjects who had comparable I.Q. levels to the experimental group, but did not participate in work-study programs. Some in the comparison group were in secondary special education programs.

Chaffin found that the salaries that could be verified by the employer differed considerably between the two groups. Twenty-three experimental subjects had a mean gross weekly wage of $90.45, while 19 in the comparison group averaged $62.84 per week. Length of time on the job was also evaluated, with the experimental group averaging 18.7 months and the control group averaging 10.6 months.

An investigation was also made of the marital status of the subjects in the experimental group. Four in the experimental group were married, as contrasted to 8 in the comparison group. Two out of the comparison group who had married lived with their parents. All of the married subjects in the control group lived independently. As a group, 32 of the 42 subjects lived with parents or immediate family. Twenty-three subjects lived alone, with spouse, with friends, or in military housing (13 experimental and 10 comparison). Three subjects, 1 experimental and 2 comparison, lived in state residential institutions.

It is interesting to note that, while the initial 1967 follow-up study strongly favored the experimental over the comparison group (92 percent to 68 percent in employment), the 1969 follow-up found the gap closing. In the 1969 study the employment rate of experimental subjects decreased to 83 percent, and the comparison group increased to 75 percent. The results of the 1969 study suggest that at least three-fourths of EMR class graduates are able to find employment of some type. Chaffin suggests that the Kansas project was at least moderately successful in that the preparation for employment may have increased earning potential for the experimental group. Six subjects in the experimental group earned $100 or more per week, and 1 subject earned $200. Four subjects had annual incomes exceeding $6,450, which Chaffin

Fig. 10-1. Along with television, listening to music is one of the primary sources of entertainment for the adult retarded.

states was the average starting salary for teachers in the Kansas City, Kansas school district during the 1969-1970 school year.

In more recent studies on the vocational adjustment of educable retarded individuals, the subjects have not appeared to be very successful. Brolin (1975) and his associates conducted a follow-up study on 71 former students and found only 21 percent functioning at an average or above average vocational adjustment; 35 percent were considered to have a fair adjustment, while 44 percent were rated as having a poor adjustment. Olshansky and Beach (1974) report that only a few over half of their trainees in a rehabilitation workshop were working a year or more after being placed on a job.

A study by Stanfield (1973) examined the quality of community life for trainable (moderately) retarded (30 to 50 IQ) individuals after graduation from a large metropolitan California school district. Of 161 graduates from the classes of 1968, 1969, and 1970, Stanfield was able to obtain information on 120 subjects. The study consisted of 65 males and 55 females ranging in age from 19 to 21. Of this group 113 (94 percent) were living with their families, 4 lived in board and care homes, 2 had been institutionalized, and 1 lived by himself. Forty percent (48) of the subjects were involved in sheltered workshops, with 80 percent earning less than $10.00 a week for full-time work. Nearly half earned less than $5.00 per week.

None of the subjects was self-supporting. Only 3 were employed outside of a sheltered workshop. One had a newspaper route earning $75.00 per week, another earned $20.00 per week as a classroom attendant, and the third earned $55.00 per week as a laundry worker. All 3 were employed part time. Two (2 percent) were employed by their fathers—one earned $10.00 per week in a window display business and the other, assisting his father who was a newspaper distribution agent, earned $300 a month (the highest paid of all subjects). Thirteen (11 percent) were involved in activity centers in the Los Angeles area.

Fifty-two of the subjects (44 percent) were not involved in postschool work or rehabilitative programs. Reasons given by parents for noninvolvement included: (1) the severity of handicap (55 percent), (2) transportation difficulties, and (3) lack of referral to jobs or postschool rehabilitation programs. Thirteen (11 percent) were involved in five different activity centers.

Ninety-four percent of the parents reported their children capable of caring for personal needs and able to protect themselves against injury. In spite of the opinion of most parents that their children could provide for themselves alone, the majority were hesitant to leave them alone for more than short periods of time. These parents indicated that they were concerned that their retarded children would not be able to handle emergencies. Approximately 90 percent of the subjects had specific responsibilities (such as picking up trash and making the bed), which the parents considered helpful.

Stanfield found that only nine sheltered workshops out of the twenty-five in the 4,069 square miles surrounding the school district would accept trainable mentally retarded individuals. As a result many who were involved in the sheltered workshops spent many hours each day in transit. The average transportation time spent daily for each workshop subject was 2 hours.

CHARACTERISTICS THAT RELATE TO THE EMPLOYABILITY OF RETARDED INDIVIDUALS

Professionals working in the area of preparing retarded individuals for the world of competitive employment are concerned with those characteristics that tend to be related to vocational success or failure. If these characteristics can be identified, vocational training programs as well as early educational programs can be developed to emphasize the positive characteristics that tend to enhance vocational success.

In comparing the characteristics of employed and unemployed individuals, Kolstoe (1961) found that intelligence was not a significant factor in employability. In his sample those with low IQ's (in the 50's) were equally successful in securing employment. Kolstoe found that academic achievement may result in higher level jobs; he also found that the most desirable age for employment was between 19 and 30. Ancillary handicaps did not preclude employment, and height and weight appeared to have no relationship to employability. Kolstoe did indicate that the employed group tended to be physically more attractive as well to have a better height-weight ratio and general health score. The employed group rated higher on cheerfulness, cooperation, respect for supervisors, ability to mind their own business, punctuality, initiative, and work efficiency. Kolstoe (1965) states that the presence of a physical handicap is less important then the appearance of a physical handicap, suggesting that the retarded should strive to avoid any unusual appearance.

Peckman (1951) cited teasing and ridicule by other workers, lack of vocational and social sophistication (such as difficulty in transportation), leaving work without notification, unwarranted sick leave, dissatisfaction with salary, poor budgeting of money, lack of initiative and job responsibility, and impulsive behavior as factors related to vocational failure among the mentally retarded. Voelker (1957) attributes job failure among the retarded to lack of punctuality, poor manners, poor personal appearance, failure to report to work regularly, and inability to get along with fellow workers.

Tarjan and associates (1959) examined reasons for failure of those retarded persons released from Pacific State Hospital in California. The progress of these individuals was followed for 4 years after their release from the institution. Those who failed vocationally did so because of inadequate work performance, problems in interpersonal relations, or voluntary return to the institution for unspecified reasons.

Cohen (1960) found postinstitutional factors related to vocational failure included difficulty with the employer, occasional pilfering, sexual problems, altering checks, and inability to account for days away from work. Some had interpersonal difficulties at home with parents and siblings. Barret, Relos, and Eisele (1965) found that vocationally successful retarded persons had higher levels of reasoning ability than the unsuccessful persons studied.

In a study of variables influencing work success for retarded individuals in Israel, Sali and Amir (1970) found that personality characteristics appeared to influence performance and output to a greater extent than IQ or specific abilities. The personality characteristic that showed the greatest relationship to the performance level was perseverance. This finding suggests that motivational factors may have one of the greatest influences on success at work for the retarded. Other variables that were highly related to work success included good motor coordination and good social adjustment.

Fiester and Giambra (1972) found that language facility and communication skills were variables related to vocational success for trainable retarded adults in sheltered workshops.

Kantner (1969) found that IQ was not a reliable predictor of occupational success or failure. His study involved 82 1967-1968 graduates from a Phoenix, Arizona special education program. Fourteen were fired from their jobs because of (1) poor punctuality or excessive absence, (2) poor attitude, and (3) not performing up to the standards of their supervisors. Only 5 subjects (6 percent) lost their jobs because of inability to perform the skill aspects of their work.

In studying postschool adjustment of educable mentally retarded individuals in Indiana, Porter and Milazzo (1958) identified what employers considered outstanding working characteristics of mentally retarded employees: (1) ability to stick to the job, (2) dependability, (3) honesty, and (4) getting along with other workers.

In examining the various reasons for occupational failure among the adult retarded, it appears rather evident that very few individuals lose their jobs because of actual inability to perform the specific tasks to which they have been assigned. Rather, failure has tended to be more related to personality factors and the inability to adjust to the job situation. Therefore, if professional workers in the field can work toward the development of strong attributes in these areas, chances of successful employment will be greatly enhanced. The development of these personality traits should not be left to the vocational level teacher or vocational rehabilitation counselor alone. At this level personality traits tend to be clearly established and at times unalterable. A conscious effort needs to be made by the entire professional team as well as parents from infancy through adulthood to develop personal attributes that will maximize the chances of occupational success. Special classes for the retarded have traditionally emphasized social and personal competencies. At times this emphasis has been at the expense of academics. While the literature gives little if any evidence that academic achievement is related to occupational success, the type and level of job may be related to the level of academic ability. A waitress, for instance, must have enough academic ability to write an order, write out a check, and total the check for the customer. It would appear prudent, therefore, to develop students to their full academic potential.

VOCATIONAL ASPIRATIONS AND ACTUAL OCCUPATIONS HELD BY THE RETARDED

From childhood and even through adult life an individual frequently fantasizes about aspirations for vocational choices. Many young girls envision themselves as housewives, mothers, or nurses. With the social liberation movements, they may in the future envision themselves in less stereotyped occupations for women. Young boys may have dreams of becoming cowboys, astronauts, or perhaps athletic superstars. While fantasy may follow a person through life, aspirations tend to become more congruent with actual abilities as the individual matures. Since an individual's life-style and ultimate personal satisfaction are often related to vocational satisfaction school, guidance, and vocational counselors attempt to direct and aid students in finding acceptable vocational choices.

The mentally retarded are not different from other children with respect to having their own vocational aspirations. Because of their intellectual limitations, these retarded individuals may find it more difficult to obtain vocational positions congruent with their aspirations. These difficulties and limitations, however, may be caused not only by their own limitations, but also by lack of imagination and creativity and by stereotyping tendencies of professionals directly related to the vocational training and placement of the retarded.

Jastak, MacPhee, and Whiteman (1963) compared vocational aspirations of retarded to those of nonretarded subjects. They found that 3 percent of the retarded and none of the nonretarded subjects desired unskilled occupations. Fifty percent of the retarded and 73 percent of the nonretarded subjects were hopeful of obtaining skilled or professional occupations. In reality, 45 percent of the nonretarded group were employed in clerical-sales, skilled, managerial, or professional positions, while the retarded group was totally excluded from these occupations. Among the employed group of retarded subjects, 40 percent held unskilled positions, as contrasted to 10 percent of the nonretarded group.

A study by the Vocational Rehabilitation Administration (1964) found approximately 75 percent of the mentally retarded in service, semiskilled, or unskilled occupations. Approximately 10 percent were employed in white-collar jobs, usually in clerical or sales positions, and less than 10 percent in agricultural or skilled positions. Other studies have also found that those adult retarded who are employed are generally engaged in service, unskilled, and semiskilled occupations rather than skilled or white collar positions (Porter and Milazzo, 1958; Peterson and Smith, 1960).

Folman and Budoff (1971) found that the more able adolescent EMR students with high learning potential tend to have lower and perhaps more realistic occupational aspirations. A higher proportion of this group aspired to blue-collar jobs than the less able students. Many of the less able aspired to jobs that were unrealistic with respect to their capabilities. Many aspired to white-collar jobs requiring post–high school and even postcollege education, suggesting fantasy or wishful thinking. The more able students appeared to have a greater understanding of the nature of their occupation choice compared to the less able.

A study by Erdman (1957) suggests that vocational aspirations of the mentally retarded may be greatly influenced by parental expectations. In studying the vocational aspirations of 98 white EMR high school boys in Wisconsin, he found that 80 percent discussed their choice of vocation with their parents as contrasted with 34 percent who had discussed vocational plans in school with teachers or counselors.

As the literature suggests, the retarded tend to have vocational aspirations similar to those of their normal counterparts. Most would prefer skilled and professional positions, while in reality the majority who are able to obtain employment end up in unskilled and service-oriented positions. It would appear that, in order to harmonize aspirations and actual jobs held, parents and professionals need to lead the retarded into more realistic goals which are within their capabilities and that are personally satisfying to them as well. Those involved in the vocational placement of the retarded need to broaden the opportunities for the retarded and avoid unnecessary stereotyping.

SHELTERED WORKSHOPS FOR THE MENTALLY RETARDED

Sheltered workshops exist throughout this country to provide occupational training and vocational opportunities for the handicapped. The National Institute on Workshop Standards defines a sheltered workshop as:

> . . . a work oriented rehabilitation facility with controlled working environment and individualized vocational goals, which utilize work experience and related service for assisting the handicapped person to progress toward normal living and a productive vocational status (1959).

Sheltered workshops tend to exist for two basic purposes: (1) to provide remunerative employment and training to prepare a handicapped individual for competitive employment and (2) to provide a permanent job placement for those individuals unable to function in competitive employment.

Fraenkel (1961) lists and discusses the six phases for a sheltered workshop rehabilitation program that are suggested by the National Association for Retarded Citizens Vocational Rehabilitation and Sheltered Workshop Committee.

1. *Screening-admissions.* A professional team of consultants screens each candidate for admission to a sheltered workshop based on educational, psychological, social, medical, and vocational records.

2. *Evaluation.* Each trainee is observed and evaluated by the workshop staff. Among the areas evaluated are the individual's interests, abilities, skills, and potential as well as social and interpersonal behavioral patterns in the vocational setting. Work samples and job explanations are also utilized to ascertain abilities and limitations of the client.

3. *Personal adjustment training.* A training emphasis is placed on the personal-social adjustment of the individual. The trainee is exposed not only to the typical work demands but also to the interpersonal demands of integrated working conditions.

4. *Vocational or job training.* The individual is placed in a particular job training situation after a careful analysis is made to assure practical goals in a vocational training program.

5. *Selective placement.* After the client has successfully completed vocational or job training, placement is made either in a workshop or in competitive employment. Placements should be made on the basis of the individual's highest level of capability.

6. *Follow-up.* The follow-up program of a sheltered workshop is an important element in the overall vocational training of the individual. Periodic

checks should be made to make sure that both employer and employee are satisfied. If any difficulties exist, intervention through counseling, special training, or a job change may be made.

Kolstoe (1965) states that ". . . the sheltered workshop stands as a contradiction. It is not self-supporting. It is not competitive. Its administrative and supervisory personnel are clinically trained, and are service rather than profit oriented." He further states that in comparison to industry, where workers are employed to produce a product, the sheltered workshop employs a product to produce workers.

Some sheltered workshops operate exclusively for mentally retarded clients, while others operate for a wider variety of handicapped individuals, such as the visually impaired, cerebral palsied, and emotionally disturbed. Some are operated by national programs such as the Goodwill Industries of America, Inc., which has over a hundred centers, and the Jewish Vocational Service agencies with over twenty locations. Other workshops are community based and may be supported by United Fund, religious groups, private endowments, or, more recently, public schools.

Typically, sheltered workshops are involved with the restoration or renewing and sale of useable clothing or household articles. These items are usually contributed through collections or strategically located depositories. Other workshop revenue comes from contracts with various businesses or industries. The Community Training Center in Salt Lake City, Utah, for example, has contracts with the Utah Travel Council and with Western Electric. The contract with the Utah Travel Council involves the sorting, packaging, and addressing of travel literature that is sent out throughout the country. The Western Electric contract calls for the salvaging and restoration of all reuseable parts of used telephones.

Workshop clients are typically compensated on a piecework basis on a rate comparable to industry workers. Thus, if the typical industry worker is paid $4.00 for ten units of work an hour, the workshop client should be paid $2.00 if production reaches five units during the entire day. Some workers are relatively productive and may earn in excess of $10.00 per day. Others are less capable and may earn less than $1.00 per day.

There are at times questions raised regarding the efficacy of providing terminal placement for those individuals earning relatively low levels of pay. From a purely economic standpoint, justification for maintaining services for these individuals may be questionable. Their wages are so low as to be of almost negligible value to themselves. Their productivity level is so low that their contribution to the employment field may also be considered nearly negligible.

The worth of involvement in a sheltered workshop should be viewed from other perspectives, however. The value of a workshop to the retarded individual's family may be considerable. The daily activities at the workshop alleviate the necessity of daily care and supervision of the retarded individual. The mother who may be otherwise required to remain home to supervise her retarded son or daughter is provided with freedom to work or engage in other activities. But perhaps the greatest value of a sheltered workshop is to the retarded individual. The particular level of remuneration is relative to the individual. Many normal individuals may question the merit of any individual working in a sheltered workshop at an extremely low wage. Yet, to the sheltered workshop worker, the $10.00 a week represents a wage and recognition for a well-performed task. While the level of performance may be subaverage in comparison to an industry worker, it nevertheless may represent near maximum effort on the part of the retarded worker. From this daily experience of working, producing, and being compensated, many retarded individuals may develop a feeling of self-worth and dignity as a contributing member of society.

SOCIAL AND PERSONAL ADJUSTMENT

In an earlier portion of this chapter we examined the overall adjustment of the retarded in the community in a review of the literature since 1919. In this section we shall explore in more detail how the retarded adult adjusts as a citizen in the community, and what factors appear to influence overall adjustment.

Sterilization

In past years sterilization has been viewed as a means of eliminating or curtailing mental retardation, preventing retarded individuals from having unwanted children, or preventing retarded individuals from having children because of their alleged incompetence. In 1927, Justice Holmes issued his famous opinion for the Supreme Court, which upheld a state compulsory sterilization law. He stated that ". . . three generations of imbeciles are enough" (Buck vs. Bell, 1927). The practice of sterilization of retarded individuals has decreased considerably in more recent years. Ferster (1966) reports that compulsory sterilization decreased from 1,643 cases in 1943 to 643 cases in 1963. In 1966, however, twenty-three states still had statutes providing for compulsory sterilization of mentally retarded individuals.

The prime targets for compulsory sterilization appear to be retarded individuals who are in the process of being released from institutions (Burt, 1973; Edgerton, 1967). In Edgerton's study of former patients of Pacific State Hospital, he found that 44 of the 48 subjects had undergone "eugenic" sterilization. During the period of their institutionalization, sterilization was considered a prerequisite to release. Form letters were sent to parents or guardians to gain consent for the procedure. These letters strongly implied that sterilization could permit parole and be in the best interest of the individual. Therefore, unless there was strong objection, the surgery was routinely performed.

By 1935, the mentally retarded constituted 44 percent of the individuals sterilized in this country; by 1946 the percentage increased to 69 percent. The rate of sterilization increased through 1937 and leveled off by 1942. The leveling off was attributable to the shortage of medical personnel during the war years (Goldstein, 1964). Gamble (1951) reported that through 1950, 26,000 retarded individuals had been rendered parolable from institutions by sterilization.

Follow-up studies of sterilized retarded individuals have generally reported favorable adjustment or at least not noticeable negative effects from the operation (Craft, 1936; Johnson, 1946). Adjustment in these studies was related to marriage, sexual changes, and incidence of sex offenses. It is interesting to note that while the subjects of the Craft study experienced no sexual changes, the incidence of sex offenses decreased dramatically. While the findings appear contradictory, they may be a function of maturity that the subjects could have developed during institutionalization or changes in criteria for a sex offense. It is possible that what was considered promiscuous behavior for younger, virile retarded persons may be considered the private business of sterilized consenting adults in a later period in life.

In Edgerton's initial study (1967) the majority of the group held negative feelings regarding the sterilization that had been imposed on them and that precluded the possibility of bearing children. The objections tended to center around three areas of concern. First, the sterilization was an indelible mark of their previous institutionalization. Second, some individuals felt deprived of children, which they wanted. Third, there appeared to be a fear on the part of many individuals that their partners would discover their infertility, which many had apparently concealed, when no offspring were produced after a period of time.

Some of the issues regarding sterilization of mentally retarded individuals are rather apparent and easy to identify. Resolution of these issues is far more complex and difficult than their identification. Some retarded individuals are either not able or unwilling to exercise birth control to avoid unwanted pregnancies. The result of some of these unwanted pregnancies may be neglected and abused children or children for whom parents must seek external financial assistance in order to provide minimal support in terms of food, clothing, and health care. In some instances sterilization prevents the procreation of other retarded children. The retarded individuals most frequently sterilized have tended to be those who are residents in institutions and particularly those in the process of being released.

A number of the institutionalized retarded are wards of the state. This condition permits the institution greater flexibility with matters regarding sterilization because parental consent may be unnecessary. Thus it appears that the institutionalized are, as suggested by Burt (1973) and by Edgerton (1967), prime targets for sterilization. This practice appears to be both ironic and discriminatory. It is ironic when and if the institutionalized retarded are routinely sterilized, since they represent the segment of the retarded population that should be of least concern regarding birth control problems. Not only are many of these individuals so socially and physically incompetent that sexual relationships represent remote possibilities, but they are among the most closely and carefully supervised members of our retarded population. The practice of sterilizing institutionalized retarded persons as a prerequisite to release appears to be highly discriminatory. They represent no greater threat to themselves and to society than the majority of the retarded individuals who are not under the jurisdiction of an institution. Yet because they have lived in institutions they are singled out and prevented from even choosing or demonstrating their relative competence or incompetence as parents.

The concern of discriminatory sterilization laws should not be limited to the institutional group exclusively. The question of whether or not society has the right to impose sterilization on any retarded individual has great relevancy to parents, professionals, and the retarded individuals themselves. Prominent jurists such as Burt (1973) and Allen (1969) suggest that involuntary sterilization of mentally retarded persons violates the individual's basic rights. It is interesting to note that two of the four unsterilized subjects in

Edgerton's study were considered successful mothers with children of normal intelligence.

A primary issue in the matter of sterilization is who decides who must be sterilized and what criterion is used to determine such a decision. Should we sterilize all retarded individuals in institutions and in the community? What are the criteria to be used for determining sufficient retardation to warrant compulsory sterilization? Should we sterilize all individuals at the trainable level or below? Should we use a cut-off of 70 or 75 IQ, which would include all educables as well? Perhaps a cut-off of 85 IQ and below would be more realistic since this level would be congruent with A.A.M.D. criteria for borderline mental retardation. Perhaps the strong advocates of sterilization could find justification for using 100 IQ as a minimum criterion for the right of having children since 100 IQ represents mean or average IQ. It should appear obvious to the reader that the setting of arbitrary criteria can be both unfair and potentially dangerous to the civil rights of every individual.

As rational individuals we must be cognizant of the realities of different life-styles and different standards of living. The standards of a good life are relative to the individual. Many middle-class individuals may consider the life-style of mildly retarded individuals as totally unacceptable. This marginal family may themselves be dissatisfied with their present life-style, but no more so than many middle-class families. What we are emphasizing is the right of an individual to exist as he sees fit, provided that his life-style does not interfere with or cause harm to anyone else. Even the previous statement is filled with ambiguities, for it would be impossible to gain complete agreement as to what constitutes interference or harm to another individual.

It should appear obvious to most individuals that in certain cases where genetic disorders exist, sterilization is a viable alternative. In instances where the intellectual capacities of an individual are severely limited, sterilization may also be in the best interests of all concerned. Capricious and prejudicial decisions disregarding the rights of mentally retarded individuals and precluding self-fulfillment must be carefully examined and, if necessary, challenged by responsible parents, professionals, and advocates for the retarded.

Marriage and the retarded

Peterson and Smith (1960) found that, in contrast to a group of normal adults, a considerably smaller number of retarded subjects married. Among the normal subjects, two and a half times as many men and three times as many women married. Divorce figures were four times as high for the retarded as for the normal group. As a group, 50 percent of the retarded subjects remained unmarried, compared to 20 percent in the normal group.

The number of children per married couples was approximately the same in both groups—about one child per married couple. There were twelve couples of which at least one partner was retarded. These couples had twelve children in public schools. Ten of these children were given intelligence tests, with eight of the ten falling within normal ranges of intelligence. One of the two children diagnosed as retarded was in a special education EMR class, and the second child was being considered for placement.

Edgerton (1967) and Edgerton and Bercovici (1976) found that marriage was highly valued among retarded subjects and was considered a highly meaningful status to achieve. In interviewing a number of former hospital patients, the desire to marry, particularly to someone not from the institution, was of paramount importance to the subjects. One subject indicated that every girl wanted to marry an individual not associated with the hospital. She indicated that she had done everything to enhance her chances such as "speaking properly," buying nice clothing, and going to nice places. She indicated that she avoided "hospital guys" (males released from the institution from which she herself had been released). She stated, "When I finally married an outside guy, I knew my troubles were over." A male subject indicated that the men from his group of former institutional subjects, including himself, had remained single because of their inability to meet nonretarded girls. He further stated that the only girls available to the men released from the institution were "hospital girls" or prostitutes.

It would appear from these studies that the retarded do desire and value marriage highly. As a group they are apparently not as successful in finding mates; this may result partly from their desire to marry nonretarded individuals or at least individuals who had had no previous association with an institution. This particular desire may be indicative of an overall desire to assume as "normal" an existence as possible.

The retarded as citizens in the community

Both the retarded individuals and the professional workers involved with them have usually sought to make retarded citizens an integral part of society. To truly become an integral part of society, one must abide by the rules and mores of the society and participate in the usual functions of citizenship. We shall examine in this section how the retarded as a group abide by the rules established by the society in which they live, and to what extent they participate in their basic rights, such as understanding of and participation in the democratic processes.

Negative behavior. Throughout the years various studies have consistently found a disproportionately high number of retarded individuals involved in criminal or delinquent activity (Moore, 1911; Goddard, 1914; Kvaraceus, 1946; Peterson and Smith, 1960).

Allen (1969) reported that a 1963 survey conducted by the George Washington University Institute of Law, Psychiatry and Criminology and the National Institutes of Mental Health received responses from 80 percent of the correctional institutions polled. These institutions housed 200,000 serious criminal offenders. The survey revealed that the percentage of retarded (using 70 IQ as a cut-off) in correctional institutions was three times as high as their percentage in the general population. In other words, approximately 9 percent of the inmate population had IQ's of 70 or below as compared to 3 percent in the general or noncorrectional institutionalized population. Nearly 1,500 inmates (1.6 percent) had reported IQ's below 55, ranging downward to an IQ of 17. The study also found a general lack of mental health resources personnel within the institutions and few special programs for the retarded. Over half the institutions had no programs of any kind, not even a special education class.

Allen's associates made further investigation by studying available data and subjects in six correctional institutions in six states. The investigation found that in most instances disclosure of the mental retardation was not made prior to judgment. Allen maintains that retardation itself is a relevant issue in determining the individual's competency to stand trial, in considering the admissibility of the confession, and in resolving the issue of criminal responsibility (insanity). Most prisoners in the sample were poor and black and had appointed counsel who had spent little time with them. The trial was often a mere formality, with 95 percent of the defendants either confessing or pleading guilty.

The study also found a significantly higher number of retarded subjects convicted for violent crimes as compared to the nonretarded group. Allen suggests that this finding should be qualified by pointing out that the retarded are, as a group, more easy to apprehend, more likely to confess, easier to convict, and probably will be incarcerated longer than the nonretarded offenders. Allen further points out that retarded offenders of less severe crimes are often committed to institutions for the retarded, thus inflating the proportion of retarded involved in violent crimes within the prison.

The results of Allen's study would suggest that our judicial system is not equal for all. The retarded can seldom afford private defense lawyers and therefore must make do with court appointed attorneys. The quality of such legal defense is a debatable issue, although we will recall that Allen's researchers found the entire trial process a mere formality.

Treatment of the retarded by law enforcers will vary from one community to another. In some communities law enforcement officers are sympathetic to the retarded, while in other communities they may be viewed as a nuisance. Possession of marijuana may be considered a serious offense in one community, and in another it may be considered too petty to be concerned with.

It appears that the retarded, who often lack financial resources and advocates, suffer in our judicial systems. There appears to be a need to develop a system in which the retarded can receive adequate legal help when they are in difficulty. The American Civil Liberties Union has long served as advocate for oppressed groups. This group, along with local associations for retarded citizens and local bar associations, can serve as effective advocates for the retarded.

While adequate legal counsel is a primary concern for the retarded, crime prevention should be an even greater concern. Freudian theory, discussed in Chapter 8, would suggest a defective superego, which if valid could explain some of the possible problems of the retarded. Parents, teachers, counselors, and other professionals need to work consistently with the retarded to help them understand: (1) legal systems, (2) community legal standards, and (3) the consequences of inappropriate behavior. Many retarded people have demonstrated their capabilities for responsible citizenship. A concerted effort could increase the number of responsible individuals and decrease the number of retarded from the ranks of correctional institutions.

Active citizenship. While special education classes often emphasize participation in social and civic responsibilities, the retarded either do not internalize what they have learned or perhaps find participation in activities such as voting too confusing. Edgerton (1967) found that none of his subjects had ever voted. Kennedy (1948) found that compared to normal subjects the retarded subjects participated less in formal organizations and voted less.

Gozali (1971) investigated the degree of knowledge and participation of 68 mildly retarded individuals in democratic political processes. The subjects ranged in chronological age from 21 to 28 and in IQ from 68 to 82. All had attended EMR school programs. Each individual was verbally given sixty questions relating to citizenship. Gozali found that most did poorly on the test, and none had even registered to vote.

Perhaps voting is not an important function for the retarded, or perhaps they do not perceive it as such. If it is not a useful and worthwhile function for the retarded, then instruction in the EMR curriculum may be a useless exercise. If, however, the retarded, particularly the mild and borderline groups, are not participating in this basic right and responsibility because of their lack of sophistication, efforts could be increased to facilitate their active participation. Curriculum could include not only an academic understanding of voting, but also some practical experience in simulation voting for public officials and even real voting within the classroom for various types of responsibilities. Perhaps groups such as the local association for retarded citizens could provide transportation and help on voting registration and other related procedures. The retarded are often on the lower end of the economic continuum. Changes in governmental status frequently have a profound effect on their lives. Voting may therefore have as much relevancy for their lives as for any other citizen in the community.

Leisure time and recreation. For many individuals, leisure time and recreation activities provide an important source of pleasure and relaxation. Many retarded adults have busy and active work schedules. For these individuals leisure time and recreational activities provide a much needed change from their daily work schedule. Other retarded adults have little if any work or regular daily activity. These individuals need recreation to escape boredom.

Stanfield (1973) found that, among moderately retarded adults, time spent in the home was typically solitary in nature. Watching television, playing records, and looking at books and magazines were listed as typical activities. Walking idly around the neighborhood was also reported as a frequent type of activity. Stanfield reported that 44 percent of his subjects were uninvolved in postschool work or rehabilitation programs. This left a large number of subjects with basically no structured daily activity. Stanfield quotes one mother as saying: "At first it wasn't too bad. He enjoyed his vacation as he called it—and then he began to ask when school would start again. I don't have the time it takes—and I don't always know what to do for him."

While 84 percent were reported to have friends, seldom were they able to interact with them. By and large, Stanfield found these friends were associated with a workshop, activity center, or social-recreation program for the retarded. Few had any friends in the neighborhood or the community at large.

Forty-six of the subjects (38 percent) participated in one or more post-school, social-recreational programs. Bowling and dances were the most frequently mentioned activities.

Stanfield concluded that with peer associations limited to sheltered workshops and activity centers and with 62 percent uninvolved in any social-recreational program for the retarded, the majority of the subjects had no social or recreational life apart from that with the immediate family.

In examining the leisure time activity of the retarded subjects, Edgerton (1967) found that they did not differ greatly from the "normal" individuals living near them in lower socioeconomic neighborhoods. Time, money, and transportation were constraints that precluded the possibility of certain types of activity. There were few hobbies and little reading, and they seldom entertained or dined in restaurants. Television was a primary source of entertainment. Other typical leisure time activities included conversation with other individuals, listening to the radio and to other music, sightseeing, or sports including swimming, bicycling, and spectator sports. In the 1976 follow-up study, Edgerton and Bercovici found the subjects had many friends, activities, and pastimes. One individual, for example, maintained a garden, a dog, and a bird and had hobbies such as painting and candle making.

While the schools provide some activities for their retarded students, the retarded adult is too often left with a lonely, inactive life. Recreational programs for adults in the community could also be made available for the retarded on an integrated basis when feasible. For others, homogeneous grouping for recreational activities may be more feasible and less threatening. The retarded are fully entitled to the pleasures that well-planned recreational activities afford. Efforts in this direction by recreational therapists, churches, parents, and local associations for retarded citizens can help to make life for the retarded more meaningful.

Attitudes of retarded adults toward mental retardation

The recent efforts toward deinstitutionalization and normalization have brought about considerable research examining the attitudes of the community, parents, and professionals toward mental retardation. What has been absent in the literature has been attempts to determine the attitudes and the knowledge the retarded have about mental retardation and the issues of integration into the community.

Gan, Tymchuk, and Nisihara (1977) developed a questionnaire with forty items equally divided into eight categories: knowledge of mental retardation, general attitude toward mental retardation, general ability, job skills, integration, rights, special needs, and personality of the mentally retarded. The statements were written in straightforward language and were to be answered on a 5-point scale from strongly agree to strongly disagree. Typical among the statements on the questionnaire were: "If a person is retarded, his or her children will also be retarded." "The worth of a human being should not be measured by how smart he or she is." "It is fine for other children to play with mentally retarded children."

Gan and her associates selected 50 mildly retarded adults ranging in age from 18 to 40 years. The purpose of the study was explained to the group, and they were informed that their participation was optional. The scale and method of response was explained in detail, and each item was read out loud. Counselors were available to assist any individual having difficulty. Two questionnaires were returned blank, while 15 others were only partially completed, suggesting lack of comprehension or inability to follow instructions. An examination of the responses of the remaining 33 participants revealed that accurate knowledge of mental retardation was demonstrated by 73.3 percent; 72.2 percent held positive attitudes toward mentally retarded individuals, 65 percent showed realistic assessment of general abilities and 79.4 percent regarding job skills. The majority (92.2 percent) strongly supported integration of mentally retarded individuals into the community, 76 percent were aware of their rights, and 78 percent were aware of their special needs within the community. The personality category showed the least amount of agreement of the eight areas sampled. A large number were either undecided or in disagreement.

The authors conclude that the study demonstrated that mildly retarded adults possess the insight and the ability to answer an attitude questionnaire. A large percentage of them possess accurate information about mental retardation and a realistic attitude toward their own needs and abilities.

RESIDENTIAL NEEDS AND ARRANGEMENTS FOR THE RETARDED ADULT

The retarded adult, as everyone else, needs some type of residential arrangement to provide for the basic necessities of life. Arrangements vary considerably depending on the severity of retardation, individual personality characteristics, age and nature of parents and family, and community resources.

Institutional living

Retarded individuals may be classified as mildly, moderately, severely, or profoundly retarded. Nearly total dependency on others may leave institutional placement as the only viable alternative for some. Other retarded individuals, whose intellectual functioning may be adequate for community living, may possess certain personality characteristics that are so disrupting to parents, relatives, and others in the community that institutional placement may also be the best alternative for them. The age of the parents may also become a factor. As parents are no longer able to care for their adult retarded children, institutional placement may become necessary. In some instances institutional living may be the only alternative for the retarded adult when community resources are inadequate. O'Connor, Justice, and Warren (1970) found that nearly three-fourths of 463 retarded adults in nineteen state institutions were eligible for community placement. In spite of their eligibility, they remained institutionalized because of a lack of community resources. Another factor that may lead to the continuation of institutionalization is the frequent use of the more able adult retarded as ward helpers. In the study by O'Connor and associates, 39.5 percent of the subjects were utilized in this manner. In this capacity they provided a useful service, relieved an overburdened staff, and helped to ease the budgeting limitations with which most institutions are faced. Utilizing the retarded adult in this manner may be justified by the possible development of more positive self-concepts of the residents through a feeling of usefulness. In spite of the possible advantages of residential work and living, all community alternatives need to be explored before any decisions are made regarding terminal residential placement.

Normalization

The principle of normalization was first articulated by Nirje (1969) and Bank-Mikkelsen (1969) and was expanded and advocated in the United States by Wolfensberger (1972). Normalization means "making available to the mentally retarded patterns and conditions of every day life which are as close as possible to the norms and patterns of mainstream society" (Nirje, 1969, p. 181). Baker, Seltzer, and Seltzer (1977) suggest that normalization has often been misinterpreted to mean the mere provision of a normative situation, such as a home in a community, will be beneficial to retarded individuals. They further suggest that the dangers in such an interpretation are obvious. Without the needed supportive services, such as training and supervision, the retarded individual may not be prepared to cope with the demands of the community. Nirje (1970) states that normalization,

> . . . will not make a subnormal normal, but will make life conditions of the mentally subnormal as far as possible, bearing in mind the degree of his handicap, his competence and maturity as well as the need for training activities and availability of services . . . the awareness that mostly only relative independence and integration can be attained [is] implied and stressed by the words "as close as possible" (p. 63).

The principle of normalization has brought with it a strong emphasis in the field of mental retardation toward deinstitutionalization. This term refers to the return of individuals residing in centers for the mentally retarded to community and home environments (Turnbull and Turnbull, 1975).

While the impetus toward deinstitutionalization has, for the most part, been generated by the sincere efforts of individuals concerned with the legal rights of the retarded, there are concerns about the movement regarding what is in the best interests of each retarded individual.

Turnbull and Turnbull suggest that the "due process" that involves institutionalization and deinstitutionalization is frequently made by the parents or guardians of the retarded person and the administrators of the institution. Often the retarded individual has no right or opportunity to voice opinions or preferences in the decision-making process. This has been based on the assumed premise that the retarded individual is incompetent to participate in these decisions. While due process is guaranteed the individual with respect to placement in special education programs, this same due process is conspicuously absent in the decision to place an individual in an institution for the mentally retarded or to deinstitutionalize the individual.

The basic premise under which many professional workers in the field of mental retardation, and parents as well, operate, is that deinstitutionalization implies a normalization process and, therefore, is in the best interest of the individual. This may be true in some instances, however, there are many considerations that must be taken into account prior to the deinstitutionalization process. It may be important to note here that while deinstitutionalization and normalization are sometimes used interchangeably, they are not necessarily synonymous. Deinstitutionalization does imply an effort toward normalization—to enable a retarded person to live in a manner as nearly "normal" as possible. *However,* the normalization concept includes not only those retarded individuals moving from an institutional setting to a less restrictive, more normal setting, but also those retarded individuals already living in the community for which a more "normal" life-style may be a worthy goal.

Turnbull and Turnbull (1975) cite a number of considerations in the deinstitutionalization process. Among the concerns they address are: the preparation for deinstitutionalization and the obligation of equivalency. While most institutions are now providing instruction and training for the transition from institutional life to community life, there is often a major concern about providing adequate preparation. There are many areas of everyday living that most individuals take for granted: shopping, crossing streets, making daily purchases, and getting transportation. Yet, unless deliberate efforts are made to provide instruction in these areas, a number of problems can develop.

In one situation a group of deinstitutionalized young adults living in a community-based home had not had any instruction regarding the use of traffic lights to cross streets and were walking against red lights. It was not until individuals in the neighborhood called the problem to the attention of the house parent that any of the professional staff realized that a problem existed.

The area of sex education is a major concern, but it is sometimes deliberately ignored. Yet, as adults in the community, these individuals will be free in many instances to conduct their personal lives as they choose. How they conduct their personal lives and the results of their interpersonal relationships may be dependent on the instruction and training that they receive in sex education. Deisher's study (1973) on institutional staff attitudes regarding the sexuality of retarded individuals suggests that there may be a substantial number of staff members who believe that residents should not be allowed to express sexual feeling or should be permitted only limited expression. While it is possible, if not probable, that more liberal attitudes have developed since this study, there is, nevertheless, the concern that those staff members who view retarded individuals primarily as asexual will not provide these individuals with adequate sex education prior to deinstitutionalization.

Another concern expressed by Turnbull and Turnbull (1975) is for the quality of deinstitutionalized care. While institutions are now carefully monitored and evaluated to meet accreditation standards, there may be limited means of evaluating the quality of deinstitutionalized care received by these individuals.

In the failure to include the retarded in decisions regarding deinstitutionalization, what the parents and the administrators consider "best" for retarded individuals may not be congruent with what the individuals consider best for themselves. The assumption that normalization is best for every retarded individual may be presumptuous on the part of professional workers in the field of mental retardation.

Deinstitutionalization has become a reality. In a class action suit on behalf of the 5,000 residents of the Willowbrook Institution in New York (New York State Association for Retarded Citizens and Parisi v. Carey, 1975), the court ordered sufficient community alternatives to reduce the institution's population to 250 persons in 6 years. Congruent with mandates on educational provisions, court rulings have stressed that the residential setting should represent the least restrictive alternative. It is incumbent on those with the responsibility of providing residential alternatives to find the setting that is truly in the best interest of the individual rather than that which is most expedient, is in the best interest of the institution or the community, or satisfies some group's social conscience. In some cases the least restrictive environment may provide for community-based alternatives. In other instances, the environment that is in the best interest of the individual and yet is the least restrictive alternative may be an institutional setting.

Program philosophies in normalization. There are a number of underlying philosophies that guide the development of community-based settings for the mentally retarded. Baker, Seltzer, and Seltzer (1977) suggest that the view that settings should provide retarded people with protection and benevolent guidance has not been entirely discarded in the move away from institutions.

Wolfensberger (1969) advocated the establishment of small community-based residences, all within regular neighborhoods and staffed with live-in house parents. Residents in these settings would utilize existing services in the community for education, work, health care, and recreation. Wolfensberger (1971) also suggested that other residential models might be appropriate, such as boarding the retarded adult with a local family, foster care, or adoption.

Fig. 10-2. Group homes usually require each resident to share in responsibilities of everyday living. (Photograph by Peter Poulides.)

Sarason (1974) emphasized what he termed "a psychological sense of community." Sarason contends that the main criterion by which any program should be developed and assessed is whether it promotes a sense of belonging, mutual responsibility and purpose, and the opportunity for individuals to be part of a group on which they can depend and to which they can contribute.

Another view is that a setting should provide intentional training for the resident. These programs emphasize providing opportunities for activities to

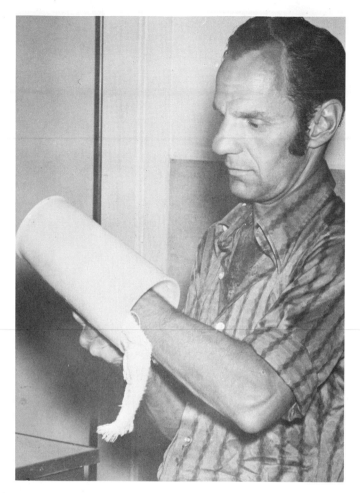

Fig. 10-3. The group home provides residents with an opportunity to learn skills for independent living.

develop skills for independent functioning in daily activities. Aanes and Haagensen (1977) draw attention to the potential problems of normalization when it is conceptualized as a means rather than a goal (end). Often unenlightened proponents of the normalization goal do not see a difference in the conceptualization of the principle and are opposed to any experiences that do not approximate that which is considered normal. Thus, some may conclude that anything normal is good and anything not normal is bad. Thorne (1975) contends that normalization as a means may actually interfere with normalization as an end or an ultimate goal of normal behavior. He argues that confusion results when a belief exists that normalized techniques (and environment) will naturally result in normalized behavior.

Models of community residences. Baker, Seltzer, and Seltzer (1977) list four major models for deinstitutionalized settings for the retarded: (1) group homes, (2) protected settings, (3) training programs, (4) and semi-independent apartments. These various settings provide a wide range of alternatives representing closely supervised to semi-independent settings.

GROUP HOMES. Within the category of group homes there is considerable variation in organizational patterns and alternatives.

Small group homes. Baker, Seltzer, and Seltzer (1977) define a small group home as a community residence with 6 to 10 residents living in a single dwelling. In their study of these small group homes they found some distinguishing characteristics. Typically, these homes are staffed by two house parents or house managers, who usually are a young married couple; they usually have an assistant to serve as a relief person for their days and times off. In some instances a house director is employed on a full- or half-time basis to handle administrative matters. These small group homes are usually integrated in residential neighborhoods. These homes emphasize programs that provide daily living experiences as similar as possible to those of nonretarded individuals. Day placements for work skill training is typical of these programs.

In their study of 132 small group homes, Baker, Seltzer, and Seltzer (1977) found that 21 percent of the residents were engaged in competitive employment, 51 percent in sheltered workshops or educational programs and 16 percent in day activity centers. The mean ages of these residents was 29, with 35 percent of the group listed as mildly retarded, 48 percent as moderately retarded, 13 percent as severely retarded, and the remaining were handicapped, nonretarded individuals.

These homes are typically financed by state funds supplemented by fees paid by the residents. As might be expected, a fairly high percentage (40 percent) met with some opposition from the community, typically neighbors.

While the failure rate for these residents in the Baker, Seltzer, and Seltzer study was notable, with nearly 19 percent returning to institutions or hospitals, 24 percent went on to live in apartments, 26.5 percent with their families, and 5 percent with foster families. In some instances these homes serve as a permanent residence for certain individuals, while in other instances they serve as an intermediate step for a more normalized situation. Small group homes in which residents contribute to group decision making may lead to superior decisions as compared to decisions made individually, and peer group discussions and decision making of day to day administrative issues may have a beneficial learning experience for retarded residents (Heller, 1978).

Large group homes. Baker and his associates (1977) identified larger group homes as having between 11 and 80 residents. They further divided these homes into three groups: small group homes with 11 to 19 residents, medium group homes with 20 to 40 residents, and what they designated as mini-institutions with 41 to 80 residents. The majority, 66, were in the medium category, 23 were in the large category, and 5 were in the mini-institution category.

Larger facilities offer some potential advantages over the smaller group homes. The larger staffs allow for greater role specialization and more free-

Fig. 10-4. Large residential homes provide an opportunity to live and work in the community while receiving necessary supervision. (Photograph by Peter Poulides.)

dom for house parents. The larger number of residents allows for more heterogenous subgrouping to provide for specialized needs of the residents. Larger facilities may also be more economical to operate. At the same time, the larger the facility the less likely it may be able to approximate a "normal" home.

Baker, Seltzer, and Seltzer (1977) found that the medium group homes utilized a variety of living accommodations for their residents. Large old homes were most frequently used. Former hospitals, former convents, and apartment houses were also used as residences. In these settings some used two husband-wife house parent teams as well as other varying support personnel, depending on size and need.

Larger group homes typically utilized very large old houses with as many as 30 rooms. These facilities were more typically found in larger cities. Baker and his associates found that residents in these larger group homes tended to be more severely retarded. Staff ratios were also generally lower than in the smaller facilities. Thus, Baker study groups concluded that a more custodial atmosphere was often the result in these facilities.

Mini-institutions, because of their size, do not fit most concepts of community residence. They were typically housed in former hospitals or in specially constructed modern facilities. In comparison to the other group homes, staffing ratio was lower, organized involvement with the outside community was limited, and rules and policies were considerably more restrictive (Baker, Seltzer, and Seltzer, 1977).

A fourth type of group house is the mixed group home, which combines other individuals, such as alcoholics, former mental patients, and former prison inmates. Wolfensberger (1972) opposed these mixed facilities on the grounds that the retarded would suffer from more negative community reactions and predicted that the retarded would model the deviant behaviors of the other residents. Baker and his associates (1977) found that the turnover rate was considerably greater, with 6 months as the average length of residence as compared to 2 years in other models. It appears that these mixed group homes serve as "half-way houses" between the institution and the outside world. One-third of Baker's sample of these homes were located in Texas where they are referred to as half-way houses.

Group homes for older adults. Group homes for older adults typically house retarded adults over the age of 50 who function at a higher intellectual level than in other models. These facilities are shared with nonretarded individuals, and more of the residents are female. Most of the facilities are privately owned, and residents are unlikely to be involved in activities outside the residence (Baker, Seltzer, and Seltzer, 1977).

PROTECTED SETTINGS. A protected setting is another option in providing housing for retarded adults.

Foster family care. Foster family care represents an attempt to provide a surrogate family for the retarded individual. Dorgan (1958) suggests that a goal of foster family care is to integrate the individual into the family setting, with the assumption that within the normal family environment and with the foster family's understanding, the individual will learn behavior acceptable to the family, and if feasible, will work. Baker, Seltzer, and Seltzer (1977) caution that a retarded person in a surrogate family may assume a dependent, childlike role; they found that those with whom placement was made, referred to their residents as "boys," "girls," or "children." Concern is therefore generated since this model may have a tendency for over protection of the retarded adult. In general, these placements provide residents with their adequate productive daytime activities and adequate opportunity to manage their physical environment, both fundamental components of normalization. Furthermore, in most instances, those who operate the foster homes generally receive a per capita fee from the state. These settings accommodate from one to six adults. Activities and quality of care to some extent is discretionary with the operators of these homes. If their goal is to make a profit, there is a danger of them spending too little on their foster residents in order to increase profits. Overly benevolent individuals, on the other hand, may spend too much, thereby depriving themselves.

Sheltered villages. A second type of protective setting for the retarded is a sheltered village. These residences for retarded adults are usually located in rural areas, typically secluded and spread out over several buildings. While rules, activities, and relative freedom within each of these sheltered villages vary, they do have one common characteristic: the retarded individual in this setting is isolated from the outside community with the philosophy that these residents are better off in isolation than being exposed to the potential failure, frustrations, and demands of the outside world. Most of these facilities are private, and a number are church supported. Fees are generally high, nearly double the cost of fees in other residential alternatives.

Of all the models explored, this alternative appears to be in greater con-

flict with the principle of normalization. Proponents of these settings argue
that the individual is better off protected and sheltered from the chaos, prejudice, and demands of society.

TRAINING PROGRAMS. The retarded individual's ability to adjust to and
cope with the demands of the community are not inate. Baker, Seltzer, and
Seltzer (1977) report that the 22 percent of all retarded individuals who returned to institutional living from community placements did so at least
partly because of their lack of preparation and training. It appears reasonable to assume that a greater degree of preparation prior to full release into
the community would greatly enhance the possibility of success. Training
programs usually fall into one of two types: community preparation programs or workshop dormitories.

Community preparation programs. Community preparation programs are
short-term residential training programs often located on the grounds of an
institution. The goal of these programs is to prepare the individual for community-based living. Many skills that the normal population takes for
granted and often learns incidentally as children, must be intentionally
taught. Typical among these skills is that of transportation (such as use of the
bus), crossing the street, handling money, shopping, working, leisure and
recreation, grooming, domestic responsibility, and interpersonal relationships.

The staff for these facilities usually have specialized training or special
responsibilities and include such specialists as a vocational rehabilitation
counselor. The progress of each individual is usually carefully charted, and
release from the institution is often dependent on the individual reaching
some predetermined competency level.

Workshop dormitories. Community residences that are administratively
and programmatically associated with vocational training are referred to as
workshop dormitories. The actual residential facility and the workshop may
be in different locations. However, the important aspect of this type of program is that both are connected administratively, and comparing these programs to community preparation programs, they have similar goals but different emphases. In the community preparation program, activities of daily
living assume the highest priority. In the workshop dormitory model, however, vocational training is given at least equal emphasis to community
living skills, and the program is oriented toward training the residents for
employment. Like the community preparation programs, the workshop

dormitory is considered a temporary or short-term program, and the resident is maintained there until ready for release for employment and community living.

SEMI-INDEPENDENT APARTMENT. All of the residential models we have discussed to this point provide 24-hour supervision for the residents. The semi-independent apartment is an exception to this characteristic and represents the least supervised, least restrictive setting of all models in which some degree of supervision is provided.

Three variations of semi-independent apartment living are suggested by Fritz, Wolfensberger, and Knowlton (1971).

1. *Apartment clusters.* Apartment clusters are comprised of several apartments in relative physical proximity to one another, functioning to some extent as a unit and supervised by a resident staff member residing in one of the apartment units.

2. *Single co-residence apartment.* Single apartments where an adult staff

Fig. 10-5. A number of more independent retarded adults live in this apartment complex with only limited supervision. (Photograph by Peter Poulides.)

member (usually college student) shares an apartment with two or three retarded roommates.

3. *Single apartment.* The maximum independence is an apartment, occupied by two or more retarded adults who are given assistance by a nonresident staff member.

These three variations provide varying degrees of independence, and individuals living in this type of residential model usually are less retarded than those living in other residential models. In this arrangement most residents are responsible for or contribute to apartment maintenance, meal preparation, and transportation to place of employment. Baker, Seltzer, and Seltzer (1977) found that 29 percent were engaged in competitive employment while 36 percent were involved in sheltered workshop activities. The risk factor for this type of arrangement appears to be great. While 24 percent of former residents went on to independent living, 23 percent returned to an institution. As stated before, more efficient preparation for independent living may curtail the failure rate.

Summary. As retarded adults move closer toward normalization, residential alternatives must be provided to meet their individual needs and differences. Many mildly retarded adults live independently in our communities. Others, however, require some degree of supervision either permanently or until they have developed those skills necessary to function independently.

For centuries the retarded have suffered neglect, ridicule, harassment, and even brutality in a society claiming to be civilized. Humankind now possesses the knowledge and the ability to eliminate some mental retardation in the future. We possess the ability to reduce the debilitating effects of mental retardation for both the individual and the family. We can educate and prepare the majority of the retarded population for useful and productive lives. For the severely and profoundly retarded, we can provide a more comfortable and humanizing form of existence. The choice is clearly ours—parents, professionals, and citizens in a potentially great society. We can reject the retarded of today and do little to prevent and ameliorate the retardation of tomorrow, or together in a multidisciplined effort we can help the retarded to become an integral part of society.

STUDY QUESTIONS

1. What is meant by, "Retarded adults exist as a paradox"?
2. What have the earlier and more recent studies of retarded adults in the community found?

3. What changes did Edgerton find in his 1976 follow-up study of his retarded subjects in the community as compared to his 1967 study?
4. What are some of the characteristics that lead to the employability of retarded individuals?
5. What are the purposes of sheltered workshops?
6. What has been the effect of sterilization on the retarded?
7. How have the retarded adjusted to marriage?
8. How do the retarded function as citizens in the community?
9. What is the principle of normalization?
10. What are the residential alternatives available to retarded adults?

REFERENCES

Aanes, D. and Haagensen, L. Normalization: attention to a conceptual disaster. *Mental Retardation*, 1978, **16**(1), 55-56.

Allen, R. C. *The retarded citizen: victim of mental and legal deficiency.* Unpublished paper. Institute of Law, Psychiatry, and Criminology, Washington, D.C.: The George Washington University. Portions of this paper published in *Legal Rights of the Disadvantaged*, Washington, D.C.: U.S. Department of Health, Education and Welfare, 1969.

Baker, B. L., Seltzer, G. B., and Seltzer, M. M. *As close as possible: community residences for retarded adults.* Boston: Little, Brown and Co., 1977.

Baller, W. R. A study of the present social status of a group of adults who, when they were in elementary schools, were classified as mentally deficient. *Genetic Psychology Monographs*, 1936, **18**, 165-244.

Baller, W., Charles, D., and Miller, E. *Mid-life attainment of the mentally retarded, a longitudinal study.* Lincoln, Neb.: University of Nebraska Press, 1966.

Bank-Mikkelsen, N. E. A metropolitan area in Denmark: Copenhagen. In R. B. Kugel and W. Wolfensberger (Eds.), *Changing patterns in residential services for the mentally retarded.* Washington, D.C.: President's Committee on Mental Retardation, 1969, Pp. 227-254.

Barrett, A. M., Relos, R., and Eisele, J. Vocational success and attitudes of mentally retarded toward work and money. *American Journal of Mental Deficiency*, 1965, **70**, 102-107.

Bradbury, W. *The adult years.* New York: Time-Life Books, 1975.

Brolin, D., Durand, R., Kromer, K., and Muller, P. Post-school adjustment of educable retarded students, *Education and Training of the Mentally Retarded*, 1975, **10**(3), 144-149.

Buck vs. Bell. *Supreme Court Reports*, No. 584, 274, U.S. 200, 1927.

Burt, R. A. Legal restrictions on sexual and familial relations of mental retardates—old laws, new guises. In F. F. de la Cruz and G. D. LaVeck (Eds.), *Human sexuality and the mentally retarded.* New York: Brunner/Mazel, Inc., 1973.

Chaffin, J. D., Spellman, C. R., Regan, C. E., and Davison, R. Two follow up studies of former educable mentally retarded students from the Kansas work-study project. *Exceptional Children*, 1971, **37**, 733-738.

Cohen, J. S. An analysis of vocational failures of mental retardates placed in the community after a period of institutionalization. *American Journal of Mental Deficiency*. 1960, **65**, 371-375.

Craft, J. H. The effects of sterilization. *Journal of Heredity*, 1963, **27**, 379-387.

Deisher, R. W. Sexual behavior of retarded in institutions. In F. F. de la Cruz and G. D. LaVeck (Eds.), *Human sexuality and the mentally retarded.* New York: Brunner/Mazel, Inc., 1973.

Dorgan, J. Foster home care for the psychiatric patient. *Canadian Journal of Public Health*, 1958, **49**(10), 411-419.

Edgerton, R. B. *The cloak of competence.* Berkeley: University of California Press, 1967.

Edgerton, R. B. and Bercovici, S. M. The cloak of competence years later. *American Journal of Mental Deficiency*, 1976, **80**(5), 485-497.

Erdman, R. L. Vocational choices of adolescent mentally retarded boys. *Dissertation Abstracts*, 1957, **17**, 2497.

Fairbanks, R. F. The subnormal child—seventeen years later. *Mental Hygiene*, 1931, **17**, 177-208.

Fernald, W. E. After-care study of the patients

discharged from Waverly for a period of twenty-five years. *Ungraded,* 1919, **5,** 25-31.

Ferster, E. Eliminating the unfit—is sterilization the answer? *Ohio State Law Journal,* 1966, **27,** 391.

Fiester, A. R., and Giambra, L. M. Language indices of vocational success in mentally retarded adults. *American Journal of Mental Deficiency,* 1972, **77,** 332-337.

Folman, R., and Budoff, M. Learning potential and vocational aspirations of retarded adolescents. *Exceptional Children,* 1971, **38,** 121-130.

Fraenkel, W. A. *The mentally retarded and their vocational rehabilitation. A resource handbook.* National Association for Retarded Citizens, 1961.

Fritz, M., Wolfensberger, W., and Knowlton, M. *An apartment living plan to promote integration and normalization of mentally retarded adults.* Downsview, Ontario: Canadian Association for the Mentally Retarded, May 1971.

Gamble, C. J. The prevention of mental deficiency by sterilization. *American Journal of Mental Deficiency,* 1951, **56,** 192-197.

Gan, J., Tymchuk, A., Nisihara, A. Mildly retarded adults: their attitudes toward retardation. *Mental Retardation,* 1977, **15**(5), 5-10.

Goddard, H. H. *Feeblemindedness, its causes and consequences.* New York: The Macmillan Co., 1914.

Goldstein, H. Social and occupational adjustment. In R. Heber and H. Stevens (Eds.), *Mental retardation.* Chicago: University of Chicago Press, 1964.

Gozali, J. Citizenship and voting behavior of mildly retarded adults: a pilot study. *American Journal of Mental Deficiency,* 1971, **75,** 640-641.

Heller, T. Group decision making by mentally retarded adults. *American Journal of Mental Deficiency,* 1978, **82**(5), 480-486.

Howe, C. E. *A comparison of mentally retarded high school students in work-study versus traditional programs.* Final report, Project No. 6-8148, Grant No. OEG-4-6-068148-1556, Washington, D.C.: U.S. Department of Health, Education and Welfare (B.E.H.), 1967.

Jastak, J. F., MacPhee, H. M., and Whiteman, M. *Mental retardation, its nature and incidence.* Newark, Del.: University of Delaware Press, 1963.

Johnson, B. S. A study of cases discharged from Laconia State School from July 1, 1924 to July 1, 1934. *American Journal of Mental Deficiency,* 1946, **50,** 437-445.

Kantner, H. M. *The identification of elements which contribute to occupational success and failure of adults classified as educable mentally retarded.* Unpublished doctoral dissertation, Tempe, Ariz.: Arizona State University, 1969.

Kennedy, R. A. *A Connecticut community revisited: a study of the social adjustment of a group of mentally deficient adults in 1948 and 1960.* Hartford: Connecticut State Department of Health, Office of Mental Retardation, 1966.

Kennedy, R. J. R. *The social adjustment of morons in a Connecticut city.* Willport, Conn.: Commission to Survey Resources in Connecticut, 1948.

Kolstoe, O. P. An examination of some characteristics which discriminate between employed and not-employed mentally retarded males. *American Journal of Mental Deficiency,* 1961, **66,** 472-482.

Kolstoe, O. P., and Frey, R. M. *A high school work-study program for the mentally subnormal.* Carbondale, Ill.: Southern Illinois University Press, 1965.

Kravaceus, W. C. *Juvenile delinquency and the school.* Yonkers on the Hudson, N.Y.: World Publishing Co., 1945.

Menolascino, F. J., Clark, R. L., and Wolfensberger, W. *The initiation and development of a comprehensive, county wide system of services for the mentally retarded of Douglas County.* (3rd ed.) A Planning Report to the Douglas County Board of Commissioners, submitted by the Greater Omaha ARC, 1970.

Moore, F. Mentally defective delinquents. In I. C. Burrows (Ed.), *Proceedings of the National Conference on Charities Correction.* Boston: George H. Ellis, 1911.

New York State Association for Retarded Citizens and Parisi v. Carey, No. 72-C-356/357 (E.D.N.Y., Apr. 30, 1975), approved 393F Supp. 715 (E.D. N.Y., 1975).

Nirje, B. The normalization principle and its human management implications. In R. B. Kugel and W. Wolfensberger (Eds.), *Changing patterns in residential services for the mentally retarded.* Washington, D.C.: President's Committee on Mental Retardation, 1969, 227-254.

Nirje, B. The normalization principle and its human management implications. *Journal of Mental Subnormality,* 1970, **16,** 62-70.

O'Conner, G., Justice, R. S., and Warren, N. The aged mentally retarded: institution or community care? *American Journal of Mental Deficiency*, 1970, **75**, 354-360.

Olshansky, S. Changing behavior through normalization. In W. Wolfensberger (Ed.), *Normalization: the principal of normalization in human services.* Toronto: National Institute on Mental Retardation, 1972.

Olshansky, S. and Beach, D. A five year follow up of mentally retarded clients. *Rehabilitation Literature*, 1974, **35**(2), 48-49.

Peterson, L., and Smith, L. L. A comparison of post school adjustment of educable mentally retarded adults with that of adults of normal intelligence. *Exceptional Children*, 1960, **26**, 404-408.

Sali, J., and Amir, M. Personal factors influencing the retarded person's success at work: a report from Israel. *American Journal of Mental Deficiency*, 1970, **76**, 42-47.

Sarason, S. B. *The psychological sense of community.* San Francisco: Jossey-Bass, Inc., Publishers, 1974.

Stanfield, J. S. Graduation: what happens to the retarded child when he grows up? *Exceptional Children*, 1973, **39**, 548-552.

Tarjan, G., Dingman, H. F., Eyman, R., and Brown, S. J. Effectiveness of hospital release programs. *American Journal of Mental Deficiency*, 1959, **65**, 609-617.

Thorne, J. M. Normalization through the normalization principle: right ends, wrong means. *Mental Retardation*, 1975, **13**, 23-25.

Turnbull, H. R., and Turnbull, A. P. Deinstitutionalization and the law, *Mental Retardation*, 1975, **13**, 14-20.

Webster's New Collegiate Dictionary, Springfield, Mass.: G. & C. Merriam Co., 1975.

Wolfensberger, W. *Normalization: the principle of normalization in human services.* Toronto: National Institute on Mental Retardation, 1972.

Wolfensberger, W. Twenty predictions about the future of residential services in mental retardation. *Mental Retardation*, 1969, **7**(6), 51-54.

Wolfensberger, W. Will there always be an institution? II: the impact of new service models: residential alternatives to institutions. *Mental Retardation*, 1969, **9**(6), 31-38.

ANNOTATED BIBLIOGRAPHY

Baker, B. L., Seltzer, G. B., and Seltzer, M. M. *As close as possible: community residences for retarded adults*, Boston: Little, Brown and Co., 1977.

A thorough review and analysis of residential alternatives for the mentally retarded.

de la Cruz, F. F., and La Veck, G. D. *Human sexuality and the mentally retarded.* New York: Brunner/Mazel, Inc., 1973.

Contains many excellent papers presented at a conference sponsored by the National Institute of Child Health and Human Development, U.S. Department of Health, Education and Welfare and Public Health Service, National Institutes of Health.

Edgerton, R. B. *The cloak of competence.* Berkeley: University of California Press, 1967.

A detailed follow-up on the lives of individuals released from Pacific State Hospital in California. Includes detailed portraits of selected subjects and the concerns of these individuals living outside of the institution.

CHAPTER 11

The aged retarded

(Photograph by Peter Poulides.)

INTRODUCTION

In some ways the content of this chapter extends the material in Chapter 10. Certainly the processes of aging is not a separate category in adulthood. There are, however, some very legitimate reasons to give special attention to the latter part of adulthood—the final phase of the life cycle. For one, interest in the process of aging and the field of geriatrics has grown dramatically in the past few years. Part of this attention has perhaps been the result of a developing society that can afford to be increasingly humanistic. However, another very strong influence has been the very visible presence of an increasing number of older persons in our midst. As our medical sophistication has progressed (and the raw physical demands for survival have diminished), the longevity of the general population has increased.

Aging, what does it mean? Who is an old person? Certainly these are questions to which most can provide some sort of an answer. An old person is perhaps one's grandmother or grandfather. An old person is one who is retired. But an old person from the perspective of a child may differ greatly from that of someone who is 45 years of age. For the most part, peoples' perceptions of age involve specific examples, probably examples from personal experience or personal frame of reference on a conceptual basis. One does not have to probe very far before it becomes evident that these answers vary a great deal. There are nearly as many answers to the questions as there are individuals to be polled. Thus the conceptual basis on which a behavioral scientist must operate must also vary. If one views aging (or the elderly) from a physiological viewpoint, a very different perspective may result than if it is addressed from a cultural viewpoint. Different individuals and characteristics *will* emerge in defining the elderly. To compound the problem further, different attitudes and philosophies will also prevail. As for other topics, this chapter will focus on a domain that is very fluid and quite complex, factors that become even more pronounced because of the primitive level of knowledge development in the area.

The particular focus of this chapter is on aging of the mentally retarded. This brings us to a second reason for providing special attention to this phase in the life cycle of the mentally retarded. It has been emphasized throughout this volume that the retarded represent one part of the complete spectrum of humanity. Although they are different in some respects, they are not in many others, and to ignore this is to be blinded by either attitude or lack of information. Thus, the process of aging cannot be denied attention for the elderly retarded any more than it can for the population in general. The major emphasis of both research and service for the retarded has been at the *childhood* level. One only has to peruse the literature to note that even at the adolescent level attention declines dramatically. This segment of the population does, however, grow up, and they grow old, and die.

RESEARCH ON AGING AND RETARDATION

There has been relatively little research conducted that specifically focuses on aging in the mentally retarded. In fact, the information available is so limited that it might be characterized as nearly nonexistent. With rare exceptions (Kaplan, 1943) interest in this area has not been evident until very recently. Although there is still an urgent need for additional study, this area does appear to be rising in terms of priority of attention.

The introductory statement presented before suggested a certain lack of clarity regarding who the aged retarded are. Some of the reasons for this lack of clarity were alluded to and will receive additional attention in this section. Research will be reviewed in an attempt to explore how the elderly mentally retarded differ and how they are similar to the nonretarded. Since we are limited in research data on the retarded, the nonretarded population occasionally will be used as a referent group.

METHODOLOGICAL PROBLEMS

A number of influences contribute to the relative absence of research in the area of aging and the retarded. Some of these factors involve interest and attitude toward the population, although recent changes appear evident. Other influences involve methodological problems encountered in conducting research on aging in general and with the mentally retarded specifically.

Some of the methodological problems encountered in investigations on aging involve fundamental research design difficulties. These have been reviewed in depth by Schaie and Gribbin (1975) and represent very serious impediments to the growth of a knowledge base regarding the process of aging. Because of their importance, these design problems will be reviewed briefly. They require consideration as one attempts to interpret existing data on the elderly and the process of growing old.

Two of the most common approaches to studying the process of aging involve the cross-sectional design and the longitudinal design. The cross-sectional design samples subjects from several age levels (for example, 40 to

49, 50 to 59, 60 to 69, 70 to 79) and compares certain measures between groups. Longitudinal studies, on the other hand, select a single sample of subjects and follow them through the years to compare behaviors at the different ages. Both approaches essentially have the goal of comparing attributes at different ages in order to determine how the aging process affects them. Although on the surface these approaches would appear appropriate for that purpose, problems have arisen that appear to make interpretation of data difficult or at least something to be undertaken cautiously.

The cross-sectional design is by far the most convenient procedure since all subjects are assessed at approximately the same time. A sample of subjects at each age level is selected and the investigator then records the desired data. As noted before, the data are then compared between age levels with the intent of suggesting that any differences between groups result from age differences (inferring the aging process). The design problem that surfaces relates to this inference or interpretation. Although it may be the case that observed differences *are* caused by age differences, there also may be another interpretation. Differences that appear, for example, between the group that is 40 and the group that is 70 years old, could be the result of the effects of sociocultural change. After all, more than a quarter of a century has passed since the older group was 40. It is quite likely (and observations of the past quarter of a century would confirm) that many social and cultural changes have occurred in such a period of time. Differences between groups may be from aging, the different sociocultural influences, or a combination of both.

Longitudinal investigations are not plagued by the problem of sociocultural change in the same fashion as cross-sectional studies. Since the same sample is followed through a period of years (even a life span) the "generation gap" differences are not as potently operative. It cannot be denied, however, that a given person makes certain behavioral changes as sociocultural influences are altered. A more serious difficulty is the problem of sample attrition over the period of the study. Because subjects are inevitably lost during the investigation, the sample available at, say, age 70, is likely to be quite different than the initial sample at 40. Thus differences might result from the fact that the sample composition differs between 40 and 70 rather than from the effects of age. This has been termed "experimental mortality" and is an inherent design problem in longitudinal studies (Schaie and Gribbin, 1975; Drew, 1976).

An additional difficulty in longitudinal studies relates to the fact that the investigation may extend beyond the life span of the researcher. This has frequently led to the use of retrospective studies that do not take direct measurement at the earlier ages but rely on retrospective reports of the data based on the memory of the subjects and others close to them. Such approaches are plagued with serious difficulties relative to the reliability and accuracy of the retrospective reports.

The methodological problems noted above are serious threats to the soundness of research on the effects of aging. They do not, however, imply that the study of aging is impossible or should not be undertaken. This section has been included for the purpose of providing the reader information concerning problems associated with reading and interpreting research on the elderly. Obviously, there are times when research results need to be interpreted cautiously in order not to generalize beyond the data generated or to make unsound inferences based on preliminary findings.

IDENTIFYING THE AGED RETARDED

Investigators studying the aging process in the mentally retarded are faced with even more difficulties than those who study aging in general. Since there has been so little research focusing specifically on this population, there is little information available to use as a point of departure. Dickerson, Hamilton, Huber, and Segal (1974) characterize the aged mentally retarded as somewhat of an *invisible group* since they are essentially invisible in the literature, both in gerontology and mental retardation.

Faced with this type of situation, researchers are forced to address some fundamental questions as they initiate study of the elderly retarded. One of the very basic questions that is raised immediately was mentioned in the initial part of this chapter—who is an old retarded person? Segal (1977) suggested that individuals 55 and over be considered as aged. This definition was reportedly agreed on because of the fact that certain federal agencies use 55 as the guideline in terms of funding programs for the elderly. There may be other factors, however, that recommend such a reduced age guideline for the retarded population.

Dickerson and associates (1974) speculated that a mentally retarded person who lives to 45 or 50 years of age is probably considered old. Such conjecture is striking primarily because a chronological age of 45 to 50, or even 55, would not typically be thought of as old in the general population. However,

Dickerson and her associates indicate that the mentally retarded may be subject to "double or triple jeopardy" with regard to the normal loss pattern associated with advancing age. This hypothesis should not be interpreted as speculation that the aging process (physiologically) is necessarily more rapid in the retarded population. These authors make clear that part of their speculation is based on factors such as where the retarded reside and what minimal services are available for the elderly handicapped.

It has been suggested that identification of the aged retarded is not as simple a task as it might appear. One obvious question pertains to the size of the population. Although there has not been a great deal of study on this topic, there has been some attention given it (Payne, 1967; Dickerson and others, 1974; Kriger, 1975). All of these investigations focused on retarded populations residing in institutions. Some interesting results were evident from these studies. For example, Payne found that 18.2 percent of the institutionalized population sampled (17 institutions in 13 western states) was over the age of 40. Kriger, on the other hand, found only a very small number of retarded persons over 40 in her study. A search of available records only produced 110 names in the entire state of Ohio (only 75 of these individuals could actually be found). These figures are particularly striking in view of the estimates of over 38,000 who should have existed, based on percentage projections.

Results such as Kriger's raise some extremely interesting questions regarding aging and mental retardation. Where are the elderly retarded? Perhaps the use of population percentage projections is inappropriate for this group. It would seem, however, that the state of Ohio (or any other state for that matter) would have more retarded individuals over 40 than were found. Are they hidden or invisible because of lack of services—and therefore not on anyone's records? Perhaps there is a lower survival rate in the mentally retarded population. Perhaps they have adapted and are no longer so evident as being retarded. These types of questions are central to the study of aging in the mentally retarded and largely remain unanswered in any definitive way.

CHARACTERISTICS OF THE AGED RETARDED

It is not surprising that a complete picture of the aged retarded is lacking. Problems encountered in the study of aging generally are compounded by additional complexities that pertain specifically to the mentally retarded.

Interest in this area is, however, growing, and some evidence is available relative to characteristics of this population.

Mental functioning

A decline in mental functioning is a characteristic that is typically associated with the aging process. Most people would agree that older people they know are frequently less mentally alert and often not as generally capable mentally as younger individuals. This type of perception also often compares the functioning of the older person on a current basis with recollections of their functioning when younger. Although there are many unanswered questions related to this perception, it is definitely a rather widely held view. One question related to our particular focus concerns the influence of the aging process on older mentally retarded people. Do retarded people experience further decline in mental functioning as they age? Does the rate of mental decline occur in a similar fashion as for nonretarded peers (if, in fact, it occurs at all)?

A few investigations have focused specifically on the mental functioning of the mentally retarded and have included older subjects in the sample (Kaplan, 1943; Thompson, 1951; Bell and Zubek, 1960). In most cases results were somewhat mixed, although some support seems evident for a decline in measured intelligence. Bell and Zubek, for example, conducted a cross-sectional study using subjects from 15 to 64 years of age. They reported that full-scale IQs seemed to hold rather well between 20 and 45 but declined thereafter. Kaplan's (1943) investigation used a different design and assessed measured intelligence of retarded individuals over 45 years of age. Subjects in his study had been tested previously, and the earlier test scores were compared with the retest performances to determine the degree to which changes were evident. An average of nearly 15 years had elapsed between testing. Although some decline in measured intelligence was noted, results did not suggest that the subjects' rate of decline was much different than might be expected of their nonretarded counterparts. In fact, certain specific performance areas showed an increased functioning over earlier assessments (for example, vocabulary performance in males).

Results of research reviewed indicate a mixture of findings, a situation that is not surprising given the limited attention to the area. In part these varying data may be the result of the different research designs and the specific samples included in the studies. The evidence does seem to *suggest* that there is a decline in mental functioning as the mentally retarded grow old— at least in terms of measured intelligence. It is not at all clear how such a decline compares with their nonretarded peers, although at least limited evidence suggests that it is not substantially greater (Kaplan, 1943). It is also not clear how specific areas of functioning that are a part of the global measured intelligence vary with age.

Another point of caution must also be considered however in relation to interpretation of these results. It is commonly agreed that situational factors, such as the testing itself, can substantially alter an individual's performance. This may involve a heightened performance or a decrement, depending on the individual and the situation. This type of influence has also been found by a number of investigators in the field of gerontology (Botwinick, 1969; Lair and Moon, 1972; Furry and Baltes, 1973; Fisher, 1973). One factor that may well result in declining test scores is the increased cautiousness that is observed in older people in general. Botwinick's results, in particular, highlighted the "risk avoidance" or greater cautiousness in the elderly (1969).

Such a characteristic as increased cautiousness would tend to present its influence most prominently in tasks where a time limit for responding was involved. It would also seem highly evident in situations that are potentially anxiety producing, such as in the presence of a nonroutine authority figure (for example, the psychometrician). Both of these conditions could logically be assumed to exist for aged mentally retarded individuals in the testing situation. If they exhibit the same increased cautiousness as older people in general (and there is no reason to expect that they would not), the timed responses required by testing might substantially negatively influence their scores. They simply may fail to respond within the allotted time.

The presence of the psychometrician may create some special concern for the elderly retarded. Kaplan (1943) suggested that the event of a mental test is an important occurrence in the life of an older retarded person (recall that nearly all the data available on the aged retarded involves institutionalized populations). He specifically indicated that this provided strong motivation for these older patients because to do poorly might result in negative consequences, and a good performance might have favorable results (such as institutional parole or release). Whereas the logic presented seems appealing, more recent studies have reported certain findings that place this line of reasoning somewhat in doubt.

A part of the investigation by Dickerson and associates (1974) involved individual interviews with older mentally retarded patients. Many of these individuals had resided in the institution for an extended period (20 to 60 years). The overwhelming perceptions of these patients was not one that would view parole or release favorably. In large part these older retarded patients were happy in the institution and tended to make comments such as, "I like it here," "All of my friends are here," "I'd be afraid to go—there is so much crime," and "I'm safe here" (Dickerson and others, 1974, p. 8). These investigators further reported that some subjects were reluctant to be interviewed because they were afraid that would mean they would have to live elsewhere. One can certainly argue that these patients' desire to remain in the institution might be based on the wrong reasons, but their perceptions would not seem disputable—they tended to feel comfortable in the institution and did not wish to move elsewhere; whether in fear of the unknown or for other related reasons. Such a perception is definitely at variance with the interpretation made by Kaplan and could easily be viewed as an attitude that might promote poorer test performance.

Other factors may also contribute to the apparent decline in mental functioning by older retarded people. It should be noted, however, that these points are largely speculative since research on these topics mainly comes from the general field of gerontology rather than mental retardation. For example, age deficits are typically evident on tasks that are paced (Taub, 1972; Kinsbourne, 1973), tasks that require a constant switching of attention (Craik, 1971), and tasks that involve free recall rather than recognition (Harwood and Naylor, 1969). Although these findings did not entail studies with retarded subjects, it is most conceivable that such results would also be evident with the retarded. Such tasks as those noted also ring quite familiar as one considers the activities included in an intelligence test.

Age deficits have also been found with tasks that require a change of learning set (Traxler and Britton, 1970). This topic is similarly an area that has not been extensively investigated with older retarded subjects. The literature does, however, suggest that retarded subjects (undifferentiated by age) are particularly susceptible to the formation of sets that tends to diminish their ability to transfer learning to other situations (Kaufman and Prehm, 1966; Drew and Espeseth, 1968). In view of these findings, it would seem reasonable to expect that older retarded people might be more susceptible to forming sets than both the younger retarded and the older nonretarded. This, of course, is speculative since specific investigation of the topic remains to be undertaken.

Research on the mental functioning of aged retarded people has been limited with regard to both depth and scope. This is perhaps most reflective of the limited research on the aged retarded in general rather than specifically a lack of interest in terms of mental functioning. We would anticipate that it may become a topic of increased activity in the future.

Social and personal functioning

It is evident from the interviews conducted by Dickerson and associates (1974) that the older retarded individuals in their sample, for the most part, did not want to live outside the institution. Their reasons for wishing to remain varied considerably in terms of specifics, as suggested by their remarks noted earlier. Most probably they had very little information concerning what life was like outside the institution, after all, the average length of institutionalization was 38 years. The institution had definitely become their home, and they seemed to view the outside world as a place of uncertainty and as a place to be feared. A review of their interview remarks does seem to reflect a theme of security in their institutional placement.

An additional theme also seems to emerge, however. These older mentally retarded patients made repeated references about being happy and about their friends. One older gentleman even made note of having been very active with "his ladies" (age unreported although he had been in the institution for 57 years). This raises some very interesting questions about the quality of life that the aged mentally retarded have. What types of social and personal life do they experience? As stated before, information on this topic is limited, although there have been some reports that provide a glimpse of life for the mentally retarded at this stage of the life cycle.

Talkington and Chiovaro (1969) reported on a pilot project aimed at programming for the special needs of the elderly retarded that was supported by Title III of the Older Americans Act. This project included over 100 older retarded individuals (institutionalized) ranging in age from 50 to 72. The description of these individuals at the beginning of the project varies somewhat from the impressions evident in the findings of Dickerson and her associates. Talkington and Chiovaro characterized their subjects as being mostly inactive, showing behavioral patterns suggesting senility and "regressive trends in self care" (p. 29). They also noted that these older retarded patients evidenced a general lack of interest and characteristic feelings of worthlessness. Although these investigators reported substantial progress as a function of their project, the description of their subjects prior to beginning the program is not a very favorable one. They noted that most of the patients in the project

Fig. 11-1. There are a variety of activities available for older retarded citizens. (Photograph by Peter Poulides.)

had been forgotten by their families or, in many cases, their families were nonexistent by virtue of death and relatives moving to other locations.

Despite the evident differences, there are some areas of similarity in the findings of Dickerson and associates and the description by Talkington and Chiovaro as noted previously. Dickerson and her colleagues also reported that several of their subjects no longer had close relatives that were alive or active in terms of visitations to the institution. One of their subjects, a female, had lived in the institution for 52 years. During the interview this woman reported that her brother had brought her to the institution when she was initially placed (an arrangement made by her mother). Since that time she had not seen her brother or her mother. This particular patient, however, represented an atypical point of view from most in the Dickerson study—she was the one woman in the sample who desired to live outside the institution.

Information in this section clearly indicates that a comprehensive picture of the social and personal functioning of the aged retarded is not available at this time. Many dimensions of this topic remain unexplored. Literature that is available presents a picture that is somewhat unexpected in terms of the general concept held by laypeople concerning growing old. Although they may not have a life in old age that most of us would choose, aged mentally retarded people do not seem to view their own lot in life as being miserable. At least many interviewed in the Dickerson study seemed relatively satisfied. Whereas this is only one source of data, it does raise some interesting questions that should provide a fertile topic for future research.

SUMMARY

Who are the aged retarded and what are their characteristics? These were general questions with which we began this chapter and in large part they remain. The final part of the life cycle of the mentally retarded is one that has had very little examination, particularly in comparison to those presented earlier in this volume. We are still faced with the question of whether or not the mentally retarded tend to age more rapidly than their nonretarded peers. In some cases retarded individuals do seem to become prematurely old. Certainly the ages under discussion in this chapter (45 to 55) are not considered old in the general population. If, in fact, this population does age more quickly, it is not at all clear whether it is due to factors related to mental retardation or to environmental factors that may be associated with mental retardation, such as poor health care.

It is interesting to note that the mentally retarded seem to be a segment of the population that does not experience the "middle age" stage of life to any marked degree. They tend to behave and are often thought of as being in somewhat of an extended childhood and adolescent phase for a large part of their lives. Whether this is because of the institutional atmosphere and consequent expectations has not been addressed or to any degree considered. Again, the need for research with comparable groups that have not been institutionalized is evident. Although the mentally retarded adult has been receiving greater attention in recent years, this period seems somewhat shortened because by the age of 45 or 50 they are considered "old." Once again the question is raised as to whether this is a function of mental retardation, the sociocultural environment, or both. Certainly the type of service patterns available to the mentally retarded impact on this phenomenon to a rather substantial degree. Literature available on this population suggests that aged retarded individuals tend to spend a very long period of life in institutions. Many who *are* discharged are placed in nursing homes—facilities that society characteristically reserves for the elderly. This very pattern of placement would seem to largely delete the middle age phase from the life of the retarded.

A further note of interest emerges regarding the placement of older mentally retarded people in nursing homes. Once in these placements, they tend to be grouped with elderly patients who are senile. Dickerson and her associates suggest that this is one phenomenon that contributes to the "invisibility" of the aged retarded. Their behaviors do not seem to be differentiated from those of elderly patients in general, and they "lose" their diagnosis of mental retardation. One obviously must question whether or not such programming practices are appropriate and in the best interests of these individuals. However, if they are (a matter not yet determined), it raises the question of the advisability of relabeling these people with a term that carries such negative connotations. As has been suggested throughout this volume, mental retardation is a complex problem that involves an interaction of many forces and influences. It is a problem that society must deal with and one that society has at least partially created. The life of the aged retarded reflects these interacting variables to no lesser extent than in earlier stages of the life cycle.

STUDY QUESTIONS

1. The aged retarded have been characterized by some as an "invisible" group. In some ways this seems to be an artifact of record-keeping, whereas in other ways it is a real phenomenon. How are these two perspectives of the invisible population related? How are they different? What are some implications for social services?
2. The general perception of older people is that they have a reduced level of mental functioning. Does this perception hold for older mentally retarded individuals? Does it seem to be more true for mentally retarded than nonretarded people? What other factors may enter the picture in terms of mental performance for older populations?

3. The study of aging is fraught with a number of difficulties relative to sound research. What are some of the problems encountered in conducting cross-sectional investigations? Longitudinal studies? How might these problems result in difficulties with regard to interpretation of results?

REFERENCES

Bell, A., and Zubek, J. P. The effect of age on the intellectual performance of mental defectives. *Journal of Gerontology*, 1960, **15**, 285-295.

Botwinick, J. Disinclination to venture response versus cautiousness in responding: age differences. *Journal of Genetic Psychology*, 1969, **119**, 241-249.

Craik, F. I. Age differences in recognition memory. *Quarterly Journal of Experimental Psychology*, 1971, **23**, 316-323.

Dickerson, M., Hamilton, J., Huber, R., and Segal, R. The aged mentally retarded: the invisible client—a challenge to the community. Paper presented at the annual meeting of the American Association on Mental Deficiency, Toronto, 1974.

Drew, C. J. *Introduction to designing research and evaluation.* St. Louis: The C. V. Mosby Co., 1976.

Drew, C. J., and Espeseth, V. K. Transfer of training in the mentally retarded: a review. *Exceptional Children*, 1968, **35**, 129-132.

Fisher, J. Competence, effectiveness, intellectual functioning, and aging. *Gerontologist*, 1973, **13**, 62-68.

Furry, C. S., and Baltes, P. B. The effect of age differences in ability–extraneous performance variables on the assessment of intelligence in children, adults, and the elderly. *Journal of Gerontology*, 1973, **28**, 73-80.

Harwood, E., and Naylor, G. F. K. Recall and recognition in elderly and young subjects. *Australian Journal of Psychology.* 1969, **21**, 251-257.

Kaplan, O. Mental decline in older morons. *American Journal of Mental Deficiency*, 1943, **47**, 277-285.

Kaufman, M. E., and Prehm, H. J. A review of research on learning sets and transfer of training in mental defectives. In N. R. Ellis (Ed.), *International Review of Research in Mental Retardation*, Vol. 2, New York: Academic Press, Inc., 1966, Pp. 123-147.

Kinsbourne, M. Age effects on letter span related to rate and sequential dependency. *Journal of Gerontology*, 1973, **28**, 317-319.

Kriger, S. F. On aging and mental retardation. In Hamilton, J. C., and Segal, R. M. (Eds.), Proceedings of a Consultation-Conference on The Gerontological Aspects of Mental Retardation. Ann Arbor: University of Michigan, 1975.

Lair, C. V., and Moon, W. H. The effects of praise and reproof on the performance of middle aged and older subjects. *Aging and Human Development*, 1972, **3**, 279-284.

Payne, D. *1,500,000 bits of information: some implications for action.* Boulder, Colo.: Western Interstate Commission for Higher Education, 1967.

Schaie, K. W., and Gribbin, K. Adult development and aging. *Annual Review of Psychology*, 1975, **26**, 65-96.

Segal, R. Trends in services for the aged mentally retarded. *Mental Retardation*, 1977, **15**(2), 25-27.

Talkington, L., and Chiovaro, S. An approach to programming for aged MR. *Mental Retardation*, 1969, **7**(1), 29-30.

Taub, H. A. A comparison of young adult and old groups on various digit span tasks. *Developmental Psychology*, 1972, **6**, 60-65.

Thompson, C. W. Decline in limit of performance among adult morons. *American Journal of Psychology*, 1951, **64**, 203-215.

Traxler, A. J. and Britton, J. H. Age differences in retroaction as a function of anticipation interval and transfer paradigm. *Proceedings of the 78th Annual Convention of the American Psychological Association*, 1970, **5**, 683-684.

ANNOTATED BIBLIOGRAPHY

Dickerson, M., Hamilton, J., Huber, R., and Segal, R. The aged mentally retarded: the invisible client—a challenge to the community. Paper presented at the annual meeting of the American Association on Mental Deficiency, Toronto, 1974.

This document represents an insightful glimpse into the world of the aged retarded. It is a report of an investigation and provides information concerning the life of the older retarded citizen who is institutionalized as well as those who have been placed in various settings in the community. Beyond the investigatory report of a study, however, this paper's value is largely found in the records of interviews with older retarded individuals. It provides perspectives from these interviews that cannot be gained in any dispassionate reporting of data. Copies of this document were provided to the authors by Dr. Robert Segal, Program Director for Social Work, Institute for the Study of Mental Retardation and Related Disabilities, University of Michigan, Ann Arbor.

Hamilton, J. C., and Segal, R. M. (Eds.), Proceedings of a Consultation-Conference on The Gerontological Aspects of Mental Retardation. Ann Arbor: University of Michigan, 1975.

This monograph represents a collaborative effort by the Institute of Gerontology and the Institute for the Study of Mental Retardation and Related Disabilities at the University of Michigan. It contains papers presented as well as workshop reports from a conference on the aged retarded conducted at the University of Michigan in 1975. The interested reader will find this valuable in terms of both the presentation of information and current thinking relative to issues involved in services to the aged retarded population.

PART FIVE

Family, social, and legal issues

CHAPTER 12

Retardation and the family

(Photograph by Peter Poulides.)

INTRODUCTION

The family is perhaps the oldest and most enduring of all human institutions. It has survived the rise and fall of civilizations and empires, wars, famine, plagues, depressions, recessions, and the constant changes of social values and systems. Typically the family is based on an emotional bond between parents and a hereditary bond between them and their children. The family may be viewed as a small system consisting of parents and children or an extended unit also consisting of grandparents and even distant relations.

Family systems are developed for various reasons. Among the more prominent reasons are the needs for security, belonging, and love. The family provides a socially acceptable vehicle to bring children into the world. Parents choose to have children for various reasons. Some do so for religious reasons, others because children provide them with a sense of security. Some individuals see children as an extension of themselves, or ego, and some perceive their children as a means to attain some degree of immortality. Others, perhaps, have children because it appears to be a normal thing to do. Unfortunately, the conception and birth of some children are unplanned, and the children are unwanted.

The advent of a new child into a family has traditionally been a happy occasion. The birth of the child marks the end of a long wait of 9 months and also the end of the anxiety associated with the pregnancy. Babies and children have such a positive connotation in our society that much of the literature neglects to mention the negative aspects of parenthood.

With rare exceptions, the arrival of a new child into a family represents some degree of intrusion. Prior to the arrival of the newborn child, family patterns usually have been established. Parents experiencing the birth of their first child may find that they must forsake much of their freedom and flexibility. Now they are not only responsible to themselves but also to the child they have brought into the world. Even families experiencing the birth of children past the first one may experience a feeling of intrusion. Children often detract from the direct relationship between husband and wife, and the arrival of additional children into the home naturally represents additional financial and emotional commitments. Wernick (1974) suggested that the arrival of the first child alters the lives of a man and woman even more profoundly than marriage itself. The center of the family shifts as attention is now focused on the newborn child, and everything becomes viewed in relationship to children in the family.

A new child in the family may have a positive or negative effect on the relationship already existing between husband and wife. The child may draw the parents closer together with a commitment toward a common goal. On the other hand, the child's presence may result in discord and conflict. The arrival of the child usually represents a dramatic change in life-style for a couple. Reiss (1971) found that a large percentage of couples indicated that there was a decline in the positive aspects of marriage with the passage of time. The decline was greatest among couples with children. Chinn, Winn, and Walters (1978) suggest a number of changes that a child will bring to the life-style of a couple. With the birth of a child, recreational and social activities might have to be curtailed or modified. Travel over extensive distances or time may become difficult because of expense, inconvenience, and sometimes the uncooperative behavior of the child. Entertainment may become a problem because of the expense or difficulty of obtaining babysitters.

Financial problems may also plague new parents. The husband or wife, typically the latter, may have to give up a job that contributes a substantial amount of family income to stay at home with the child. Initially the mother may react positively to her new role, only to find later that the daily routine is boring, and the lack of adult companionship and interaction is lonely and frustrating. Even if the mother is eventually able to return to gainful employment, the net income is still curtailed in most instances because of the expense of child care. The financial stress created by the additional expenses of maintaining a child may require one of the parents, usually the father, to take a second job. The physical and emotional stress of the added work and the reduced time together may cause additional stress in family relationships.

Couples with children at times find that their childless friends lack sympathetic understanding about the needs and nature of children and parenthood. This may result in a change in friendship patterns, marking an end to a relatively independent and carefree life-style. Housing needs may change significantly. The small but adequate apartment suddenly becomes inadequate. The comfortable and socially convenient "adults only" apartment complex must be vacated for one that is less to their tastes. A two-seat sports car may no longer be practical, since the required additional room for the child and the child's belongings may dictate a larger, more practical, but less enjoyable mode of transportation.

The list of complications, inconveniences, expenses, and changes in life-styles brought on by a new child is endless. Many, if not all, of these negative aspects of parenthood are often overshadowed by the sheer joy and pleasure that the child brings to the new parents. The displeasures of diaper changing and the sleepless nights, owing to the infant's crying, may tend to fade away with the first smile, the first step, and the first spoken word. With these first accomplishments, parents may begin to envision a fruition of their dreams and hopes of parenthood—healthy, bright, capable, beautiful children doing all the things that the parents did or wished they could have done.

The retarded child's delayed maturation may preclude the exhibiting of skills associated with normal development. Developmental delays in these children may retard their abilities to smile at their parents, mimic voices, or take their first steps at the times when more normal infants do.

The parents of retarded children may find few of the typical joys that compensate for the frustrations and inconveniences imposed by a child. Dreams and hopes regarding the child's future are often shattered. The child who was to represent an extension of the parents' egos serves instead as a deflation of their egos. Such a child may serve as a threat to the parents' self-esteem, their feelings of self-worth and dignity. Many individuals view the procreation of normal, healthy children as one of the main purposes of existence. In producing a handicapped child, they may view themselves as failures in what they consider one of their most fundamental purposes in life.

While a child's handicap does not necessarily preclude the pleasures of parenthood, the satisfaction that may be realized by accomplishments of the child may be overlooked and overshadowed by the frustrations the parents experience. There are many satisfying experiences that parents of handicapped children can enjoy. The handicapped can accomplish realistic goals that parents may set for them or that they set for themselves. Professionals working with parents of the retarded can serve a useful function by facilitating the recognition of these accomplishments (Chinn, Winn, Walters, 1978). Parental reaction to the advent of a retarded child may be unpredictable. Reactions are based on feelings, and for the parents, the magnitude of their feelings and reactions is as great as they perceive the problem to be.

There is no response, reaction, or feeling that can be considered typical, mature, good, or bad. It is unlikely that professional workers in the field of mental retardation can predict accurately their own responses to having a retarded child unless they have already endured such an experience. Parental reactions vary because of their feelings of frustration, hurt, fear, guilt, disappointment, ambivalence, or despair. The feelings and perceptions of these parents may not be congruent with those of the professional workers. They need not be. However, awareness, acknowledgement, and recognition of the parent's feelings and state of being will greatly facilitate parent-professional interaction.

Chinn, Winn, and Walters (1978) suggest that the professional worker is involved with the retarded child by choice. Interaction is limited. Even for the teacher who may spend a 6-hour day with the retarded child 5 days a week, interaction is comparatively limited. Parents have the child every day and every night. There are no weekends or Christmas, spring, and summer vacations to escape the reality of having a retarded child. There is often no time or date that the parent can look to that signals the child's entry into independent living and their freedom of parental responsibilities and obligations.

As suggested earlier, the advent of any newborn represents some degree of intrusion in the family setting. With the arrival of a retarded child, it is intensified. The retarded child will require more attention and care and frequently greater expense to the family. The normal attention and time given to the husband or wife and to the other children may be diverted to the handicapped child, who appears to be in greater need.

In this chapter we shall address ourselves to the impact of the retarded child on the family, the needs of the child, the needs of the parents, the needs of the siblings in the family, and, finally, the decision regarding institutionalization.

THE IMPACT OF THE RETARDED CHILD ON THE FAMILY

Rosen (1955) suggested five stages through which many parents of retarded children progress from the time they first sense or become aware of a problem until the time they accept the child on a realistic basis. We shall list these five stages and refer to them as we progress through the chapter, examining the retarded child's relationship to the family. They are as follows:

1. Awareness of a problem
2. Recognition of the basic problem
3. Search for a cause
4. Search for a cure
5. Acceptance of the problem

It would be appropriate at this stage to examine some of the variables that affect a family's reaction to the problem of mental retardation. The degree of severity is always an important variable. A mildly retarded child may not have any physically distinguishing characteristics that might suggest mental retardation. As we shall discuss in a subsequent chapter, many parents are unaware that the child is retarded until academic failure occurs in the public schools. The degree of impact, frustration, or disappointment does not necessarily correlate directly with the degree of deficiency, however. Parents of severely retarded children whom we interviewed have sometimes indicated that, while the initial impact was severe, it was perhaps easier for them to acknowledge their problem than for other parents whose children were mildly retarded. The mental retardation is obvious to the parents of severely retarded children, and acknowledgement (not necessarily acceptance) generally comes quickly.

The religious background of the parents may also be a variable related to the degree of impact of mental retardation on the family. We shall discuss this in more detail later in the section on religious counseling. The etiology and age of onset are important variables. Physical traumas that may permanently impair a child who has developed normally may be more debilitating to the parents than congenital retardation.

The socioeconomic and intellectual levels of the family may also be factors in the degree of impact generated by mental retardation. Some families who exist in lower socioeconomic levels may place less emphasis on cognitive development and skills and, at times, more emphasis on the development of physical attributes. This may be particularly true when members of the family work primarily in occupations that have greater physical rather than cognitive demands. In a situation, however, in which a family places great emphasis on cognitive development and members of the family work primarily in professional settings requiring a higher level of education and cognitive functioning, reactions may be quite different. A retarded child born into a family where education and white collar jobs are held in high regard may present a greater threat and disappointment to the family.

For the parents of severely and profoundly retarded children, awareness of the problem and recognition of the basic problem (Rosen, 1955) may come simultaneously. Moderately and mildly retarded children may not have physically distinguishing characteristics that readily identify them as mentally retarded. With these children the parents may have an awareness of an existing problem when the child fails to develop or progress as anticipated.

The problem may be more obvious to those parents who have had other children that have developed normally.

For many parents, while there may be some indications of inconsistent growth and developmental patterns, the actual problem does not manifest itself until the child is in school, fails academically, and is evaluated and declared retarded by the school psychologist. When the parents are informed that their child is retarded, they may acknowledge the condition or recognize it for what it is, or they may resort to a variety of defense mechanisms in order to aid their egos in coping with the problem. The initial impact may take several forms. It may result in some sort of a transient stress disorder, particularly for the parents, or it may even have a permanent debilitating effect on the entire family unit.

Farber (1960) suggests that the advent of the retarded child need not create a family crisis, although this is a potentiality. How the event is defined by the family will determine whether or not a real crisis exists. Chinn (1979) states that whether or not an event becomes a crisis depends on three basic conditions: (1) the nature of the event, (2) the resources of the family, and (3) how the family defines the event. There are few families, however, in which the stigma of mental retardation imposed by our society will not cause the event to be interpreted as a crisis. The professional can help the family to cope with the crisis and hopefully to minimize it. By examining the resources of the family, including role structure, emotional stability, and previous experiences with stress, the professional can help the family utilize the strengths in its resources to effectively deal with the problems.

Parental reactions

The reactions of parents when they recognize the existence of mental retardation in their child is highly unpredictable. A child represents the extension of the parent's self, and the birth of a defective child can represent a serious threat to, or even damage, the parental ego (Kravaceus and Hayes, 1969; Ryckman and Henderson, 1965). Children are physical productions of their parents. If something is good about a child, this may be viewed by some as a reflection of the good in one or both parents. If the child is "bad" or there is something wrong, this may be viewed as a negative reflection on the parents. Parents may also tend to view their child as a source of vicarious satisfaction. They often hope to see their children achieve physically, educationally, professionally, and financially as they themselves would like to have done, to fulfill their own denied dreams. Thus, mentally retarded children may cause their parents extreme disappointment because of their inability to meet such expectations. Parents also have tendencies to believe that they can "transcend" death through their children. Their children provide them with a legacy and some measure of immortality. They may believe that the retarded child deprives them of this particular desire, creating even further frustration.

Defense mechanisms

When individuals consider their security to be threatened, they tend to defend against the offending force. There are many forms of defense mechanisms; some are considered relatively immature, whereas others are more sophisticated, sociably acceptable, and mature. The use of defense mechanisms, such as *denial* and *projection of blame*, are generally regarded as immature and are often frustrating and difficult for professional workers to cope with.

Denial. We have already suggested that the birth of a retarded child poses serious threat, insult, and even injury to the parental ego. Human beings have developed a system of defense mechanisms to protect or minimize damage to the ego. In order to defend against the debilitating effect of the retarded child on the ego or self-concept, parents sometimes resort to the defense mechanism of denial. Kanner (1953) suggested that this common reaction, especially during the initial stage of adjustment, provides a form of self protection against the painful realities. Parents may minimize the degree of handicap or simply deny that any problem exists (Safford and Arbitman, 1975). They therefore close their minds to their child's limitations or, as Begab (1966) suggested, may explain their child's limitations by implying laziness, indifference, or lack of motivation.

While the use of defense mechanisms is normal, and denial is common, it is generally considered one of the less mature and less socially acceptable defense mechanisms. It is one that can be both useless and destructive. It is useless because the refusal to accept the reality of their child's handicap will not make the problems disappear. It is destructive because it impedes the child's own acceptance of limitations and may prevent necessary training and therapy (Wentworth, 1974).

Denial symptoms are both frustrating and exasperating to the professional. Because the parents (sometimes only one parent) refuse to recognize the conditions for what they really are, programming for services and treatment is frequently delayed and sometimes never receives attention. Because most state laws require parental consent prior to placement of a child in special education, the retarded child whose parents deny that the problem exists may be excluded from any special educational programs. Denial may also deprive the child of necessary medical treatment, which only adds to the frustration of professionals endeavoring to help the family.

While the denial process strains the relationship between parents and professionals, the latter should always be cognizant of the extreme emotional stress placed on the family and should realize that, for the present time, this immature defense mechanism may be the only one that the parents are capable of using. With time, patience, and continued support, the professionals may eventually help the parents to face reality and to realize that the birth of the retarded child need not stigmatize their lives nor cast any doubts on their integrity as adequate parents or human beings.

Projection of blame. When mental retardation continues to be evident for long periods or is severe, denial may not be a viable means to defend the egos of the parents. Other defense mechanisms are at the disposal of the parents; for example, the projection of blame. Frequently, the targets for attack are individuals who may be responsible for causing the parents considerable frustration and sometimes agony. Their negative feelings may be justified in some instances, but not for the reasons for which they are projecting their blame. Physicians are frequently the object of parental attack. Attacks are often directed at the allegedly incompetent obstetrician. Some of the common types of attacks toward obstetricians include: "If only the doctors had taken better care of my wife (or me) before the baby was born, they would have known something was going wrong and could have prevented it"; "If only the doctor had not taken so long to get to the hospital, help would have been there early enough to keep something from happening"; "If they'd had enough sense not to use so much anesthesia . . ." (Wentworth, 1974). The other allegedly "incompetent" physician to whom attacks are directed is the pediatrician who "did not attend to the child properly immediately after birth or failed to treat an illness or injury adequately." The majority of these attacks are not justified, since the mental retardation may not be a function of inadequate or incompetent medical care. Parent hostility may be more frequently justified in the inadequate and sometimes even improper counseling on the part of the physician. While skilled in the medical aspects of their practice, physicians are often ill-equipped to counsel parents adequately because of either lack of preparation in counseling skills or lack of knowledge of the resources available for the care and treatment of retarded children.

When the retardation is evident and thus can be diagnosed at birth, it is usually the responsibility of the attending physician, the obstetrician, or the pediatrician to inform the parents of the situation. The task of informing parents that their child is retarded may be viewed by some as difficult or unpleasant, and physicians have frequently been criticized for not assuming this professional responsibility adequately. Farber (1968) suggests that family physicians often feel a sense of guilt that they are in some way responsible and have failed the family. If Farber's contention is accurate, it may explain in part the numerous incidents in which parents complain bitterly that their physician either resisted or failed to inform them of the true nature of the problem. Typically, these parents complain that the physician indicated that their child would eventually catch up. Farber cites two examples of physicians failing to adequately inform parents. In one situation the mother found out by reading the diagnosis on the nurse's chart where "mongoloid" had been indicated. In another situation the attending physician recommended that the newborn child remain in the hospital for "reasons of health." Six weeks later another physician called the mother over the phone, informed her that the child was retarded, suggested institutionalization, and indicated that he would assist in the placement.

Other professionals who may be subject to criticism or parental attacks are school psychologists or social workers who may have the primary responsibility of informing parents that their children have been psychologically evaluated, diagnosed as mildly retarded, and should be placed in a special education class. It may also be the responsibility of these individuals to secure the necessary written parental consent for special class placement. How tactfully and skillfully the counseling is conducted with the parents may have a decided effect on the parental reactions and attitudes toward the school. Even if the counseling is carried out as professionally as can be expected, frustrated parents may still use the psychologist or social worker as a scapegoat, projecting blame on them. The individuals in the school setting most likely to receive the brunt of the projected blame from parents are former teachers. Particularly when no medical etiological data are available, parents may tend to place the blame of the child's retardation on the previous teachers for their alleged failure to "teach" their child adequately. The teachers may indeed be guilty of failing to meet the needs of the child educationally or even of failing to refer the poorly performing child for psychological evaluation. It is highly unlikely, however, that these teachers are in any way responsible for the mental retardation itself.

We have suggested that parents at times project the blame for their child's mental retardation on various professionals. In most instances the attacks are without justification. At times, however, frustration and anger toward these professionals may be justified because of their inadequacies in providing for the needs of the *parents* of the retarded child. When this is the case, the projection of blame may tend to be more of a displacement reaction. In other words, blame may be justified, but not for the expressed reasons.

Other reactions

There are a number of other parental reactions that may be considered common. It should be noted that, while these reactions are common, not all parents exhibit these reactions, and exhibiting one of these reactions does not necessarily imply that others are present or should be anticipated. Chinn, Winn, and Walters (1978) suggest that among the common parental reactions are fear, guilt, mourning or grief, withdrawal, rejection, and acceptance.

Fear. The unknown generates anxiety in the individual. Anxiety in turn may generate fear. There are so many unknowns that the parents of retarded children face that fear is a natural and common reaction. While the professional worker may be familiar with the etiology, nature and prognosis of mental retardation and the available resources for dealing with it, many of the parents may have barely heard of the condition prior to the birth of the child. Some of the fears and concerns may seem completely absurd to the professional worker. Yet these fears are genuine and must be acknowledged, heard with sensitivity, and responded to appropriately. Until the parents are provided adequate information, the fears will persist. Unfortunately, answers are not available for all of the questions the parents need to have answered, and a certain amount of anxiety may always be present. Among the common fears or questions are, "What caused this handicap, and if we choose to have other children, will they be retarded too?" "How will our friends and relatives feel about us and the child?" "Will we always have to take care of the child or is self-care and independence possible someday?" "What will this do to our family?" "Who will take care of the child when we are no longer able?" These are merely a few of the many questions that the parents need to have answered. As Froyd (1973) suggests, the parents lack knowledge and experience and thus have no conceptual background on which to base their hopes or control their fears. The professional worker can have many of the answers readily available and thus can respond to the parents' questions. Many of the questions can be anticipated, and professional workers need to be able either to answer the questions or provide available resources where the answers can be found.

When the parents are informed that the child is handicapped, a certain amount of basic information should be provided in most instances. There is a danger in providing the parents with too much information when they are already so overwhelmed with the fact that the child is handicapped. They may be unable to integrate any more information at that time. There is an equal amount of danger in providing the parents with inadequate information when they need it. As the professional worker gains experience in working with parents, an ability to sense the needs of the parents will develop. Careful follow-up can provide parents with additional information as warranted.

Guilt. Human nature at times dictates that blame for wrongdoing be assessed somewhere. To many, the birth of a retarded child represents wrongdoing. The child who is handicapped is abnormal. Some individuals, who feel that everything should be orderly and logical, maintain that to be abnormal is wrong, and someone or something is responsible for this wrong. Parents sometimes follow this line of reasoning, and when they are unable to place blame somewhere else, they turn it on themselves. They begin to look for and eventually find something in their lives or their behavior that may seem to be responsible for this handicapping condition in their child. When they look hard enough, something may eventually turn up, which will seem to them a logical reason. Guilt may be in the form of self-incrimination for past wrongs with punishment in the form of the child with a handicap. Guilt may follow more logical lines. It is even possible that the parent, however unintentionally, may be responsible for the handicapping condition. An example is rubella syndrome, where the mother's development of German measles may lead to the birth of a child with retardation or another handicapping condition.

Guilt can serve some useful purpose in such cases if it prevents the recurrence of certain inappropriate behaviors. Usually, however, guilt is insidious and debilitating. Assuming the blame will not make the handicap disappear, and intense feelings of guilt can erode the parents' positive self-concept. Guilty parents are difficult to work with, and guilt is very difficult to dispel. Professionals working with parents who are experiencing feelings of guilt can help them to channel their energies into more productive activities.

Mourning or grief. When the realities have set in and the parents begin to realize fully what has happened, they may react with grief or mourning. Grief is a natural reaction to situations that bring extreme pain and disappointment. We all grieve when we lose something that we cherish or value. The birth of a child with a handicap represents a loss of a dream and a hope—for a normal healthy son or daughter. It may also represent the loss of the parents' positive self-image. To the parents, this birth may seem more like a death. In some instances parents may react to the birth of the retarded child with death wishes (Hart, 1970; Begab, 1966). Hart cites a father's reaction shortly after the birth of a child with Down's syndrome. The father stated that he felt as if he was in mourning and should be dressed in black. Other parents either consciously or unconsciously wish for the death of their retarded child. Begab states that it is not uncommon for parents to harbor death wishes toward their retarded child, particularly when the child becomes burdensome and they wish to be relieved of this burden. Hart suggests that some parents will institutionalize a retarded child immediately after birth, announce that the child was stillborn, and even place an obituary notice in the newspaper. Some parents unconsciously wish for their retarded child's death, preoccupied with thoughts of "when the child dies," or "if the child should die." Many of these parents would deny their death wishes if confronted, as they are unable to acknowledge these hidden wishes on the conscious level. Grossman (1972) suggests that these death wishes may also be functioning among normal siblings. Another group of parents, however, are consciously aware of their death wishes and may or may not be willing to indicate these feelings publicly. More recently, however, a growing number of individuals have been willing to risk public censure by refusing to grant permission for life-saving surgery or medical treatment that would prolong the life of their retarded child. While such decisions raise many moral and ethical questions, only these parents know the true extent of the emotional, financial, and physical hardships they have had to endure. Judeo-Christian ethic tends to place a high value on human life. The medical profession with its Hippocratic oath obligates most physicians to sustain life even when it appears unproductive and futile. In recent years the alternative decisions regarding the course of action for parents of retarded children has increased by society's growing acceptance of deviancy and the increasing sanction of the individual's right to choose between life and death. The difficult issue of who holds the responsibility for life and death decisions has yet to be resolved. Furthermore, individuals confronted with the awesome decision frequently do not have sufficient information regarding the potential quality of life the child might have at the time that the critical decision must be made. These complex problems and issues are discussed in considerable detail in Chapter 14.

Withdrawal. There are times when we want and need to be alone, away from others. We can be alone physically, or we can have others around us and still be alone because we choose to shut others out of our thoughts and out of interaction with us. Being alone gives us a kind of freedom—freedom to think by ourselves, to rest, meditate, and do things in our own private world. Solitude can be therapeutic. It can give us a break from the pressures that surround us—away from everyone else's problems and away from the world of others we choose not to be with. We can be alone in our office or home, even though we are surrounded by people. We can be alone by detaching ourselves emotionally from the presence of others, or we can allow our thoughts to be somewhere else. We can be alone physically by going for a long walk or by jogging on the beach. We can shut the door, take the telephone off the hook, turn on the television, and be alone.

Being alone can allow us time to put our thoughts in order, to put together our confused personal world and concerns. It can give us time to analyze our problems, work them through, and decide a plan of action. Being alone is a form of withdrawal. Withdrawal can have therapeutic value, as it can be a part of a total healing process. It is a normal reaction, and one that is typical for parents of children with handicaps (McKibbin, 1972).

Although therapeutic in many instances, withdrawal can be potentially damaging. Withdrawal is a form of isolation, and prolonged isolation can be harmful. Parents may choose to isolate themselves because of their feelings of shame and guilt. They may unfortunately withdraw from the friends, relatives, professional workers, or activities that may facilitate the healing process. By withdrawing, the parent can construct a protective barrier of space and silence against outside pain, if not against the hurt inside. Staying away from social functions protects against "nosy" questions about the children and the family. Keeping away from restaurants and other public places keeps "critical eyes from staring at the retarded child."

Rejection. Perhaps one of the most common but delicate parental reactions to deal with is that of rejection. The term parental rejection tends to carry with it such a negative connotation that any parent who has been described as rejecting is frequently stereotyped and prejudged not only as an incompetent parent but also as an incompetent individual devoid of the humanistic values that we allegedly hold in high regard. If we are to equate rejection with negative feelings parents may direct toward their children, then parents who do not at sometime or another reject their child would be a rare exception. As we examine the everyday dynamics that go on between parents and their children, we find many instances in which the child's behavioral patterns exceed the tolerance level of the parents. Thus, if children of normal intelligence frequently elicit responses of negative reaction from their parents, we can clearly understand how a retarded child with limitations and additional problems will frequently cause some form of parental negativism. However, it is rejection to extreme degrees that we are considering. Gallagher (1956) defines parental rejection as "the persistent and unrelieved holding of unrealistic negative values of the child to the extent that the whole behavior of the parent toward that child is colored unrealistically by this negative tone." Gallagher further states that there are four general ways in which parental rejection is expressed:

1. *Strong underexpectations of achievement.* In this particular type of rejection, the parents have so devalued the child that they minimize or ignore any positive attributes. Gallagher suggests that the child often becomes aware of these parental attitudes, begins to have feelings of self-worthlessness, and behaves accordingly. We thus have what is often referred to as a "self-fulfilling prophecy."

2. *Setting of unrealistic goals.* Parents sometimes set goals so unrealistically high that they are unattainable. When the child fails to reach these unrealistic goals, the parents can then justify their negative feelings and attitudes on the basis of limited performance.

3. *Escape.* Another form of rejection may include desertion or running away. It may be quite open and obvious, such as the parent who simply leaves the family and moves out of the home entirely. Other types of desertion may be more subtle—the parent is so occupied with various responsibilities that there is little if any time to be at home with the family while the child is awake. This could take the form of "demanding special projects at the office" or perhaps the demands of "various responsibilities at the church." Others may seek to place the child in a distant school or institution

when comparable facilities are available near the home. We would like to emphasize strongly that placement of a retarded child in an institution should not be equated with parental rejection. Many, if not the majority, of institutional placements are made with full consideration of the best interests of both the child and the family.

4. *Reaction formation.* When the parent tends to deny negative feelings and publicly presents completely opposite images, this may be classified as a reaction formation defense mechanism. The negative feelings of the parents are contrary to their conscious values, and they cannot accept themselves as anything but kind, loving, warm parents. For example, parents who resent their retarded child may frequently tell friends and relatives how much they love their child.

Gallagher suggests that many parents are in an untenable position when dealing with professionals. If they express their honest feelings of not liking their child, they are condemned as rejecting parents. If they indicate that they like and love their retarded child, they may be suspected of manifesting a reaction formation.

Gallagher further suggests that, because of the negative connotation that "parental rejection" carries with professionals, it is important to distinguish between primary and secondary rejection. Primary rejection is the result of the unchangeable nature of the child. Thus, it is generally the personality dynamics of the parents rather than the behavior of the child that determines parental attitudes. Secondary rejection, on the other hand, is the result of the behavioral manifestation of the child that results in the negative attitudes of the parents. Thus in primary rejection, the parental rejection can be modified or may cease if only parental attitudes are modified. In secondary rejection, parental rejection may be altered if the child's behavior is modified. Gallagher suggests that in working with parents it would be easier for the professional if the type of rejection could be readily identified. Unfortunately, this is not a simple task, and a considerable amount of time may be necessary before the parents reveal their true emotional attitudes and values. Gallagher states that it is therefore safer to assume that the rejection is of a secondary variety until and unless the parents indicate otherwise.

•   •   •

When parents discover that their child is mentally retarded, they typically undergo a transient stress disorder. A transient stress disorder is a form of emotional disturbance. It is a common and natural outcome of an inordinate amount of stress. Nearly everyone experiences transient stress disorders at some time in life. They can develop through the loss of a loved one or can be caused by other emotional traumas, such as divorce or the loss of a job. Fortunately, they are temporary. We are usually able to adjust, and the disorder is alleviated. If, however, the problems are not resolved, the disorder may persist. Hopefully, the reactions we have examined that may be symptomatic of a transient stress disorder will be worked through as the parents have time to resolve their feelings.

As professionals, we would find our task far simpler if all parents of retarded children could love their children and could accept and value them for what they are in spite of their limitations. Unfortunately, this is an unrealistic expectation, and we must honor their feelings of frustration and hurt, realizing that it is not we, but the parents who must cope with the problem each day. If we as professionals are to give the parents support, we must per-

Fig. 12-1. The parents' acceptance of the retarded child and of themselves is a major step toward normalization in the family. (Photograph by Peter Poulides.)

mit withdrawal and grief, if that is what is needed. We cannot dictate feelings. We can only point out choices, alternatives, consequences, and possible directions after the feelings have been honored and resolved. Hopefully, when time has had an opportunity to exercise its healing powers, the parent will arrive at the stage of acceptance.

Acceptance. Acceptance (Rosen, 1955) is the final step in the long difficult road to adjustment for the parent. Acceptance can develop in three areas: (1) acceptance that the child has a handicap, (2) acceptance of the child, (3) acceptance of self. Acceptance of the child is a major and critical step in the healing and growing process. This step implies a recognition of the value of such children for who they are. They are children first and most important of all. They have feelings, wants, and needs like other children. They have the potential to enjoy life and to provide enjoyment for others. They can set, or their parents can set for them, realistic, attainable goals. The attainment of these goals can bring satisfaction, pride, and pleasure to the parents and the children themselves. They are people, very real and important people.

The entire process of reaching self-acceptance is a long and difficult one for the parents. It is filled with pain, frustration, self-doubt, and ego-shattering experiences. Somehow, in spite of all the hurts and debilitating experiences, the parents can emerge with a firm conviction that they are parents of a very special child. They are individuals worthy of respect from others and from themselves. Their integrity as worthy members of the human race has not been diminished; instead, it has been enhanced. They have not only endured a major crisis but have grown into a stronger, wiser, and more compassionate human beings.

NEEDS OF PARENTS

Parents of retarded children have a number of special needs; many of them are unmet. When they are met, however, adjustment is facilitated. Some of these important needs, which require the awareness of professional workers and parents themselves, are presented in this section.

Communication

Perhaps the greatest need parents of children with handicaps have is for effective communication. Effective communication implies understanding and support. These parents must have their feelings and their needs recognized and understood by each other, friends, family, and professional workers. It's important for them to know that they have support from those who care about them. Support implies recognition of their needs and assistance in meeting these needs. This does not always imply agreement. At times a parent's perceptions of a problem may be faulty. Appropriate support may be in recognition of the parents' feelings and helping to resolve them without bringing harm to anyone.

In communicating effectively the parents need to receive as well as to send messages accurately. Parents require information presented in a clear concise manner. This needs to be done in terms that they can understand, rather than in what is often meaningless professional jargon. Parents often feel ambivalent when receiving information from professional workers. They want the truth because they know they must have it to deal with their problems effectively. At the same time they do not want to hear the truth if it is too painful. Recognizing this ambivalence can be very helpful and can also clarify the professional's own ambivalence.

Parents are often concerned about the future development of the child. They want to know how and when the child will develop and what the prognosis is for the future. Gayton (1975) suggests that many professional workers take a "don't worry about it now" attitude and label the parents as "overanxious" if they persist. He warns that if the professional worker does not provide the parents with reliable information or direct them to responsible sources, they may search on their own. In searching on their own they may find outdated material with misconceptions about the handicaps. Parents need to be provided with accurate information as early as possible to alleviate their anxiety and to provide them with a feeling that they are doing something to help (Gayton and Walker, 1974). Mattson and Agle (1972) suggest that this information-seeking behavior of parents results in "control through thinking" and allows the parents to master their anxiety and feelings of helplessness.

Regretfully, too many professional workers talk down to parents in a patronizing, authoritarian manner. They sometimes feel that the parents lack comparable educational status or sufficient experience or background to understand. Because of these attitudes, many of these professionals communicate poorly and at times fail to communicate at all. Occasionally they may even withhold pertinent information. While professional terminology may be a useful tool in note taking, record keeping, and communicating with other professionals, it may be an obstacle to understanding in situations that involve parents. Information that cannot be understood is useless to parents (Gorham, 1975).

It is true that some parents may lack comparable educational status. This does not mean, however, that they are unworthy of good communication. It is also true that the parents may lack experience and background. The professional worker, however, should be aware that these parents may soon have more experience and background than most professionals. Many parents will someday be better informed about etiological matters concerning their child than most physicians. They may also be more informed and skilled in dealing with certain types of behaviors exhibited by their children than most special education teachers.

Understanding the etiology of retardation

In Rosen's (1955) five stages of parental development, the search for a cause is the third stage, and search for a cure is the fourth stage. When the retarded child is diagnosed and the parents recognize and acknowledge the condition, there is frequently a tendency to attempt to find the cause of the condition. This search may lead them in one of two directions—to a theological explanation or to a medical explanation.

Religious counseling and theological explanation. In a time of crisis and difficulty, people frequently turn to religion for comfort, assurance, and sanction. Some seek assurance that they are not to blame, others seek some help in picking up the "broken pieces of their life." It is interesting to note, however, that Wolfensberger and Kurtz (1969) found that in most studies even religious parents of the retarded have found little guidance and comfort from their spiritual leaders. They suggest that the inadequate religious guidance is a function of the interpretation of mental retardation primarily as a medical problem. The authors suggest that the problem may be partially a function of the lack of training and information that the clergy has at its disposal when counseling parents of handicapped children.

Stubblefield (1965) suggests that mental retardation can develop into a theological crisis. The degree of crisis may be directly related to the religious background of the parents. While the advent of a retarded child could either weaken or strengthen religious beliefs, the particular faith of the parents may also affect their responses to the event. The parents' religious orientation may be directly related to the degree of acceptance of the retarded child.

Studies by Farber (1959) and Zuk (1959) suggested that religious affiliation may influence a family's reaction to a handicapped child. Both studies suggested that Roman Catholic families tend to be more accepting of a retarded child than either Protestant or Jewish families. While family acceptance of mental retardation may be a function of religious affiliation, acceptance may be more closely related to the theological explanation for the occurrence of the event. Hutchinson (1968) suggested that Catholics consider redemption as a continual process, thus humanity will continually experience suffering in redemption for its sins. This was not to imply that the advent of a particular child represented atonement for the sins of the particular parents involved, but rather for all humankind. Neal (1968), a Methodist, suggests that the handicapped child is a function of nature missing its mark. Christiansen (1969), expressing a Mormon point of view, indicates that retarded individuals are part of a divine plan—their premortal existence was as whole spirits, and their presence on earth is merely temporal and for a short period of time in comparison to eternity. He contends that when they leave their earthly existence they will again assume a more perfect existence. Jewish rabbis tend to indicate that there is no classical theological explanation. The event occurred.

It is not our intention to present a comprehensive overview of theological explanations of mental retardation. Even the explanations within specific denominations or religious groups may vary with the individual theological interpretation of each religious leader. Rather we are attempting to indicate that there are divergent theological views. Often suggested by laymen but emphatically denounced by the clergy and religious leaders is the contention that the retarded child represents divine retribution for either or both of the parents' present or past sins. Such a position is emotionally debilitating to parents, and as Stubblefield (1965) indicates, "belief that retardation is the punishment by God creates extreme guilt and prevents parents from realistically planning for the retarded child. In any counseling with parents, professionals should exercise extreme caution in avoiding any suggestion of this particular view."

Considering the divergent theological views, one can perhaps understand why reactions of parents with different religious affiliations may vary. Those who have no theological explanation may find acceptance far more difficult than parents who are convinced that the retarded child is part of a divine plan. Thus some devout parents view the retarded child as a religious responsibility. Some view themselves as martyrs, ready to accept the responsibility

as "a God-given cross to be borne patiently and submissively" (Kravaceus and Hayes, 1969). These various positions inevitably have a direct
effect on the relationship between parents and child, parent and parent, and parents and other children, which we shall discuss later in the
chapter.

Our basic concern is in the quality of religious counseling. As stated earlier, the clergy has tended to view mental retardation as more of a medical
than a religious problem. Perhaps this position may be correct. However, it
does not negate the need for sound religious counseling in relationship to
mental retardation. It would appear that the professionals within the field of
religion and designated religious leaders are generally in need of a better
grasp of the problems involved in counseling parents of handicapped children. A greater amount of time could profitably be spent during divinity
school training in the area of pastoral counseling as it relates to addressing
the problems of handicapped children. In addition, it would appear necessary for these individuals to clearly conceptualize within their own minds
what their church and they personally believe to be the theological implications involved in this matter. As these implications are conceptualized, there
is a distinct need to formulate a plan for counseling the parents to enable
them to deal with any anxiety as it relates to guilt and how the church can
aid them in their time of trauma. In order to fulfill such a plan, each of these
individuals should explore the various programs, facilities, and agencies to
which they can refer the parents. Finally, each religious leader should initiate, if it has not already been done, an affirmative action program to provide
religious programs within the Sunday school, confirmation classes, and so on
to accommodate the handicapped. If religious institutions are to reflect the
social conscience of society, definitive and affirmative actions must be taken
to educate their congregations about exceptional children and to provide
effective programs for them as well.

Medical explanation. Hopefully parents will be able to resolve many, if
not all, of their anxieties as they relate to religion. But parents will also need
information regarding medical etiology. In some cases diagnosis is relatively
simple, as in Down's syndrome or some physical trauma. The counseling,
however, must be done with great skill to alleviate or minimize any feelings
of guilt associated with the child's condition. The mother of a child with
rubella syndrome should be freed from her anxieties as they relate to her
being "responsible" and thus blaming herself.

Usually counseling related to etiology will be done by a physician or a geneticist. Parents will be concerned primarily with the possibility of having a second retarded child. When physical trauma caused by an accident or infection is involved, counseling is less difficult. When the counseling involves risk taking and mathematical odds, where genetic problems have caused the initial case of mental retardation, the task becomes more complex. Parents may listen to the geneticist explain the mathematical odds, but often they will want the professional to make the decision for them concerning whether or not they should have another child. Any professional, whether a geneticist, teacher, or psychologist, who is approached by parents for advice of this nature is taking a risk of later being a scapegoat should the parents have another retarded child. Any pregnancy involves some degree of risk. The odds, the risks, and the possible consequences should be clearly articulated by the professionals. After the information is given, the decision whether or not to have another child is rightfully that of the parents. It is they who will share the joy of a normal child or bear the consequences of a handicapped one.

Searching for a cure

When the parents of a retarded child have had their basic needs met with respect to concerns for the cause of their child's condition, they will usually investigate the possibility of some type of remediation or cure. Unfortunately, in the majority of cases their prospects for a complete cure are remote. In some conditions, when the retardation is a function of emotional disorders or environmental deprivation, some remediation techniques may be prescribed, such as psychotherapy or environmental stimulation and enrichment. If treatment is prescribed early enough, some positive results are possible.

In certain types of medical conditions, such as galactosemia or phenylketonuria, dietary controls can minimize the extent of damage. Physical therapy and speech therapy can be prescribed to improve functional level. In many instances the prescribed treatments may improve the intellectual as well as the functional level and even improve the child's score on standardized tests of intelligence. Seldom, however, is it possible to move these children out of the ranges of mental retardation into what we could classify as a normal range of intelligence.

As professionals we must be acutely aware of the desperate nature of the feelings of many parents at this particular stage. Some may, if the financial resources permit, take the child from one clinic to another hoping to receive the type of diagnosis they want to hear. We as professionals have the responsibility to help protect these parents from unscrupulous individuals who will willingly diagnose the child as "learning disabled" or anything else the parents may wish to hear and provide special remediation programs at a great expense, with few if any positive results. When parents seek sanctions for questionable treatment programs, it would appear that the most prudent approach would be to refer them to professionals whose judgments have been noted for their reliability or to organizations such as the American Association for Mental Deficiency or the National Association for Retarded Citizens.

Searching for help

One of the most fundamental needs of parents of retarded children is to be made aware of the various services at their disposal. Many of these parents are in a state of confusion and find that many of the professionals they contact are unable to give them advice beyond their own area of expertise. Physicians are able to provide medical information, and the schools, educational information; but each may be limited in their ability to provide other types of information. Probably one of the best sources of information is the local association for retarded children, which is frequently an affiliate of the National Association for Retarded Citizens. The membership of these organizations is comprised of anyone interested in promoting the welfare of the retarded; however, the majority of the membership usually consists of the parents of retarded children. These organizations serve two very useful functions for parents. First, it makes them aware that they are far from being the only ones in the world with their seemingly unique problem. Within the group they will find other parents who have experienced the same type of frustration they are presently experiencing and who can share with them the various methods they have worked out to cope with these problems (Meadon and Meadon, 1971). In addition, these more experienced parents as well as the professional staff can give advice regarding the various services available for their child. Parents with older retarded children can help the other parents anticipate future development (Gayton, 1975).

If the community is so small that there is no local organization, the parents can contact the office of the state association to obtain the necessary information and to find out where the nearest local affiliate is located. Parents may write directly to the National Association for Retarded Citizens (see

Appendix), from which a considerable amount of helpful literature is available. Furthermore, local school districts should be willing to provide parents with information about the nature and purpose of their special education programs. Parents need to know precisely what the goals of the special education program are and what can be anticipated at each level as the child progresses through the years.

Maintaining normal family functioning within the family unit

One of the more important needs of the families involved with retardation is for the family unit to maintain normal functioning as nearly as possible. There are many problems that may hinder such functioning. First, the parents may be so guilt ridden for having produced the retarded child that they feel they must dedicate every moment of their lives to the child's welfare. Unfortunately, these intense feelings of obligation may interfere with normal interactions of the parents with each other, with their normal children, and with their friends and relatives. Second, the additional financial burden of the retarded child may hinder normal expenditure for recreation and other activities and even for necessities. Third, the problems of care may be of such a nature that the parents are either unwilling or unable to find someone to provide the necessary supervision while they engage in even minimal recreational or social activities.

The three problems mentioned are not uncommon. Professionals counseling the parents need to help the parents dissipate their feelings of guilt or at least minimize them. They must be helped to realize that the advent of a retarded child should not destroy normal family relations. Few if any would want these relations destroyed. At times, however, parents are so intensely engrossed with their care for the retarded child that they become oblivious to the needs of other family members, including their own. Gayton (1975) suggests that the reality burdens of the child with a handicap make social and recreational enjoyment much more difficult to attain. He also suggests that the withdrawal tendencies of the parents tend to serve as a model for other family members and may convey to them that the handicapping condition is something to be ashamed of and hidden.

When the financial burdens created by the birth of the retarded child reach an extent that recreational and social activities are interfered with, parents should be counseled and directed toward the many types of activities available at a minimal cost, or at times, no cost. Care for the retarded child can be made available if various resources are tapped. Perhaps there are not any individuals available to care for the child in the manner parents would like to have the child cared for, but people can be taught, and parents should make every effort to seek out individuals who are willing to learn. Parents may be willing to share baby-sitting responsibilities with other parents of retarded children who may be more in tune with the routine and needs of the retarded child. Although it is a sensitive issue, which will be discussed in a later section, normal siblings may occasionally assume some responsibility while parents maintain some degree of social life.

The ability of the family to maintain some degree of normal socialization may be partly a function of the degree of acceptance by the entended family and by the neighbors within the community. Barsch (1968) and Farber (1968) found that the wife's side of the family tended to be more accepting and supportive. Farber indicated that the husband's mother tended to blame her daughter-in-law for the birth of the retarded child. Barsch and Farber both suggested that parents of retarded children appear to be able to maintain positive relationships with the neighbors. Some parents had to contend with misperceptions and suspicions regarding retarded children. It appears that successful integration with the extended family and with neighbors may well be a function of educating these other two groups, as well as the retarded child's immediate family, toward acceptance of the child and about associated problems. In essence, while the advent of a retarded child into the family creates many additional burdens and problems, life within the family unit must continue in a manner that will provide optimum opportunity to develop and maintain sound mental health for everyone involved.

Planning for the future

Perhaps one of the greatest concerns of parents of a retarded child is what the future holds for their child when they are no longer able or available to provide care. In the early years, the retarded child usually lives at home and is entitled to attend public school until the maximum attendance age is reached (often 21 years). At this age the retarded individual may not function socially and intellectually as an adult, but the responsibility of the schools has ended. If vocational rehabilitation services are available, then there is some assistance that may continue.

Parental concerns often center around where and how the child's needs ultimately will be met. The thought of forcing the child into an institution after spending a large number of years in the community and family setting may be difficult for parents to accept. While normal siblings have frequently been called on to assume the responsibilities of their parents, it is neither fair to them nor their own families to have this responsibility imposed on them unless it is by their own choice.

It may be in the best interest of the child if parents are able to make necessary arrangements for continued maintenance and other matters through carefully planned provisions, such as trusts that specify care. Whereas this view of maintenance focuses on providing funds, parents can at least have some assurance that their child will be adequately provided for when they are no longer able. Through reliable organizations, parents who are interested in providing a trust for their child can usually locate an attorney with this particular expertise. For the mildly retarded, plans can be made to develop the child to a reasonably productive and independent life. For the moderately retarded and those more seriously handicapped, specific provisions must be made.

NEEDS OF THE RETARDED CHILD

Children with mental retardation above all else are children. Their retardation, while having an influence on their lives, is secondary to their needs as children. They are more like normal children than they are different, and, therefore, have all of the basic needs of normal children.

Communication

Among the primary needs of the retarded child is the need for communication. Like their parents, such children need clear, concise, understandable messages. Many are far more perceptive than they are given credit for being. They can sense when things are wrong and when they are presented with half-truths. They, more than anyone, must be able to deal with their limitations. Some need to know what their limitations are and how their limitations will affect their lives. They need to know how they can make the best of their lives and how to reach their full potential for a meaningful existence.

Professional workers and parents have often been guilty of minimizing the feelings of children. The child's personal feelings are as important and valid as an adult's. Parents and professional workers frequently fail to include children in the decision-making process, yet the decisions affect them more than anyone else. Adults are sometimes prone to speak about the child,

Fig. 12-2. Communication is one of the fundamental needs of the retarded child. (Photograph by Peter Poulides.)

when present, in an uncomplimentary manner, as if the child can neither hear nor understand what is being said. The retarded child needs straightforward and congruent messages from others with respect to their feelings. Limited in understanding abstractions and less able to pick up cues, a retarded child is often confused by subtle insinuations, silent treatments, and other indirect cues that are often presented in an effort to change others' behaviors. If a particular behavior is unacceptable to the parent or professional worker, the child needs to know it. The child needs to know why it is unacceptable and what can be done to remediate the problem. Shielding the child from the truth usually serves no useful purpose and may damage the child's ability to grow.

Acceptance

Acceptance is one of the basic needs of humans (Maslow, 1954). Retarded children are no different in this need from anyone else. They need to be accepted as worthy individuals, both by others and from their own personal views.

We have already discussed parental rejection. The severe loss of self-esteem, feelings of inadequacy, and depression can make it difficult for the parent to love the child. Physical stigmata and/or lack of normal responsiveness may also retard the normal attachment of parents to a child (Gayton, 1975). The effects on the child are insidious, and many retarded children desperately seek someone with whom they can identify. They need good models, and the professional worker can help to provide these models. While the professional worker cannot make anyone like someone else, the groundwork for acceptance can be laid. With the mainstreaming of retarded children into classes with normal children, acceptance is even more crucial. By carefully educating the child's classmates and teachers about the child, fears of the unknown may be dissipated, leaving the way open for acceptance. The professional worker can and should be an individual who exudes a feeling of warmth and acceptance. By finding and capitalizing on the positive attributes of the child, the professional can assist the parents in realizing the worth of the child and can help bring about acceptance, which is Rosen's final stage as noted at the beginning of this chapter (Rosen, 1955).

Freedom to grow

Every retarded child, no matter how severely handicapped, has the ability to grow. It is the responsibility of the parents and the professional worker to provide the fertile environment and the proper atmosphere for the child to grow to full potential.

In a discussion of variables that affect the learning and thinking competency of the sensory impaired child, Chinn and Chinn (1979) discuss two important variables that are also applicable to the development and adjustment of the retarded child. The range and variety of potential experiences and activities may be unduly limited. Families of retarded children may assume that because the children are retarded they cannot appreciate experiences that normal children do. However, unless the parents provide them with a wide variety of experiences, their learning and adjustment may be greatly curtailed. Parents sometimes are easily embarrassed and at times are overly sensitive to what others may think when their child's behavior is observed in public. Unless retarded children have the opportunity to visit the zoo, ride a bus, and eat in a restaurant, they will be deprived of important experiences that all children should have for maximum social development.

A second important variable affecting adjustment is a balance of control within the child's environment. The child who, unnecessarily, is completely dependent on the "normal" members of the family may develop an attitude of helplessness and a loss of self-identity. It is often far easier for a parent to dress a retarded child, for example, than it is to teach the process of dressing. The latter may be a long and painful experience. However, when the child has accomplished this, another level of independence has been achieved, and self-concept has probably improved. The other extreme is equally insidious. A retarded child who completely controls and dominates the environment by overwhelming an overly patronizing family with unreasonable demands also fails to make an acceptable environmental adjustment. As the child learns to interact successfully with the family and to participate in it and to accept responsibilities, these learned experiences are usually transferred into the educational setting, peer group relationships, and other social contacts later in life.

NEEDS OF THE NORMAL SIBLINGS

While the writers in the field of mental retardation have focused a great deal of attention on the effects of a retarded child on parents, the effects on the normal siblings have in the past been ignored or relegated to a secondary level of importance. In more recent years considerable attention has been focused on this important subject. Researchers and writers have become increasingly more aware that the birth of a retarded child may have direct consequences on the overall development of other children in the family.

The literature has addressed itself to questions such as: "How does the retarded child affect the development and adjustment of normal siblings?" "What are the attitudes of the normal siblings toward the retarded child?" "What factors influence these attitudes?" "What are the fears and concerns of the normal siblings, and how can the negative effects be avoided or minimized?" We shall attempt to touch on some of these crucial questions and to provide, in the annotated bibliography, several excellent sources for further explanation of this and other topics in this chapter.

In an attempt to ascertain the attitudes of normal siblings toward their handicapped brother or sister, Barsch (1968) provided a group of parents with a checklist of possible normal sibling reactions or attitudes. While there were occasional indications of some resentment, the majority of the parents indicated that their normal children had favorable attitudes toward the handicapped child. It is quite possible, however, that these parents may have been insensitive to the real feelings of their normal children or that they could not accept negative feelings toward the retarded child either from themselves or from their other children.

Farber (1968) states that parents tend to assign a status to each child in the family commensurate with his or her perceived abilities. Typically, the status tends to be based on chronological age. As a child grows older and actual abilities become more apparent, there is occasional readjustment of roles and expectations. Regardless of birth order, the retarded child eventually becomes the youngest child socially. Normal siblings at times are under pressure to assume more responsibility and act older than they actually are. In a study of severely retarded children and their normal siblings, Farber found that the latter's relationship with their mother was adversely affected by the handicapped child's high degree of dependency. Younger normal and retarded children tend to be treated on a more equal basis, but as they grow older, the normal siblings assume a superordinate position in the relationship. Farber found that siblings who, as younger children, had limited interaction with their retarded brother or sister were less affected than those who had interacted freely.

Schild (1976) suggests that one of the potential problems faced by normal siblings is the unrealistically high expectations for them by parents, who are trying to compensate for the retarded child's deficiencies.

Communication

The advent of a retarded child is a total family problem. As such, the normal children in the family need to be involved in the total family communication process. Too frequently the decisions related to the retarded child are made without prior discussion or explanation to others in the family, yet they affect the entire family. The other children have many feelings about their retarded sibling; they also have feelings and concerns about themselves. They need to feel free to communicate these feelings to their parents.

Sometimes parents relate to the normal children with good intentions but with poor techniques. They do what they think is best for the family, but what they do may not have a positive outcome or be in the best interest of the family unit. If, however, they can communicate what they are doing and why they are doing it, the unpleasantness of the situation may at least be understandable to the normal children.

Normal siblings must also deal with peer reaction such as teasing and ridicule. These problems may come at an age when the normal child lacks the maturity and understanding of the situation to resolve them effectively. Parents sometimes compound the frustration and confusion of the normal children by refusing to discuss with them the problems of mental retardation (Grossman, 1972). Many parents are so overwhelmed with the burden of dealing with their own problems and identity with respect to their retarded child that they are ill-equipped to recognize the needs of their other children. Often they are unable to recognize or to help them in the many stresses and traumas created by the presence of the retarded child.

Schreiber and Feeley (1965), working with normal adolescent siblings of retarded children, developed a group process whereby ten of these siblings met bimonthly for sessions lasting an hour and a half for an 8-month period. During the sessions many concerns emerged. Among the concerns expressed were:

1. How do you tell friends about your retarded brother or sister?
2. How do you deal with your parents when they have not discussed the problems of mental retardation and the implications for the family?
3. How do you deal with those who speak offensively about the retarded?
4. Are parental expectations of normal sibling roles fair to all involved?
5. What is the responsibility of the normal children to the retarded child in the event of parental death?
6. What do you do when parents have no affection toward the retarded child?
7. Does retardation in the family lessen the prospects of marriage and is it hereditary?

Grossman (1972) conducted a similar type of group interaction program for adolescents. It was interesting to note that some of the problems encountered in establishing the group were directly related to lack of parental cooperation. These adolescents were dependent on their parents for transportation, and lack of parental cooperation in this area precluded participation. It appeared that many of the apprehensive parents were fearful of their children revealing family secrets during the sessions. Many of the concerns expressed by this group were similar and in some instances identical to those raised in the Schreiber and Feeley (1965) study. Some of the concerns expressed by the participants in Grossman's group included:

1. Apprehension about being identified with the retarded child
2. Lack of understanding of what the retarded sibling's capabilities were, such as how much the child knew and could understand
3. When acting as parent substitutes, how to discipline the retarded child

Begab (1963) suggested that older siblings be recognized as an essential element in family adjustment and that they be included in the study, treatment, and interpretation phases of the case-work process. Because parents often find it difficult and painful to share their knowledge regarding the retarded child with normal children, there may be a tendency to avoid discussion. Begab strongly urges counseling to take the form of family counseling rather than just parental counseling. This process would facilitate communication between parents and normal children, allowing them both to express their concerns. While Grossman (1972) suggested that exaggerated attention to the handicapped condition or overintellectualization can result in some adverse effects, it appears that the more the family understands the condition, the better they are able to cope with it.

Wentworth (1974) reported that normal siblings unequivocally stated that the most important advice to parents was to be honest. Sound parent-child relationships are built on trust. Trust is developed when parents and children are both secure in their feelings that their relationship is built on honesty. They need to know what caused the handicap, just how severe the disability is, why the retarded child needs special care and treatment, and what the prognosis is. Wentworth further suggests that questions be answered as truthfully as possible, according to the child's age and level of comprehension.

Unlike many functional disturbances, the problem of mental retardation as a family concern can usually be traced to a particular point and time when retardation is identified. Thus, if professionals, such as nurses, physicians, theologians, psychologists, and teachers will work toward providing the types of counseling and therapeutic services needed, chances for adjustment by both parents and normal siblings will be maximized.

Attention

Another great need for the normal sibling is that of attention. The accounts of neglected normal siblings in families with a child with a handicap are endless. These normal children are neglected for a number of reasons. They are neglected because the parents are sometimes overwhelmed with the responsibilities of caring for the retarded child. The parents neglect their normal children at times because they may be so filled with guilt that they feel they must devote all their time to the handicapped child. Parents sometimes neglect their normal children because they are attempting to escape from the entire family, which is such a threat to their self-esteem. They may even neglect their normal children because they operate under the assumption that they are unfit as parents because they have produced a child whom they view as defective. Other children may suffer because their parents *are* incompetent as parents and would not have given them adequate attention regardless of the situation. These children are often in desperate need of attention. If they are unable to secure the attention they need at home, they may secure it in socially unacceptable ways at home, at school, and in the community as well.

Acknowledgment of feelings without guilt

One of the primary needs of the normal sibling is to be able to acknowledge their own feelings without guilt. We have already stressed how the retarded child may be a drain on family resources both financially and emotionally. It is only natural that some negative feelings on the part of the normal siblings will develop. One of the most comprehensive studies on the normal siblings of retarded children was done by Grossman (1972). Her research was conducted with four groups of university students. Two groups were students from a private university. These groups included normal brothers of retarded children as one group and normal sisters of retarded children as a second group. The other two groups were obtained from a community college and consisted of normal brothers of retarded children and normal sisters of retarded children. Students participated in the study on a voluntary basis and received a small amount of remuneration for their time spent on the project. It should be emphasized that not all eligible subjects contacted agreed to participate; that is, some normal siblings of retarded children declined to participate. Some assumptions may be made that those agreeing to participate may have tended to represent groups that had more positive attitudes toward mental retardation, with some of those with more negative attitudes eliminating themselves from the study.

Grossman found that the students from the private university tended to come from the more affluent families that could be considered upper socioeconomic class. The parents tended to have a high educational background and held positions of high occupational status. Subjects from the community college, however, tended to come from lower middle socioeconomic families and had already or were in the process of obtaining a higher level of educational preparation than their parents. Because of the economic status of the families of the students from the private university, the retarded child presented no particular financial burdens on the family. There were no limitations financially for any services for the retarded children nor were there any limitations with respect to domestic help.

Grossman found that the parents of students from the private university tended to shield their normal children as much as possible from the inconveniences of a retarded sibling. The males in the group had had little direct contact with the retarded child compared to the females, who tended to be more involved with and participated in child-rearing activities of younger siblings and the retarded child to some extent. Males in the community college sample also tended to be uninvolved with the handicapped sibling. Many were involved with full- or part-time jobs and were financially independent from their parents. Some were married and had their own families to be concerned with. Of the four groups, they appeared to be the least involved with the retarded sibling. Females from the community college, however, appeared to be the most involved of the four groups with their retarded siblings. Some had major roles in the child-rearing responsibilities, with some serving as mother surrogates. Some felt they knew more about caring for the retarded child than their parents did and may indeed have possessed greater skills, having had preparation in special education classes as well as volunteer work with retarded children in the community.

With the 83 university subjects, Grossman attempted to determine if the impact of the retarded child had an adverse or a positive effect on the normal siblings. (The reader will recall that the study was conducted on a voluntary basis with some eligible subjects declining or deselecting themselves from the study. We may speculate that a higher percentage of those not participating may have represented those with more negative feelings or attitudes.) Grossman found that 45 percent of the subjects benefited from the experience of having had a retarded child in the family. These individuals tended to have a greater understanding and tolerance for people in general and for the handicapped in particular. They were more sensitive to prejudice and its consequences and had a greater appreciation for their own good health and intelligence. Grossman's findings support those of Kramm (1963), who found that 76 percent of 50 families with children with Down's syndrome indicated that they had benefited from having a retarded child.

Farber (1968) suggested that normal siblings who interact regularly with the retarded child and, at times act as parent surrogates, internalize welfare norms and tend to opt for the more altruistic vocational choices emphasizing "devotion of mankind" and "devotion to worthwhile causes." Farber further states that the effect of the retarded child on normal siblings may even influence marriage choices. Normal siblings who maintain close relationships to their retarded brother or sister may not consider anyone as a marriage partner who demonstrates little tolerance for the handicapped child.

Grossman, however, found that an equal number of subjects sampled were judged to be affected negatively by the experience of having a handicapped sibling. Some of the negative effects noted included shame, a sense of being tainted or defective, and a sense of guilt for being the child who was not retarded or for having negative feelings toward their retarded siblings. Some indicated resentment toward the disrupting influence on the family unity, such as stress on parental relationships and neglect of normal children in the family.

Resentment. The resentment that Grossman alludes to is a common and natural reaction on the part of a normal child with a retarded sibling. While the reaction is typical and normal, many parents, as well as children, who hold these feelings of resentment do not realize that such feelings are to be expected. It is important that the parents and these normal siblings be assisted in dealing with these feelings in an emotionally constructive manner.

Hunter, Schucman, and Friedlander (1972) suggested that a normal child in the family may develop feelings of anger toward the retarded sibling. Anger may be felt because of the lack of personal attention received and the apparent favoritism shown toward the child with a handicap. Resentment may develop because the handicap prevents the family from going on certain types of outings; because treatment, therapy, special schooling, and so on place financial constraints on the family; and because the normal child may have to assume certain types of unpleasant responsibilities such as baby-sitting. The normal child may even wish for the other child's death or at least that the retarded sibling would just go away (Grossman, 1972; Gordon, 1975).

Guilt, fear, shame and embarrassment. The normal sibling may have guilt feelings. These feelings of guilt may occur because of negative feelings toward the retarded child. Guilt feelings may even be present because the sibling was fortunate enough to be normal and the other child handicapped.

The normal child may also feel fear. When younger, normal siblings may be fearful that they too may become retarded. As they become older, they may be fearful that they too may have children with handicaps. They may also be fearful that someday, when the parents are no longer able to provide care, they will have total responsibility for the handicapped sibling (Grossman, 1972). Grossman suggested that younger normal siblings tend to have fears and anxieties and may even fantasize. She cites an example of one child who, after the retarded child had been institutionalized, had fears that a "boogey man" would take her away. Schreiber and Feeley's work, along with Grossman's, suggests that there are many concerns and fears that normal siblings have that somehow must be dealt with adequately either by the parents or through professional help. Younger children who do not have accurate information may develop fears and fantasies.

The normal sibling often has feelings of shame and embarrassment. They may be embarrassed to be seen in public with their sibling, embarrassed to tell their friends, embarrassed to bring their friends home, or embarrassed to have a date pick them up at their home. It is understandable why a teenager may be reluctant to be picked up at the house by a friend if a retarded sibling is ill-mannered and exhibits unpredictable behavior.

Wentworth (1974) suggested that embarrassment is perhaps the second most prevalent emotional reaction that nonhandicapped siblings experience. She further suggests that the degree of embarrassment may be a function of the age of both the handicapped and nonhandicapped child and the type of handicap the child has. A younger child with a handicap presents an image of a helpless individual to be "mothered." It may be easier for the normal children and their peers to accept the child at this age. As retarded children become older, more difficult to control, and lacking in the "cuteness" evident as a child, they can be a much greater source of embarrassment. Older children, particularly in their adolescent years, become more cognizant of and more easily influenced by peer approval. Because teenagers can be cruel in their remarks, normal siblings may become increasingly embarrassed as tackless remarks are made about a brother or sister with a handicap.

• • •

In summary, the needs of normal siblings in the family are often overlooked. Careful guidance by parents and professional workers can lead to a healthy adjustment to the problems created by the presence of the retarded child.

INSTITUTIONALIZATION

The decision to institutionalize a retarded child is both difficult and complex; it affects the retarded child, the parents and siblings, and perhaps close family friends and the extended family. With the development of new special education programs and other community-based programs, the decision regarding whether or not a child should be institutionalized has become even more complex. In the past when few if any community-based facilities and programs were available to parents, many retarded children were routinely institutionalized. The development and refinement of these programs have now negated much of the rationale previously used for institutionalization and provide families with viable alternatives.

Special education classes for trainable and educable retarded individuals are now available in almost every community large enough to warrant the maintenance of such programs. As P. L. 94-142 is implemented, educational programs will also be available in the community for the more severely retarded children. In addition, vocational rehabilitation programs and sheltered workshops have made it possible for many more retarded individuals to maintain useful and productive lives in the community.

The percentage of mentally retarded individuals in institutions is relatively small. It is estimated that at most 4 percent (Farber, 1968; Wolfensberger and Kurtz, 1969) of the nearly 6 million retarded individuals in the United States live in institutional settings. However, while the percentage is small, the total numbers of individuals living in institutions approaches nearly a quarter of a million people. This number represents a significant amount of financial expenditure for both the families and the states and a significant number of individuals involved in the operating processes of institutions.

There are many variables that may contribute to a decision to institutionalize a retarded child. The mentally retarded child, however, is no less in need of emotional support from the family than the child with normal intellectual potential. If the retarded individual is to maximize potential, the same kinds and qualities of support must be available as to the normal child. The best types of institutions are the ones that can provide the emotional needs ordinarily given in the home. Even the best institutions and the most conscientious staff members are often inadequate as parent surrogates (Slobody and Scanlon, 1959). The efficacy of institutional treatment recently has received closer scrutiny because of the negative findings about the realities of institutional life (Blatt and Kaplan, 1966; Baumeister, 1970).

While the effects of poor institutional care can depress cognitive development (Tizard and Tizard, 1971), there is also support for the contention that institutional care can have a more positive effect than poor home care (Tizard and Rees, 1974). Certain efforts have been made to improve the level of institutional care. In 1964, the American Association of Mental Deficiency published *Standards for State Residential Institutions for the Mentally Retarded* to assist in the evaluation of residential schools. A decade ago, however, few institutions met the AAMD standards (Hubbard, 1969). While problems still exist, many improvements nationally have been made to improve the quality of care and services (Helsel, 1971; Saltz, 1973).

Institutionalization often has been justified as being for the good of the family. Yet there is evidence that in some instances the retarded child actually benefits parents and normal siblings (Grossman, 1972; Kramm, 1963). Institutionalization is contrary to the American value system. Our society values children as a means of actualization, cohesiveness, and togetherness in family interaction. The family is viewed as a primary socializing agent, and the removal of a member of the family to an institution means that the individual will cease to function as a sociological member of the family and that socialization will take place somewhere else (Wolfensberger and Kurtz, 1969).

We in no way wish to imply that institutionalization is an improper or inadequate means of management for the retarded child. We fully acknowledge the vast improvements in the past decade with respect to institutional facilities, programming, care, and quality of staff. We would like to emphasize, however, that the decision to institutionalize should be made with due deliberation, that it be made only after all alternatives have been explored, and that it be made by the parents, who are the ones who must live with the child or with the decision to institutionalize.

Early institutionalization

The practice of recommending early institutionalization for the retarded has not been uncommon among physicians. Some are able to convince the fathers immediately after birth that early institutionalization is in the best interest of the family and that the mother not be allowed to see the child (Beddie and Osmond, 1955; Jolly, 1953). Such advice is generally given with good intention in an effort to avoid any ill effects on older siblings and to avoid maternal attachment, which will make the institutionalization even more difficult. Unfortunately, much of the advice is given without careful consideration of the effects of such a decision on the parents, the family, and the child. Preventing the mother from seeing the child may leave the mother with severe anxieties regarding the "monstrous" child she has conceived. Even if the parents do decide on institutionalization, seeing the child permits a certain degree of closure regarding the status of the child. Many parents are surprised to find that the retarded child is not as atypical as they may have fantasized.

Often the advice of the physician for early institutionalization is made without awareness of available community resources (Giannini and Goodman, 1963). Frequently the recommended institutionalization of an infant may be neither practical nor feasible for the family. State institutions may have long waiting lists and may be unable to accommodate the family for a considerable period of time. The cost of private institutions may be prohibitive for the family or may require such financial sacrifices as to negate the suggested advantages to the normal siblings (Jolly, 1953).

Parents are entitled to as much information as possible regarding the nature of their child's condition, as well as all of the alternatives. Parents who know more about their child's condition are more prone to be accepting. Stone (1967) found that well-informed parents of children with Down's syndrome were not only more accepting, but were less likely to institutionalize the child.

Home and community care for the retarded child may not be a viable alternative in some instances. Institutionalization may become necessary when the behavior of the child in the community, the physical and emotional strain on the parents, or some other form of crisis to the child or family does not permit continuation of home care (Begab, 1955). When such a decision is made, both the family and the child should be prepared for this critical experience.

Precommitment services

Unfortunately many of those individuals advising parents to institutionalize their child are lacking in their understanding of the personality and behavioral characteristics of the retarded child and are relatively uninformed about institutional programs and facilities (Begab, 1955). Thus, while giving advice to institutionalize, they are ill-equipped to help the family and child prepare themselves intellectually or emotionally for the admission. Parents in the process of institutionalizing their child may need assistance in working through their feelings of guilt and anxiety. Their guilt may be precipitated by feelings of inadequacy or failure to meet the needs of their child in the home. Anxiety may frequently be a function of the uncertainties concerning the care and treatment the child will receive in the institution.

When a decision in the best interest of all the parties involved has been made to institutionalize a child, the professional counselor should help the family to see how the decision is best for the child as well as for the other members of the family. The professional can also help to alleviate the accompanying feelings of guilt. The counselor or the institutional staff should help the parents in their understanding of the institution's facilities and programs and how their child will fit into them.

Parents should be advised of various means of minimizing the trauma on the actual day of commitment. The higher level retarded child can be better prepared if visits are made to the institution prior to commitment. In this fashion the child can become acquainted with the facilities, programs, staff, and, to some degree, other children. It may be advisable to make several visits during which the child is allowed to interact with the staff and other residents and possibly to participate in activities. The day of commitment may be traumatic for the entire family, regardless of the amount of preparation, but familiarity with the facility may reduce the trauma.

After institutionalization

After a child is placed in the institution, families tend to settle into one of several patterns. One type of family completely cuts itself off from the retarded child. Once placement has occurred, the child is essentially forgotten, perhaps never to be seen or visited by the family again. A second type of family lives in constant ambivalence, sometimes seemingly unconcerned, overly concerned at other times. Some of these parents vent their frustrations and guilt feelings by finding every conceivable fault with the institution. A third type may be extremely supportive both to the child and to the institution, working diligently to help the institution in constructive ways (Wolfensberger and Kurtz, 1969).

Many families wait through long frustrating months or even years until a vacancy finally allows them to place their retarded child. During this long wait many begin to perceive the institution as the answer to all their problems. After the placement there may be a considerable amount of letdown when they find that all their problems have not dissipated. The normal siblings may still quarrel, the daughter who projected blame on the retarded child remains unpopular, or strained relationships between parents may continue (Dittman, 1962).

Even after institutionalization in the best interests of all concerned, many problems must be resolved. Some of these include feelings of guilt for having "abandoned" their child and determining how to maintain a satisfactory relationship with their child, both while in the institution and when a home visit occurs. Counselors should be keenly aware of the postcommitment concerns and problems that may arise and should be prepared to help the family resolve these problems.

Emerging trends

There appear to be several trends emerging with regard to the programming and the role of the institution for the mentally retarded. As more community programs become available, an increasingly larger percentage of retarded children have been kept at home. As previously suggested, the advent of P.L. 94-142 will provide more educational services in the community, thus giving many parents a greater number of options. In most instances, institutions have moved in the direction of services for the more severely retarded (Payne, Johnson, and Abelson, 1969).

Previously, many institutions were referred to as colonies. These colonies were often located in remote areas, isolated from the population centers. Instead of the term colony, many have changed their names to training schools. The residents are referred to as residents or students rather than patients or inmates. Many of the newer facilities are built close to major population centers where the residents are closer to their families and also closer to available rehabilitation programs. Older institutions may be nearby simply because of expansion of the cities themselves, so they are no longer remote. Many of these institutions now have excellent training programs as well as special education programs. The term training school implies that learning is taking place. These programs are made available to residents when there appears to be some feasibility for special programs. Now that many are closer to the larger population centers, the institutions have been able, in most instances, to recruit qualified professional staff members, such as social workers, rehabilitation counselors, dentists, physicians, psychologists, nurses, certified teachers, physical and recreational therapists, and physical educators. With the availability of these professional workers, research as well as programming has benefited. Some children previously relegated to a useless existence are now being developed beyond their functional expectancy levels through intensive therapy programs and special techniques such as behavior modification.

Some institutions are operating effective rehabilitation programs with the expectancy of returning many of their residents to the community. Some institutions are also operating satellite community-based group homes to facilitate rehabilitation and the individual's transition from the institution into the community. In essence we are seeing better physical facilities in institutions, but more importantly, a shift in direction with regard to their purposes and services. While taking a proportionately larger number of more severely retarded children for custodial care, the institutions have also developed competent professional staffs to provide high-quality services for the severely retarded residents and have begun training programs for the more able.

SUMMARY

In summary, we feel that institutionalization is a viable alternative for some families. In some instances, the family situation may be such that institutionalization is the best alternative. We strongly support, however, the position that the decision to institutionalize is rightfully that of the parents, that adequate counseling be provided prior to and after institutionalization, and that all the community resources be explored before a final decision be made.

We have examined how the advent of a retarded child can affect the integration of a family unit. Parental reactions are varied and are not always predictable. Parents, retarded children, and normal children all have specific needs. One need common to all three is for effective communication; they all need clear and concise communication that they can understand. They also need support from one another when possible and from professional workers in dealing with their feelings.

The decision concerning institutionalization is difficult and complex. There are no standard answers that will be appropriate for all situations. The improvement of the quality of institutional care, as well as new community programming, have given parents greater options, but may also serve to make it more difficult to reach a decision.

The relationship between the retarded child and the family is frequently a difficult one. If, however, the professional team can provide quality comprehensive services, many of the needs of the parents, the retarded children, and the normal siblings can be met; and the traumatizing effect of the child's presence can be minimized, while the positive aspects are enhanced.

STUDY QUESTIONS

1. What are some of the typical reactions of parents to the birth of a retarded child?
2. Why is communication such a primary need for parents, retarded child, and normal siblings?
3. How and why does religion affect parental reaction?
4. What is meant by the need of the retarded child for freedom to grow?
5. What does the literature suggest regarding the effect of a retarded child on normal siblings?
6. Who should decide whether or not a retarded child should be institutionalized? What variables should be considered in making the decision?
7. What can be done to alleviate the trauma of institutionalization?

REFERENCES

Barsch, R. H. *The parent of the handicapped child.* Springfield, Ill.: Charles C Thomas, Publishers, 1968.

Baumeister, A. A. The American residential institution: its history and character. In A. A. Baumeister and E. C. Butterfield (Eds.), *Residential facilities for the mentally retarded.* Chicago: Aldine-Atherton, Inc., 1970.

Beddie, A., and Osmond, H. Mothers, mongols, and mores. *The Canadian Medical Association Journal,* 1955, **73**, 167-170.

Begab, M. J. Precommitment services in a training school for mental defectives. *American Journal of Mental Deficiency.* 1955, **59**, 690-697.

Begab, M. J. Casework for the mentally retarded case work with parents. *The mentally retarded child: a guide to services of social agencies.* Washington, D.C.: U.S. Government Printing Office, 1963, pp. 58-68.

Begab, M. J. The mentally retarded and the family. In I. Philips (Ed.), *Prevention and treatment of mental retardation.* New York: Basic Books, Inc., 1966.

Blatt, B., and Kaplan, F. *Christmas in purgatory.* Boston: Allyn & Bacon, Inc., 1966.

Chinn, P. C., and Chinn, P. L. The child with learning problems. In P. L. Chinn, *Child health maintenance: concepts in family centered care.* (2nd ed.) St. Louis: The C. V. Mosby Co., 1979.

Chinn, P. C., Winn, J. and Walters, R. H. *Two-way talking with parents of special children: a process of positive communication.* St. Louis: The C. V. Mosby Co., 1978.

Chinn, P. L. *Child health maintenance: concepts in family centered care.* (2nd ed.) St. Louis: The C. V. Mosby Co., 1979.

Christiansen, J. *Theological implications of having a handicapped child.* Panel discussion, Salt Lake City: University of Utah, 1969.

Dittman, L. L. The family of the child in the institution. *American Journal of Mental Retardation,* 1962, **66,** 759-765.

Farber, B. Effects of a severely mentally retarded child on family integration. Monograph, *Society for Research in Child Development,* 1959, **24**(2).

Farber, B. Family organization and crisis: maintenance of integration in families with a severely retarded child. Monograph, *Society for Research in Child Development,* 1960, **25**(1).

Farber, B. *Mental retardation: its social context and social consequences.* Boston: Houghton-Mifflin Co., 1968.

Farber, N. W. *The retarded child.* New York: Crown Publishers, Inc., 1968.

Froyd, H. E. Counseling parents of severely visually handicapped children. *New Outlook for the Blind,* 1973, **67:** 251-257.

Gallagher, J. J. Rejecting parents? *Exceptional Children,* 1956, **22,** 273-276.

Gayton, W. F. Management problems of mentally retarded children and their families. *Pediatric Clinics of North America,* 1975, **22**(3), 561-570.

Gayton, W. F., and Walker, L. J. Family management of Down's syndrome during the early years. *Family Physician,* 1974, **9,** 160-164.

Gordon, S. *Living fully,* New York: The John Day Co., 1975.

Gorham, K. A. A lost generation of parents. *Exceptional Children,* 1975, **41**(8), 521-525.

Giannini, M. J., and Goodman, L. Counseling females during the crisis reaction to mongolism, *American Journal of Mental Deficiency,* 1963, **67,** 740-747.

Grossman, F. K. *Brothers and sisters of retarded children.* Syracuse, N.Y.: Syracuse University Press, 1972.

Hart, N. W. Frequently expressed feelings and reactions of parents toward their retarded children. In N. R. Bernstein (Ed.), *Diminished people.* Boston: Little, Brown and Co., 1970.

Helsel, E. D. Residential services. In J. Wortis (Ed.), *Mental retardation: an annual review.* New York: Grune & Stratton, Inc., 1971.

Hubbard, J. E. *Results of team evaluations in 134 state residential institutions in the U.S.* Final Project Report to the Division of Mental Retardation, 1969.

Hunter, M. H., Schucman, H., and Friedlander, G. *The retarded child from birth to five: a multi-*disciplinary program for the child and family. New York: The John Day Co., 1972.

Hutchinson, G. *Theological implications of having a handicapped child.* Panel discussion, East Texas State University, 1968.

Jolly, D. J. When should the seriously retarded be institutionalized? *American Journal of Mental Deficiency,* 1953, **57,** 632-636.

Kanner, L. Parents' feelings about retarded children. *American Journal of Mental Deficiency,* 1953, **57,** 744-755.

Kramm, F. R. *Families of mongoloid children.* Publication No. 401, Washington, D.C.: U.S. Children's Bureau, 1963.

Kravaceus, W. C., and Hayes, E. N. *If your child is handicapped.* Boston: Porter Sargent, Publisher, 1969.

Maslow, A. H. *Motivation and personality,* New York: Harper & Row, Publishers, 1954.

Mattson, A., and Agle, D. P. Group therapy with parents of hemophiliacs. *Journal of the American Academy of Child Psychiatry,* 1972, **11,** 558-571.

McKibbin, E. H. An interdisciplinary program for retarded children and their families. *American Journal of Occupational Therapy,* 1972, **3,** 125-129.

Meadon, K. P., and Meadon, L. Changing role perceptions for parents of handicapped children. *Exceptional Children,* 1971, **38**(1), 21-26.

Neal, C. *Theological implications of having a handicapped child.* Panel discussion, East Texas State University, 1968.

Payne, D., Johnson, R. C. and Abelson, R. B., *Comprehensive description of institutionalized retardates in the western United States,* Boulder, Colo.: Western Interstate Commission for Higher Education, 1969.

Reiss, I. L. *The family system in America.* New York: Holt, Rinehart and Winston, Inc., 1971.

Rosen, L. Selected aspects in the development of the mother's understanding of her mentally retarded child. *American Journal of Mental Deficiency,* 1955, **59,** 522.

Ryckman, O. B., and Henderson, R. A. The meaning of a retarded child for his parents: a focus for counselors. *Mental Retardation,* 1965, **3**(4), 4-5.

Safford, P. L., and Arbitman, D. C. *Developmental intervention with young physically handicapped children.* Springfield, Ill.: Charles C Thomas, Publisher, 1975.

Saltz, R. Effects of part-time mothering on I.Q.

and S.Q. of young institutionalized children. *Child Development*, 1973, **44**, 166-170.

Schild, S. The family of the retarded child. In R. Koch and J. C. Dobson (Eds.), *The mentally retarded child and his family.* (Revised ed.) New York: Brunner/Mazel, Inc., 1976.

Schreiber, M., and Feeley, M. Siblings of the retarded: a guided group experience. *Children*, 1965, **12**, 221-225.

Slobody, L. B., and Scanlon, T. B. Consequences of early institutionalization in mental retardation. *American Journal of Mental Deficiency*, 1959, **63**, 971-974.

Stone, N. D. Family factors in willingness to place the mongoloid child. *American Journal of Mental Deficiency*, 1967, **72**, 16-20.

Stubblefield, H. W. Religion, parents and mental retardation. *Mental Retardation*, 3(4), 8-11.

Tizard, B. and Rees, J. A. A comparison of the effects of adoption, restoration to the natural mother, and continued institutionalization on the cognitive development of four-year-old children. *Child Development*, 1974, **45**, 92-99.

Tizard, J. and Tizard, B. The social development of two-year-old children in residential nurseries. In H. R. Shaffer (Ed.), *The Origins of Human Social Relations.* New York: Academic Press, Inc., 1971.

Wentworth, E. H. *Listen to your heart: a message to parents of handicapped children.* Boston: Houghton Mifflin Co., 1974.

Wernick, R. *The family.* New York: Time-Life Books, 1974.

Wolfensberger, W., and Kurtz, R. A. Religious and pastoral counseling. In W. Wolfensberger and R. A. Kurtz (Eds.), *Management of the family of the mentally retarded.* Chicago: Follett Publishing Co., 1969.

Zuk, G. H. The religious factor and the role of guilt in parental acceptance of the retarded child. *American Journal of Mental Deficiency*, 1959, **64**, 139-147.

ANNOTATED BIBLIOGRAPHY

Chinn, P. C., Winn, J. and Walters, R. H. *Two-way talking with parents of special children: a process of positive communication.* St. Louis: The C. V. Mosby Co., 1978.

Provides a background on family systems, principles of communication and semantics as it affects the communication process. Provides the reader with a communication process in dealing with parents, children, and other professionals and gives examples of putting the process into action.

Gordon, T. *Parent effectiveness training.* New York: Peter H. Wyden, Inc., 1970.

An excellent book with suggestions of interaction and communication skills that parents can develop to deal more effectively with their children.

Grossman, F. K. *Brothers and sisters of retarded children.* Syracuse, N.Y.: Syracuse University Press, 1972.

A publication reporting the findings of Grossman and her colleagues in their research on normal siblings of retarded children.

Wentworth, E. H. *Listen to your heart: a message to parents of handicapped children.* Boston: Houghton Mifflin Co., 1974.

Although written primarily for parents, this book written by a parent of a child with a handicap can provide some valuable insights to the professional worker. It explores both the reactions to having a child with a handicap and the needs of the family.

Wolfensberger, W., and Kurtz, R. A. *Management of the family of the mentally retarded.* Chicago: Follett Publishing Co., 1969.

A comprehensive book of readings dealing with various aspects of the family of the retarded child.

CHAPTER 13

Legislative and legal issues

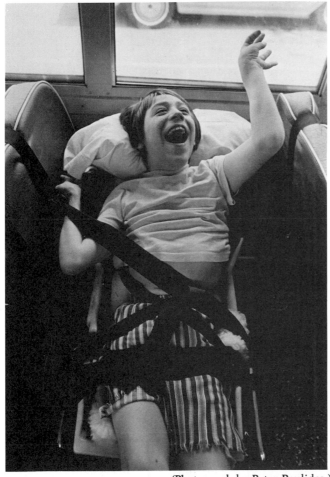

(Photograph by Peter Poulides.)

INTRODUCTION

A chapter on legal and legislative issues in such a book as this would have been almost unheard of in the not-so-distant past. In fact, many texts published within the past 10 years neglected this area; or if a section were included, the orientation was geared toward historical aspects with perhaps only a passing reference to legislation. Today it is inconceivable that texts relating to the exceptional child would omit the dramatic changes that have occurred, particularly in the past few years. Although, the seeds of change were planted many years ago, we in special education, have only recently become significantly involved in the legal and legislative arena.

The use of the law to influence social changes in the United States is not a recent event. Gilhool (1976) stated that "In going to the courts, exceptional citizens have joined an old tradition in the United States. That tradition, the use of the courts to achieve social change, to achieve justice, dates back at least to 1905 when W. E. B. Dubois and his associates founded the National Association for the Advancement of Colored People (NAACP)" (p. 16). The interaction between the legal system and special education advocate groups is producing profound changes that will undoubtedly influence our society for generations to come.

One fact must be kept in mind by all concerned with the legal issues as they relate to the exceptional person. That fact is that even though our involvement in legal and legislative actions are of recent occurrence, nothing essentially new is being proposed. The change represents a belated recognition by society that exceptional persons have not been dealt with fairly and that "The right to be human, based upon principles of equality, is applicable to all individuals" (Drew, Hardman, and Bluhm, 1977, p. 101).

If a society is to remain viable, there has to be a direct correspondence between the laws of that society and the equal application of those laws to all citizens. The fact that this has not always been the case is apparent to anyone with even a cursory understanding of history. However, it is not whether a nation, through its laws, has always fairly applied those laws, but whether a country has ensured the open access to the laws for redress of grievances—both for the individual and the group. The recent legislative and legal activity is evidence that the rights of the exceptional person at long last are being recognized and responded to in a manner that has far-reaching implications for all persons.

This chapter is not intended to provide an exhaustive account of the varied political, economic, and social issues that have led to recent legislative and legal actions. The emphasis of this chapter is to examine some historical antecedents that have influenced recent legislation and court decisions; provide a detailed review of current legislation; discuss related legal aspects; and in conclusion, identify some educational-legal issues that will be of continuing concern.

HISTORICAL ANTECEDENTS

There is no direct mention in the Constitution or the Bill of Rights about education as either a right or a privilege. All educational concerns come under the framework of promoting health, morals, comfort, and general welfare. The purposes of education have been many and varied and have been influenced by many factors, such as the prevailing philosophy of the times, economics, and political influences. There has been a general agreement that the schools have the responsibility to prepare students to take their place in society. The New Hampshire Supreme Court in *Fogg v. Board of Education* (1912) ruled that

> The primary purpose of the maintenance of the common school system is the promotion of the general intelligence of the people constituting the body politic and thereby increase the usefulness and efficacy of the citizens, upon which the government of society depends. Free schooling funded by the state is not so much a right granted to pupils as a duty imposed upon them for the public good (p. 174).

Such rulings laid the groundwork for later court decisions that further delineated the states' responsibility for all citizens in regard to education. Public education functions as an arm of the state in which schools perform those activities delegated to them by the state, namely, the education of future citizens. It is a given that such delegation of power places education squarely in the center of the political process with all of its related pressures and varied interest groups. This is evident in our history as well as by current laws that have been enacted by federal and state legislatures. It is obvious that schools are both a social institution and a governmental function and are affected by society's awareness of needs as influenced by changing political climates.

There has been a relatively long history of actions by the federal government that relate to the handicapped. In a chapter such as this there is no need to provide a historical accounting of all such legislation. For the interested reader LaVor (1976) provides a succinct accounting of federal legislation con-

cerning exceptional persons. There is a need, however, to trace some events
that have been direct antecedents to the current state of affairs.

Since World War II, for example, there has been a decided change relative
to legislative and legal involvement in the area of special education, and with
the mentally retarded in particular. This has involved a variety of individuals and groups who may be characterized as "significant others" and has
been the result of many factors. Such influences as (1) the impact of the barbaric practices toward minorities in Nazi Germany, (2) the multitude of
maimed and crippled soldiers returning from World War II and the Korean
and Vietnamese "wars," (3) the advent of economic prosperity, (4) a national
recognition that being disabled does not mean lack of worth to both the community and the individual, (5) the involvement of parent groups, and (6)
advances in both the medical and social sciences, which in serendipitous
fashion stimulated interest in mental retardation. Additional impetus has
resulted from the highly visible accomplishments of individuals disabled in
some way (such as Helen Keller, President Franklin D. Roosevelt) along with
public admission by notable public figures that handicaps that were previously embarrassing occurred in their families (President John F. Kennedy's
mentally retarded sister, Senator Hubert Humphrey's mentally retarded
granddaughter, Senator S. I. Hayakawa's mentally retarded son, and others).
All of these influences, and others, have interacted to bring about actions that
are historically unprecedented.

Public education provisions for the handicapped, including the mentally
retarded, parallels to a considerable degree the establishment of minority
group rights in the United States. Specifically, we can begin with *Roberts v.
the City of Boston* (1849). This case concerned the denial of admission of
Sarah Roberts to a school for whites. The court ruled that Sarah was not
being denied instruction by being refused admission to the school in question. There was no consideration given to the possibility of lack of equal
quality or future educational consequences. This decision set a precedent for
related exclusionary cases in the years to come. The importance of the Roberts decision was that it was not based on the quality of the education provided but on whether some educational experience was available.

School boards have the power to assign pupils to particular schools, unless it is shown to be so arbitrary as to negate the efficacy of the placement
(Williams v. Board of Education). Most educational legal decisions involving the exceptional child have been exclusionary rather than facilitative. The

rational has been the "protection" of the schools rather than concern about the educational and social needs of the "undesirable" child. A philosophical change, in a social sense, began to occur in this country in the early part of the twentieth century. Two cases are of particular importance: *Beattie v. State Board of Education* (1950) and *State Board of Education v. Petty* (1950). Although neither of these cases involved mentally retarded individuals, they are important as precedents for later decisions. The first case, *Beattie v. State Board of Education,* concerned a cerebral palsied boy excluded from a public school class because of his condition, which, it was argued, caused a depressing effect on his classmates and his teachers. Although the schools had recommended placement in a school for the deaf and speech defective (quantitative), he was refused enrollment in the regular school program (qualitative). The boy refused such placement, a position that was supported by his parents. An appeal was made to the local school superintendent, who asked for a ruling from the State Superintendent of Public Instruction for Wisconsin. After no firm direction was given by the state school Superintendent, the school refused to allow the boy enrollment in his grade in the public school. The critically important factor in this case was the action of the jury in the municipal court of Antigo, Wisconsin, where the issue was first deliberated outside of the public school arena. The jury ruled in favor of reinstating the boy in the public school. This decision signaled a change in that, for one of the first times, the rights of a student were emphasized over the traditional view that "defective" children were to be segregated. Although this municipal court decision was overruled on appeal to the Wisconsin Supreme Court, an important dissenting opinion was written. This dissenting opinion was based on two important, and later significant, reasons; namely, that the school board should yield to public opinion as represented by the municipal court jury and that the boy's physical appearance and related behaviors (cerebral palsy) did not have a harmful effect or infringe on other children's right to an education.

The second case (*State Board of Education v. Petty,* 1950) occurred in Iowa. In this case an argument almost diametrically opposite to the *Beattie v. State Board of Education* (1950) issue was heard. The school board sought permission from the parents to place their child in a school that would best meet his educational needs. The court decision directed the parents to place the boy, who was deaf, in the state school for the deaf. The parents refused and instead placed him in a rural school near where they lived. An appeal was heard by the Iowa Supreme Court based on the parents' contention that it had not been proved the boy could not be educated in the public rural school. After expert testimony the Iowa Supreme Court unanimously ruled that the boy would have to be enrolled in the school for the deaf. This case is important in that it established a handicapped child's right to an education. The Court stated "It is our conclusion that the best interests of the child would be served by his attendance at a school where education could be adequately developed in the light of his handicap."

A dramatic change of events occurred in 1954 that was to have far-reaching effects on education. The case has become known as *Brown v. Board of Education of Topeka* (1954). The issue was segregation and the concomitant "equal opportunity" in a qualitative sense. The Supreme Court in reaching its decision stated:

> Today education is perhaps the most important function of state and local governments. Compulsory school attendance laws and the great expenditure for education both demonstrate our recognition of the importance of education to our democratic society. . . . In these days, it is doubtful that any child may reasonably be expected to succeed in life if he is denied the opportunity of an education. Such an opportunity, where the State has undertaken to provide it, is a right which must be made available to all on equal terms. . . . We conclude that in the field of public education the doctrine of "separate but equal" has no place. Separate educational facilities are inherently unequal. Therefore, we hold that the plaintiffs and others similarly situated for whom actions have been brought are, by reason of the segregation complained of, deprived of the equal protection of the laws guaranteed by the Fourteenth Amendment (p. 492).

The effect of *Brown v. Board of Education* on special education has been profound. The importance rests primarily with the fact that the decision stated unequivocally that education is a "right" and must be ". . . available to all on equal terms." This decision removes any argument that education is a privilege and in effect has opened the doors to all children to a free and appropriate education. Subsequent legislation (for example, P. L. 93-380, P. L. 94-142), which will be discussed in a later section, has provided support for the rights of the handicapped by protecting them against discrimination solely on the basis of a handicapping condition. This legislative activity has emphasized such areas as access to public facilities, procedural due process, least restrictive placement, free and appropriate education, and nondiscriminatory evaluation.

In the past 10 years there have been a multitude of court cases involving special education, either directly or indirectly. These cases have focused on matters relating to architectural barriers, classification, commitment, criminal law, custody, education, employment, guardianship, intelligence testing, limitation of treatment, sterilization, voting, and zoning. The interested reader who wishes to delve into the status of such court cases in the various areas should consult *Mental Retardation and the Law*.

In 1967 in *Hobson v. Hansen*, Judge J. Skelly Wright ruled that placing children in different tracks based on performance on various tests during their early school years violated the equal protection clause of the U.S. Constitution. In reviewing this case, Judge Wright found that there was a disproportionate number of blacks in special education classes and stated:

> The evidence shows that the method by which track assignments are made depends essentially on standardized aptitude tests which, although given on a system-wide basis, are completely inappropriate for use with a large segment of the student body. Because these tests are primarily standardized on and are relevant to a white middle class group of students, they produce inaccurate and misleading test scores when given to lower class and Negro children. As a result, rather than being classified according to ability to learn, these students are in reality being classified according to their socioeconomic or racial status, or—more precisely—according to environmental and psychological factors which have nothing to do with innate ability (p. 514).

On appeal in *Smuck v. Hobson* (1969) the Court of Appeals supported Judge Wright's ruling that abolished a tracking system in the District of Columbia public schools.

One of the first cases involving classes for the mentally retarded was heard in the Superior Court of Orange County, California (*Arreola v. Board of Education*, 1968). This case was brought to trial on behalf of 11 Mexican-American children and sought to prohibit special education classes for the educable mentally retarded unless the following three conditions were met: (1) that a hearing be held prior to placement (due process), (2) that the use of intelligence tests allow for cultural differences, and (3) that the curriculum be educationally sound and provisions for retesting be periodically scheduled.

Beginning in 1970 a number of other cases that directly involved classes for the mentally retarded were contested in the courts. In *Spangler v. Board of Education* (1970), the United States District Court for the Southern District of California found that the Pasadena schools had a "racial imbalance" in both the faculty and student bodies, had used intelligence tests that were both inaccurate and unfair, and had increased segregation by a disproportionate number of black students being assigned to "slow classes." A case filed in the Massachusetts Federal District Court in the same year (*Stewart v. Phillips*, 1970) also related to testing and minority students. In this case, for the first time, monetary damages were included in the grievance of the plaintiffs (poor and black). It was alleged that pupils placed in classes for the mentally retarded based on a single IQ score on tests that were discriminatory had been irreparably harmed.

Again in 1970, in *Diana v. State Board of Education*, the United States District Court for the Northern District of California concluded that there had been a denial of equal educational opportunity for nine Mexican-American children. The plaintiffs maintained that they were placed in classes for the educable mentally retarded on the basis of tests (Wechsler and Stanford-Binet Intelligence Tests) that were culturally biased. Since the children were from homes in which Spanish was spoken, it was argued that undue discrimination had occurred because: (1) the children were tested in English and (2) tests had been standardized on Anglo-American children. Therefore, placing the children in classes for the educable mentally retarded was a denial of equal educational opportunity and was discriminatory. Ross, DeYoung, and Cohen (1971, pp. 7-8) noted that it was agreed that the following conditions must be met in future placement decisions:

"1. All children whose primary home language is other than English must be tested in both their primary language and English.

2. Such children must be tested only with tests or sections of tests that do not depend on such things as vocabulary, general information, and other similar unfair verbal questions.

3. Mexican-American and Chinese-American children already in classes for the mentally retarded must be retested in their primary language and must be reevaluated only as to their achievement on nonverbal tests or sections of tests.

4. Each school district is to submit to the state in time for next school year a summary of retesting and reevaluation and a plan listing special supplemental individual training which will be provided to help each child back into the regular school class.

5. State psychologists are to work on norms for a new or revised IQ test to

reflect the abilities of Mexican-Americans so that in the future Mexican-American children will be judged only by how they compare to the performance of their peers, not the population as a whole.

6. Any school district which has a significant disparity between the percentage of Mexican-American students in its regular classes and in its classes for the retarded must submit an explanation setting out the reasons for this disparity."

A related and essentially a follow-up case was *Covarrubias v. San Diego Unified School District* (1971). This case was filed on behalf of 17 minority students (5 Mexican-Americans and 12 blacks) who were enrolled in educable mentally retarded classes in the San Diego School District. The basis of the case also was denial to equal education because of cultural bias of the Wechsler and Stanford-Binet Intelligence Tests relative to placement. The difference in this case was that monetary damages were requested, similar to *Stewart v. Phillips* (1970). The rationale for this request was that the school district deprived the students of equal protection under the law. It was also requested that special education classes be discontinued until testing approaches could be altered to account for cultural influences.

Also, in 1970 the Association of Black Psychologists requested that the San Francisco School Board impose a moratorium on both intelligence and ability testing of black children. The basis of their presentation was the issue of inappropriate norms and content validity of standardized tests used with black children. This issue was brought to the courts in the latter part of 1971 in *Larry P. v. Riles* (1971) and *Ruiz v. State Board of Education* (1971). In these two cases, both class action suits, the contention was that the tests used were discriminatory when used to place and maintain minority children in classes for the mentally retarded. In the *Larry P. v. Riles* (1971) case, which was filed in behalf of six black elementary-aged children in San Francisco, the plaintiffs' argument was that the children were not mentally retarded but were victims of tests that failed to account for their ethnic background. The lawyers requested that the public schools be required to: (1) assess black children with tests that would take into account their cultural background, (2) prevent placement of black children in special classes on the basis of inappropriate tests, (3) direct the San Francisco public schools to reevaluate all black children presently enrolled in classes for the mentally retarded by using nondiscriminatory tests, (4) remove any indication of the plaintiffs ever having been in classes for the mentally retarded, (5) require the schools to ensure that a proportionate distribution of blacks in special education classes for the retarded are in line with black children in the total population, and (6) declare that the assignment of black children on the basis of discriminatory tests be a violation of the Fourteenth Amendment of the U.S. Constitution. In 1972 a preliminary injunction was issued by the presiding judge that stated that black children could not be placed in educable mentally retarded classes on the basis of IQ tests as traditionally administered. The preliminary injunction was supportive of the six points made by the plaintiffs, as indicated above. As of this writing, this case is still undergoing hearings.

In *Ruiz v. State Board of Education* (1971) the plaintiffs' contention was that scores on group IQ tests were recorded in the children's cumulative folders, and this practice not only influenced teachers' attitudes but also influenced counselors relative to academic advising and placement of children in classes for the educable mentally retarded. Further, it was charged that the group IQ tests did not take into account the children's background and that such group tests were inadequate measures of ability. This case was filed on behalf of Mexican-American children.

Probably two of the more important cases in regard to providing free, appropriate education for the handicapped, have been *Pennsylvania Association for Retarded Children (PARC) v. Commonwealth of Pennsylvania* (1972) and *Mills v. Board of Education of the District of Columbia* (1972). In referring to the precedent set in *Brown v. Board of Education* (1954) the courts in both of these cases ruled that when a state has assumed the responsibility to provide public education, it must make it available to all on equal terms. In the PARC decision the courts ruled that Pennsylvania had a constitutional duty to provide a free public education to all retarded children in the Commonwealth. The court reasoned that all mentally retarded children can benefit from educational and training programs and, therefore, there was no rationale for exclusion of such children from the educational system. This case has caused a number of similar class action suits, which collectively led Congress to enact P. L. 93-380, the Education Amendment of 1974.

In *Mills v. Board of Education of the District of Columbia* (1972) the court ruled that the Board of Education has the obligation to provide specialized education that would be of benefit to the child. The court further held that to deny equal education to the mentally retarded is a violation of due process of the law. Therefore, it is illegal to suspend, expel, or reassign children without prior hearing and without a periodic review.

Other educationally related cases that have been landmark court actions include: *Wyatt v. Stickney* (1972), *Jackson v. Indiana* (1972), *Souder v. Brennan* (1973), and *Wyatt v. Aderholt* (1974). In *Wyatt v. Stickney* (1972) it was established that the mentally retarded had the right to treatment in the least restrictive environment. This includes the right to: (1) an individualized treatment program, (2) an environment that is psychologically and physically humane, (3) a qualified and adequate staff, and (4) programs that are offered in the least restrictive way possible. The case that ensured due process relative to commitment was *Jackson v. Indiana* (1972). The court ruled that to commit a person to an agency (for example, a state institution or a mental hospital) until recovered could in effect be a life sentence without recourse to appeal. Therefore, this would be a denial of both equal protection and due process. It was the court's decision that persons who were not competent to stand trial must either be released or be civilly committed. In a related case (*Souder v. Brennan*, 1973) it was ruled that persons in state institutions could not be subjected to involuntary servitude. It was required that work records of patient-laborers in state institutions be kept and that their rights be explained to them.

The preceding review of important court cases is representative of a multitude of legal actions that have been litigated over the past several years. As noted earlier, there are many others that have not been examined since an exhaustive review of such material far exceeds the scope of an introductory text.

FEDERAL LEGISLATION

As a direct result of the court cases reviewed in the preceeding section, the United States Congress has enacted a number of laws that are having, and will continue to have, a tremendous impact on education. In this section the authors review major legislation passed by the federal Congress and review two major public laws that are of particular importance because of educational provisions for the mentally retarded: P. L. 93-380 and P. L. 94-142.

Legislation: 1965 to 1973

The decision to review federal legislation acts beginning in 1965 is not to be interpreted as an indication that previous laws are unimportant. Indeed, laws passed prior to 1965 have had significant effects on educational provisions for the handicapped and in establishing vocational rehabilitation programs. In regard to mental retardation, certainly P. L. 85-926 (1958) and

P. L. 88-164 (1963) were indications of increased federal involvement in these areas. However, it was not until the early 1960's that legislation at the federal level was generated that had profound impact nationally. For the interested reader, a review of past legislation by the federal Congress is provided as an appendix to this chapter.

Federal aid to education became a fact of life beginning in the middle 1960's with P. L. 89-10, Elementary and Secondary Education Act, (ESEA, 1965). Public Law 89-10 represented, for the first time, a commitment by the federal government to improve public school education in the United States. This law included assistance to local public schools in terms of meeting the needs of children designated as "educationally deprived." A companion bill, P. L. 89-313 (1965), amended a section of P. L. 89-10 (Title I) and provided for support of children in state-operated (or supported) schools that served the handicapped but that had not been included, for funding purposes, under the original act.

The Elementary and Secondary Education Act was amended in 1966 (P. L. 89-750). A section of the act (Title VI) made funds available to states in order to expand programs and better meet the needs of handicapped children. Also under this act, a National Advisory Committee on Handicapped Children was instituted to advise the Commissioner of Education. It was during this period that Congress established the Bureau of Education for the Handicapped (BEH) to be the responsible office for administering all education programs for the handicapped.

In 1967 ESEA was again amended (P. L. 90-247) to provide more programs for the handicapped. It was recognized that, despite ESEA, a number of handicapped students were still being excluded. Public Law 90-247 amendments, therefore, specifically designated funds for the handicapped (Title III) and to assist state education agencies expand their programs for the handicapped. In P. L. 90-576, Vocational Education Amendment of 1968, the Congress required that at least 10 percent of each state's vocational education funds coming from the federal government be allocated for the handicapped.

Experimental preschools and early education programs for the handicapped were highlighted in 1968 with the passing of P. L. 90-538, Handicapped Children Early Education Assistance Act. Also, in 1969, P. L. 91-60 was passed, which established a National Center on Educational Media and Materials for the Handicapped.

A direct precursor to P. L. 93-380 and P. L. 94-142 was P. L. 91-230 (1970), specifically, the amendment creating the Education of the Handicapped Act (EHA) (1971). Part B of EHA provided grants to states (and trust territories) to assist their initiation, expansion, and improvement of programs for the education of handicapped children. In addition, P. L. 93-112, Rehabilitation Amendments of 1973, extended and recodified the Vocational Rehabilitation Act first passed in 1943 (P. L. 78-113). In the 1973 amendment (P. L. 93-112), Congress included a section that prohibits discrimination on the basis of mental or physical disability (Section 504). This law effects every federally assisted program or activity in the United States. Major features of this law included: (1) state rehabilitation agencies giving priority to individuals with the most severe handicaps and expanding and improving services to these same individuals, (2) instituting written rehabilitation programs for each client, (3) authorizing states to develop a Consolidated Rehabilitation-Developmental Disabilities Plan, (4) studying the role of sheltered workshops for rehabilitation and employment of the handicapped, (5) studying the coordination of programs for the handicapped, (6) forbidding discrimination against qualified handicapped persons in federally assisted programs, (7) establishing a federal Interagency Committee on Handicapped Employees, (8) providing a client assistance program, and (9) developing an interagency board to assure compliance with the Architectural Barriers Act (1968).

The final regulations were in effect June 3, 1977; and by July 5, 1977, all institutions receiving financial assistance from the Department of Health, Education and Welfare (HEW) were required to return an Assurance of Compliance with this law. During the balance of 1977 all agencies submitted data that ensured: (1) that existing facilities would be accessible to the handicapped, (2) that agencies that receive funds from HEW and that employ 15 or more persons do not discriminate on the basis of handicap, and (3) that any structural changes required in existing facilities would be identified and a plan developed to ensure their completion. During 1978 HEW required that all agencies receiving HEW funds complete a self-evaluation process that would involve handicapped individuals and organizations. Also, all public schools (elementary and secondary) must provide a free, appropriate education for all qualified handicapped students by September 1, 1978. By June 2, 1980, all structural changes in existing facilities to accommodate handicapped persons must be completed.

Legislation: 1974-1978

This section will review those public laws that are having and will continue to have a significant impact on education and our society in the coming years. It will be obvious that the laws have historical references stemming from identified needs generated in developing programs, legislation, and court decisions.

P. L. 93-380, Education Amendments of 1974. Public Law 93-380 extended and amended the Elementary and Secondary Education Act of 1965 and subsequent amendments, the Education of the Handicapped Act, and a number of other education statutes emanating from the federal Congress. This public law encompassed some rather significant implications for the handicapped. Included in this law were provisions for significantly increased funding designed to assist states in meeting "right to education" requirements imposed by courts and legislatures. Also, this legislation required states to develop plans for implementing educational opportunities for all handicapped children, including procedural safeguards (nondiscrimination) in identification, evaluation, and placement of the handicapped and retaining the handicapped in regular classrooms whenever possible. Additionally, P. L. 93-380 included sections on aid to state-supported schools, a provision that allowed handicapped children in an appropriate program to be counted as one and a half children for computation purposes and up to 20 percent of formula monies for adult education to be used for educational programs for institutionalized persons.

P. L. 93-383, Housing and Community Development Act of 1974. In P. L. 93-383 the 93rd Congress revised all major housing legislation that had previously been passed in congressional sessions. Several aspects of this law had impact on the handicapped, including provisions that assume the handicapped, along with the elderly, have financial assistance from the Department of Housing and Urban Development (HUD) in leasing adequate housing and that authorize HUD to make government loans for housing the elderly and the handicapped. As a part of this governmental involvement, HUD was authorized to award grants for special demonstration projects for the purpose of designing housing for persons with special needs.

P. L. 93-156, Rehabilitation Act Amendments of 1974. This legislation authorized the President to call a White House Conference to investigate problems of handicapped citizens and to propose administrative and legislative recommendations for handling these problems.

This law also included several amendments to the Rehabilitation Amendment of 1973 (P. L. 93-112), such as providing a broader definition of "handicapped." The definitional emphasis was changed from that of handicaps related to employment or vocational objectives to one that focused on limitations of functioning level in one or more of an individual's main life activities. Also, vocational rehabilitation clients must be provided the opportunity to be involved in decisions affecting their program, and the requirements for written rehabilitation plans were refined in providing services for each client.

P. L. 93-647, Social Service Amendments of 1974. Public Law 93-647 involved a complete revision of federal and state social services program agreements. The following goals were set forth relative to the handicapped:

1. Economic self-support to prevent, reduce, or eliminate dependency
2. Self-sufficiency to reduce and prevent dependency
3. Prevention of abuse, neglect or exploitation or both children and adults unable to protect themselves
4. Provision of community-based, home-based, or other less intensive and more natural care of individuals to prevent inappropriate institutional care
5. Referral, admission, and other services to institutionalized persons when other types of care are not feasible or appropriate

The law also specified requirements for the states to submit plans to the Department of Health, Education and Welfare that include: fair hearing restrictions of client information, identification of responsible state agencies, and other factors that would ensure proper care of persons being served by vocational rehabilitation programs. A lack of state compliance might result in termination of funding or withholding of a percentage of federal funds.

P. L. 94-142, Education for All Handicapped Children Act (1975). The enactment of P. L. 94-142 represents a culmination of activities by both parents and professionals through legal and legislative means. In many ways it is a continuation of what Dimond (1973) termed "the quiet revolution," that essentially had its beginnings in the civil rights movement of the 1950's.

As is apparent in the preceding sections of this chapter, P. L. 94-142 does not represent a totally new concept relative to requirements or the involvement of the federal government in determining education rights. In fact, this legislation includes much of what was involved in P. L. 93-380, the Education Amendment of 1974, and Section 504 of P. L. 93-112, Rehabilitation Amend-

Fig. 13-1. With the passage of P. L. 94-142, all children are entitled to a free and appropriate education. Schools must find appropriate means to provide transportation for all children. (Photograph by Peter Poulides.)

ment of 1973. This law builds on previous actions and underscores the statement of the National Advisory Committee on the Education of the Handicapped that, "In law and as national policy, education is today recognized as the handicapped person's right" (1976, p. 143).

Public Law 94-142 was signed into law by President Ford (albeit reluctantly) on November 28, 1975, after it received overwhelming Congressional support (Senate vote, 87 to 7, and House of Representative vote, 404 to 7). President Ford's reservations were not with the objectives of the Act, but were about the cost of implementation and additional federal encroachment on state and local domains. As with any such far-reaching legislation, the critical factor is sound and responsible implementation of the law. This will be discussed further in the concluding section of this chapter.

Four major purposes of the Education for All Handicapped Children Act have been identified:

Fig. 13-1, cont'd. For legend see opposite page.

1. *Full education opportunities.* The goal is to provide all handicapped children with a free and appropriate education. Priorities are given to children not being served and those children who are severely handicapped.

2. *Procedural safeguards.* The Act specifies policies and procedures for safeguarding the due process rights of parents and children. Similarly, educational agencies are protected by the same procedural safeguards. These safeguards include:

    a. The right to be fully informed and included in all decisions concerning identification, evaluation, educational planning and programming, and program evaluation

b. The assurance that placement decisions will not be based on biased or discriminatory data

c. The assurance that educational placement will be in the least restrictive setting, that is, with nonhandicapped children whenever and wherever possible

d. The right to have access to and control over all educational records and assurance of the confidentiality of such information, that is, not released without parent permission

e. The right to appeal decisions made by the schools regarding any facet of the child's educational program

f. The right to obtain an independent evaluation of the child

g. The child's right to be represented by surrogate parents for those children who are wards of the state or whose parents or guardians are unknown or not available

3. *Appropriate education.* In order to ensure that each eligible handicapped child receives an appropriate education, the law requires that an individualized educational plan (IEP) be developed. The criteria of eligibility relates to those children who meet the statutory definition and who are in need of special education and/or related services. The definition includes those children who are "mentally retarded, hard of hearing, deaf, orthopedically impaired, other health impaired, speech impaired, visually impaired, severely emotionally disturbed or children with specific learning disabilities who by reason thereof require special education and related service" (P. L. 94-142, 1975, Sec. 4, a, 1). Not all children who are disabled need or require special education, since they can successfully attend school without additional assistance. An IEP would not be required for these children. The Act defines the IEP as follows:

> A written statement for each handicapped child developed in any meeting by a representative of the local educational agency or an intermediate educational unit who shall be qualified to provide, or supervise the provision of, specially designed instruction to meet the unique needs of handicapped children, the teacher, the parents or guardians of such child, and, whenever appropriate, such child, which statement shall include (A) a statement of the present levels of educational performance of such child, (B) a statement of annual goals, including short-term instructional objectives, (C) a statement of the specific educational services to be provided to such child, and the ex-

tent to which such child will be able to participate in regular education programs, (D) the projected date for initiation and anticipated duration of such services, and appropriate objective criteria and evaluation procedures and schedules for determining, on at least an annual basis, whether instructional objectives were being achieved. (P. L. 94-142, 1975, Sec. 4, a, 19.)

This aspect of P. L. 94-142 is obviously one of the most critical components of the Act. It is a plan of action and a statement of goals for the child, developed by the school in conjunction with the parents of the child. It is not a contract, although school districts are legally responsible for ensuring that special educational services are provided. The IEP is not a day-by-day instructional map, but a plan that delineates needed special educational services that are appropriate for the child.

4. *State assistance.* In order to implement P. L. 94-142 the federal government will provide supplementary monies, guidelines, and technical assistance to state and local educational agencies. The purpose of this assistance is to ensure that an equal educational opportunity is provided for all handicapped children needing services.

During the 1977 to 1978 school year, all states in compliance with the law received assistance based on the number of children (ages 3 through 21) receiving services. Additional allocations were possible for service provisions for the preschool handicapped. A ceiling on the number of handicapped children (ages 5 through 17) was set at 12 percent for each state. Federal financial assistance to the states is based on a payment formula that specifies a gradually increasing percentage. The formula was derived on the national average expenditure per child multiplied by the number of handicapped children in each state who receive special education and related services that are publicly augmented. The percentages of financial assistance are as follows: 1978, 5 percent; 1979, 10 percent; 1980, 20 percent; 1981, 30 percent; 1982 and subsequent years, 40 percent. In dollar amounts these percentage figures translate into approximately 300 million dollars in 1977-1978 and to over 3 billion dollars by 1982 of federal contributions toward implementation of the Act. There is, however, an inflationary-deflationary clause that allows for adjustments related to the national per pupil expenditure averages.

This review of P. L. 94-142 is admittedly an overview of the Act. It is not intended to provide all of the specific ramifications and implementation procedures and problems. The interested reader is urged to read the original law and guidelines available through the Bureau of Education for the Handicapped. Also, a number of articles and books have been written that delineate in specific detail all aspects of this Act. For example, *Exceptional Children* has published a series of articles aimed at providing the reader with a necessary orientation.* Also, a number of articles have been written on various facets of the law (Abeson and Zettel, 1977; Ballard and Zettel, 1977; Ballard and Zettel, 1978a; Ballard and Zettel, 1978b). Other available literature on the subject would include articles in *The Exceptional Parent* (such as Saranson and Doris, 1977); edited monographs (such as Schipper, Wilson and Wolf, 1977; Weintraub, Abeson, Ballard, and LaVor, 1976).

Continuing legal and legislature activities

This section does not attempt to provide a comprehensive review of current and proposed legal or legislative activities. To do so would perhaps be misleading and inappropriate because of the changes that can and do occur in legal proceedings and the legislative process and the problems associated with monitoring such activities.

We strongly believe that persons involved in, and concerned about, special education should be knowledgeable about legal and legislative activities. However, knowledge without active commitment and demonstrated activity in the legal and legislative process is an acceptance of the status quo. The court battles and the legislative actions that have been reviewed in this chapter attest to the power that committed individuals can have in influencing the direction of laws for obtaining the rights of the handicapped and for providing better education for all. A debt of gratitude is owed by all handicapped children, their parents, and special educators to those persons and organizations that have led the way thus far in ensuring that the constitution is a viable document and in demonstrating that the "system" can be made more responsive.

For some it is a comfortable position to "cop-out," claiming that the political arena is far too big (or dirty, or self-serving, or unresponsive for them) to become involved in it or to have influence on it; the material reviewed here should effectively counter such a position. For others, it may be comfortable to note that gains have been made in behalf of the handicapped, and there is no reason personally to become active; this review should also point out that

---

*Exceptional Children, Nov. 1976, Issue 3, Vol. 43 was devoted entirely to federal programs for the special child.

even though the "battle" for the rights of the handicapped (and indeed all persons) has been engaged, the "war" is far from over. For perhaps a third group, a comfortable position is to continue to leave such political activity to their colleagues in terms of carrying the banner of human rights; a cursory understanding of history (for example, Nazi Germany) should be ample demonstration that a lack of commitment to civil rights by all persons can be disastrous. In the United States, for example, it was not until 1954 *(Brown v. Board of Education)* that education was established as a *right*. A fourth group may counter and say that such laws as have been enacted are too expensive and that further action may financially be impossible. Such a position has merit in a society of "competing equities." However, this argument must be envisioned not only by a recognition of priorities but also by the evidence that there is a significant return in earning power generated by employment of the mentally retarded (Conley, 1976). Without an emphasis being placed on the rights of *all* citizens, we must ask what kind of society we will have. To the authors and their colleagues, priority must always be given to the human condition.

THE LEGISLATIVE PROCESS

This section is oriented toward providing a description of the legislative process and identifying various publications and organizations that the interested person can refer to for continual updating of the status of court decisions and congressional bills that are in committee or possibly will be forthcoming.

A discourse on all of the ramifications involved in the legislative process would be far too lengthy and probably not very effective in communicating the essence of the process. Therefore, we will attempt to provide a description of the basic structure involved, in initiating legislation through the final approval of a bill. Although the illustration is at the federal level, the same process is typically applicable to local and state governments. The process can be a lengthy, time-consuming activity, but in many respects this can be healthy (as well as destructive) in ensuring that the various viewpoints about legislation are heard, considered, responded to, and thoughtfully evaluated.

1. *Initiating legislation.* New legislation can be introduced by the President (or governor or mayor) or by the Congress. The initial idea, however, can be originated from either within the governmental structure or from the community. Indeed, all new or revised legislation begins with a perceived need.

If the concept is considered to be of sufficient importance, a legislator or the President begins the process of determining (through the legislative staff, executive staff, or appointed task force) its viability. This involves developing considerable documentation in order to establish a purpose, a need, a delineation of implications relative to extant laws, and its constitutionality.

During, and as a part of, this translation of an idea into a proposal, there would be continuing contact and dialogue with "significant others" as to their reactions, concerns, and possible support. These "significant others" would be both from inside and outside of government. Assuming that all the details are worked out, that the federal (or state) agency that would be administratively responsible is identified (for example, Department of Health, Education and Welfare), and that sufficient legislative and community support is generated to ensure its initial acceptance, the proposal can be introduced in either the House or the Senate via the committee having initial responsibility for reviewing proposed bills.

2. Legislative procedures. After being referred to the responsible committee (in either House or Senate or both) the proposed legislation is again studied and researched, and hearings are held involving persons from both inside and outside the governmental structure. Legislative subcommittees may be established to look at various aspects of the proposed bill to ensure a thorough examination of all of its facets. It should be apparent that at any stage of this truncated description, the process can be discontinued because of lack of viability or continued support.

Assuming, again, that all of the hurdles are successfully negotiated through continued support, compromise, or revision of difficult parts, the next step is the introduction of the bill into the House and Senate. The bill is identified in the House by a number signifying its sequential place in the number of bills being introduced in that session (for example, H. R. 128 would indicate it would be the 128th bill to be considered by the House). The Senate would identify the proposed bill by a similar designation (such as S. 72).

At the appropriate time the bill reaches the floor of the House and the Senate (not necessarily at the same time) and again is reconsidered in detail. Amendments can be offered and can be accepted or rejected. The bill can then be returned to committee (either House or Senate or both) where it can languish and die or can be returned with modifications for reconsideration by the Congress.

If the proposed act is passed by the Congress, it is given a designation such as Public Law 94-142 (P. L. 94-142). This indicates that this is the 142nd law passed by the 94th Congress. The next step is the President's accepting it by signing the bill into law, returning it for further consideration by the Congress, or vetoing of the proposed act. A President's veto can be overridden by two-thirds vote of both houses, and the bill can become law.

While this rather simplistic account of the legislative process delineates the major events leading to the enactment of a bill into law, it is recognized that considerable flavor has been lost. For a much more animated accounting of the process the reader is referred to LaVor's (1976) delightful chapter entitled, "Martin Hatches an Egg: A Fairy Tale Describing the Way Laws are Made."*

Suggested references

An attempt to provide a listing of pending legislative and court proceedings would not be feasible given their continual tenuous nature. The reader would be better served by our providing a listing of sources that are geared to a continued updating of legislative and legal events. Suggested, but certainly not all-inclusive, reference sources would include:

1. *Mental Retardation and the Law: A Report on Status of Current Court Cases.* This publication is issued quarterly under the aegis of the U.S. Department of Health, Education and Welfare, Office of the Assistant Secretary for Human Development, President's Committee on Mental Retardation, Washington, D.C. 20201.

2. *Programs for the handicapped.* This publication is now oriented toward providing a cross-section review of governmental activities that relate to the handicapped. Office for Handicapped Individuals, 338 D., Hubert H. Humphrey Building, 200 Independence Ave., S. W., Washington, D.C. 20201.

3. *American Association on Mental Deficiency.* This association has a broad range of professional interests that are oriented toward the mentally retarded, including legislation. Their address is 5101 Wisconsin Avenue, N. W., Washington, D.C. 20016.

4. *Council for Exceptional Children (CEC).* This Council is involved in all

---

*LaVor, M. L. Martin hatches an egg: a fairy tale describing the way laws are made. In F. J. Weintraub, A. Abeson, J. Ballard, M. L. LaVor (Eds.), *Public policy and the education of exceptional children.* Reston, Va.: The Council for Exceptional Children, 1976a, Pp. 259-329. This book also includes six other very germane chapters that are highly recommended.

areas of exceptionality. As such, they have been very influential in legal and legislative activities at the local, state, and federal levels. Contact Policy Implementation, Governmental Relations: Unit, CEC, 1920 Association Drive, Reston, Va. 22091.

5. *The National Association for Retarded Citizens.* This organization is involved in a wide variety of activities related to retarded citizens. The Association's membership is composed of both parents and professionals. Their address is 2709 Avenue E, East, Box 6190, Arlington, Tex.

6. *Federal government.* Copies of all federal laws may be obtained by writing to the House of Representatives, or the Senate, Document Room, U.S. Capitol, Washington, D.C. 20510. Be sure to include the public law number in your written request. Also, copies of all public laws can be found in any law library.

7. *National Center for Law and the Handicapped.* For information concerning legal rights of the handicapped, the Center can be contacted at 1235 North Eddy Street, South Bend, Ind. 46617.

8. *Mental Health Law Project.* Their address is 1220 19th Street, N.W., Suite 300, Washington, D.C. 20036.

9. *Closer Look.* This publication is put out by the Office of Education, Department of Health, Education and Welfare, Washington, D.C. 20201.

10. *American Bar Association (ABA).* Their address for specific information on retardation and the law is Mental Disability Legal Resource Center, 1800 M. Street, N.W., Washington, D.C. 20036.

11. *Educator's Legal Service Institute for Learning.* The address is 171 Saybrook Industrial Park, Old Saybrook, Conn.

Related legal issues

There are a number of issues that impinge on the life of the mentally retarded citizen that have not been directly addressed in the preceeding sections. While there are some obvious areas of overlap, the legal status of mentally retarded persons in a number of areas are unique and historically influenced. Many of the rights that most of us take for granted are still important factors for the mentally retarded.

Housing. As a result of legislation and legal decrees, such as that reviewed previously, there is an increasing regard for independent living arrangements for the mentally retarded as well as for the handicapped in general. The concept of *normalization*, in particular, has stressed both physical and social integration of the retarded, of which housing is one important dimension (Wolfensberger, 1972). The mainstreaming concept implies the least restrictive placement in an educational sense, but the concept has much more far-reaching implications that affect society in general. It has been demonstrated over the years that the retarded person can be successfully integrated into the community (Baller, 1936; Charles, 1958; Miller, 1965; Baller, Charles, and Miller, 1967; Edgerton, 1967, 1976). This is not to say that problems do not exist, but it does indicate that they are not insurmountable with appropriate supplementary services. Despite such evidence, there appears to be a continued reluctance by communities to incorporate mentally retarded individuals in their midst. Examples include nationwide problems in establishing half-way houses, hostels, and other arrangements in residential neighborhoods.

One recent study regarding attitudes is of particular importance. Trippi, Michael, Colao, and Alvarez (1978) conducted a study to investigate attitudes of landlords toward prospective mentally retarded tenants. The results of this study indicated that of 100 persons advertising rentals, 52 stated the apartment was not available after finding the prospective tenant was mentally retarded; 47 attempted to discourage the prospective retarded renter by downgrading the apartment in some way; only one person responded in such a way as to indicate an intent in renting to a retarded person. In conclusion, the authors stated that, "It appears that programs designed to replace public misconceptions and negative attitudes with more accurate information and positive experiences must be placed high on the list of priorities for helping the handicapped" (Trippi, Michael, Colao, and Alvarez, 1978, p. 443).

Marriage. As a result of the eugenics movement at the turn of the century there has been manifested a fear in the United States concerning the marriage of mentally retarded persons (Blanton, 1975, p. 178). The reaction has been excessively responded to by many states in enacting laws prohibiting marriage of mentally retarded persons. Krishef (1972) reported that, in a state by state survey, 24 percent of the states prohibited marriage of retarded persons; 37 percent had no law; 6 percent permitted such marriages; no information was available for 29 percent of the states; and no reply was reported for 4 percent of the states in the survey.

One study of importance in this area was conducted by Floor, Baxter, Rosen, and Zisfein (1975). The authors found that marriage between formerly institutionalized retarded persons can be successful, but there were some difficulties, primarily stemming from lack of preparation (a condition not unknown to the nonretarded population). Their survey found "... that about 50% of the couples studied can sustain a marriage for several years with a reasonable degree of competence, and that children do not, at least in the first few years, serve as an overwhelming burden" (Floor, Baxter, Rosen, and Zisfein, 1975, p. 37). By comparing married versus single persons who had been institutionalized, the authors found that the single person demonstrated a greater number of personal and social problems than those who had married. Related articles tend to show that retarded individuals, although not without problems, can and do respond adequately to marriage, particularly if they are well adjusted (Peck and Stephens, 1965; Katz, 1968; Bowden, Spitz, and Winters, 1971; and Mattinson, 1970). However, Whitcraft and Jones (1974) in their survey study found that of 652 respondents (parents, professionals, and others) 53 percent believed that retarded individuals could not carry out a successful marriage, and 59 percent believed that retarded persons could not be successful in rearing children.

Sterilization. Coupled with the problems of marriage and the influence of the eugenics movement in the early 1900's is the issue of sterilization of the mentally retarded. Krishef (1972) reported that at the time of his survey, 24 states permitted sterilization and only two states prohibited sterilization of retarded persons. The other states had no extant law (two did not reply to the survey). Of those states having laws in effect, all required consent in some form (parent, guardian, the retarded person, court, agency, or a combination of these). In this regard Krishef states that, "the lack of mandatory sterilization procedures seems to reflect a concern for the rights of the individual." (Note, however, the issues related to consent for sterilization discussed in Chapter 14.)

The study conducted by Whitcraft and Jones (1974) of 652 respondents, found that 85.8 percent were in favor of voluntary sterilization of the mentally retarded. Addressing both the marriage and sterilization issues, Whitcraft and Jones (1974) supported the research of Reed and Reed (1965) in recommending the following justification for revision of outdated state statutes with regard to sterilization:

"1. Any possible humane method of prevention of mental retardation must be utilized. Voluntary sterilization could reduce the incidence of retardation by 50% in one generation (Reed and Reed, 1965, p. 7).

2. Obligations and responsibilities of parenthood appear beyond the ca-

pacities of mentally retarded persons and may negate potentially successful adjustments to independent community living.

3. The normal expression of sexuality of retardates could be viewed with equanimity by parents, counselors, and others if the complications inherent in possibilities of procreation were not involved" (Whitcraft and Jones, 1974, p. 33).

That the above is true is certainly subject to much debate, particularly the reliance on the questionable research of Burt (1958, 1967).

Voting. Several articles have addressed the topic of the rights of the retarded with regard to voting (Osborne, 1975; Gerard, 1974; Cleland, Swartz, McGaven and Bell, 1973). The general trend of the research indicates that with adequate preparation and instruction, the retarded can and do responsibly carry out this citizenship right. However, Kokaska (1972) found that most retarded adults do not exercise their voting rights.

A survey of the 50 states and the District of Columbia by Olley and Fremouw (1974) indicated that 20 states have laws that permit the retarded to vote unless they have, by legal action, been judged to be legally incompetent. Twenty-two states have not provided regulations for exercising the voting privilege by retarded persons. Four states did not respond to the survey, and the other five states have informal procedures with certain restrictions.

Licenses. Two areas are of particular importance for the mentally retarded under this heading: driver's licenses and licenses that are required for certain jobs. In our society the inability to drive is a particularly incapacitating problem both for mobility and for employment requiring a driver's license. Under the Department of Transportation there are several divisions that are oriented, at least partially, toward assisting the handicapped. The trend toward road signs that pictorially provide information about road conditions and warnings are of particular importance to nonliterate persons. For example the Office of Driver and Pedestrian Education and Licensing (Department of Transportation) have developed audio techniques to assist functional illiterate groups. The mentally retarded are not prevented from obtaining driver's licenses because of retardation. The criterion is competence to safely drive an automobile, motorcycle, or other type of vehicle.

Obtaining special licenses for particular jobs is again not prohibited because of retardation per se; the criterion is the ability of the person to perform competently. Adequate training and subsequent performance is the key, as it is for everyone.

Contracts. Although there may be initial concern by some banks, loan companies, or other loaning agencies about a retarded person's loan application, this is not the most important criteria. As with anyone else, the important factor is the ability of the person to engage in a contract relative to fulfilling the obligations contained in the agreement. The danger is one of lack of understanding of the contractual agreement, but this is not much different, if at all, from the problems encountered by naive persons. Education concerning the pitfalls of purchasing a car, television, or other large items, is again the key. The emphasis in the past few years on consumer rights serves to highlight the fact that all of us are naive at times and need assistance regarding contractual agreements.

Crime and delinquency. In the late 19th and early 20th century it was generally concluded that crime and related antisocial behaviors were highly correlated with low intelligence. Many of our statutory laws were developed during this period (President's Committee on Mental Retardation, 1977, p. 118). Those individuals judged to be mentally retarded were more often victims of the law than citizens with rights. One of the reasons for this was the application of the law in a rather rigid, inflexible manner, without a differentiation between retarded persons and the rest of the population.

It goes without saying, perhaps, that this is a very complex area involving judgments on competence to stand trial, the relationship between intelligence and criminal behavior, the retarded person's understanding of right and wrong, and a host of other related factors. In a review of research in this area, Menolascino (1974) found that there is no clear-cut relationship between mental retardation and crime. There appears to be a stronger relationship between environment and the incidence of criminal behavior than between retardation and crime (Morris, 1948; Allen, 1970). Related articles in this area that should be reviewed for additional insight include Allen, 1966, 1968a, 1968b, 1968c; Brown and Courtless, 1967, 1971; Marsh, Friel, and Eissler, 1975; Biklen, 1977; President's Committee on Mental Retardation, 1977.

Education. Legal and legislation issues have been discussed both in this chapter and throughout the book. Therefore, this subsection does not attempt a summary, but addresses that aspect of law relating to due process, particularly the concept of administrative hearings. Under P. L. 94-142, there is an administrative process that is oriented toward attempting to provide due process steps to assist children, parents, and school representatives in resolving educational concerns without initially resorting to civil court involvement. The concept employed in the process has been referred to as "impartial hearings."

The procedural aspects of this approach include any placement, evaluation, program changes, education plan development, or exclusion from a program. Either the child, parents (or surrogate parents), or school can request an impartial hearing if the problem cannot be resolved between the school and the parents. The appointment of an impartial hearing officer to hear both sides of the issue with full disclosure of the facts as perceived by both sides is the initial step. The decision of the impartial hearing officer is considered to be binding on all parties. However, appeal procedures to the State Board of Education is an option of either the parents or the school. After review by a panel (usually composed of trained impartial officers) appointed by the state, a recommendation is provided either to sustain, modify, or reject the impartial hearing officer's decision. The panel's recommendation is to the appropriate state body (usually the State Board of Education), who is responsible for making the final administrative decision. Of course, the parents or the school have recourse to civil court if they desire to pursue a more favorable decision.

SUMMARY AND COMMENTS

The material reviewed in this chapter reflects a new era for special education with many far-reaching implications for our society. The involvement of the legal profession and legislative bodies with education is an example of a cross-disciplinary interaction that has been utilized to end discrimination toward the handicapped. It is a well-recorded fact that the treatment of mentally retarded persons has been exclusionary and has denied their rights as citizens. However, the passing of laws and various court actions are but one aspect of the total problem. It is one thing to authorize monies to implement the laws, but it is quite another to appropriate the necessary funds to implement what the laws require. In the same vein, only half the effort has been expended in the passing of laws; the other half is in the field of education, particularly special education, generating the necessary administrative procedures to effectively comply with the law.

The enactment of legislation will not, however, accomplish the task alone. There is an additional influence that must become operative for the laws to be effective and to actually end discrimination against the handicapped.

That influence is the crucial attitudinal changes required of us all in meeting the spirit of the law. This may, in the long run, be the most difficult task of all, but certainly not an impossible one. The attitudinal difficulties are many and varied and are the least controllable variable relative to the spirit of the law. There are several concepts that may need to be rethought by educational professionals. Perhaps, the most important one is a definition of education. Since many children who were previously excluded now have a *right* to education, public schools are going to be faced with additional responsibilities. If education is defined in only an academic sense, which is certainly a core concept, then many handicapped children are not going to "fit" in a restricted educational definition. However, if education can be defined as bringing people to a higher level of functioning than they were before, then both severely-profoundly retarded and gifted children can be conceptually, administratively, and functionally included. A second factor that relates to attitudinal difficulties is the need for all people to learn to look beyond the label and see the *person* behind the demonstrated disability.

The nondiscriminatory aspects of the laws should assist us in accepting and understanding the handicapped. Exclusionary practices have tended to separate and make "different" persons an unknown, and hence, an "anxiety-fear" phenomenon has developed in many cases. This "anxiety-fear" is demonstrated both concretely and abstractly in many reactions of "normal" people to a retarded person. A concrete example of this involves concern about the criminal tendencies, suspected sexual proclivities, and other subjectively implied deviancies about this population. Such commonly held misconceptions have great attitudinal impact in regard to housing. Hopefully, the inclusion of the handicapped into the mainstream of our society will assist in negating these "anxiety-fears." Perhaps by providing early contact, we can promote a gradual understanding of the handicapped as people who have the same needs for love, respect, care, and nurturing as everyone else.

There are additional concerns in implementing the law that are of major importance. It is the opinion of many that the time-lines for compliance are too restrictive. On the one hand, it is argued that after many decades of demonstrated curtailment of citizenship rights of the handicapped, we must move with haste. This point is well taken and certainly backed by evidence. However, as Drew (1978) has pointed out in discussing the "least restrictive placement" dimensions of the law, we may be attempting to implement without full understanding. That is, accepting the concept without fully exploring the complexities of least restrictive placement may actually detract from implementation and have unfavorable long-range implications. Drew identifies three major problem areas that influence the full realization of the concept: (1) its impact on the total educational community, for many regular educators see it as something new being imposed on them; (2) the enthusiastic reaction by others, particularly special educators, that the time is appropriate and everything must be done to implement least restrictive placement; and (3) a "paper compliance" by many school districts that embrace the concept in theory but in which little is actually changed from a program standpoint. It can be argued that all of the "i's" are not dotted or the "t's" crossed and we are in a "showdown" period, which is certainly true. It may also be argued that we cannot wait until everything is in place before proceeding with full *implementation* of, and *compliance* with, the law. There is little debate about the truth of these arguments. At the same time, without major concern for the long-term ramifications, we may be doing more harm than good. This is not to be construed as a negative reaction, but as a concern that we do not promise more than can be delivered. There is a serious possibility that in our use of the concepts:

> . . . we commit serious errors in being so apparently casual concerning these matters (casual as if we *understand*; many are not casual in their exuberance). I believe that we *must* be thoughtful, thoughtful concerning meaning, thoughtful concerning implications, and *preeminently* thoughtful about our outcomes in regard to these concepts. This is the only way, in my opinion, that we can be fully effective in understanding the context in which we operate and hopefully, in the implementation of *the law*. (Drew, 1978, p. 2.)

The concern here is that, without such thoughtfulness, we may be the recipients of a "backlash" that can be counterproductive to what is right, needed, and backed by law. Without proper concern and caution, and by promising too much, handicapped children can be the unfortunate recipients of our conceptual mistakes.

STUDY QUESTIONS

1. There has been a strong relationship between civil rights and the rights of the handicapped. Trace this development, demonstrating the close ties between these two areas, particularly education as a right versus a privilege.
2. The court cases involving special education and the rights of the retarded have been discussed in the chapter. Examine these court cases and identify the major points of litigation involved.

3. Public laws are based on precedents established in prior laws and litigation. Review the court cases and the public laws, and trace the connection between them and P. L. 94-142.

4. There are some concerns about the long-range implications of recently passed public laws. Discuss the problems associated with the implementation of P. L. 94-142 as it relates to educational implications.

REFERENCES

Abeson, A., and Zettel, J. The end of the quiet revolution: the Education for All Handicapped Children Act of 1975. *Exceptional Children,* 1977, **44**(5), 114-128.

Allen, R. Toward an exceptional offenders court. *Mental Retardation,* 1966, **4**(1), 3-7.

Allen, R. Legal norms and practices affecting the mentally deficient. *American Journal of Orthopsychiatry,* 1968a, **38**(4), 635-642.

Allen, R. The mentally retarded offender: unrecognized in court and untreated in prison. *Federal Probation,* 1968b, **32**(3), 22-27.

Allen, R. The law and the mentally retarded. In F. T. Menolascino (Ed.), *Psychiatric approaches to mental retardation.* New York: Basic Books, Inc., 1970.

Arreola v. Board of Education, 160-577, Superior Court, Orange County, Calif., 1968.

Ballard, J., and Zettel, J. Public law 94-142 and section 504: what they say about rights and protections. *Exceptional Children,* 1977, **44**(3), 177-185.

Ballard, J., and Zettel, J. Fiscal arrangements of public law 94-142. *Exceptional Children,* 1978a, **44**(5), 333-337.

Ballard, J., and Zettel, J. The managerial aspects of public law 94-142. *Exceptional Children,* 1978b, **44**(6), 457-462.

Baller, W. R. A study of the present social status of a group of adults who when they were in elementary schools were classified as mentally deficient. *Genetic Psychology Monographs,* 1936, **18**, 165-244.

Baller, W. R., Charles, D. C., and Miller, E. L. Midlife attainment of the mentally retarded: a longitudinal study. *Genetic Psychology Monographs,* 1967, **75**, 235-329.

Beattie v. State Board of Education, City of Antigo, 169 Wis. 231, 172 N. W. 153, (1950).

Biklen, D. Myths, mistreatment and pitfalls: mental retardation and criminal justice. *Mental Retardation,* 1977, **15**(4), 51-57.

Blanton, R. Historical perspectives on classification of mental retardation. In N. Hobbs (Ed.), *Issues in the classification of children,* Vol. 1, San Francisco: Jossey-Bass, Inc., Publishers, 1975.

Bowden, J. Spitz, H., and Winters, J., Jr. Follow-up of one retarded couple's marriage. *Mental Retardation,* 1971, **9**(6), 42-43.

Brown v. Board of Education, 347 U.S. 483, 74 Sup. Ct. 686 (1954).

Brown, B., and Courtless, T. The mentally retarded in penal and correctional institutions. *American Journal of Psychiatry,* 1968, **124**(9), 1164-1170.

Brown, B., and Courtless, T. *The mentally retarded offender.* Rockville, Md.: National Institute of Mental Health, Center for Studies on Crime and Delinquency, 1971.

Brown, B., and Courtless, T. *The mentally retarded offender.* Washington, D.C.: The President's Commission on Law Enforcement and Administration of Justice, 1976.

Burt, C. The evidence for the concept of intelligence. *British Journal of Educational Psychology,* 1955, **25**, 158-177.

Burt, C. The inheritance of mental ability. *American Psychology,* 1958, **13**, 1-15.

Charles, D. C. Ability and accomplishment of persons earlier judged mentally deficient. *Genetic Psychology Monographs,* 1953, **47**, 3-71.

Cleland, C., Swartz, J., McGaven, M. and Bell, K. Voting behavior of institutionalized mentally retarded. *Mental Retardation,* 1973, **11**(4), 31-35.

Conley, R. Mental retardation—an economist's approach. *Mental Retardation,* 1976, **14**(6), 20-24.

Covarrobias v. San Diego Unified School District, 7-394, Tex. Rptr., 1971.

Diana v. State Board of Education, C-70, 37 RFP, N. D. Cal., 1970, 1973.

Dimond, P. The constitutional right to education: the quiet revolution. *The Hastings Law Journal,* 1973, **24**, 1087-1127.

Drew, C. J., Hardman, M. L., and Bluhm, H. P. *Mental retardation: social and educational perspectives*, St. Louis: The C. V. Mosby Co., 1977.

Drew, C. J. Least restrictive alternative: a concept in search of definition. Paper presented at the 102nd annual convention, American Association of Mental Deficiency, Denver, Colo., May, 1978.

Edgerton, R. B. *The cloak of competence: stigma in the lives of the mentally retarded*. Berkeley, Calif.: University of California Press, 1967.

Edgerton, R. B., and Bercovici, S. M. The cloak of competence: years later. *American Journal of Mental Deficiency*, 1976, **80**, 485-497.

Floor, L., Baxter, D., Rosen, M., and Zisfein, L. A survey of marriages among previously institutionalized retardates. *Mental Retardation*, 1975, **13**(2), 33-37.

Fogg v. Board of Education, 82 Atl. 173, 1912.

Gerard, E. O. Exercise of voting rights by the retarded. *Mental Retardation*, 1974, **12**(2), 45-47.

Gilhool, T. K. Education: an inalienable right. In F. J. Weintaub, A. Abeson, J. Ballard, and M. L. LaVor (Eds.), *Public policy and the education of exceptional children*. Reston, Va.: The Council for Exceptional Children, 1976.

Hinkle, V. R. Criminal responsibility of the mentally retarded. *American Journal of Mental Deficiency*, 1961, **65**(4), 434-439.

Hobson v. Hansen, 269 F. Supp. 401 (D.D.C. 1967).

Jackson v. Indiana, 406 U.S. 715, 1972.

Katz, E. *The retarded adult in the community*. Springfield, Ill.: Charles C Thomas, Publisher, 1968.

Kokaska, C. J. Voter participation of the EMR: a review of the literature. *Mental Retardation*, 1972, **10**(5), 6-8.

Krishef, C. H. State laws on marriage and sterilization of the mentally retarded. *Mental Retardation*, 1972, **10**(3), 36-38.

Larry P. v. Riles. C-71-2270 U.S.C., 343 F. Supp. 1306 (N. D. Cal. 1972).

LaVor, M. L. Federal legislation for exceptional persons. In F. J. Weintraub, A. Abeson, J. Ballard, and M. L. LaVor (Eds.), *Public policy and the education of exceptional children*. Reston, Va.: The Council for Exceptional Children, 1976a.

LaVor, M. L. Martin hatches an egg: a fairy tale describing the way laws are made. In F. J. Weintraub, A. Abeson, J. Ballard, and M. L.

LaVor (Eds.), *Public policy and the education of exceptional children*, Reston, Va.: The Council for Exceptional Children, 1976a.

Marsh, R. L., Friel, C. M., and Eissler, V. The adult m. r. in the criminal justice system. *Mental Retardation*, 1975, **13**, 21-25.

Mattinson, J. *Marriage and mental handicaps*. Pittsburgh: University of Pittsburgh Press, 1970.

Menolascino, F. J. The mentally retarded offender. *Mental Retardation*, 1974, **12**(1), 7-11.

Mental retardation and the law: a report on status of current court cases. Washington, D.C.: U.S. Department of Health, Education and Welfare, President's Committee on Mental Retardation.

Miller, E. L. Ability and social adjustment at midlife of persons earlier judged mentally deficient. *Genetic Psychology Monographs*, 1965, **72**, 139-198.

Mills v. Board of Education of the District of Columbia, 348 F. Supp. 866 (D.D.C. 1972).

Morris, J. V. Delinquent defectives—a group study. *American Journal of Mental Deficiency*, 1948, **52**(4), 345-369.

National Advisory Committee on the Education of the Handicapped. *The unfinished revolution: education of the handicapped*. Washington, D.C.: U.S. Government Printing Office, 1976.

Olley, G., and Fremouw, W. The voting rights of the mentally retarded: a survey of state laws. *Mental Retardation*, 1974, **12**(1), 14-16.

Osborne, A. G., Jr. Voting practices of the mentally retarded. *Mental Retardation*, 1975, **12**(3), 15-17.

Peck, J. R., and Stephens, W. B. Marriage of young adult male retardates. *American Journal of Mental Deficiency*, 1965, **69**(6), 818-827.

Pennsylvania Association for Retarded Children v. Commonwealth of Pennsylvania. 334 F. Supp. 1257 (E.D. Pa. 1971).

Petty v. Petty, 41 N.W. 2, 672 (1950).

President's Committee on Mental Retardation. *Mental Retardation: past and present*. Washington, D.C.: U.S. Government Printing Office, 1977.

Reed, S. C., and Reed, E. *Mental retardation: a family study*. Philadelphia: W. B. Saunders Co., 1965.

Roberts v. City of Boston, 59 Mass. (5 Cushing) 198 (1849).

Ross, S. L., Jr., DeYoung, H. G., and Cohen, J. S.

Confrontation: special education placement and the law. *Exceptional Children*, 1971, **38,** 5-12.

Ruiz v. State Board of Education, Calif., 1971.

Saranson, S., and Doris, J. The Education for All Handicapped Children Act (Public Law 94-142): what does it say. *The Exceptional Parent*, 1977, **7**(4), 6-8.

Schipper, W. V., Wilson, W. C., and Wolf, J. M. Public education for the handicapped. In E. Sontag (Ed.), *Educational programming for the severely and profoundly handicapped*. Reston, Va.: The Council for Exceptional Children, Division on Mental Retardation, 1977, Pp. 6-13.

Smuck v. Hobson, 408 F.2d. 175 (1969).

Souder v. Brennan, 367 F. Supp. 808 (D.D.C. 1973).

Spangler v. Pasadena Board of Education, 311 F. Supp. 501 (C.D. Cal. 1970).

Stewart v. Phillips. 70-1199-F. (D. Mass. 1971).

Trippi, J., Michael, R., Colao, A., and Alvarez, A. Housing discrimination toward mentally retarded persons. *Exceptional Children*, 1978, **44,** 430-433.

Weintraub, F. J., Abeson, A., Ballard, J., and LaVor, M. L. (Eds.), *Public policy and the education of exceptional children*. Reston, Va.: The Council for Exceptional Children, 1976.

Whitcraft, C. J., and Jones, J. P. A survey of attitudes about sterilization of retardates. *Mental Retardation*, 1974, **12**(1), 30-33.

Williams v. Board of Education, 79 Kan. 202., 99 Pac. 216, 22 L.R.A. (N.S.) 584 (1908).

Wolfensberger, W. *The principle of normalization in human services*. Toronto: National Institute on Mental Retardation, 1972.

Wyatt v. Aderholt, 368 F. Supp. 1382, 1383 (M.D. Ala. 1974).

Wyatt v. Stickney, 344 F. Supp. 387, 344 F. Supp. 373 (M.D. Ala. 1972).

ANNOTATED BIBLIOGRAPHY

Kindred, M., Cohen, J., Penrod, D., and Shafer, T. (Eds.) *The mentally retarded citizen and the law*. New York: The Free Press, 1976.

This volume, sponsored by the President's Committee on Mental Retardation, is a comprehensive review of the legal status of the mentally retarded. The editors have included the work of over 65 lawyers, educators, and social scientists. Four sections are included: (1) personal and civil rights of the mentally retarded, (2) rights of mentally retarded citizens within community systems, (3) institutionalization and the rights of mentally retarded citizens, and (4) the mentally retarded citizens and the criminal correctional process.

President's Committee on Employment of the Handicapped. *A handbook on the legal rights of handicapped people*. Washington, D.C.: U.S. Government Printing Office, 1977.

A variety of topics (civil rights, housing, education, insurance, and others) are attended to in this pamphlet. The Committee responded to each topic by providing brief statements of the law followed by the national or state (Virginia and Maryland) law.

President's Committee on Mental Retardation. *Mental retardation: past and present*. Washington, D.C.: U.S. Government Printing Office, 1977.

A historical through present-day report of national involvement concerning mental retardation is presented. All aspects of the problem at both state and federal levels are addressed including: inheritance of a hundred years, the growth of federal programs, action in the states, the role of higher education, the economics of mental retardation, and others. This compilation is the tenth annual report of the President's Committee.

Weintraub, F. J., Abeson, A., Ballard, J., and LaVor, M. L. *Public policy and the education of exceptional children*. Reston, Va.: The Council for Exceptional Children, 1976.

This book is a highly recommended resource for anyone desiring in-depth material related to legislative legal issues related to special education.

APPENDIX

MAJOR FEDERAL LEGISLATION FOR EDUCATION OF THE HANDICAPPED: 1827-1975

The following listing of major federal legislation affecting the handicapped is adapted from LaVor (1976, pp. 103-111). It was thought that this material would be of particular importance to the reader in associating titles with public law numbers and as a historical overview of congressional actions.

Public law	Title	Enacted
19 8	An Act to provide for the location of the two townships of land reserved for a seminary of learning in the territory of Florida, and to complete the location of the grant to the Deaf and Dumb Asylum of Kentucky	1/29/1827
29-11	An Act to extend the time for selling the lands granted to the Kentucky Asylum for teaching the deaf and dumb	2/18/1847
33-4	An Act to establish in the District of Columbia a Government Hospital for the insane	3/3/1855
34-5	An Act to establish the Columbian Institution for the deaf and dumb	2/16/1857
34-46	An Act to incorporate the Columbian Institution for the Instruction of the Deaf and Dumb and the Blind	2/16/1857
35-59	An Act to amend the "Act to incorporate the Columbian Institution for the Instruction of the Deaf and the Dumb and the Blind"	5/29/1858
35-154	An Act making appropriations for sundry civil expenses of the government (first appropriations bill)	6/12/1858
38-52	An Act to authorize the Columbian Institution for the Deaf and Dumb and Blind to confer degrees	4/8/1864
38-210	An Act making appropriations for sundry civil expenses of the government for the year ending June 30, 1865 and for other purposes	7/2/1864
38-50	An Act to amend an Act entitled, "An Act to incorporate the Columbia Institution for the Instruction of the Deaf and the Dumb and the Blind"	2/23/1865
39-167	An Act making appropriations for sundry civil expenses of the government for the year ending June 30, 1868 and for other purposes	3/2/1867
39-169	An Act to amend existing laws relating to Internal Revenue and for other purposes	3/2/1867
45-186	An Act to promote the education of the blind	3/3/1879
55-HR4304	An Act regulating postage on letters written by the blind	7/7/1898
58-171	An Act to promote the circulation of reading matter among the blind	5/27/1904
59-288	An Act to modify the requirements of the Act entitled "An Act to promote the education of the blind," approved 3/3/1879	6/25/1906
62-336	An Act making appropriations for the services of the Post Office Department for the fiscal year ending June 30, 1913, and for other purposes	8/24/1912
65-178	Vocational Rehabilitation Act (for discharged military personnel)	6/27/1918
66-24	An Act providing additional aid for the American Printing House for the Blind	8/4/1919

Public law	Title	Enacted
66-236	An Act to provide for promotion of vocational rehabilitation of persons disabled in industry or otherwise and their return to civil employment	6/2/1920
66-384	An Act providing additional hospital facilities for patients of the Bureau of War Risk Insurance and of the Federal Board for Vocational Education, Division of Rehabilitation, and for other purposes	3/4/1921
67-47	An Act to establish a Veterans' Bureau and to improve the facilities and services of such bureau and further to amend and modify the War Risk Insurance Act	8/9/1921
67-370	An Act amending Subdivision 5 of Section 302 of the War Risk Insurance Act	12/18/1922
68-197	An Act to authorize an appropriation to enable the Director of the United States Veterans Bureau to provide additional hospital facilities	6/5/1924
68-200	An Act to amend sections 1, 3, and 6 of an act entitled, "An Act to provide for the promotion of vocational rehabilitation of persons disabled in industry or otherwise and their return to civil employment"	6/5/1924
68-218	An Act to incorporate the United States Blind Veterans of the World War	
68-242	World War Veterans' Act of 1924	6/7/1924
69-584	An Act to amend the Act providing additional aid for the American Printing House for the Blind	2/8/1927
69-655	An Act to amend paragraph (1) of section 22 of the Interstate Commerce Act by providing for the carrying of a blind person, with a guide, for one fare	2/26/1927
71-317	An Act to amend an Act entitled, "An Act to provide for the promotion of vocational rehabilitation of persons disabled in industry or otherwise and their return to civil employment"	6/9/1930
71-787	An Act to provide books for the adult blind	3/3/1931
72-222	To amend an Act entitled "An Act to provide for the promotion of vocational rehabilitation of persons disabled in industry or otherwise and their return to civil employment," approved June 2, 1920, as amended	6/30/1932
72-439	To amend section 1 of the Act entitled, "An Act to provide books for the adult blind," approved 3/3/31	3/4/1933
73-214	To amend the Act entitled, "An Act to promote the circulation of reading matter among the blind," approved April 27, 1904, and Acts supplemental thereto	5/9/1934
74-139	To authorize an increase in the appropriation for books for the adult blind	6/14/1935
74-271	Social Security Act	8/14/1935
74-732	To authorize the operation of stands in federal buildings by blind persons, to enlarge the economic opportunities of the blind, and for other purposes	6/20/1936

Public law	Title	Enacted
75-37	To provide special rates of postage on matter for the blind	4/15/1937
75-47	To authorize an increase in the annual appropriation for books for the adult blind	4/23/1937
75-184	To amend the Interstate Commerce Act (seeing eye dogs)	7/5/1937
75-339	To amend the Act approved August 4, 1919, as amended, providing additional aid for the American Printing House for the Blind	8/23/1937
75-412	United States Housing Act of 1937	9/1/1937
75-523	To amend the Acts for promoting the circulation of reading matter among the blind	5/16/1938
75-739	To create a Committee on Purchases of Blind-made products and other purposes—Wagner-O'Day Act of 1938	6/25/1938
76-118	To amend the Act entitled, "An Act to provide books for the adult blind," approved 3/3/31	6/7/1939
76-379	Social Security Act Amendments of 1939	8/10/1939
76-562	To amend the Act entitled "An Act to provide books for the adult blind" approved 3/3/31	6/6/1940
77-270	To further amend the Acts for promoting the circulation of reading matter among the blind	10/14/1941
77-330	To permit seeing eye dogs to enter government buildings when accompanied by their blind masters, and for other purposes	12/10/1941
77-726	To amend section 1 of the Act entitled, "An Act to provide books for the adult blind," approved 3/3/31, as amended	10/1/1942
78-16	To amend Title 1 of Public Law Number 2, 73rd Congress, March 30, 1933, and the Veterans Regulation to provide for rehabilitation of disabled veterans, and for other purposes	3/24/1943
78-113	Vocational Rehabilitation Act Amendments of 1943	7/6/1943
78-235	To provide revenue, and for other purposes or "The Revenue Act of 1943"	2/25/1944
78-338	To amend the Act entitled, "An Act to provide books for the adult blind"	6/13/1944
78-346	Servicemen's Readjustment Act	6/22/1944
79-661	To amend the Act entitled, "An Act to provide books for the adult blind	8/8/1946
79-719	Social Security Act Amendments of 1946	8/10/1946
80-471	Revenue Act of 1948	4/2/1948
80-617	To amend the Civil Service Act to remove certain discrimination with respect to the appointment of persons having any physical handicap to positions in the classified civil service	6/10/1948
80-642	To maintain status quo in respect of certain employment taxes and social security benefits pending action by Congress on extended social security coverage	6/14/1948

Public law	Title	Enacted
81-162	Authorizing an appropriation for the work on the President's Committee on National Employ the Physically Handicapped Week	7/11/1949
81-290	To permit the sending of braille writers to or from the blind at the same rates as provided for their transportation for repair purposes	9/7/1949
81-734	Social Security Act Amendments of 1950	8/28/1950
82-308	To restore to seventy pounds and one hundred inches in girth and length combined the maximum weight and size limitations for appliances or parts thereof, for the blind, sent through the mails	4/9/1952
82-354	To amend the Act approved 8/4/1919 as amended, providing additional aid for the American Printing House for the Blind	5/22/1952
82-446	To amend the Act entitled, "An Act to provide books for the adult blind"	7/3/1952
82-590	Social Security Act Amendments of 1952	7/18/1952
83-420	To change the Columbian Institution to Gallaudet College, define its corporate powers, and provide for its organization and administration and other purposes	6/18/1954
83-531	To authorize cooperative research in education	7/26/1954
83-565	Vocational Rehabilitation Amendments of 1954	8/3/1954
83-761	Social Security Amendments of 1954	9/1/1954
84-825	To amend the Interstate Commerce Act in order to authorize common carriers and such attendants at the usual fare charged for one person	7/27/1956
84-880	Social Security Amendments of 1956	8/1/1956
84-922	To amend the Act to promote the education of the blind, approved March 3, 1879, as amended, so as to authorize wider distribution of books and other special instructional material for the blind, to increase the appropriations authorized for this purpose, and for other purposes	8/2/1956
85-308	To amend an Act entitled, "An Act to provide books for the adult blind"	9/7/1957
85-840	Social Security Amendments of 1958	8/28/1958
85-864	National Defense Education Act of 1958	9/2/1958
85-905	To provide in the Department of HEW a loan service of captioned films for the Deaf	9/2/1958
85-926	To encourage expansion of teaching in the education of mentally retarded children through grants to institutions of higher learning and to state educational agencies	9/6/1958
86-372	Housing Act of 1959	9/23/1959
86-778	Social Security Amendments of 1960	9/13/1960

Public law	Title	Enacted
87-276	To make available to children who are handicapped by deafness the specially trained teachers of the deaf needed to develop their abilities and to make available in individuals suffering speech and hearing impairments the specially trained speech pathologists and audiologists needed to help them overcome their handicaps	9/22/1961
87-294	To amend the Act to promote the education of the blind, approved March 3, 1879, as amended, so as to authorize wider distribution of books and other special instruction materials for the blind, and to increase the appropriations authorized for this purpose, and to otherwise improve such Act	9/22/1961
87-543	Public Welfare Amendments of 1962	7/25/1962
87-614	To authorize the employment without compensation from the Government of readers for blind Government employees, and for other purposes	8/29/1962
87-715	To provide for the production and distribution of educational and training films for use by deaf persons, and for other purposes	9/28/1962
87-765	To establish in the Library of Congress a library of musical scores and other instructional materials to further educational, vocational, and cultural opportunities in the field of music for blind persons	10/9/1962
87-838	To amend the Public Health Service Act to provide for the establishment of an Institute of Child Health and Human Development	10/17/1962
88-156	Social Security Act Amendments of 1963	10/24/1963
88-164	Mental Retardation Facilities and Community Mental Health Centers Construction Act of 1963	10/31/1963
88-242	To authorize the President to issue annually a proclamation designating the first week in March of each year as "Save Your Vision Week"	12/30/1963
88-443	Hospital and Medical Facilities Amendments of 1964	8/18/1964
88-628	To authorize the President to proclaim October 15 of each year as "White Cane Safety Day"	10/6/1964
88-641	Social Security Amendments of 1964	10/13/1964
88-650	Social Security Amendments of 1964	10/13/1964
89-10	Elementary and Secondary Education Act of 1965, as amended	4/11/1965
89-36	National Technical Institute for the Deaf Act	6/8/1965
89-97	Social Security Amendments of 1965	7/30/1965
89-105	Mental Retardation Facilities and Community Mental Health Centers Construction Act of 1965	8/4/1965
89-109	Community Health Service Extension Amendments of 1965	8/5/1965

Public law	Title	Enacted
89-239	Heart Disease, Cancer and Stroke Amendments of 1965	10/6/1965
89-258	Captioned Films for the Deaf Act	10/19/1965
89-313	Federal Assistance to State Operated and Supported Schools for the Handicapped	11/1/1965
89-333	Vocational Rehabilitation Act Amendments of 1966	11/8/1965
89-522	An Act to provide books for the adult blind	6/30/1966
89-511	Library Services and Construction Act Amendments of 1966	7/19/1966
89-601	Fair Labor Standards Amendments of 1966	9/23/1966
89-614	Military Medical Benefits Amendments of 1966	9/30/1966
89-694	Model Secondary School for the Deaf Act	10/15/1966
89-749	Comprehensive Health Planning and Public Health Services Amendments of 1966, "Partnership for Health"	11/3/1966
89-750	Elementary and Secondary Education Act Amendments of 1966	11/3/1966
89-752	Higher Education Act Amendments of 1966	11/3/1966
90-31	Mental Health Amendments of 1967	6/24/1967
90-35	To amend Title V of the Higher Education Act and re-designate it as the Educational Professions Development Act	6/29/1967
90-99	Vocational Rehabilitation Amendments of 1967	10/3/1967
90-154	To amend the Library Services and Construction Act	11/24/1967
90-170	Mental Retardation Amendments of 1967	12/4/1967
90-174	Partnership for Health Amendments of 1967	12/5/1967
90-206	Postal Revenue and Federal Act of 1967	12/16/1967
90-247	Elementary and Secondary Education Amendments of 1967	1/2/1968
90-248	Social Security Amendments of 1967	1/2/1968
90-391	Vocational Rehabilitation Amendments of 1968	7/7/1968
90-415	To increase size of the Board of Directors of Gallaudet College	7/23/1968
90-458	To establish a register of blind persons in the District of Columbia, to provide for the mandatory reporting of information concerning such persons and for other purposes	8/3/1968
90-480	Elimination of Architectural Barriers to Physically Handicapped	8/12/1968
90-489	Establishment of National Eye Institute	8/16/1968
90-538	Handicapped Children's Early Education Assistance Act	9/30/1968
90-574	Health Services and Facilities Amendments of 1968	10/15/1968
90-575	Higher Education Amendments of 1968	10/16/1968
90-576	Vocational Education Amendments of 1968	10/16/1968
91-17	To authorize the President to issue a proclamation designating the first week in June of 1969 as "Helen Keller Memorial Week"	5/28/1969

Public law	Title	Enacted
91-61	To provide for a National Center on Educational Media and Materials for the Handicapped and for other purposes	8/20/1969
91-69	Older Americans Act Amendments of 1969	9/17/1969
91-172	Tax Reform Act of 1969	12/30/1969
91-205	To insure that certain federally constructed facilities be constructed so as to be accessible to the physically handicapped	3/5/1970
91-209	To extend the Migrant Health Act for three years, and provide increased authorization therefor	3/12/1970
91-211	To provide grants for construction of community mental health centers	3/13/1970
91-230	To extend programs of assistance for elementary and secondary education	4/13/1970
91-375	Postal Reorganization Act	8/12/1970
91-442	To broaden National Employ the Handicapped Week to apply to all handicapped workers	10/8/1970
91-453	To provide long term financing for expanded urban mass transportation programs	10/15/1970
91-490	To revise certain criteria for handling mentally retarded persons in the Forest Haven Institution in the District of Columbia	10/22/1970
91-517	Developmental Disabilities Services and Facilities Construction Amendments of 1970	10/30/1970
91-572	To improve family planning services and population research activities of the federal government	12/24/1970
91-587	To authorize Gallaudet College to maintain and operate the Kendell School as a demonstration elementary school for the deaf	12/24/1970
91-596	Occupational Safety and Health Act of 1970	12/29/1970
91-609	Housing and Urban Development Act of 1970	12/31/70
91-610	To extend for one year the authorization for various programs under the Vocational Rehabilitation Act	12/31/1970
91-695	To provide assistance in developing and administering lead-based paint elimination programs	1/13/1971
92-28	Wagner-O'Day Amendments	6/23/1971
92-58	Military Medical Benefits Amendments	7/29/1971
92-178	Revenue Act of 1971	12/10/1971
92-223	Intermediate Care Amendments of 1971	12/28/1971
92-316	Free or reduced-rate transportation for the blind	6/22/1972
92-318	Education Amendments of 1972	6/23/1972
92-336	Social Security Benefit Increase	7/1/1972
92-345	Maternal and Child Health Amendments	7/10/1972
92-424	Economic Opportunity Amendments of 1972	9/19/1972
92-515	Rights of the blind and other physically handicapped in the District of Columbia	10/21/1972

Public law	Title	Enacted
92-563	National Advisory Commission on Multiple Sclerosis Act	10/25/1972
92-595	Small Business Investment Act Amendments of 1972	10/27/1972
92-603	Social Security Amendments of 1972	10/30/1972
93-29	Older Americans Comprehensive Services Amendments of 1973	5/3/1973
93-42	National Autistic Children's Week	6/15/1973
93-45	Health Programs Extension Act of 1973	6/18/1973
93-53	Maternal and Child Health Amendments	7/1/1973
93-66	Renegotiation Act Amendments	7/9/1973
93-76	Committee for Purchase of Products and Services of the Blind and Other Handicapped	7/30/1973
93-87	Federal Aid Highway Act of 1973	8/13/1973
93-112	Rehabilitation Amendments of 1973	9/26/1973
93-113	Domestic Volunteer Services Act of 1973	10/1/1973
93-146	Amtrak Improvement Act of 1973	11/3/1973
93-151	Lead-based Paint Poisoning Prevention Amendments	11/9/1973
93-233	Social Security Amendments of 1973	12/31/1973
93-256	Supplemental Security Income Benefits	3/28/1974
93-269	General Education Amendments	4/18/1974
93-326	National School Lunch and Child Nutrition Act of 1974	6/30/1974
93-335	Extend Food Stamp Eligibility to SSI Recipients	7/8/1974
93-348	National Research Act	7/12/1974
93-358	Wagner-O'Day Act Amendments	7/25/1974
93-368	Foreign Equipment Import Duty (Social Security rider)	8/7/1974
93-380	Education Amendments of 1974	8/21/1974
93-383	Housing and Community Development Act of 1974	8/22/1974
93-415	Juvenile Delinquency and Prevention Act of 1974	9/7/1974
93-484	Import Duty on Horses (Social Security rider)	10/26/1974
93-503	National Mass Transportation Assistance Act of 1974	11/26/1974
93-516	Rehabilitation Act Amendments of 1974	12/7/1974
93-561	March of Dimes Month	12/30/1974
93-640	National Arthritis Act of 1974	1/4/1975
93-641	National Health Planning and Resources Development Act of 1974	1/4/1975
93-643	Federal-Aid Highway Amendments of 1974	1/4/1975
93-644	Community Services Act of 1974	1/4/1975
93-647	Social Services Amendments of 1974	1/4/1975
94-44	To extend SSI to continue food stamp eligibility for recipients	6/28/1975
94-142	Education for All Handicapped Children Act	11/28/1975

CHAPTER 14

Social and ethical issues

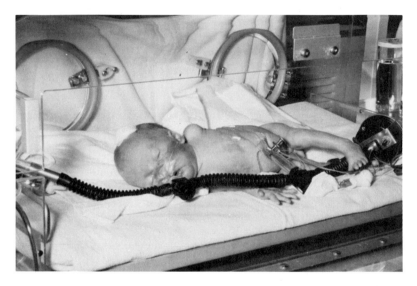

(From Chinn, P. L. *Child health maintenance: concepts in family centered care.* (2nd ed.) St. Louis: The C. V. Mosby Co., 1979.)

One fact that has become increasingly obvious as we have proceeded through this volume is that mental retardation is an extremely complex phenomenon. Although this has been explicitly stated in earlier chapters, the stark emphasis provided by the study of retardation presents a more dramatic commentary than written language can ever transmit. There are few if any simple answers; there are varying philosophies and often conflicting viewpoints and value systems. It seems only appropriate that the concluding chapter of this book examine what is perhaps the most fluid of all areas: social and ethical issues related to mental retardation.

In some ways, social issues and considerations are central to the mental retardation problem and have been throughout history. As noted in earlier chapters, attitudes toward and the treatment of retarded individuals have always reflected the prevailing philosophies concerning human existence and human worth. Such philosophies are the source of what we know as ethics, the rules that guide the ". . . determination of what is good or bad" (Tymchuk, 1976, p. 44).

Many of the issues that are discussed in this chapter have recurred in the philosophies and prevailing actions of societies throughout human history. During certain periods they have represented routine practices that were unquestioned since they were accepted as being in harmony with the best interests of the human species and civilized society. Modern civilization has, however, publicly abhorred earlier attitudes and practices, such as euthanasia, or mercy killing, and has decried its perpetrators as inhumane and barbaric. At the same time that this public representation has been put forth, many of those actions that have been so loudly denounced have been quietly continued. Only recently have public statements and examinations of these practices been forthcoming, breaking what Duff and Campbell termed a "public and professional silence on a major social taboo" (1973, p. 894). Although these authors were specifically discussing the withholding of care from defective infants, others have described a variety of treatment conditions and practices that are equally dramatic (Blatt and Kaplan, 1966; Horan and Mall, 1977). As public awareness has been heightened, many have been shocked, not only by the actions and conditions that exist but also by the realization that we are in some sense a hypocritical society. It is now our task to progress from the stage of being shocked to one of serious examination of our fundamental values concerning what is right and important in this society and to determine the most effective means to achieve the desired outcomes. Additionally, we must balance these considerations with our ability and willingness to pay. This chapter attempts to initiate that process of examination.

INTRODUCTION

Consideration of social and ethical issues in relation to any topic requires some exploration of the philosophic foundations of society. Our day-to-day activities seldom include any conscious consideration of philosophy and in many quarters it has become fashionable to vocalize indifference or even unfavorable attitudes about its place in contemporary civilization. Regardless of how we view philosophy, each of us operates on the basis of some set of guiding principles, whether explicit or implicit, that form a general code of ethics governing our behavior. Further, any code of ethics that is reasonably consistent, is derived from a philosophy concerning what life is about.

Tymchuk (1976) summarizes two philosophic positions that he views as important in an examination of social and ethical issues related to mental retardation. These philosophies—utilitarianism and formalism—represent extreme polarities in terms of viewpoints regarding the rights and worth of individuals in society. Utilitarianism holds that an individual has "only those rights granted him by the larger society," whereas formalism maintains that it is the individual ". . . with basic rights which can be neither abrogated nor curtailed by society and the individual's rights are superordinate to those of society" (Tymchuk, 1976, p. 45). Neither of these two extremes is workable in pure form in a complex society such as ours. Exclusive subscription to a pure form of utilitarianism leads to the group with the greatest power tending to continue in power and often expanding their position by substantially limiting the rights of those with less power. Pure formalism also presents a dilemma in that as the rights of some are made more distinct, this very action tends to result in the reduction of the rights of others. A serious problem that must be confronted and debated involves the determination of where on the continuum between these two extremes we can operate comfortably. This is an enormously difficult question but one that must be seriously addressed if we are to ensure human rights in a reasonable fashion.

One of the topics to be discussed in this chapter has previously been mentioned, that being euthanasia. Euthanasia is defined in *Webster's New Collegiate Dictionary* as "the act or practice of killing individuals that are hopelessly sick or injured for reasons of mercy." This topic, although not unknown to most people, was recently brought dramatically into the public eye by the case of Karen Ann Quinlan, a 22-year-old New Jersey woman whose life was being maintained by means of an artificial support system. For nearly a full year from the time of her admission to the hospital in April 1975, Karen remained in a coma-like state with her life being apparently sustained by a respirator and tubal feeding. At the time of the New Jersey Supreme Court decision in March 1976, it was the opinion of all individuals involved that there were no medical procedures available that would facilitate Karen's recovery and that termination of artificial support would result in almost immediate death. This case entered the courts because of a disagreement between Karen's family and the attending medical personnel. Her parents, after much agony and soul searching, had requested that the life support system be terminated. The physicians involved refused to take this action. To make a complex case even more difficult, after cessation of life support, Karen Quinlan continued to survive, and, in fact, was moved to a nursing home.

The frequency with which treatment is withheld and patients are allowed to die is not well documented on a general basis, although some investigations have been conducted with specific populations (Duff and Campbell, 1973). It is, however, a commonly known fact among hospital personnel that decisions "not to resuscitate" occur on a regular basis. The practice is sufficiently common that most hospitals use some type of "Code 90" sticker that indicates that the patient is to receive no intensive care or resuscitation (Fletcher, 1973).

The general topic of euthanasia is certainly one that warrants a great deal of attention. More directly related to our present area of inquiry, however, is the practice of euthanasia with mentally retarded individuals. As later discussions will indicate, attention to this issue (at least in terms of published material) has focused most heavily on euthanasia with newborns who are or appear to be retarded at birth. This type of action usually involves a request on the part of the parents to withhold some sort of routine surgical or medical treatment that is needed for the infant to survive. If the physician agrees to the request, the newborn usually dies.

The practice of life management is far more widespread than most of us realize but is not typically open for public discussion. Robertson (1975, p. 214) characterizes it as ". . . now common practice for parents to request, and for physicians to agree, not to treat" infants who are defective at birth. Duff and Campbell (1973) investigated the background in 299 consecutive deaths that were recorded in a special-care nursery and found that 43 of them involved the withholding of treatment. This figure represents over 14 percent of the sample studied. Other cases have come to light since Duff and Campbell published their findings. Robertson characterizes the withholding of treatment from handicapped infants as a procedure that "is rapidly gaining status as 'good medical practice' " (1975, p. 214).

One's initial reaction to the topic of euthanasia may be rather straightforward—that it is a barbaric practice and should not be permitted. Unfortunately, it is not quite that simple. It is an issue that is plagued with incredible complexities from many different perspectives, which are discussed more fully in later portions of this chapter.

One of the factors that influences the complexity of social and ethical problems has been indirectly mentioned previously in the discussion of formalism philosophy. It was noted that one dilemma presented by pure formalism involves the curtailment of the rights of some individuals or segments of society as the rights of others are emphasized. This dilemma has been termed the *competing equities* issue (Boggs, 1977) and is presenting some very perplexing problems in contemporary society generally and particularly in the area of handicapped citizens' rights. For example, the competing equities issue enters into the controversy of the euthanasia topic previously discussed. Some would contend vigorously that it makes little sense to expend the extraordinary resources necessary to maintain life support for a terminally ill patient when such resources are so badly needed by others. Another part of this same contention involves the sentiment that such valuable resources as expensive equipment and medical talent should be deployed in a manner that will generate the most benefit for society. This viewpoint, which rings familiar to the utilitarian philosophy, would tend to diminish greatly the resources available for society, such as for terminally ill, aged, and mentally retarded citizens.

The competing equities issue also comes into play with philosophical viewpoints that are not clearly in the utilitarian vein. For example, formalism is very much in evidence as some call for the maximum possible effort to maintain life support for infants who are severely handicapped at birth. This position is often based on the infant's right to life, which, from the formalism viewpoint, cannot be abridged in any fashion by anyone. Competing equities are evident as one considers the potential conflict between the rights of the infant and the rights of the parents. Some have argued that the psychological, social, and economic burdens imposed by the care for a mentally retarded child are so extreme that parents should have the right to choose another alternative, particularly when extraordinary life support measures are involved. Thus the rights of parents and the rights of handicapped infants present a potentially conflicting situation—one that is complex and without easy answers.

The competing equities issue is by no means limited to the area of euthanasia. The concept rings a very familiar note to most of us in our daily lives. Further discussion in later sections highlights the manner in which it becomes relevant to many social and ethical considerations in the field of mental retardation.

It is evident from this brief overview that the social and ethical issues to be addressed in this chapter range over a wide variety of topics. They represent complexities and controversies that defy simple solution. It is not the purpose of this chapter to attempt to present answers or to assume that one position on a given issue is more appropriate than another. In most cases the proponents on both sides are not only earnest in their viewpoints but also are armed with legitimate arguments to support their opinions.

THE LIFE CYCLE: ISSUES AND ETHICS

Although many of the topics to be discussed are not limited to a given age group, certain patterns are evident that relate to different stages of the life cycle. The remaining portions of this chapter are therefore organized in the life-cycle format represented by the rest of the book. Discussions focus on ethics and issues at the prenatal stage and those particularly relevant to the early postnatal years, the school years, and adulthood. Certain issues, such as competing equities, transcend life-cycle stages and are examined as relevant throughout the chapter.

Prenatal ethics and issues

The prenatal period of the life cycle presents some uniquely difficult ethical questions. Since we are referring to the time before a child is born, we are addressing the task of prevention of mental retardation. The concept of preventing retardation historically has had a very favorable ring to it and continues to sound like an extremely laudable goal. However, some of the means that may be involved in attaining this end have been controversial to say the least. From some perspectives they hit at the very core of morality and, therefore, become prominent as social and ethical issues.

Genetic screening and counseling. Previous chapters have made note of certain disorders that are associated with inherited conditions or predispositions. Some of these represent conditions in which the probability of occurrence increases because of family origin (such as Tay-Sachs disease). Others become more probable because of the age or condition of the parent(s) (such as Down's syndrome). Many professionals believe that genetic screening and counseling should be routine when such situations exist. Although this is quite logical when viewed from the perspective of preventing mental retardation, such suggestions have raised concern and objections on the part of some segments of the population. Some view genetic screening and counseling as an interference with individual rights and freedom to mate and reproduce by choice. These objections strike particularly sensitive chords when they relate to conditions associated with certain ethnic or family origins, such as in sickle-cell anemia and Tay-Sachs disease. It is understandable how such procedures could be viewed as discriminatory and aimed at reducing the reproduction of certain ethnic groups. However, such a perspective goes far beyond the purpose typically defined and associated with genetic screening and counseling.

Genetic screening has been defined as ". . . a search in a population for persons possessing certain genotypes that (1) are already associated with disease, (2) may lead to disease in their descendants, or (3) produce other variations not known to be associated with disease." (National Academy of Sciences, 1975, p. 9). Since our current discussion is focusing on the prenatal period, the second genotype is of immediate concern.

The resulting action from genetic screening is genetic counseling for those parents or potential parents involved. Genetic counseling for such individuals includes providing information concerning the condition, the frequency with which it occurs (if possible, translated into the probability of occurrence in the situation at hand), and what behavioral and physical characteristics might be expected if it does occur. All of these areas should be dealt with, including various reproductive options. The genetic counselor must also be prepared to answer all questions openly and completely in order for the parent to become fully informed concerning the problem being faced.

The fundamental purpose of such screening and counseling is to ensure that the parents or potential parents are thoroughly informed regarding the genetic disorder under consideration. It is *not* the counselor's task to make a decision for them. If the information provision and discussion approach is adhered to, the argument of discrimination and interference with individual rights is largely disarmed. It would seem that parents are even better prepared to exercise their rights if they are fully aware of the potential outcomes and options. As with most emotionally charged issues, however, this point of view does not prevent some from continuing to put forth arguments against genetic screening and counseling.

Prenatal assessment. The prenatal developmental period presents other difficult ethical questions in addition to those already discussed. Since we are referring to the *in utero* period, one of the most immediate problems relates to assessment and resulting actions. The discussion in Chapter 4 indicated that there are a variety of techniques currently available that permit prenatal assessment of fetal status (for example, amniocentesis, fetoscopy). This is an area, like genetic screening, where technological developments have made significant strides in recent years. It can also be anticipated that such developments will continue, permitting even greater accuracy in diagnostic capability. As with many such accomplishments, technological developments in prenatal fetus assessment can also present certain dilemmas.

In Chapter 4 the authors took the position that evaluation should not be conducted unless it has a purpose. This was presented as a basic assumption underlying assessment that runs counter to the practice of merely evaluating because it is the popular thing to do. In this earlier context we were most directly referring to assessment that, if one subscribes to the above assumption, *must* result in some action related to service delivery (such as educational programming). If we are to remain consistent, the same assumption must be considered in the case of prenatal assessment.

Abortion. Viewing the preceding assumption in relation to prenatal assessment, one is immediately faced with the types of action that might result. If prenatal assessment indicates either that the fetus is, or is likely to be, defective, one alternative that might be considered is abortion. There may be no single topic that has received public attention that has been, and remains, as controversial as abortion. Some factions have contended vigorously that the practice of abortion is nothing less than murder. This notion is based on the view that a life exists, with human rights and human qualities, from the time of conception or shortly thereafter. On the other side of the issue there is a substantial segment of the population that maintains, with equal vigor, that abortion should be an option for any woman who so desires, under any circumstances. This viewpoint is based on the generic proposition that a woman has the right to be in control of her body and that being forced to continue an unwanted pregnancy is a violation of that right.

As the abortion issue is approached in relation to mental retardation, perspectives seem to be altered somewhat. A portion of the population still voices a blanket opposition to abortion. However, this position is held far less strongly and is represented by fewer individuals than when the issue relates to a nonhandicapped fetus. Some who would not favor abortion in a general sense, either by virtue of religious or personal philosophy, are ready to accept the practice in the context of handicapping conditions. In many cases this shift in perspective is not limited to mental handicaps but is generalized more broadly to any handicapping condition.

This type of philosophic shift is not limited to the issue of abortion. As we proceed through this chapter on social and ethical issues we will encounter similar phenomena in relation to other topics. Reconciliation of the apparent inconsistency in philosophic position has not, for the most part, been seriously undertaken by our society. In some ways this may be viewed as an indictment of society in general and specifically those who represent this type of an inconsistent philosophy. Such an indictment, however, would seem to serve little productive purpose. It is more important to realize that belief systems are somewhat fluid as they are operationalized.

Regarding our current topic, many people hold certain beliefs concerning such practices as abortion when they are considered in the context of mental retardation. These beliefs may be quite different than their general posture relative to abortion. Abortion *is* one alternative action that may be taken if prenatal assessment indicates that the developing fetus is defective. It would seem that, in all cases, the belief system of the parents involved should prevail as a decision is made whether or not to abort. This may present some conflict with the attending medical personnel if *their* personal value system is opposed to the practice of abortion. When such a situation does occur, the physician should inform parents of their right to seek the services of other medical personnel if they so desire.

The decision to abort a defective fetus is obviously in conflict with the position that such practice should not be permitted under any circumstances. This latter viewpoint is often based on the belief that the fetus has a right to life that cannot be abridged by anyone for any reason. Those who are more inclined to abort a defective fetus often argue that the quality of life for the handicapped individual is likely to be so diminished that no one would choose to live under such circumstances. This, of course, puts them in the position of deciding what the fetus would or would not choose if that action were possible (a point the opposing faction is quick to emphasize). A further point of contention involves the effect of a handicapped child on the parents and siblings. In many cases the immediate and continuing financial, psychological, and social burdens are extreme and impact on the family in an undesirable fashion. Those who would favor abortion contend that parents should at least have the option to decide. Of course the opposing view counters with the right of the unborn fetus to life regardless of the consequences for others.

The conflict characterized by the opposing value systems is not reconcilable because the disagreement is so fundamental. It is a situation where we are faced with competing equities that probably cannot be resolved to the satisfaction of both sides.

Ethical issues during the early years

Ethical issues related to mental retardation during the early years are fully as complex as those encountered at the prenatal stage. Some of these have been noted briefly in the introductory sections of this chapter, others have not. In all cases the issues involve agonizing problem situations, without easy or simple solutions. As with previous portions of this volume, the period from birth to 5 years of age is considered when we are discussing the early years.

Each developmental period is critical, in one fashion or another, to a child's overall growth process. The first 2 months after birth, usually termed the neonatal period, is our first focus for discussion. Chapter 5 indicated that many authorities view the first half of the neonatal period as the most dangerous in the total life span. Many of the developmental processes that were underway prenatally remain uncompleted and are continuing at an extremely rapid rate. Additionally, the infant is now without the protective environment provided by the mother's womb. Until a more complete arsenal of defenses is developed, the baby is perhaps more vulnerable to hazardous influences than at any other time.

Life management issues. The first few hours after birth and the first month of extrauterine life also represent a prime setting for one of the most controversial ethical issues relating to the life of a handicapped infant. It is during this period when chances may be greatest that consideration is given to withholding treatment for infants who are diagnosed as defective. As indicated in the introductory sections of this chapter, this practice is often termed euthanasia, although there are some important distinctions between euthanasia and the decision "not to prolong life," as we shall see in later discussion.

Ethical issues. It is not surprising that there are some important parallels between the ethical reasoning applied to abortion and that pertaining to decisions about postnatal survival of an infant. If one is to be philosophically consistent, the same arguments and posture that are presented in relation to abortion should also be used in connection with the practice of euthanasia. To some degree this is the case although we have already witnessed considerable fluidity in ethical reasoning and can expect more as we examine further issues.

The polarized viewpoints described previously for abortion are also encountered in the issues of postnatal survival. Ramsey (1973), for example, holds that abortion should not be an option even when prenatal assessment indicates that the fetus is severely defective or diseased. It is his contention that whatever arguments are used to justify abortion may also be used to support "infanticide" or the killing of infants. Ramsey's argument is not based on the position that we *would* commit a given act. He is essentially saying that there is no distinct moral difference between infanticide and abortion and that if we would not practice the former then we should not practice the latter.

Similar consistency is evident on the opposite side of the issue, which is perhaps best expressed by Joseph Fletcher (1973). He not only maintains that it is appropriate but suggests a moral obligation to abort a fetus that is diagnosed as defective. Fletcher further contends that the same reasoning holds for the practice of euthanasia with defective infants.

As would be expected, there are a variety of philosophical positions that fall somewhere between these two extreme points of view. John Fletcher, for example, supports an approach that "accentuates parental freedom to participate in life-and-death decisions independently in both the prenatal and postnatal situations, accepts abortion of a seriously defective fetus, but disapproves euthanasia of defective newborns" (1975, p. 75). It is his viewpoint that there are "morally relevant differences between abortion and euthanasia" that must be considered (p. 76).

Fletcher discusses three points that he views as representing these differences. His first consideration involves the fact that the infant now has a separate physical existence from the mother, which was not the case on a prenatal basis. This situation places the infant in the position of being a patient with independent rights for care and support. The essence of Fletcher's point is that the newborn has an independent status and can and should be considered separately from the mother. On the other hand, the prenatal fetus does not have independent status, so, he maintains, the status of the fetus *should not* be considered separately. Fletcher's second point relates closely to his first. Since the newborn is separate physically from the mother, it is now much more accessible than was the case prenatally. Fletcher argues that this places a greater obligation on the physician to heal and relieve suffering. Fletcher's third point rounds out what he sees as the morally relevant differences between abortion and euthanasia. In this context he notes a major difference in parental acceptance and loyalty to the unborn fetus when compared with the newborn. It is his contention that parental loyalty to the newborn is much stronger than that attached to the unborn fetus.

The above points are presented to support Fletcher's position, which accepts abortion but views euthanasia with disfavor. He notes two further points that argue against euthanasia that are frequently discussed and debated in the context of this complex issue. The first of these points is the obvious danger of euthanasia when practiced by unprincipled individuals. His second point is the inherent danger in changing societal attitudes toward the birth of infants from one of great caring to one of accepted selective euthanasia.

It should be pointed out that, throughout the discussion of John Fletcher's point of view, the term euthanasia has been used. This is because of the fact that he is very careful to use that term when examining the rationale for his position. For Fletcher and many others interested in this area, the term euthanasia has a very specific connotation.

In many situations with seriously defective infants the decision that is being faced is more one of whether or not to "prolong life" than actual euthanasia. These two terms convey different meanings, which may have considerable importance from both legal and moral standpoints. Euthanasia suggests mercy killing, or the beneficent termination of a life that may otherwise continue. According to George Fletcher, failure to prolong life, on the other hand, conveys the idea of not "artificially lengthening a life that would otherwise end" (Fletcher, 1968, p. 119). These differences, although appearing subtle to some, clearly become a part of the controversy as we proceed to examine this issue.

Legal issues. From a legal standpoint the distinction between euthanasia and a decision not to prolong life is essentially the difference between *acts* and *omissions*. Euthanasia, as described above, involves the act of terminating a life that would continue if the act was not committed. Not to prolong life, on the other hand, involves omission in that the physician fails to act and permits death to occur. George Fletcher (1968) notes that the act of terminating life is first degree murder in the eyes of the law, regardless of motive. The legal view of omitting action depends on the relationship of the physician to the other person. If the individual is a *patient* that has a reasonable expectation that the physician will provide treatment, failure to do so is legally no different than acting to terminate a life. If the individual is not a patient the physician is not *legally* bound to intercede in the same fashion. Fletcher also points out that "there is a significant gap between the law in theory and the law in practice" (1968, p. 120). He cites only one case where a physician was brought to trial for a euthanasia act. In this case the physician was acquitted even though he admitted performing the act and his nurse testified as a witness. With regard to acts of omission the gap between theory and practice seems even greater. Fletcher notes that no cases can be found where a physician has been found either criminally or civilly liable for deciding not to prolong life.

The absence of case law pertaining to acts of omission seems particularly significant when viewed in the context of a defective newborn. Since there is usually an attending physician during and after birth, it seems that the establishment of the patient status on the part of the infant is automatic. As mentioned previously, if the physician omits life-saving action with a patient that has a reasonable expectation of treatment, the law views this no differently from an act to terminate life. What appears clear is that, in practice, society has chosen to look the other way when decisions not to prolong life are made. Further, it appears that this is particularly true when the situation involves a defective newborn. Even John Fletcher modifies his position on postnatal practice under such circumstances. He states that "allowing the infant to die by withholding support while relieving pain is a decision, in my view, that can be ethically justified for reasons of mercy to the infant and relief of meaningless suffering of the parents and medical team" (1975, p. 77). He is careful to qualify this position, however, by using such terms as "cases of terribly damaged newborns for whom death is the desirable outcome when therapy either is not available or will only prolong the ordeal" (p. 77). Thus Fletcher remains more reluctant than some to permit postnatal management of life in this fashion even in the cases involving handicapped infants. This is not the case with many physicians and ethicists dealing with this issue.

The preceding discussion clearly illustrates the discrepancy between the theoretical legal view and the practiced legal view of postnatal life management. This seems to raise the question of whether or not the theoretical legal view should be changed. If society has implicitly determined that selective euthanasia and decisions not to prolong life are within acceptable zones of behavior, then one might wonder why the formal statements of those acceptable zones (law) are not redefined. As might be expected, this issue has been raised.

The study by Duff and Campbell (1973) was of particular importance because it provided at least a limited public data base concerning the frequency with which treatment is withheld from handicapped infants. After examining their data and the ethical ramifications thereof, Duff and Campbell turned to the legal issues in their final statements. They took the rather strong position that if withholding treatment from severely handicapped infants is a "violation of the law, we believe the law should be changed" (1973, p. 894). Others have preceded this position with considerable debate concerning the legislation of voluntary euthanasia (Kamisar, 1958; Williams, 1958; Williams, 1966). Thus it is evident that the topic of changing the law has received some attention from both sides. The logic in favor of changing the law is perhaps deceptively simple when presented as it was in relation to the acceptable zones of behavior given above. There are, however, some persuasive arguments against such change.

One of the arguments against changing the laws lies with the extreme difficulty of developing legal standards that can be effectively operationalized. One might expect that legislation removing criminal liability for decisions to withhold treatment would be very narrow in its definitions. Those that are most reluctant to speak of these issues use such terms as "terribly diseased," "tragically deformed," and "hideously damaged." However, even if legislation were developed with very strict and narrow criteria, application of legal standards by society and the development of case law has a way of continuously expanding the legal jurisdiction. Both Fletcher (1968) and Burt (1976) note that there is great difficulty in distinguishing between the clear cases and those that are less clear. For example, Robertson (1975) suggests that treatment might be withheld from "profoundly retarded, nonambulatory hydrocephalics who are blind and deaf" (p. 267). To this Burt responds by asking, ". . . what about those only blind? only deaf? and so on" (p. 439). This illustrates the difficulty of defining standards that can be effectively operationalized from a legal standpoint. Regardless of the care with which definitions are prepared, there will always be the "next hard case" that does not quite fit the description and requires professional judgment.

Burt also presents other persuasive points to argue against changing the laws. One of his points involves a change in attitude that frequently occurs when court arguments are made over issues that are specifically authorized by legislation. Experience has shown that litigation relating to acts specifically addressed by legislation often involves arguments presented in a fashion that might be characterized as cool, rational, and dispassionate. Burt clearly believes that the dispensing of life or death is an issue that we cannot afford to treat in a dispassionate manner. His concern is that explicit authority, such as that which might be found in legislation, would place life and death decisions for defective newborns in a context where either choice might be made with equal ease. Burt believes that this should not be the case and that death decisions should be reached reluctantly. It is his contention that the current state of affairs promotes that reluctance as a result of the mere existence of potential criminal liability.

The description of Burt's arguments might suggest that he is firmly opposed to the withholding of treatment. This is not the case. It should be emphasized that he is in opposition to changing the law and thereby specifically authorizing such action. He places this position squarely in the arena of social and ethical issues by noting:

> I am not suggesting that existing values must not change or that no self-respecting physician would ever or should ever withhold treatment from a newborn. Rather, I am suggesting that if we are evolving toward new values in this matter, we must do so gradually, hesitantly, and looking backward to what we have been, as often as we look forward to imagine what we will become (p. 446).

Burt's arguments warrant serious consideration regardless of whether one holds a similar position or not. One does not have to search very far into the past to discover topics and issues that have experienced an expansion of what is authorizable. Some of the topics, such as abortion and euthanasia, are discussed, examined, and practiced in manners that would have been viewed as clearly beyond the realm of possibility 20 years ago. In some cases technological advances have occurred that seem to have subtly governed philosophical changes. In other areas it is not altogether clear what influences have fostered such changes, but we still find ethical considerations being examined that would previously have been thought wildly impossible. Perhaps nowhere is there reason to give pause as much as there is in the issues of postnatal life management.

Life management decisions. In "looking both backward and forward" as we examine our values there are several immediate questions that arise in relation to life management. Although there may be many other issues, one is promptly faced with how life management decisions are made, who makes such decisions and under what circumstances, and about whom such decisions will be made. Some examination of this latter question has been previously debated and presented. In most cases those who debate the issues of life management are discussing infants who are extremely damaged or defective at birth. However, such terms as "extremely" are adjectives that may be broadly defined and are subject to differing interpretations.

THE JOHNS HOPKINS CASE. In at lease one case that received considerable visibility, substantial debate might occur relative to the degree of handicap that the infant represented. This involved a case that occurred at Johns Hopkins Hospital with a two-day-old full-term male infant who had facial characteristics and other features leading to a clinical impression of Down's syndrome. No cardiac abnormalities were evident but a greenish vomiting commenced shortly after birth. X-ray examination indicated the existence of an intestinal obstruction that was clinically labeled as duodenal atresia.

It is important to momentarily discuss the duodenal atresia to place this case in perspective. Diamond (1977) reviewed this specific case and examined the issues involved in medical intervention through surgical correction of the intestinal obstruction. He stated that the problem could be corrected with a survival rate of about 98 percent and that acute appendicitis with newborn infants has a higher mortality rate. Diamond pondered the ethics and value structure that would *require* performance of this "virtually risk-free operation" on a nonhandicapped infant does not place the same obligation in the case of a handicapped infant.

In the Johns Hopkins case there was an intestinal obstruction that could be surgically corrected with negligible risk. The infant reportedly had no additional complicating factors other than the clinical impression of Down's syndrome. Is Down's syndrome an example of an "extremely" handicapping condition? This may be a debatable issue. Some would answer in an unqualified affirmative manner. Others might note the potential intellectual range of Down's syndrome children and would disagree. The answer is not clear-cut, although one factor that may come into play occasionally is that Down's syndrome is *visually* evident. The decision in the Johns Hopkins case was to withhold treatment. Following discussion with the parents, the surgical correction of the duodenal atresia was not performed, and all feeding and fluids were discontinued. Fifteen days later the infant died of starvation and dehydration.

There are many ethical issues raised by the Johns Hopkins case. One can certainly question the humaneness of permitting an infant to starve to death over a 15-day period. This is a particularly difficult question since the decision not to operate made it impossible for the infant to receive food and fluids in a normal manner. However, the issue concerning the degree of handicap represented by Down's syndrome is equally provocative in terms of our question regarding on whom life management decisions will focus. It is questionable that Down's syndrome necessarily "fits" with the adjectives of extremely, terribly, or tragically handicapped. Some Down's syndrome children may reach a level of intellectual functioning that would be classified as moderate or even mild mental retardation.

The possibility that mildly or moderately retarded infants are vulnerable to negative life management decisions raises serious concerns. This is particularly true in the context of earlier discussions about proposals to enact legislation authorizing selective life management. It was noted before that application of legal standards by society and the development of case law has a tendency to continuously expand legal jurisdiction. Even in the absence of legal authorization, use of advancing technology frequently seems to desensitize society to encroachment on value structure boundaries. These tendencies should be carefully considered as we heed Burt's plea that we look both backward and forward as we evolve new values in the matter of life management. Will future life management decisions include the mildly handicapped? This may already be the case where the handicap is visible such as with Down's syndrome. Will future life management include the election of a particular sex on the part of parents? Perhaps only beautiful infants will receive favorable decisions. These suggestions are clearly repugnant and wildly impossible; however, many of the topics that society once thought were wildly impossible are currently viewed as accepted practice by some. This discussion is not presented in order to take a position on life management practices, a point that should be emphasized forcefully. Instead it is meant to provoke the most serious examination possible of the social and ethical issues related to such treatment alternatives with mentally retarded individuals.

Decisions—who and how. The earlier questions posed included how life management decisions are made, and who makes such decisions and under what circumstances. In part these issues are related to the discussion just presented. However, certain other points warrant at least brief attention in terms of these questions.

Both the "how" and "why" questions are not answered simply. Shaw (1977) presents a series of case vignettes from his pediatric surgery practice, as well as others, that exemplify the difficulties posed by life management decisions with handicapped newborns. His presentation includes attention to both who and how, with an emphasis on what he terms "informed consent." He notes that patients, when they are adults and mentally competent, have the right to be fully informed about proposed medical treatment. It is generally agreed that such patients then have the legal right to accept or reject that treatment and, in fact, to reject *any* treatment. When the patient is a minor, however, or not judged to be mentally competent, the decision process is vastly altered. In the case of handicapped infants, the parents have the right to "informed consent" but do not have sole decision-making prerogatives. It is Shaw's contention that the parents' decision is "subject to review when physicians or society disagree with that decision" (1977, p. 76). His statement concerning review by physicians and society specifically addresses situations when the parents' decision involves the *rejection* of treatment. It is clear from published reports that this is the case in terms of public decision-making. It would be patently unacceptable for medical personnel to publicly reverse a parental decision to prolong life. Off the record, medical personnel do, however, report cases where unilateral (but not public) decisions are made to withhold treatment in certain circumstances.

CONSENT. The act of consent is not as simple as suggested by the term "informed consent." Although informed consent is a term that has achieved popular usage, it is a misnomer. The American Association on Mental Deficiency viewed the problems of consent as sufficiently significant that a special task force was commissioned to examine the complexities of this topic. This effort resulted in publication of the AAMD *Consent Handbook* (Turnbull, 1977), which examines consent in a detailed manner and from both definition and application standpoints.

Although consent has specific meanings in a variety of contexts, the ramifications of consent often result in legal interpretations. This is certainly the case in the context of the current discussion. The AAMD *Consent Handbook* defined consent principally as a legal concept. From this standpoint there are three elements of consent that must be considered: capacity, information, and voluntariness. For the most part these three elements must be present for consent to be effective. It is also important to realize that consent is seldom if ever permanent and may be withdrawn at almost any time. Generally the act of withdrawing consent must also include the three elements of capacity, information, and voluntariness.

The elements of consent are of particular importance in the context of our discussion of life management decisions with handicapped infants. The AAMD *Consent Handbook* defines the first element—capacity—in terms of three factors: the person's age, the person's competence, and the particular situation. Both legally and logically the infant does not have the capacity to consent specifically on at least two of these factors. A person under the age of majority (generally 18 years) is legally incompetent to make certain decisions. Likewise, it is clear that the infant does not have the developed mental competence to understand and give consent. Thus in terms of capacity, the parents, legal guardians, or other persons acting on behalf of the parents have the authority to consent for the infant.

The second element of consent—information—also must receive careful consideration. The *Consent Handbook* discusses this element in the following manner:

> . . . the focus is on *"what" information is given and "how" it is given* since it must be effectively communicated (given and received) to be acted upon. The concern is with the *fullness* and *effectiveness* of the disclosure: is it designed to be fully understood, and is it fully understood? The burden of satisfying these two tests rests on the professional (p. 8).

The last sentence of this quotation is particularly important in terms of life management decisions with handicapped newborns. Clearly the giving or withholding of consent rests primarily with the parents, but in a sense such decisions are the joint responsibility of parents and medical personnel. In order for the element of effective information to be present, it is the physician's responsibility to see that the information about the infant's condition is designed to be fully understood and *is* fully understood.

The third element of consent—voluntariness—also has great relevance in the context of our discussion of life management decisions with handicapped newborns. Although voluntariness may appear to be a simple concept, subtle influences in the process of giving or withholding consent make it far from simple. In discussing voluntariness the AAMD *Consent Handbook* notes that the consenting individual must be "so situated as to be able to exercise free power of choice without the intervention of any element of force, fraud, deceit, duress, over-reaching or other ulterior form of constraint or coercion" (p. 10). This places even further responsibility on the physician. The information provided must be complete and without explicit or implicit inclusion of personal judgment. This may be particularly difficult since physicians are typically viewed as power figures by the lay public, and they certainly are not without their own feelings or inclinations in such situations. It may also be the case that the parents are highly vulnerable to persuasion immediately after the birth of a handicapped infant.

Life management in terms of euthanasia or withholding treatment from handicapped infants may be one of the most complex social and ethical issues related to mental retardation. The preceding discussion has illustrated the individual agonies involved in these decisions and has also suggested that societal value structures are under stress in such situations. Perhaps nowhere is the concept of competing equities so evident. The rights of the infant and the rights of the parents may be in direct conflict depending on the values and attitudes of the parents. Such conflict is not a new observation for those who work with retarded children and their families. What may be new or unique is the stark realization that the decisions being made involve a degree of seriousness that is totally unfamiliar to most of us—the actual dispensing of life or death.

Other issues. The neonatal period and the remaining portion of the early years also represents a high-risk time for other actions involving a mentally retarded infant. Some of these actions also come under consideration as we examine social and ethical issues. If a child is definitely identified as being mentally retarded during this period of time, it is quite likely that a visible clinical syndrome is evident (Down's syndrome) or that the handicap is in the moderate to severe or profound range. More often than not a mildly retarded child without physical evidence of a problem is not diagnosed with any degree of certainty until formal schooling begins. Parents of this latter type of child may have some concerns about developmental delays but these are often private concerns that frequently remain in the back of their minds and are either not discussed or are rationalized and denied. However, parents of children who are diagnosed as mentally retarded during their early years must address the issues of care and early education on a more immediate basis, which often raises ethical considerations that are emotionally laden and cause extraordinary stress.

Institutionalization decisions. The type of care and where such care is going to occur frequently surface as considerations with children who are diagnosed as retarded during their early years. One issue that often arises with such children is whether or not they should be institutionalized. This is always an agonizing choice for parents and frequently is made doubly difficult by the type and amount of information on which they can base their decision. The discussion in Chapter 4 indicated that prediction of a child's ultimate level of functioning is extremely difficult during the very early periods of life. Although predictive accuracy improves as the child grows older, assessment procedures that are useful during infancy are quite unreliable in terms of later functioning. Additionally, parents of very young retarded children are often interacting with medical personnel as their primary source of information. Historically physicians have had too little training to effectively meet this challenge, although significant efforts have recently been made in many medical schools to include such preparation. Assessments of such children by physicians have consequently been subject to considerable error, particularly when there is also a physical handicap or defect present (Drew and Hardman, 1977; Hardman and Drew, 1977). For example, research by Pearson and Menefee (1965) indicated that pediatricians consistently underestimated the level of intellectual functioning of such individuals, which resulted in a tendency to recommend institutionalization more frequently.

There are a variety of social and ethical issues involved in this situation. One immediate consideration pertains to the inclination to recommend or at least favor institutionalization based on estimates of the degree of handicap by medical personnel. Although Pearson and Menefee's sample included older individuals, their findings give rise to concern with the handicapped infant as well as the young handicapped child. The more generalized concern relates as much as anything to the apparent magnitude of consistent error in estimates by pediatricians. Their results indicated that approximately two-thirds of the assessments were close to one full standard deviation away from administered standardized test scores. This coupled with their report that pediatricians *consistently misjudged* and *underestimated* the level of functioning heightens the concern even further. This type of data base would seem to be a rather uncertain basis for the decision to institutionalize.

A brief note to moderate the potential interpretation of this discussion seems in order before proceeding. First of all, it was mentioned previously that *recent* efforts have been evident to improve the preparation of physicians for working with handicapped individuals and their families. The current authors have observed significant leadership by some medical personnel responsible for preparation programs, which are excellent and appear to be having a substantial impact. Some pediatricians involved in teaching hospitals have become extremely knowledgeable about education of handicapped individuals and have done a great deal to foster an interdisciplinary team effort with special education and psychology. The fact remains, however, that *many* medical personnel who are currently in practice were trained prior to the advent of this concern. Their level of knowledge and the nature of their approach to handicapped children remains unknown on an individual basis but *may*, as a group, reflect the type of findings reported by Pearson and Menefee.

Placement of a young retarded child in an institution once again raises the issue of consent and the three elements that must be present for consent to be effective. As with our previous discussion, effective consent must include capacity, information, and voluntariness. The parents must give consent with these three elements functionally present in order for institutionalization of the child to be legitimate. In the context of the previous discussion, the element of information raises particular concern. The parents may be interacting with medical or other professional personnel who are not properly equipped to provide a complete and appropriate data base for decision making. There has been little consequence in the past for professionals who have provided inadequate information or advice in terms of a child's placement. Turnbull and Turnbull (1975) note that such immunity may be approaching obsolescence as parents and advocates for retarded individuals undertake litigation to alter decisions previously made on inadequate information or advice. They further suggest that malpractice might be an appropriate and emerging concept for other professions besides medicine.

INSTITUTIONAL CONDITIONS. No decision for treatment or placement of a retarded child should be undertaken casually or without full consideration of its ramifications. This seems to be particularly the case when the decision involves potential placement of a retarded child in a residential institution. Such a decision involves perhaps the most restrictive placement possible and represents a dramatic removal of the individual from the societal mainstream. Although this type of placement is appropriate in certain situations, when inappropriate, the outcomes can be very detrimental.

Residential institutions historically have had a very poor image as treatment and habilitation agencies for retarded persons. While some of this poor image may be undeserved or from extenuating circumstances, conditions in institutions have often been undesirable and in some cases they have been deplorable. Burt (1976) considers them "warehouses for human beings, if anything, an understated depiction of many, perhaps most, of these large-scale, geographically isolated institutions" (p. 441). Others have portrayed the conditions in institutions in equally dramatic and unfavorable terms (Blatt and Kaplan, 1966). A judiciary subcommittee of the United States Senate conducted five days of hearings during the summer of 1977 while considering legislation on the civil rights of institutionalized persons (S. 1393). The hearings resulted in over 1,100 pages of testimony and exhibits by individuals involved with the mentally retarded either as professionals or as other interested parties. These pages include extremely graphic descriptions of institutional problems and conditions, much of which is most unfavorable.

The desirability of institutional placement may thus be questioned on arguments of unacceptable conditions alone (although the restrictiveness of placement raises additional questions). The assignment of any human being to live in some of the subhuman conditions that have existed raises serious issues of societal values. Fortunately, as noted earlier, others have raised and continue to raise such questions in a number of public forums, and dramatic changes are underway. Some of these changes have been initiated by institutional personnel themselves, whereas others have emerged as a result of efforts by advocates for retarded citizens. In general there is a diminishing propensity to commit very young children to institutions. This represents a very favorable move in view of the assessment difficulties that have previously been discussed. It also reduces the likelihood that institutionalization will occur on the basis of inadequate information and increases the probability that other treatment alternatives will be given more serious consideration. Although these favorable changes are underway, it is important for society to continue examination of its value structure relative to services for mentally retarded individuals. Was it by intent or by neglect that the deplorable institutional conditions were allowed to evolve? Does it represent an implicit statement of society's philosophical position on the value of human life or a statement of belief that retarded individuals are somehow "less human"? Such questions are much like those posed earlier; they have no single or simple answers.

A final note is in order relative to institutional placement in general and to the particular context of the early years. The issue of competing equities once again makes its presence very much felt. Here, as before, the competing equities question may place the handicapped child in a polar position with the parents and the rest of the family. On one hand there is the right of the retarded child to live and develop in the best environment possible. On the other hand one must consider the impact on the family. What effect does the child's presence (and the presence of the handicap) have on the parents and any nonretarded siblings that may be a part of the family constellation? In many cases the impact is unknown at the outset, and reports have varied all the way from favorable to essential destruction of the family unit. One factor is a constant in this consideration, there *is* an impact that is not minimal.

Ethical issues during the school years

In part, social and ethical issues that surface during the school years are similar to some that have been discussed in earlier parts of this chapter. Competing equities, consent, and placement issues are not limited to a particular age level. In fact, they are so fundamental that they can be observed in nearly all arenas of service delivery to handicapped individuals. However, the manner in which these issues emerge is altered considerably by the context of different phases of the life cycle.

Placement issues. The placement of mentally retarded children in educational settings raises a variety of issues, including generic philosophical questions as well as those related to the manner in which implementation is undertaken. A certain amount of historical contexting is helpful in examining both philosophical and implementation questions. The major portion of this discussion, however, examines the issues that are more current and those that might be anticipated in the future.

Earlier sections of this book have discussed in detail the educational programming for mentally retarded children and youth. From these discussions it is clear that one of the placement alternatives involves what some have termed "pull-out" programs. Such programs are characterized by removing the retarded child from the educational mainstream and providing essentially the complete educational experience in a situation that is isolated from the child's nonhandicapped peers. Examples of this type of placement include self-contained special education classes, special schools, and residential institutions. Earlier sections have noted that such placements exist as alternatives but should be viewed as existing *on a continuum* with others that involve specialized programming for the child *within* the educational mainstream. This view is not one that has prevailed from a historical perspective.

Special classes and other "pull-out" programs for mentally retarded children have a long history. The first public school special classes in the United States were organized in 1896. Enrollment in such programs increased at a steady rate until only recently. By 1922 there were over 23,000 children enrolled in special classes, and by 1958 this number had increased to over 196,000 (Mackie and Robbins, 1960). The increase in special classes for retarded children was based on the belief that such placement was more beneficial than maintaining them in regular classroom settings. As noted in earlier chapters, both the data and logic supporting this as the sole approach to educating handicapped children has been seriously questioned in recent years. Without recounting the details presented in Chapter 9 we can briefly summarize current thinking by referring to Deno's cascade of services model (1970) and the basic principles of P. L. 94-142. These sources suggest that handicapped individuals should be treated and educated as closely as possible to the mainstream of society. In the context of our present discussion this would focus on the formal educational process.

Much of the current thinking regarding the education of handicapped children has been captured in P. L. 94-142, which was discussed in Chapter 13 on legal issues and responsibilities. As suggested by this earlier discussion, P. L. 94-142 is an extremely complex piece of legislation that raises many questions and issues. One of these issues relates specifically to the placement of handicapped children in the least restrictive appropriate educational environment. This concept is very different from the logic that supported "pull-out" programs as the primary means for educating mentally retarded children. It emphasizes a continuum of service alternatives and requires that education agencies develop procedures to assure that handicapped children are educated with nonhandicapped children to the degree that it is appropriate. The least restrictive placement concept thus emphasizes that special classes, separate schooling, or other removal of handicapped children from the regular educational environment should be alternatives of choice *only* when the child's handicap is such that satisfactory education cannot be accomplished in regular classes, even with the use of supplementary aids and services. There are many issues that are raised by the least restriction principle. Many of these have been raised in earlier chapters on the school years and legal issues. Additionally, the least restriction principle has raised several questions and issues that appear to warrant attention in the context of social and ethical domains.

LEAST RESTRICTION PRINCIPLE. One of the issues raised by the least restriction principle represents a somewhat fluid combination of competing equities and the formalism-utilitarianism philosophical conflict. As suggested earlier, the formalism philosophy presents a dilemma in its pure form because as the rights of some are made more distinct, the environment of others is often impinged. This dilemma is nearly definitional in the way it relates to competing equities. Education of mentally retarded children in least restrictive placements may create some of these exact problems. For example, least restrictive placement will mean that a rather substantial number of mildly retarded children will have their primary placement in regular classrooms. Even with supplementary aids and ancillary services that may be available, they will require certain additional in-class attention, which the teacher may not be accustomed to providing and perhaps may require certain skills that the teacher may not have acquired. Such a situation is described in a tentative fashion, but it is clear that many teachers face this expectation with great anxiety.

In many parts of the country, teacher expectations relative to least restrictive placements have emerged in contract negotiations between school districts and teachers' bargaining organizations (that is, unions and professional associations). For example, in some areas teacher organizations have taken the stand that class size must be reduced by three nonhandicapped children for *each* handicapped child that is placed in the regular classroom.

This raises an immediate question of where those three nonhandicapped children will be placed. If a regular class had three handicapped children enrolled, it would result in the displacement of nine nonhandicapped children under this type of plan. Such an arrangement could easily result in a significant increase in the number of classrooms, and even schools, in a district. This instantly gives rise to the issue of cost and also the possibility of increased bussing. When these matters are considered, the competing equities problem emerges very significantly. Taxpayers are already less than enthusiastic about the portion of their income that is being absorbed by public education. Parents of nonhandicapped children will have some legitimate reasons for irritation as *they* are asked to pay more while their children are shifted from class to class (or are bussed).

The difficulties described represent only one instance where we face the competing equities issue in the schooling of mentally retarded children. The dilemma is found squarely on the philosophical questions raised by formalism in our complex society. When we make more distinct the legitimate rights to an appropriate education for some, this very act may impinge on those same rights of others. The social value question at stake is at once simple and complex: who sacrifices? Is it a matter of requiring that all be equally disadvantaged or all equally advantaged? Or do we turn to a utilitarian philosophy wherein an individual only has those rights granted by society at large (the privileged)? It may be possible for society to ensure an appropriate education for all handicapped children without significantly imposing a disadvantage on nonhandicapped children. This cannot, however, be accomplished without a cost, and society must determine if it is willing to pay that cost. The least restriction principle places a strain on societal values in that this question cannot go unanswered. This is a tall order for a social structure that is not accustomed to addressing such difficult questions in an orderly manner.

Appropriate education issues. The language of P. L. 94-142 raises many questions that can be discussed in the context of social issues related to the school years. A complete examination of these matters far exceeds the scope of this chapter and, in fact, this volume. However, one particular piece of the language is strikingly provocative. The term "appropriate" was mentioned in the discussion of least restriction; least restrictive *appropriate* placement. This term is found in several parts of the legislation and is essentially intended to connote a qualitative description of the educational programming.

The placement and educational program should be *appropriate* for the nature and degree of the handicap.

The facet of the legislation dealing with appropriate education may be problematical from at least two standpoints. The first relates to the term itself. *Appropriate,* like many such adjectives, is a general term that is subject to a wide variety of definitions. Although this is characteristic of legislative language, the range of implemental or operational outcomes is as varied as the number of individuals responsible for implementation. This brings us to the second problem with the term appropriate. Public law 94-142 is a revolutionary piece of legislation. Some have suggested that it is *so* revolutionary that it may die of its own weight because it may be too difficult to actualize the changes required on a mass basis. Consequently, professionals have been so engaged in responding to its major and obvious tenents that the term "appropriate" has been largely ignored. This presents a significant dilemma because the *appropriateness* of the educational or treatment program was the essential raison d'etre for the legislation. In fact, an *appropriate* education is a fundamental assumption that underlies the consumer-public's support of public education in general. Some responses to the concepts of P. L. 94-142 have seemed to ignore appropriateness to such a significant degree that ethical questions appear to be raised. Drew (1978) described example situations that give rise to such concerns, specifically related to least restrictive placement. One of these involves what he terms a "paper compliance" in which efforts are more concentrated on making a child's program *look* appropriate on paper than ensuring the *actual* appropriateness of the program. Although such situations have existed in the past, it seems that efforts are intensifying with the advent of the federal legislation.

The type of activity represented by paper compliance certainly detracts from the effectiveness of educational programming, the fundamental purpose of the legislation. It also brings into question the professional ethics of those who undertake such plans. Initial reaction to this type of compliance may be much like that suggested in the context of life management—that it is unethical practice and should not be permitted. Whereas most of us would agree in principle, this problem, like those we have discussed previously, is plagued with complexities that make a simple solution difficult.

Although one cannot excuse paper compliance, it is not difficult to understand some of the reasons why such responses occur. First of all, the public schools are not generally well equipped to implement P. L. 94-142 on a widespread basis. Chapter 13 outlined in detail the major principles of the law.

This is a massive piece of legislation, which, if interpreted and implemented literally (as intended), means immense changes in most school districts. In many cases these changes require personnel and skills that are not currently available. In fact, some of these resources might not be available by the time that compliance is required even *if* the schools had the financial capability to buy them. Thus, from the perspective of those who are charged with the responsibility of implementation, the task often seems overwhelming. Once again, while we may not excuse or condone paper compliance, it is not difficult to see how this response occurs.

Additional factors add to the complex issue of providing "appropriate" educational programming as defined in P. L. 94-142. This is a prescriptive piece of federal legislation, which, from many educators' viewpoint, is being imposed on them by outsiders. This *outside* imposition has at least two sources from the perspective of many who are required to comply. First of all, many regular elementary and secondary educators view the law as being imposed on them by special education. This is not exactly met with favorable reaction since one segment of the profession (and a smaller one at that) is dictating what appropriate education is to another, larger, segment of the profession. The outside imposition perspective also becomes evident because this is a federal law that dictates certain matters about how education will be conducted at the state and local levels. This raises the immediate question of whether or not such a definition of appropriate education is federal intervention in states' rights.

These factors, as well as others, contribute in a variety of ways to the development of paper compliance plans and other procedures that are highly questionable in terms of fostering appropriate educational programming for handicapped children. Prior to their examination it may have been rather easy for us to declare such approaches unethical and contrary to the fundamental purpose of education. Their discussion may not lessen this concern in regard to the ultimate benefit for retarded children. Such discussion does, however, highlight the complex nature of the situation. Appropriate education, least restrictive placement, competing equities, and states' rights are merely samples of the issues that make social value questions related to the school years difficult and without simple solutions. Although in a different context, the philosophical and operational differences are no less complicated nor more easily resolved than those we confronted in the early years.

Consent. The introductory comments to this section stated that consent was an issue that is also relevant to the school years. Parents must be actively involved in the decision process that results in changing the educational program for their child. In terms of our specific focus—the mentally retarded child—this process includes consent for assessment or diagnosis as well as any programming changes that might occur as a result of such assessment.

Consent in the context of the school years involves the same basic principles that were discussed previously with regard to life management decisions. In order to be effective, parental consent for all action, including assessment and programming, must include the three elements of capacity, information, and voluntariness. As before, consent is seldom if ever permanent and may be withdrawn at nearly any time. The educator who is attempting to obtain consent carries a heavy burden—just as the medical professional did in our previous discussion—in terms of ensuring that the three elements of consent are present.

One element of consent that is altered somewhat in the context of the school years is capacity. For the most part, capacity to consent for the mentally retarded child must remain with the parents as before. From a strictly legal standpoint, the capacity to consent does not rest with the child because of age (under the age of majority) and lack of mental competence to fully understand the nature and consequences of consent. However, good practice would suggest that a blanket assumption of incapacity throughout the school years is inappropriate. Specifically, older retarded individuals (adolescents or young adults) who are functioning at a near normal level may be quite capable of participating in the consent process. Depending on the situation and the individual, they may be able to give consent directly or they may best give consent concurrently with a third party, such as the parents. The likelihood that a third party *must* participate in consent is raised if the information is complex or if the individual appears less able. As before, the process of obtaining effective consent is one that involves the exercise of considerable judgment. There are few set rules that one can follow to relieve the need for exercising solid professional judgment. The burden of obtaining *effective* consent rests heavily with the professional, a situation that may create a certain amount of discomfort but one that must obtain if the rights of retarded individuals are to be adequately protected.

Ethical issues during adulthood

The social and ethical issues that surface during adulthood ring very familiar following the discussions of earlier sections in this chapter. Many of the generic principles, the philosophical differences, and the agonizing social questions remain relatively constant. As before, however, the manner in which these issues emerge is altered considerably by the context of the adult years. A comprehensive discussion of all social and ethical issues that are relevant to the mentally retarded adult is far beyond the scope of this chapter. Consequently, we focus on those that hopefully will promote the most serious questioning on the part of the reader.

The emergence of certain social and ethical issues during the adult years is not surprising. Questions related to marriage, reproduction, and sterilization, if they are to arise, most logically become considerations during this part of the life cycle. As with most of the issues discussed in this chapter, these topics have been subject to considerable controversy.

Sterilization issues. Although the topics related to life management decisions are complex, the issues surrounding sterilization of retarded individuals are no less perplexing. Controversy surrounding sterilization has a very long history, and the legal authority related to sterilization varies throughout the country. This section does not recount the history nor the legal basis since those have previously been addressed. Our focus here is an analysis of the issues per se.

ARGUMENTS FOR AND AGAINST. One of the ways to approach the topic of sterilization is to examine how and why mentally retarded individuals receive different consideration than their nonretarded peers. Both the historical controversy and the legal authority to sterilize the mentally retarded (see Chapter 13) clearly indicate that different consideration *is* given. For example, although voluntary sterilization of nonretarded citizens is mostly viewed as an individual prerogative (as a means of birth control), involuntary sterilization laws pertaining generally to nonretarded citizens are essentially unheard of. A variety of justifications have been advanced to support sterilization of the mentally retarded. Krishef (1972, p. 36) summarizes these arguments as those that hold sterilization to be: "(1) in the best interest of society and the state, (2) in the best interest of the retarded individuals, and (3) in the best interest of the unborn children." As with other issues examined in this chapter, there are also those people who express strong opposition to sterilization of mentally retarded individuals. Arguments on this side of the issue are varied and include: (1) concern about the potential misuse of legal authority to sterilize, (2) some evidence that certain of the pro-sterilization arguments noted before do not consistently hold true, and (3) concern about the rights of the retarded individual and the manner in which the process is undertaken. Each of these areas represents a serious societal question and issue that warrants examination.

The first pro-sterilization argument held that sterilization of the mentally retarded was in the best interest of society and the state. This is a particularly difficult premise, depending on how one views the support for it. This proposition may also exemplify, perhaps more clearly than any other issue, how the best interest of the state may come into conflict with rights of an individual. One very important basis for the "benefit to society and state" argument involves a reduction in the numbers of retarded individuals in the population. In a very real sense this is another approach to the prevention of mental retardation. Proponents of this position point to the fact that such a reduction would decrease the number of citizens that require extra services from society and thereby would lessen the cost burden for such care on the state and the taxpayers. This argument would seem to be based on a utilitarian philosophy since such savings, if they were to occur, could be redirected to those societal needs that might ultimately result in greater productive return to the general public.

One question that is immediately raised concerns the degree to which such a practice would actually result in reduced incidence of mental retardation? The answer to this question is anything but obvious. If sterilization is viewed as preventing only the transmission of inferior or damaged genetic material, the reduced incidence would appear quite minimal. Mental retardation that can be directly attributed to genetic causation represents a rather small proportion of the total mentally retarded population. Furthermore, those individuals whose mental retardation can be attributed to genetic causation are more likely to be functioning at lower levels; some in the severe to profound range. For a number of reasons one can make the case that such individuals are less likely to be engaged in procreation acts to begin with. The difficulty with this entire line of reasoning becomes evident when one views the broad perspective of mental retardation. First of all, earlier sections of this volume have examined the nature-nurture controversy in considerable detail relative to the development of intelligence (and mental retardation causation). It is clear from these earlier discussions that determination of environmental influences cannot be accomplished with great precision. It is also evident that the environment *does* have a significant impact on mental retardation causation, particularly in the milder range of handicap. Thus sterilization is not solely focusing on the transmission of inferior genetic material.

Thus the question remains, to what degree would a massive sterilization program reduce the incidence of mental retardation? Although the answer must remain somewhat speculative, there are some data available. Bass (1967) makes reference to a Danish program that involves genetic counseling and voluntary sterilization of the retarded. This program, directly aimed at preventing reproduction by retarded individuals, had been in operation for 25 years at the time of Bass's research in 1967. Results suggested that the incidence of mental retardation was reduced by "approximately 50% a generation" (p. 45). Bass also cited the work of Reed and Reed (1965), who suggested a similar reduction in incidence might be expected if voluntary sterilization were to become widely accepted in the United States.

Although limited, the literature cited above does suggest that a rather substantial reduction in the incidence *might* be expected if sterilization of mentally retarded individuals were conducted systematically. This might appear to lend support to the "best interest of society" argument. It is evident, however, that our complex and diverse society is not willing to accept such a practice in a single-minded fashion. The reasons for this are as many and varied as our culture itself.

One very strong influence is our apparent unwillingness to overrule the rights of individuals in favor of the rights of the larger society in any blanket fashion. One of the individual rights that seems to loom very large in this regard is the right of procreation. As early as 1921 the importance of this individual right was noted in legal interpretation of the federal Constitution. At this time the Michigan attorney general issued an opinion, based on the Constitution, which held that the right to have and retain the power of procreation was second only to the right to life itself (Price and Burt, 1976). It is generally accepted that such a fundamental individual right can only be abrogated on a voluntary basis by the individual involved. One must then ask the question regarding how compulsory sterilization laws came to exist in certain states? Obviously, in these situations the interests of the state were deemed to supercede the rights of the mentally retarded.

CONSENT ISSUES. Even voluntary sterilization of the mentally retarded presents some complex questions both conceptually and with regard to implementation. The moment we move into a voluntary status with respect to sterilization we are once again faced with the question of consent. The concept of consent in the context of sterilization is not different from consent generally and must include the three elements of capacity, information, and voluntariness. Consent in the context of sterilization does, however, present some interesting implementation problems that we have not encountered in earlier discussions.

The element of capacity was discussed earlier with particular focus on the person's age and competence. As mentioned previously, a person under the age of majority is legally incompetent to make certain decisions. Since our main focus in this section is the adult years, age will not be a substantial consideration with regard to the capacity element. Competence does, however, become an issue. The basic question is whether or not a retarded adult has the mental competence to understand what sterilization is and what the implications are. This would not seem to be an answerable question in a general sense. It would seem most logical to consider each case individually, depending on the person's level of functioning. However, some would disagree vigorously. A decision concerning sterilization has been described as being so "complicated and extraordinarily important" that many individuals who are of normal intelligence are perhaps not competent to fully comprehend its implications (Baron, 1976, p. 273). Whereas this may be true for only some nonretarded individuals, it does seriously raise the competence issue in the situation where a mentally retarded person is involved. Baron is emphatic, however, in his contention that the opinion of the retarded person being considered for sterilization should not be ignored. He states that "although the consent of the candidate should not be considered alone to be sufficient basis for sterilization, it should certainly be considered important evidence along with such other evidence as is available, that sterilization is in fact in his best interest" (p. 273).

The natural place to turn for assistance in obtaining consent would seem to be the parents (or legal guardians) of the retarded individual. This has been the case in our earlier discussions of other procedures requiring consent. It is assumed that they will consider such decisions with the best interests of their ward being the first and foremost concern. This may not, however, be a sound assumption with respect to sterilization. In fact, Murdock (1974) suggests that "parents or guardians often have interests that conflict with those of the retarded child. The parents of a retarded child may have understandable fears that the grandchild will also be retarded. Moreover, the parents may perceive a danger of their retarded child proving to be an unfit parent, and might wish to avoid the risk of shouldering responsibilities of grandchildren . . ." (p. 917). If such a situation does exist it is clear that parental input in the consent process may not be motivated solely by consideration of the candidate's best interest.

Baron (1976) indicates that there has been a noticeable tendency for the courts to intervene and review parental decisions regarding consent for sterilization. The court's interest is that of ensuring that the retarded individual's best interests are protected and are the sole determining factor influencing the sterilization decision. This presents a very difficult dilemma, one that makes the consent process extremely complicated. Court intervention itself is complicated. In order to assure objectivity the court must be presented with information and arguments on both sides. This requires that advocates for both sides be present in court and be equally informed and articulate regarding the manner in which they inform the court. It further requires that the arguments on both sides include *all* relevant information and that information that is presented be *limited* to the issues pertaining to the "best interests" of the retarded individual. This latter point eliminates the presentation of information or arguments relating to either the state's interests or those of the parents.

This brief discussion represents only the "tip of the iceberg" in terms of the complex issues related to consent for sterilization. Although we began our examination with a focus on the element of capacity, the elements of information and voluntariness very quickly became intertwined in the considerations. This discussion highlights the manner in which issues can become extremely complicated as attempts are made to protect individual rights. It also raises other social questions that are not easily answered. Do the parents' rights and interests have no value? What about the interests of the state? The concept of competing equities becomes very evident in situations where the rights and interests of all parties are not in harmony. These are very familiar questions, reminiscent of the extreme philosophical differences that were presented in the beginning of this chapter.

Marriage issues. The issues pertaining to marriage of mentally retarded adults are closely related to sterilization and are often considered together. Marriage issues are perhaps not as legally complicated (that is, consent) since an irreversible medical procedure is not involved. Possibly the overriding issue or questions in this area rests with the mere existence of laws restricting marriage of retarded individuals. As indicated in earlier chapters, there are many states with laws that place some type of restriction on the right to marry for those classified as mentally retarded. One has to ask why these laws exist. Are these laws aimed at the protection of the individual or are they basically for the protection of society?

The above question is presented by the current authors in a spirit of issue examination. For some, the evidence is so compelling that objective examination of this issue is tantamount to ignoring the manner in which such laws were developed. Wolfensberger (1975) discusses restrictive marriage laws as a part of society's need to prevent procreation by mentally retarded individuals. Credence for this perception certainly arises from the observation that 56 percent of the states have both sterilization and restrictive marriage laws in common (Krishef, 1972). If not credence, certainly intrigue is added to this examination by the wording of early legislation cited by Wolfensberger (1975). He references an 1895 bill passed by the Connecticut House of Representatives. It reads as follows:

> Every man who shall carnally know any female under the age of forty-five years who is epileptic, imbecil, feeble-minded, or a pauper, shall be imprisoned in the State prison not less than three years. Every man who is epileptic who shall carnally know any female under the age of forty-five years, and every female under the age of forty-five years who shall consent to be carnally known by any man who is epileptic, imbecile, or feeble-minded, shall be imprisoned in the State prison not less than three years (p. 40).

Wolfensberger also notes that a law to prohibit marriage of "feeble-minded and insane" was proposed at the national level in 1897 and received a great deal of support. One could interpret the above wording from either perspective (that is, individual or societal protection) since specific mention of the intent is absent. There is little question regarding intent, however, as Wolfensberger continues. The commentary historically seems to be captured by Wilmarth in 1902 whose focus was on the "abatement of this evil" and a search for ways to accomplish it (Wolfensberger, 1975, p. 40).

It does seem that society's interests were paramount, at least historically. One must raise the question of whether or not this is still the case. Some of these old laws remain on the books. What about current legislation? Are current laws and efforts merely more carefully disguised attempts to protect the best interests of society or are they really aimed at achieving some balance between the rights of individuals and the rights of our larger culture? There are strong arguments on both sides.

The questions and issues discussed throughout this chapter are not pleasant topics. They represent areas that we might wish to avoid. They are, however, social and ethical questions of great importance. These are issues that test the strength of societal fabric. We cannot ignore what seems to be the fundamental question—are mentally retarded individuals considered subhuman, or at least less deserving of the rights of the rest of humanity?

STUDY QUESTIONS

1. Duff and Campbell (1973) have taken the position that if nontreatment of certain infants is in violation of the law, then the law should be changed. How does this position fit with formalism philosophy? How does it fit with utilitarianism philosophy? What are your views, and why do you believe the way you do?
2. It appears that selective abortion and nontreatment of defective infants are more common practices than the general public knows. Who should make these judgments that are literally life and death decisions? On what basis(es) did you determine your response?
3. Public education in this country is largely supported by taxpayers. Special services for mentally retarded children often cost a great deal more than educational services for their nonretarded peers. To what degree do you think that parents of nonretarded children should be held responsible for the increased costs of educating mentally retarded children? On what basis do you believe as you do?
4. Sterilization of mentally retarded adults is often justified on the basis of the general welfare of society and the state. In many cases it appears that the best interests of the state and the best interests of the retarded individual may be in conflict. Whose interests should prevail and why?

REFERENCES

Baron, C. H. Voluntary sterilization of the mentally retarded. In Milunsky, A., and Annas, G. J. (Eds.), *Genetics and the law.* New York: Plenum Publishing Corp., 1976, Pp. 267-284.

Bass, M. S. Attitudes of parents of retarded children toward voluntary sterilization. *Eugenics Quarterly,* 1967, **14,** 45-53.

Blatt, B., and Kaplan, F. *Christmas in purgatory.* Boston: Allyn and Bacon, Inc., 1966.

Boggs, E. M. *Competing equities: an issue raised by, but going beyond, Section 504.* Memorandum to the Legislative and Social Issues Committee of the American Association on Mental Deficiency, Jan. 1977.

Burt, R. A. Authorizing death for anomalous newborns. In Milunsky, A., and Annas, G. J. (Eds.), *Genetics and the law.* New York: Plenum Publishing Corporation, 1976, Pp. 435-450.

Deno, E. Special education as developmental capital. *Exceptional Children,* 1970, **37,** 229-237.

Diamond, E. F. The deformed child's right to life. In Horan, D. J., and Mall, D. (Eds.), *Death, dying and euthanasia.* Washington, D.C.: University Publications of America, Inc., 1977, Pp. 127-138.

Drew, C. J. *Least restrictive alternatives: a concept in search of definition.* Paper presented at the 102nd Annual Convention, American Association on Mental Deficiency, Denver, May 1978.

Drew, C. J., and Hardman, M. L. *The PMR multihandicapped: a review on retardation and physical handicaps.* Paper presented at the Third Annual Western Research Conference on Mental Retardation, Carmel, Calif., Mar.-Apr. 1977.

Duff, R., and Campbell, A. Moral and ethical dilemmas in the special-care nursery. *New En-*

gland Journal of Medicine, 1973, **289,** 890-894.

Fletcher, G. P. Legal aspects of the decision not to prolong life. *Journal of the American Medical Association,* 1968, **203,** 119-122.

Fletcher, J. Ethics and euthanasia. In R. H. Williams (Ed.), *To live and to die: when, why, and how.* New York: Springer-Verlag, 1973, Pp. 113-122.

Fletcher, J. Abortion, euthanasia, and care of defective newborns. *New England Journal of Medicine,* 1975, **292,** 75-78. Quotes reprinted by permission.

Hardman, M. L., and Drew, C. J. The physically handicapped retarded individual: a review. *Mental Retardation,* 1977, **15**(5), 43-48.

Horan, D. J., and Mall, D. (Eds.), *Death, dying, and euthanasia.* Washington, D.C.: University Publications of America, Inc., 1977.

Kamisar, Y. Some non-religious views against proposed "mercy-killing" legislation. *Minnesota Law Review,* 1958, **42,** 969-1042.

Krishef, C. H. State laws on marriage and sterilization of the mentally retarded. *Mental Retardation,* 1972, **10**(3), 36-38.

Mackie, R. P., and Robbins, P. B. Exceptional children in local public schools. *School Life,* 1960, **43,** 14-16.

Murdock, C. W. Sterilization of the retarded: a problem or a solution? *California Law Review,* 1974, **62,** 917.

National Academy of Sciences. *Genetic screening: programs, principles and research.* Washington, D.C., 1975.

Pearson, P. H., and Menefee, A. R. Medical and social management of the mentally retarded. *General Practitioner,* 1965, **31,** 78-91.

Price, M. E., and Burt, R. A. Non-consensual medical procedures and the right to privacy. In Kindred, M., Cohen, J., Penrod, D., and Shaffer, T. (Eds.), *The mentally retarded citizen and the law.* New York: The Free Press, 1976, 94-112.

Ramsey, P. Abortion. *Thomist,* 1973, **37,** 174-226.

Reed, E. W., and Reed, S. C. *Mental retardation: a family study.* Philadelphia: W. B. Saunders Co., 1965.

Robertson, J. A. Involuntary euthanasia of defec-

tive newborns: a legal analysis. *Stanford Law Review,* 1975, **27,** 213-269.

Shaw, A. Dilemmas of "informed consent" in children. In Horan, D. J., and Mall, D. (Eds.), *Death, dying and euthanasia.* Washington, D.C.: University Publications of America, Inc., 1977, Pp. 75-90.

Turnbull, H. R., III. (Ed.) *Consent handbook.* Washington, D.C.: American Association on Mental Deficiency, 1977.

Turnbull, H. R., III, and Turnbull, A. P. Deinstitutionalization and the law. *Mental Retardation,* 1975, **13**(2), 14-20.

Tymchuk, A. J. A perspective on ethics in mental retardation. *Mental Retardation,* 1976, **14**(6), 44-47.

Williams, G. L. "Mercy-killing" legislation—a rejoinder. *Minnesota Law Review,* 1958, **43**(1), 1-12.

Williams, G. L., Euthanasia and abortion. *University of Colorado Law Review,* 1966, **38,** 181-187.

Wolfensberger, W. *The origin and nature of our institutional models.* Syracuse, N.Y.: Human Policy Press, 1975.

ANNOTATED BIBLIOGRAPHY

Horan, D. J., and Mall, D. (Eds.) *Death, dying, and euthanasia.* Washington, D.C.: University Publications of America, Inc., 1977.

This edited volume provides comprehensive coverage of the topics of death, dying, and euthanasia. The reader interested in more information on these topics will find the book to be an invaluable resource. It is most likely the most comprehensive and provocative volume on these topics to date.

Turnbull, H. R., III. (Ed.) *Consent Handbook,* Washington, D.C.: American Association on Mental Deficiency, 1977.

This is an invaluable volume both from a standpoint of educating and as a reference for the practitioner. A brief book, it provides a comprehensive examination of the issues involved in obtaining consent. The interested reader will find the *Consent Handbook* to be the only volume of its kind and an invaluable resource for further information on this complex topic.

Author index

Subject index